REVELATION
THROUGH
SCIENCE

REVELATION THROUGH SCIENCE

Evolution in the Harmony of
Science and Religion

James G. Martin
With Original Illustrations by James G. Martin Jr.

Library of Congress Control Number: 2016913671
ISBN: Hardcover   978-1-5245-3608-4
             Softcover   978-1-5245-3609-1
             eBook   978-1-5245-3610-7

Print information available on the last page.

Rev. date: 01/24/2017

To order additional copies of this book, contact:
Xlibris
1-888-795-4274
www.Xlibris.com
Orders@Xlibris.com
703122

Dedication

To Dottie and our family.
To those who taught us.

TABLE OF CONTENTS

PART ONE

PART TWO

PART THREE

PART FOUR

FOREWORD TO
Revelation Through Science

By Earl R. Mac Cormac

James G. Martin, governor, scientist and believer, has written an extraordinary book in clear prose exploring the relationship between science and religion. Believing that science has become a modern expression of Divine Revelation, this book reviews a variety of topics: a history of the warfare between science and religion including the church's rejection of Galileo's contention that the earth revolved around the sun; the challenges of Darwin's theory of evolution to a universe created by God; and agnostic and atheistic contentions that creation was random. Beyond these historical reviews, expository chapters of modern astronomy, geology and paleontology, physics, biology, organic chemistry and biotechnology and genomics are presented.

Disclaiming that science can tell us about God, Dr. Martin believes that science can contribute to our understanding of how God created the world. A contemporary theological interpretation of Biblical creation stories does, however, reveal and confirm God's actions in the world. References are also made to parallel creation stories found in Islam, Buddhism and Hinduism.

Throughout this impressive work, historical and contemporary references to many other works on science and religion are presented along with pictures and diagrams illustrating scientific and religious principles and theories. *Revelation Through Science* can be read in three ways:

- first, one can read from beginning to end following the argument that science informs and enhances religious belief;
- second, one could read a number of chapters exposing different sciences and learn not only issues of science and religion, but also contemporary details of those sciences; and

- third, beginning at the end with the author's own beliefs and read backwards, thereby learning how a religious belief is confirmed by discoveries in science.

The most notable new contribution to our understanding of how science affects religion comes in discussions of organic chemistry. Drawing upon an understanding of right-handed and left-handed organic molecules and the right-handed spiral of DNA and RNA, the mathematical possibilities that these configurations could have come about randomly seems impossible and argues for design and order confirming theological convictions of God's creation of the world.

A colleague of Governor Martin once said that the reason people voted so enthusiastically for him in his two successive gubernatorial terms and his preceding six terms as a Congressman resulted from the public perception that "what you see is what you get." The trait continues in this volume as Martin explicitly expresses what he believes and carries on a pleasant and insightful conversation with the reader. Interestingly, he describes in a late chapter how his training as a chemist affected his legislative actions in Congress.

Comments and Endorsements

"*Revelation Through Science* makes the case for how science, including its recent discoveries, has supported the theory that a living and benevolent God was clearly involved in creation. It is another important chapter in the long conversation between science and religion."

Douglas W. Oldenburg
Columbia Theological Seminary, President Emeritus

"The chemical intricacies of life are so mind-boggling that it is difficult to imagine that they came about entirely by chance. In this lively, and at times even whimsical account, chemist Jim Martin reasons that there is a divine hand behind the long evolutionary process that has created intelligent life on earth."

Owen Gingerich
Harvard-Smithsonian Center for Astrophysics, author of *God's Universe.*

"Jim Martin takes us on a fascinating journey through the history of science. This is not a dull read—it's understandable and entertaining. As scientist, teacher, politician, Martin understands the deep and often heated public debates over faith and reason, science and religion. He is passionately (and winsomely) convinced there need be no conflict. He believes that God speaks both through the book of Scripture, and the book of nature. His wide-ranging description of the many pointers to purpose is impressive. Believers and skeptics alike may find here reason to pause, think, and perhaps re-think. It should be widely read."

Leighton Ford
President, Leighton Ford Ministries

"In *Revelation Through Science*, Dr Martin skillfully crafts a colorful mosaic of humanity's quest to understand itself and its origins. His mosaic depicts a tree of many branches drawing sustenance from the same roots – the roots of *revelation*. By charting the triumphs and limitations of science from the Big Bang to the emergence of life from inorganic matter, Dr Martin challenges the reader with the proposition that science is *"a modern and valid means of revelation of God's great power."* Irresistible reading, especially in the clarity it brings to the issues for the non-scientific reader!"

Joseph B.H. McMillan
British jurist, author of *A 'Final Theory' of God*

REVELATION
THROUGH SCIENCE

Prologue: Modern Revelation

Introduction

Many of us grew up with a supposition that is widespread in American society: that science and religion, and the philosophies that undergird each, are intellectually separate and, in the view of some, intractably opposed. Many Americans have accepted the notion that one cannot in good conscience believe in both what the Bible tells us and what science tells us. Historically, that view goes back to the Reformation and Galileo's bold defense of the sun-centered universe, which offended some theologians and Aristotelian philosophers. Today's dispute, however, ignores the issues upon which the Inquisition found Galileo guilty of "vehement suspicion of heresy." Today's battleground is not about whether the earth is fixed and central, or moves around the sun while spinning on its own axis. That was settled 350–400 years ago to everyone's satisfaction, with no residual threat today to anyone's belief in Biblical inerrancy.

For some sectors of modern society, the taproot of discord was planted a century and a half ago with the publication of Charles Darwin's *Origin of Species*, and the debate over the scientific validity and theological implications of his transformational theory of evolution. On one side, atheists have seized upon the strong fossil and genomic evidence for gradual evolution, coupled with geologic and radiochemical evidence of the age of the earth, as being sufficient to explain how we got here without any help from supernatural origin or intrusion. Diametrically on the opposite side, "creationists" defend their literal interpretation of every related passage of Holy Scripture with arguments intended to refute the fossil evidence of variation and natural selection of species. Some go further, disputing the evidence that the earth is old enough for such slow evolution to proceed by trial and error to the extent that it has. Agnostics have found in this deep controversy enough grounds for skepticism to take comfort in awaiting a resolution; while

1

many theistic believers have finessed the whole thing as an insoluble clash of semantics between two separate but equivalent domains of truth. No one is totally happy with the standoff.

The relationship between science and religion has itself *evolved* in the intervening centuries. There has been a shift toward reconciliation between these two realms of perceived fundamental truth. In this book, we will consider how that relationship has changed and where it seems to be going, and examine the underlying basis for this progress. For this purpose, the author offers material from professional disciplines other than his own (chemistry and politics), and must acknowledge the difficulty in ensuring that each topic reflects the most recent research and understanding. An effort has been made to reflect scientific disputes when and where appropriate. There are chapters with topics from astronomy, physics, geology and paleontology, biology, and biochemistry, in which certain crucial issues in those fields contribute to the question of how we got here.

A good deal of that material overlaps the field of chemistry, but most of it is so specialized within its own subject discipline that my attempts to summarize may be inadequate, or even surpassed by new discoveries. Interpretations that are written for the educated nonscientist may seem oversimplified to the expert in the subject. To whatever extent modification is required, it will comfort this writer that you will have gained thereby a clear example of the way science works. As long as the scientific method is pursued, old ideas and theories will be revised or rejected. If my secondhand interpretation of others' fields stirs you to read more about their topics, an earnest purpose will have been served.

Style and Structure of this Book

At this point, an interruption is in order to anticipate several somewhat unorthodox features, one of which just appeared. It is generally considered improper for an author's remarks guiding or engaging the reader to be parsed in the second person. I suppose the use of third-person indirection serves to comfort the reader that the remark is more general and not personal. In the preceding paragraph, I directed my commentary to the second-person pronoun, you, because my purpose is to reach you personally, to engage your mind toward an understanding of science, its power and its limitations. After all, *Revelation through Science* is written for the educated **non**scientist. It is likely that some of the material may be too obtuse for you (not some impersonal third person), and I want you to feel that it is acceptable to skim over a difficult section if it seems overwhelming, perhaps to return later before leaving the chapter in which it appears. While writing, my mind is not focused on some impersonal other, but on you. That is how I teach, from the other end of the log.

Each chapter is intended to be free-standing so that you are welcome to take them in any order that interests you. Frequently, an important topic is cross-referenced to other chapters or specific pages, where a more detailed explanation might be found. The organization of the sequence of chapters may concern you that they are not in strict chronological order. Instead, the material is organized by broad disciplines, like astronomy and then physics. This structure develops the material more logically, without regard to whether Charles Darwin's work (chapters 7 and 8) preceded that of Edwin Hubble (chapter 4), which it surely did.

One other device needs clarification. From time to time, there will be a short section that is interesting apart from the cosmological point being developed. Such "asides" are presented in brackets and indented to indicate that they may enlighten but are not essential, and in the hope that this practice will not be a distraction.

From Conflict to Reconciliation

The Biblical account of creation in chapter 1 is a necessary perspective for subsequent chapters. There are, after all, two versions in the *Book of Genesis*, and other creation insights occur elsewhere in the Bible. To the extent that theologians sometimes reach different scholarly interpretations, it is likely that this layman's brief summary will raise an objection or two. The way I see it, if we all shared identical views there would be no need for more than one of us to do all the thinking.

Chapter 2 presents a condensed review of how the comfortable relationship between theology and early science prior to Copernicus and Galileo was shaken by the latter's observations with the newly invented telescope. The resulting conflict was essentially an argument among Christians who differed in their adamant adherence or objection to Aristotelian authority. Once that rift settled down, as compelling evidence from Kepler, Galileo, and Newton came to be accepted, there followed a peaceful era of more than two centuries, broken by the publication of Charles Darwin's *Origin of Species*, followed five years later by his *Descent of Man* (chapters 7 and 8).

Today's dispute over Darwin's theory of evolution (chapters 9 and 10) is driven by the necessity perceived by some good Christians to defend their literal interpretation of *Holy Scripture* against the scientific evidence that we got here via a very slow process of evolution. Creationists have objected to evolution, insisting that all known species (and the fossil record) were "fixed" in their present form during six "days" of creation, and that the earth is 6,000–10,000 years old. Some atheists reveled in the conflict with this branch of religious orthodoxy, not wasting the opportunity to bash believers with solid scientific evidence that the earth is 4.5 billion years old and the universe is 13.7 billion years old; and that all species (extant and extinct) have evolved from protobiotic, common ancestry in the span of three billion years. It seems ironic that these opposing sides agree on the shared dictum that one cannot and must not believe in both God and evolution, although they arrive from aggressive and implacably opposed ideologies.

For the last ninety years, creationists have pressed sympathetic state legislatures to prohibit teaching evolution in public schools. Failing that, they demand "equal time" for teaching something called "creation science" as an alternative to science if evolution is taught. This fight has not gone well for them. Federal courts, citing the "establishment" clause, have consistently upheld the First Amendment to the U.S. Constitution against the imposition of religious tenets and dictates masquerading as science (chapters 9 and 18).

Grown weary of the argument over whether one must choose between religion and science, other Christians have asserted a simple dichotomy that the two domains are separate and coequal, with no inherent conflict. This view has given comfort to those who respect both science and religion, but has persuaded neither the atheist nor the creationist adversaries. From this "peaceful coexistence" armistice, there has emerged a recent movement of theistic scientists, who contend that the deeper science takes us into the nature of things, the more we find "evidence for belief," to use the elegant phrase of Francis Collins. They contend that the world is fine-tuned for life and its evolution of intelligent, self-aware humans, and that there is a diminishingly remote probability that this could have happened by chance or coincidence. Could creation, then, have purpose?

Chapter 5 will review this concept of "anthropic" fine-tuning with an impressive array of examples that have been put forward by theistic physicists, astronomers, and geologists. Later chapters will present more examples derived from the fields of biology, chemistry, and biochemistry, some of which originated herein. You can make up your own mind about all of this as you ponder which leap of faith makes more sense to you.

4

As a change of pace, you will find chapters intended to provide relief from the heavier work. A brief biographical sketch of the incomparable Tycho Brahe (chapter 3), an account of the Tennessee "monkey trial" of John Scopes (chapter 9), and some surprising reflections on the search for extraterrestrial intelligence (SETI, chapter 17) are tangential to the overall subject, but are more narrative and less technical in style, as are the short biographies of Galileo and Darwin (chapters 2 and 7, respectively). I could not resist a chapter on the contemporary partisan politics of science (chapter 18), which may not add a lot to the reconciliation of science and religion, but it is certainly relevant. After that, following good pedagogic practice, the final chapter will recapitulate the question:

Must science be an impediment to faith . . . and if so, whose faith?

Dozens of thoughtful and talented writers on all sides have weighed in with their compelling rationales to resolve the controversy, or at least defend a viewpoint. Recent decades have seen the emergence of the more reconciling position of theistic scientists: that science has revealed not only (a) how God provided for so many different species with unarguably common anatomic and genomic similarities, but also (b) a growing list of highly improbable coincidences that point to the work of a supernatural Creator. What can I add to that except repetition?

The late great Congressman Morris "Mo" Udall (D-Arizona) often lamented that the day's debate had reached the repetitious point "where everything has been said, but not everyone has said it." One might argue that enough has been written on this subject, to which my response would be that not many chemists have yet contributed to the conversation about the interrelationship between science and religion from the distinctive view of our discipline. Perhaps more ought to become engaged, with points to be made and refuted. Chemistry yields a rich lode of material that indicates the purposefulness of life. It is not expected that this book will end the debate with soft or loud "Hosannas" (see Mencken in chapter 9), but it would serve a good purpose if it were provocative enough to draw friendly fire from chemists who see it similarly or differently.

Challenging others to join the discussion, however, is not the main objective of writing *Revelation through Science*. The intended reader is the nonscientist who has at least a modest education, and who cares about the apparent conflict between science and religion. My ideal is to write at that level while keeping it acceptable to the expert: to introduce a concept and carry the reader to a deeper understanding of some fascinating scientific discoveries and what they mean. Unavoidably, some material may seem opaque and difficult to comprehend because it is difficult to describe in familiar metaphors. At that point the reader could just say "Wow!" at the impenetrable majesty of it and move on to the next paragraph. That will be all right.

There is a glossary of terms (pages 393 ff.) in language paraphrased from dictionaries. It and the index of names and topics (pages 409 ff.) may help you retrieve a special context. The intent, however, is not to make you a trained scientist (if you are not one already), but to help you see that there is, and need be, no irreconcilable conflict between two "alternative universes" of science and religion.

I am grateful to friends who were willing to read chapters critically so that I could have the benefit of their expertise and insights. Professor Anthony Abbott dissected some of the early drafts for improvements in style and clarity, returning later as final editor, a debt payable only in friendship. Professor Eric Carlson reviewed chapters on astronomy and physics, saving me from a number of misinterpretations. A similarly elegant evaluation from Professor Malcolm Campbell critiqued the material on biology and evolution. The Reverend John Rogers read the Biblical and theological passages, which clearly needed the help of expert guidance. Jane Shaw edited several chapters for style and clarity. Professor Earl Mac Cormac, scientist and ordained minister, read the entire first draft manuscript, with valuable comments on its overall effect and many particulars. Professor Owen Gingerich critiqued the final draft. What an inordinate privilege to have corrective input from these esteemed scholars! My revisions may not always have ended up quite where they pointed me, but only because it is difficult to translate complex ideas to the nontechnical reader while presenting conflicting views in a fair and reasonable context. I am more than grateful for the skills and patience of Ben Arby, Kim Oliver, John Briones, Sarah Perkins, and Cheryl Ishigaki at Xlibris as they and their colleagues guided me through the unfamiliar labyrinth of publishing.

Unable to rely upon the veracity of copyright trails for most of the illustrations found in the Internet, I was fortunate to have sired a clever amateur cartoonist, James Martin Jr. He has enhanced my rather expansive explanations with often imaginative sketches, of which I am proud. I believe you will find them illuminating and entertaining, and especially memorable for their whimsy. Other family members read parts for comprehensibility.

Ultimately, what matters is what you think. You may want to put it down after each chapter to let the ideas sink in and ferment. Hopefully there is enough entertainment value in each chapter to bring you back for the next. Even better if it moves you to read others' perspectives on this vital subject. Are you ready for a mind-stretching challenge?

It would seem fair to provide you with a simple, concise statement of what I believe, in the interest of transparency. Each reader can decide what to make of the interactions between science and religion, but nothing is served by being oblique about my faith. Here's what I believe about the Holy Bible:

- It is the revealed Word of God in narrative, symbolic, and poetic form.
- It reveals the relationship between God and all humankind.
- It is our best guide to faith and practice, to belief and worship.
- It is not a science textbook, having been written long before modern science.

As to science, I believe, further, that

- Modern science is our best method for discovering and understanding nature.
- Science, and evolution in particular, need not be an impediment to faith.
- Science <u>reveals</u> God's processes of evolution and His timeframe of creation.
- For theistic believers, science is a contemporary mode of **Revelation**.

More than that, when we get into the accumulating scientific evidence of evolution, you will see why I believe there is an infinitesimally remote probability that we got here by chance. You are not compelled to accept this claim or its theological implication, but it might be worth your while to think about it. There is an old saying that if you are walking through the woods and see a turtle perched atop a fence post . . .

. . . you know it didn't get there by itself.

Disclaimer: No turtle was injured in the preparation of this book.

Revelation
Through
Science

Part One

Chapter 1

Creation and the Bible

The Heavens declare the glory of God,
and the firmament showeth His handiwork.
                                    ——Psalm 19:1

Th'unwearied sun from day to day, does his Creator's Pow'r display,
And publishes to every land the work of an Almighty Hand.
                              ——Excerpt from Joseph Addison (1712)
                              "The Spacious Firmament on High"

One day is with the Lord as a thousand years, and a thousand years
as one day.
                              ——Second Peter 3:8 (cf. also *Psalms 90:4)*

Old Testament authors were not scientists. The subject did not exist until
the third century BC, dating from when Eratosthenes demonstrated
evidence that the earth was round. Thus, they had no way to know
that the earth revolves around the sun or that the earth rotates about
its own axis. After all, modern science didn't emerge until several
thousand years later with Galileo's studies of motion and his "spyglass"
observations. Galileo himself had a useful insight: "The Bible tells us not
how the heavens go, but how to go to Heaven!" He wrote it in Italian, of
course, but it translates rather well.

The Biblical Canon

All sixty-six books of the Holy Bible were written before AD 150. Old
Testament texts date from about 1000 to 160 BC, with most of the New
Testament having been written down between AD 60 and 125. The
Second Epistle of Peter and the *Third Epistle of John* may date from

slightly later. Other texts, often with different perceptions, were written after the first century, although the *Gospel of Thomas* could have been written contemporaneously with much of the canonical New Testament.

A great deal of scholarship has been devoted to a number of noncanonical texts, as have several commercially successful fictional accounts. Some have found it to be a useful fiction to attribute the inclusion of some texts and the crucial exclusion of others to the Council of Nicaea (AD 325), commissioned by Roman Emperor Constantine after his conversion to Christianity. While this assembly did purge groups that were considered heretical, the process of selecting and deselecting canonical Scripture was pretty much complete by then (although it continued to foment for another two decades).

Among the early Christian communities there were efforts to determine which texts were authentic accounts of the life of Jesus Christ and of the early Christian church, and to distinguish these from ones that were suspect. The earliest known document of this kind is a manuscript known as the *Muratorian* fragment (*circa* AD 170). By the year 200, there was general agreement among the various congregations in favor of the current twenty-seven books, while they suppressed other texts with different accounts and doctrines. The rediscovery at Nag Hammadi of many of these "discredited" Gnostic gospels and letters shows that not everyone had accepted the censors' consensus. It also resumed the ancient debate over the range of interpretations of the divinity and humanity and acts of Christ, and to discern which of them were authentic and worthy of belief.

It is interesting to note that this canonical selection process was not a novel departure for those early Christian communities. The same process had been going on for centuries among rabbinical scholars to affirm which books constituted the accepted *Masoretic Text*, also called the Tanakh. After decades of changing views as to what was canonical and what was merely acceptable for edification, the question was settled as to which books were worthy to be included. There is one tradition that this was done at the Synod at Jamnia in AD 70, but other authorities believe wide consensus was reached 110 years earlier, during the preeminence of the Hasmoneans (around 40 BC), a controversy far beyond my reach.

One may devote a lifetime of study to these conflicting texts in order to discern the revealed Word of God. Judgments were made in the second century—that are still being questioned in the twenty-first century—to differentiate between true revelation from God and the wishful and heretical imagination of mortal men. Sometimes the trail is blurred and indistinct.

Science is Revelation

My purpose is to raise a different question: was revelation cut off from us around AD 200? Was that the end of it? Or does God continue to reveal new understandings to us, both among the priesthood and among us ordinary individuals? The thesis of this book is that one such mode of continuing revelation might be found in the scientific journals and instruments of discovery. The more we unravel secrets of the physical, chemical, and biological nature of matter and of life, the better we can understand and appreciate the creative power of God. Nonbelievers are free to reject all of this as a "leap of faith," but may find that their own tenets require intellectually comparable ballistic trajectories.

Science is revelation of a modern kind. Science does not reveal anything about the essence of God or His purpose for us, nor can it do so. Science cannot even ask useful questions about purpose, or why we are here. Science cannot measure and describe these kinds of questions, important as they are. But science definitely can ask questions about how God made us, how life emerged from non-life and evolved so many varieties, and the highly detailed nature of how we are structured, and the function of each body part.

It is important to understand that science rarely gives us answers that are settled and final. Each theoretical explanation is one that expresses behavior or structure in mathematical and/or metaphorical terms to help us understand. "After further review" (as the football referee says), there will be modifications that either confirm, improve, or replace a theory, as new evidence accumulates.

One of the great strengths of the Scientific Method is that each theory generates a great deal of research aimed at disproving or amending its explanation. When successive experiments are unable to dislodge a theory, and the more assaults that it withstands, the greater its acceptance and its impact grows. Each experimental test that fails to falsify or discredit a theory thereby adds to its luster and inspires confidence. Contrary evidence that is inconsistent with the prevailing theory may lead us to a better concept. This potential for falsifiability drives basic research to seek better models and explanations.

Science can and does reveal for the believer a partial understanding of how God, in His wisdom and power, assembled the universe within very precisely critical parameters for success (see chapter 5). Science also reveals part of the process for the first origins of life, the rather abrupt appearance later of most body forms (which we call *phyla*), and therefrom the slow, gradual emergence of higher genera and higher species, culminating in one singular species of sentient, self-aware creatures, endowed with the unique capability for discovering and reasoning about these very questions.

Science has debated the evidence of the age of the universe, and has concluded that there was one singular and profound instant of creation 13,700,000,000 ± 100,000,000 years ago. Furthermore, there is inescapable evidence that the sun, Earth, and the rest of our little solar system were created 4.5 billion years ago, after a supernova laced the surrounding space with heavier elements that could make rocks and living organisms. Science has studied geologic strata and fossil deposits, the variations among plants and animals, and the submicroscopic molecular structure of DNA, and concluded that all species have evolved from single-cell primordial life by a process we call evolution.

When it comes to these kinds of questions, the theist finds science to be modern revelation of how God did it. You are free to "Believe It or Not," but faith does not require rejection of the best science . . . or *vice versa.*

Science continually fills in more gaps in our understanding of nature. Therefore, we must be cautious not to think we can prove the existence of God by invoking supernatural explanations for any facts that contemporary science has not yet explained. This potential fallacy has been described as the "God of the Gaps" syllogism (page 170). If God is found in the gaps of science, what happens if new discoveries fill in the gaps? At the same time, as science is able to fill in many gaps, more gaps become apparent. Therefore, we must be equally cautious not to accept the atheistic claim that science disproves God. Science can neither ask nor answer that question. Nevertheless, science has given us a great deal of evidence that can be interpreted by believers as revelation of God's power.

It is instructive that all of the recorded histories of the earliest known civilizations show that among their fundamental achievements was finding a dependent relationship with a beneficent, although sometimes demanding, supernatural presence. This concept would generally be depicted as a personage or being, greater than mortal, having vast powers.

Few civilizations missed this perception that some power, beyond them or their understanding, was engaged with them. Because the priesthood that developed in each culture had the responsibility and authority to interpret this power and relationship for the masses, a symbolism of pictures or some phonetic device was developed to keep a record of what was known and of the rituals that seemed beneficial.

Different conceptions of this deity emerged in different communities of our early ancestors. That was because different signs were encountered within the experiences of different civilizations. Some interpreted a need for human sacrifice; others did not. For some, sacrificial animals were acceptably sufficient.

It was inevitable that early humans would overreach in their various interpretations of evidence and mystery. Some would find it convenient to explain a great variety of phenomena by concluding that there were multiple gods, each with special and unique powers. One pervasive Abrahamic tradition evolved as a belief in one God and an absence of any others. This monotheism is fundamental to the belief and teaching of Judaism, Christianity, and Islam. There remain great differences, but whether one prays to Jehovah (Yahweh), God, or Allah, the essentials are the same, yet with differing explanatory texts and directives.

In the Beginning . . . *Genesis 1:1*

Let us take a moment to review the Biblical account of the Creation story. We will see a number of uncanny coincidences between the *Genesis* sequence of events and what we understand from modern astronomers' interpretation of the "Big Bang" theory of instantaneous creation and the study of numerous fossils preserved from prehistoric times. The overall correspondence is not perfect, but is good enough to make one wonder how the ancient writers could have supposed something close to the scientifically correct sequence of events.

I particularly like the imagery in the version from *The Living Bible*, a compilation of paraphrases of various English-language translations published by Tyndale House Publishers (1971). Notice especially the phrasing of the second verse.

1. *When God began creating the heavens and the earth,*
2. *The earth was at first a shapeless, chaotic mass, with the Spirit of God brooding over the dark vapors.*
3. *Then God said, "Let there be light." And the light appeared.*

Compare this with the majesty of the *New King James Version* (Thomas Nelson Publishers, the source of all subsequent passages from the Bible) for the same verses:

1. *In the beginning God created the heavens and the earth.*
2. *The earth was without form and void; and darkness was upon the face of the deep. And the Spirit of God was hovering over the face of the waters.*
3. *Then God said, "Let there be light;" and there was light.*

While this was not based upon the methods or technologies of science, even the scientist can marvel at this description of the "Big Bang" of creation as revealed by modern astronomy. Science does not tell us what existed before that. Although some have offered mathematical speculations, it is not likely that science will ever have the means to probe time and space from before that instant of enormous release of matter and energy. The technologies of science have no way to pierce that veil of mystery because no physical evidence remains, but the writers of *Genesis* have given us a pretty good idea. *Then God said, "Let there be light;" and there was light.*

In chapter 4, we will look more deeply into what science reveals to us about this moment of creation and when it occurred. We will see that during its brief, initial epochs, it was so dense as to have no shape or texture, and would have been dark until expansion reduced the density to the point that photons of light could escape. We will also consider how everything that has happened since then had its origin in that first instant: every star, every planet, every rock, and every living creature. Before we explore that path, let's see first what the Bible says about it.

It is believed by many scholars that this magnificent story had its origins in the Babylonian epic of creation. The Hebrews would have been quite familiar with this story during their exile in Babylon, the kingdom that occupied much of the territory now known as Iraq. As it was approximately bounded by the Tigris and Euphrates rivers, it was also known as Mesopotamia (from the Greek for "between the rivers"). The Israelite nation could have received the creation story much earlier from the Canaanites.

In any case, the message was recast in monotheistic terms. A second version of creation developed around a somewhat different sequence of events found in the second and third chapters of *Genesis*. Some of the underlying concepts and beliefs of the times are expressed more poetically in other passages of the Old Testament.

There has been some dispute among scholars as to the intended meaning of the Hebrew word *yom*, which in the singular form and context means "day." Some contend that it can also mean a much longer period of time, as in an era, depending on the context. Others say that in *Genesis*, the use of *yom* is the singular and in all other uses in the Old Testament this refers to a single day. Those who take the broader view respond that in the six times of creation in *Genesis*, there is no article (such as *heh* or the prefix *ha* for "the") in the number for the successive time periods, thus allowing the epochal interpretation. Either way, it is likely that the writer of *Genesis* was expressing this in the best way that anyone could comprehend and accept at the time, long before the revelations from science.

The most familiar Biblical account of creation is the opening narrative of *Genesis 1:1–2:3*. This contrasts somewhat with the different account of creation in *Genesis 2:4–3:21*. Taken together, they have the same theological message: the heavens and the earth did not preexist or create themselves out of nothing. This was the act of a Supreme Being, the Architect and Builder of all that is. If one wishes to go beyond that for a literal interpretation of Scripture, there is a choice to be made whether *Genesis 1* or *Genesis 2–3* is the one absolute, inerrant text. What then do we say about the other?

Genesis 1:1–2:3 is the familiar account of six days (*yom*) of creation followed by a seventh day of rest. The first day is a concise but reasonably good statement of the Big Bang in its initial fraction of a second (see chapter 4) through the end of the so-called Photon Epoch. Day Two produced waters above and below the firmament, which was termed "heaven." Day 3 gathered the waters, allowing dry land to arise, bringing forth grass and "herb yielding seed." As we shall see in later chapters, a lot was going on if we accept the fossil evidence. Day 4 brought lights in the firmament, the sun, moon and stars. The writer of *Genesis* perceived that these stages of creation would precede the origin of animal life.

The best astrophysical evidence would place the events of Day 4 necessarily earlier than the events of Day 3, but the subsequent narrative is mostly compatible. For example, Day 5 saw the first appearance of aquatic animals, in full agreement with the timetable of fossil records. "Let the waters bring forth abundantly the moving creatures that hath life" is certainly relevant to the unique proliferation of unprecedented oceanic animal body forms in the Cambrian Explosion. However, it has been noted that the "great whales and every winged fowl" would conflict with the chronological order according to fossil evidence. Day 6, "let the earth bring forth cattle, creeping things, beasts of the earth…" Then man was made and given dominion over all. It is a quibble, but recent fossil evidence unknown to the writers of *Genesis* shows that birds first arose some 250 million years after animal life migrated out of the oceans onto dry land. Whales and dolphins resulted from a gradual return of dry-land predecessors to a water habitat. By the end of that Day 6, mankind was formed and given dominion over all creatures. The earliest anthropological indication of humans herding animals would be 18,000 years ago, followed 6,000 years later by the earliest known cultivation of wheat and rice.

One may reach various conclusions as to whether these early written accounts of creation, taken from the best understanding of their time, are controverted by science, or *vice versa*. One could point to the few particular anomalies to make a case for conflict, or point to the considerable similarity of most particulars of Biblical chronology to science. Having one day out of seven as a day of rest was a particularly beneficial practice that reflects the development of civilized communities of just the last few thousand years. Even that ideal has suffered somewhat as recent decades have shaped a more pluralistic, secular society.

There's a different creation story when we compare *Genesis 1* with the more spiritual account in *Genesis 2*. In *Genesis 2:4–17*, a mist watered the earth, and man was created out of the ground to till the earth in order for plants to grow, followed by trees for his food. Adam was put in charge of the garden in Eden, and given every beast of the field and fowl of the air for sustenance and company. This account continues with the creation of woman, and, in *Genesis 3*, her encounter with the serpent, the forbidden fruit, and its consequences. While this tells a different story, the basic message is the same. The world and all its inhabitant creatures were created by one God, and He showed a clear interest and special involvement in the one sentient species of humans.

Christians might prefer the richly symbolic expression from the opening stanzas of the *Gospel of John*:

1. *In the beginning was the Word, and the word was with God, and the Word was God.*
2. *The same was in the beginning with God.*
3. *All things were made by Him; and without Him was not any thing made that was made.*
4. *In Him was life; and the life was the light of men.*
5. *And the light shineth in darkness; and the darkness comprehended it not.*

Other Biblical Texts

Professor William Brown of Columbia Theological Seminary in Decatur, Georgia, describes the first *Genesis* narrative as mankind being brought forth "out of God." The second *Genesis* story of creation has mankind being brought forth <u>by</u> God "out of dirt." Taken together, they allow some room for interpretation. Dr. Brown has analyzed seven different creation accounts. In addition to the two *Genesis* stories, he identifies:

(a) the Leviathan story in *Job 38–41*, and other poetic references in
(b) *Psalm 104* (with its parade of the animals),
(c) *Proverbs 8:22–31* (with the concept of Woman = Wisdom),
(d) *Ecclesiastes 1:2–11* (with its geocentric concept), and
(e) *Isaiah 40–55* (the new creation).

Brown believes that *Genesis I* is best understood as "poetic, religious, and metaphoric," but not scientific. Since much of Scripture was written in contemporary vernacular of its time, he suggests we can get a feel for that by reading P.K. McCary: *The Black Bible Chronicles*, her adaptive paraphrase of the Bible in today's ethnic street language. It is reminiscent of an earlier collection of folk sermons, *God's Trombones*. *Genesis 1–3* should be taken as the poetic depiction of God's relation to mankind, and not always literally.

<u>Leviathan Story: *Job 38–41*</u>. God speaks reprovingly to Job, asking him to consider how mankind came to be on Earth and became beneficiary of the world full of plants and animals, including leviathan. There follows a divine account of numerous species. The purpose of this would appear to be a successful effort to lead Job to accept a measure of humility. Having survived great afflictions, Job had become self-righteous and proud. In its final scene, Job is rewarded, having learned some hard lessons, although this happy ending could be due to a merger with a second text.

Psalm 104. *1. Bless the Lord, O my soul* is the antecedent for verse 5: *Who laid the foundations of the earth, that it should not be removed forever.* This hymn to God's creation reflects the understanding that the earth must be fixed and immovable. It was among the arguments advanced against Galileo.

Proverbs 3:19–20 is also short and sweet: *19. The Lord by wisdom hath founded the earth; by understanding hath he established the heavens. 20. By his knowledge the depths are broken up, and the clouds drop down the dew.*

Proverbs 8:22–31. In this passage, "In Praise of Wisdom," the first person singular is none other than Wisdom, and she is speaking to us with a different account of creation:

22. *The Lord possessed me in the beginning of His way, before His works of old.*
23. *I was set up from everlasting, from the beginning, or ever the earth was.*
24. *When there were no depths, I was brought forth; when there were no fountains abounding with water.*
25. *Before the mountains were settled, before the hills was I brought forth:*
26. *While as yet He had not made the earth, nor the fields, nor the highest part of the dust of the world,*
27. *When He prepared the heavens, I was there: when He appointed the foundations of the earth:*
28. *When He established the clouds above: when He strengthened the fountains of the deep:*
29. *When He gave to the sea His decree, that the waters should not pass His commandment: when He appointed the foundations of the earth:*
30. *Then I was by Him, as one brought up with Him: and I was daily His delight, rejoicing always before Him;*
31. *Rejoicing in the habitable part of His earth; and my delights were with the sons of men.*

Ecclesiastes 1:2–11 is terse but memorable:
6. *The sun also rises, and the sun goes down, and hastens to the place where it arose.*

Isaiah 40–45 contains these verses:
40:12. *Who has measured the waters in the hollow of His hand, measured heaven with a span and calculated the dust of the earth in a measure, and weighed the mountains in scales and the hills in a balance?*
40:22. *It is He who sits above the circle of the earth, and its inhabitants are like grasshoppers, who stretches out the heavens like a curtain, and spreads them out like a tent to dwell in.*
40:26. *Lift up your eyes on high, and see who has created these things . . .*
42:5. *who created the heavens and stretched them out, who spread forth the earth and that which comes from it, who gives breath to the people on it . . .*

*45:18. who created the heavens, who is God, who formed the earth
and made it, who has established it, who did not create it in
vain, who formed it to be inhabited.*

Creation in Other Religions

The essential message in the Judaic story of creation is about the creative
power of God. This same concept of one Divine Creator as the first
cause of the world is affirmed in other religions as well. The Islamic
account in the Quran has certain similarities, which is not surprising
given its Abrahamic tradition. The Creation theme is not presented in
a singular flowing narrative, as the concepts are distributed among
separate passages. There are many helpful English-language summaries
of the Quran on the Internet. One easily comprehended presentation
of its message is in the Internet site *About.com* as summarized by the
Muslim writer named Huda.

The six days of creation as expressed in *Genesis I* is also found
in the Quran (10:3): Allah "created the heavens and the earth and all
that is between them in six days." While the Hebrew word for "day" is
yom, with scholarly dispute as to its literal meaning, the corresponding
Arabic word *youm* is said to be a unit of time that can be a day or many
thousands of days, although semantic disputes are always imaginable.

In a passage foreshadowing what astronomers call the time before
the **Quark Epoch** (chapter 4), the Quran (21:30) tells us that *the heavens
and the earth were joined together as one unit, before We clove them
asunder.* In the same verse (21:30), *Allah made from water every living
thing.* Science certainly supports that original habitat.

Allah then *turned to the sky, and it had been smoke. He said to
it and to the earth: "come together . . ."* (41:11) Again, this seems
reminiscent of what astronomers describe as the period of condensation
of dust and gases into stars and planets (chapter 4).

The intent of these verses seems to be not to define the history
of creation, but to reveal the essence that creation had Divine origin.
Elsewhere (45:3), *Verily, in the heavens and the earth are signs for those
who believe.* This clearly presages what I consider to be revelations from
science.

In contrast to the Abrahamic faiths, polytheistic Buddhism allows
a concept of continual creation, destruction, and regeneration, implying
that the quintessential world has always been there. These traditional
tenets are being modified to accommodate scientific discovery. The
ancient core belief in a flat world of concentric circles is yielding to a

Copernican cosmology under the leadership of Tibet's Dalai Lama. Not only is our solar system part of the Milky Way Galaxy, among billions of other galaxies observed in this universe, Buddhists also believe there are multiple universes beyond our observation. In their view, all universes are continually going through the processes of birth, growth, and death in endless cycles. Overall, there is no beginning and no ending.

Hinduism also teaches that our observed universe is but one of an innumerable host of universes, continually being created by Lord Brahma. It envisions vast spans of time, but there is no absolute beginning or ending of time. There is a preordained, all-pervasive order in and for everything. These beliefs are found in ancient Sanskrit texts, including both the *Upanishads* and the *Vedas*. The former guide the understanding of ultimate reality (Brahman), while the *Vedic* hymns guide the proper ritual activity. From one *Upanishad*, the *Fourth Brahmana*, creation and evolution derive from ultimate reality:

In the beginning was only Being, One without a second.
Out of himself he brought forth the cosmos and entered into
everything in it.

We will see below how these conceptions of multiple universes are being accepted or hypothesized by a number of very prominent scientists. Nevertheless, there is wide acceptance among contemporary astronomers of the evidence that a singular moment of creation of this one universe occurred, as in the "Big Bang" Theory, with Earth being formed much later in cosmological time (chapters 4 and 11).

Theological Reflections

Is it too radical for us to open our minds to the idea that science is not so antithetical to religious belief, but presents partial, modern revelation of how God created our world? In this book we will consider examples from astronomy, physics, geology, biology, organic chemistry, and biochemistry. Not only will we see that science can reveal God's ways within the natural world, but also that science presents evidence pointing to some guiding purpose in creation and in life. This is controversial. While it might not persuade atheists to accept religious faith, it could well cause some to question their own "leap of faith."

The contributions of science to these ultimate questions do not favor one religion over another. Science cannot ask such questions, much less answer them. Above all, **as much as we would wish science to show us**

the essence of God, we must discipline ourselves to accept that it is beyond the methods of science to do so. Presbyterian theologian and preacher John Rogers reminds us,

> *In the Reformed (Calvinist) Tradition, we confess that because God is God and we are finite, sinful creatures, we cannot comprehend God except as far as God accommodates himself to our limitations. God must in some way descend to meet our capacities, and has done this to the extent that the created order tells of his handiwork.*

In John Calvin's view, our knowledge of God from what we see in nature is knowledge of his works. Science does not reveal God's essence, which remains a mystery even to those who confess and worship him. Calvin wrote:

> *We know the most perfect way of seeking God . . . is to contemplate him in His works whereby he renders himself near and familiar to us and in some measure communicates himself. (Institutes I, v.9)*

Rogers again cautions that our scientific observations can only point us "to know **that** God is but not **who** God is." Reformed theologian Emil Brunner expressed it equally succinctly, "The world, with a million fingers, points to God, but it cannot reveal God." To the Christian, that essence of God is revealed most clearly in Jesus Christ. Turning again to Calvin, in his *Commentary on Colossians 1:15*, we read:

> *For Christ is the image of God because He makes God in a manner visible to us . . . He is revealed to us in Christ alone, where we may behold Him as in a mirror.*

My purpose here is not to engage in proselytizing for my faith, but to clarify the basic limitations of what I believe to be scientific revelation. The eminent theologian Karl Barth has written:

> *What man can know by his own power according to the measure of his natural powers, his understanding, his feeling, will be, at most, something like a supreme being, an absolute nature, the idea of an utterly free power, of a being towering over everything. This absolute and Supreme Being, the ultimate and most profound, this "thing in itself," has nothing to do with God. It is a part of the intuitions and marginal possibilities of man's thinking, of man's*

contrivance. Man is able to think this being; he has not thereby thought God . . . God is always the One who has made Himself known to man in His own revelation, and not the one whom man thinks out for himself and describes as God. (Dogmatics in Outline, 1959, p.23)

Or as the prophet (*Isaiah 55:8–9*) declared millennia before:

For my thoughts are not your thoughts, neither are your ways my ways, says the Lord. For as the heavens are higher than the earth, so are my ways higher than your ways and my thoughts than your thoughts.

The foregoing citations are not meant to disparage the revelation that comes to us through science, for that wellspring has great value. Rather, it is to remind us that the strengths and limitations of science are understood by theologians and prophets, and should not be misunderstood by scientists.

We are left with many questions. Does the Old Testament, with its two *Genesis* stories of creation, tell us about the age of the universe? The Bible itself does not say. We will see in chapter 11 how Bishop Ussher reached his conclusion that Creation occurred in 4004 BC, and consider whether his method (even with contributions from Johannes Kepler and Isaac Newton) is sufficient to reject all scientific evidence to the contrary.

Did God long ago stop speaking to us about all this, or could science open to us a modern Revelation? What can the age of rocks tell us about the Rock of Ages? What can we learn from astronomy and the orbiting Hubble and Kepler telescopes about the age of the universe? Was it all created for us? Can science find evidence, if not proof, of God?

Our search for answers begins with a condensed biographical account of the celebrated paragon of science, Galileo Galilei.

I want to know how God created this world.
I want to know His thoughts. The rest are details.

———Albert Einstein

Chapter 2

Galileo Galilei (1564–1642)

In the history of human civilization, there are figures of truly towering importance whose achievements and ideas have transformed society. The fields of artistic, religious, literary, political, and military innovation are rich with such heroic characters. In the field of science, we also can point to many great eminences whose works have transformed the ways that we understand the nature of matter and energy, of life, and of the universe. One could make a case that a few individuals have led such major changes in how we observe nature and interpret its structure and behavior that their enormous contributions stand out far above all others. One short list might name Galileo Galilei, Isaac Newton, Charles Darwin, and Albert Einstein. This lineup is somewhat top-heavy with three physicists and one naturalist-biologist. Perhaps you might devise an interesting alternative roster.

This chapter distills only a fraction of the life and work and times of Galileo. His departure from the old ways of thinking about motion and structure generally, and planets in particular, was so vast a change in methods of observation, careful measurement, and interpretation that Albert Einstein deemed Galileo to be "the father of science."

It is important in discussing the historic disorientation between science and religion to first understand the infamous Galileo Affair. His methods and discoveries and personality led him into a titanic clash with many of his Aristotelian colleagues as he found evidence at odds with their orthodox views. His zeal and audacity had taunted and embarrassed the philosophical establishment and earned for him too many adversaries in scholarly circles. His contemporary Aristotelians occupied the academic hierarchies of the Roman Catholic universities, holding a near monopoly on accepted wisdom. So it was inevitable that his claims would bring Galileo into vigorous, if unsought, conflict with his Catholic Establishment.

Galileo was not merely a rare genius of consummate brilliance. He also had a strong propensity for scholarly dispute, often enticing his adversaries into public debate, then demolishing them by exposing the flaws in their argument. His ideas were often contrary to accepted Aristotelian views. He was an iconoclast in a world of icons. Gali*leo* was truly a "Lion in a Den of Daniels." In many ways, this would inexorably prejudice his peers against him and deny him a fair and unbiased hearing.

Galileo had pioneered the quantitative study of motion. By rolling balls slowly down a grooved incline, he measured the relative time for objects to roll multiples of a primary distance down an incline, and derived a simple mathematical formula for acceleration that was independent of their mass. He published a variety of thought experiments to illustrate the fallacy of the Aristotelian idea that heavier objects must fall faster than lighter objects. If two cannonballs of different sizes were to fall at different velocities, what happens if they are chained or welded together? If one cannonball is cut into two fragments of different sizes, would they fall at different velocities?

[In case you were wondering, there were mechanical clocks available for approximating the time of day, but were not accurate enough for Galileo's work. He devised a "water clock" for measuring relative time. Water from a large elevated reservoir flowed down a pipe through a valve that was opened as the ball started rolling, and shut off as the ball passed a predetermined distance. The weight of the water collected for each distance was his surrogate for its elapsed time. Precision was improved by repetition, averaged for each unit of distance. He found that the weight of water collected for a ball to traverse a given distance was proportional to the square root of the distance. In other words, distance fallen (d) was proportional to the square of time (t), or $d = kt^2$ where k is the proportionality constant.

To visualize this, if the slope of an incline is such that the ball will descend one foot in one second, it will fall four feet in two seconds, and nine feet in three seconds. In this example, note that the ball falls one unit of distance in the first second, three more units in the next second, and five units of distance in the third second. Isaac Newton took this to define the acceleration due to gravity.

An apocryphal story attributed to his biographer Vincenzo Viviani even had Galileo dropping rocks and cannon balls of different sizes from the Leaning Tower of Pisa to taunt his rivals and distract their meditation as they walked by. Lacking corroboration, modern historians write it off as a fiction, but what a great story!]

Into this heated climate of scholarly rivalry, Galileo brought forth his remarkable discoveries about the moon, the stars, and our planetary system. Perhaps, had Galileo shown a bit more diplomacy and a little less hubris in his collegial relationships, his conclusions might have been more open to consideration by the philosophical and ecclesiastical establishments, and more readily accepted. Had he impressed and inspired his contemporaries to follow his example, he might have freed up his own time for fresh inquiries. Instead, he was met with vigorous opposition as he took far too much pleasure in aggravating his academic peers by proving them wrong. His every victory in these skirmishes made his adversaries even more determined to bring him down.

The Telescope (or the Dutch *Trunke*)

Before Galileo, astronomers made their observations of stars and planets visible to the unaided eye, using calibrated hinged shafts to measure angles between pairs and groups of them, and from each to the various points on the horizon. One giant among them, the incomparable Danish astronomer Tycho Brahe, compiled an enormous collection of data of such precision that for decades afterwards Johannes Kepler and other mathematicians would rely upon his measurements for calculating the planetary orbits (see Chapter 3).

The telescope, and Galileo's innovative use of it, dramatically changed astronomy, and was the single transformative instrument that launched the scientific revolution. It changed the view (so to speak!) of seventeenth-century natural philosophers as to humans' place in the vast universe. One historian, Marcia Bartusiak in her book *The Day We Found the Universe*, has put it in the most wonderful perspective: "The universe got bigger and bigger until it is beyond our comprehension."

[Galileo did not invent the telescope, by the way. That distinction is somewhat obscured in the historical record, but is presumed to have been the invention of Hans Lipperhey, a German-Dutch lens maker who demonstrated his three-power telescope to the Dutch Parliament in 1608. Whether he was the original inventor is a matter of some dispute, as his patent application was stymied by claims of two other Dutch spectacle makers (Metius and Janssen).

In Padua, Galileo had read about this clever toy, and concentrated on how to improve its technology in order to profit from the mercantile and military market. With his new appreciation of optics, he later took another contemporary Dutch invention and improved it to make the first compound microscope that could be adjusted for sharper focus.]

Galileo had been one of the first, along with one Thomas Harriot of England, to turn the "spyglass" toward the night sky. What he saw was so astonishing that he published his discoveries in *The Starry Messenger* (1610). For whatever reason, Harriot kept his observations pretty much to himself, and consequently had little impact on the scientific revolution that his Italian counterpart ignited.

Galileo began with the obvious: taking a closer look at the moon and planets. The field of his telescope was only about a third of the diameter of the moon, so he focused on features near the "terminator" between light and dark. That was an amazing start, for this technique readily revealed shadows of its ridges and craters. These shadows meant that the moon was not illuminated by its own inner light, but simply reflected the light from the sun. More controversial, of course, were Galileo's claims that the moon was not a pure crystalline sphere as generally believed, but had a decidedly pock-marked surface. It had blemishes!

Galileo was equally amazed to find that the Milky Way was not what it seems even today to the unaided eye: a vast streak of luminous gas. In every direction it became resolved by his telescope into discrete points of light coming from a mass of stars. I would encourage you to try it with your best binoculars on the next clear night, especially if the moon is not up. You do not need binoculars with high magnification, as the important feature is that they can gather far more light than can your eye alone and show you many thousands more stars. You can't say you've seen everything until you see this!

This picture of the Milky Way constituting the entirety of the universe prevailed for over three centuries. That perspective changed when Edwin Hubble, with far greater light-gathering capacity and magnifying power, discovered (1929) that spiral nebulae likewise were not gaseous clouds, but remote, giant galaxies of stars in their own right.

Of greater intrigue, Galileo observed that Jupiter had four moons in tow, prancing along through space. The number of celestial lights moving across the background of stars was raised abruptly to eleven from the mystical seven where it had stood since early antiquity. By following their changing positions across a series of nights, it was evident that they were revolving in orbits about Jupiter, just like our moon. Note that his moons more often are diagrammed NOT in a straight line. Owen Gingerich has demonstrated that this is due to the plane of their orbits being tilted slightly down to our line of sight. (If there's no hazy glare from the moon or city lights, good binoculars might enable you to see and monitor Jupiter's largest four moons from night to night, as did Galileo.)

This was a serious matter. If Jupiter could move through the heavens without losing its four moons, might not Earth also be able to move about while retaining its moon? Galileo rewarded his sponsors among the Medici family by naming these moons in their honor. Accordingly, Jupiter's four he called the Medician Moons, although we may call them Galilean Moons.

Galileo's Observations of Four Moons of Jupiter
Draft of Letter to Leonardo Donati, Doge of Venice
Credit: University of Michigan Special Collections Library;
Licensed under CC BY 4.0

Most important of all, from November 11, 1610 until January 1, 1611, Galileo observed Venus with great care. He discovered that it had the same phases as our moon, which would prove that Venus orbited around the Sun.

Consider his evidence from Venus. It had been accepted as part of the orthodox Ptolemaic geocentric order of planets that Venus could be only on the near side of the sun <u>or</u> only on its far side, but could not penetrate what were thought to be concentric spheres that nested the sun and Venus in their respective orbits. If Venus were always on the near side between Earth and the sun, its reflected light would never be able to show a full-faced reflection, but could only reflect a crescent of light. If Venus were exclusively on the far side beyond the sun, it would always be full, or nearly so. Galileo observed that in fact Venus displays all possible reflection phases, just like the familiar phases of the moon, phenomena possible only if Venus revolves around the sun. This would support the sun-centered planetary system espoused by Copernicus.

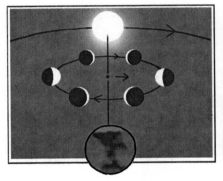

Geocentric version with Sun
beyond the epicycle of Venus

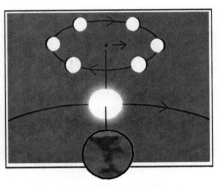

Geocentric version with the
epicycle of Venus beyond the Sun

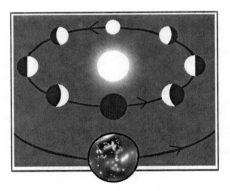

Heliocentric Phases of Venus
as observed by Galileo

One more remarkable discovery was the demonstration that the sun rotated about its own axis. Galileo had first observed sunspots, and found that they moved in a pattern across the surface and disappeared, only to reappear later, often in the same pattern. This he interpreted to mean that the entire sun was not a fixed object with the same face always toward us, but was spinning like a ball.

This phenomenon can be observed *if you promise to be very careful.* Let me emphasize as strongly as I can that you must never look directly at the sun, and certainly not with the much higher light-gathering power of a telescope or your binoculars. That will surely blind you by scorching your retina. One way to examine the sun is to hold your binoculars at about knee level, with the large lenses pointed to the sun. That will project an image of the sun down on the ground, or better yet on a cardboard that you have inclined there for the projected image. In this way, you will not be looking directly at the sun but at its image on the ground. Examining that projection, you might see small black dots within its bright circular image. Check them tomorrow and they will have moved.

Some have written that when Galileo took his telescope to the Jesuit College of Rome in 1611 for a demonstration, his hosts refused to look through it. Well, some did look, for the Jesuits encouraged astronomy. In fact, Galileo wrote of this occasion: "I have been received and shown favor by many illustrious cardinals, prelates and princes of this city."

The acclaim may not have been unanimous, for most astronomers of that day still had questions that Galileo could not then answer. Not only was Galileo not rejected, but he was elevated to membership in the Academy of Lynxes, a prestigious private society of scientists. At that time, scholars were free and eager to teach the Copernican concept in Catholic universities without incident, other than the usual academic discourse.

There is no doubt that Galileo's discoveries, and his boldness in pressing them upon the world, gave his adversaries the ultimate weapons they needed for putting him in his place. They lodged their complaints that Galileo's ideas were not only anti-Aristotelian but contravened Scripture. Galileo, of course, would not flinch at this rising danger as he met each objection with withering logic and evidence.

[Some have categorized this affair by saying that Galileo was tried and convicted of the sin of opposing Catholic dogma that the sun and all known planets revolved around the fixed center of Earth. One flaw in that oversimplified statement is that the Roman Catholic Church had no such dogma. Dogma is a statement of faith or doctrine which all are required to accept and believe in order to remain in good standing. No concept of the structure of the solar system or any other scientific question has ever been held as dogma by the Catholic Church.]

Heresy?

No one since Galileo has been subject to anything like the Inquisition as a result of scientific views. Preceding him, however, there was the deeply disturbing case of former Friar Giordano Bruno, who was convicted of heresy and burned at the stake in Rome (1600). As was the practice at the time, if the Church found someone guilty of heresy, he was then turned over to the civil authorities to dispose of him. The easy conclusion was that Bruno was executed because of his belief in the heliocentric concept of Copernicus, but it now seems a bit more complex. In an unrelated historic note, Bruno taught briefly at Padua, where he was an unsuccessful candidate for the chair in mathematics, awarded instead to Galileo Galilei.

Bruno did endorse Copernicus's idea of a central sun, and argued that it was just another star, albeit much closer to us. He believed there were thousands of other suns in the heavens, many with habitable planets like ours. Beyond this, he came to the belief that God was neither more nor less than the entirety of nature and the universe—a belief system we now call **pantheism**. These views placed him at odds with the Church on matters of dogma with regard to the Holy Trinity, the divinity of Jesus, and the virgin birth. Compounding the problem was his belief in the "atomism" of unseen fundamental particles as the basis of all matter, a concept that was then thought to conflict with the doctrine of transubstantiation of the elements of the Eucharist. Pantheism and atomism were the more likely bases for his heresy conviction, but the message was clear: proceed with caution!

For that matter, the heliocentric theory initially had been mostly well-received by the Catholic Church when it was first published by Nicolaus Copernicus very shortly before his death in 1543 AD. Young Copernicus had been appointed a canon at Frauenburg Cathedral, a post requiring no particular priestly duties. Nevertheless, his *On the Revolutions of the Celestial Spheres* was devoutly and shrewdly dedicated to Pope Paul III, and published just as death's pilot ushered Copernicus into safe harbor.

This was not the first time this sun-centered idea had appeared. Around 250 BC, Aristarchus, a noted Greek philosopher from the Island of Samos, reasoned that the sun and stars were fixed, and that Earth moved in a circle around the sun while spinning about its own axis.

Archimedes recognized that this would require the universe to be much larger than was then believed, because Earth's motion would cause parallax shifts in the angles of observed stars unless they were extremely far away from us.

The fledgling solar system was rejected, and Aristarchus was deemed a lunatic ("sol-a-tic" might be more appropriate), because his fixed sun was inconsistent with the fixed-earth idea of Aristotle from a hundred years earlier. Aristotle had envisioned a set of concentric spheres (later thought to be crystalline) as the mechanism holding the sun, moon, planets, and stars in orbs circling about the earth, and it was too great a departure to think of the earth crashing through these celestial spheres. On the unequalled strength of Aristotle's enormous reputation, this error held up for almost two thousand years. Incidentally, the Bible makes no mention of concentric crystalline spheres.

We and our ancestors have the biased perspective of being on Earth, so everything else is "out there." So it was quite natural for early civilizations to accept readily the impression that we were at the center of everything. The authors of the Old Testament texts would certainly see it that way. They had no means to discover any rotational or translational motion of the earth. To them, it was simply obvious that the earth was not moving under their feet. Even today, we speak metaphorically of "sunrise" and "sunset."

This comfort zone was given further credibility *circa* AD 140 when the Egyptian-Roman astronomer and geographer Claudius Ptolemaeus ("Ptolemy") wrote his thirteen-part astronomical encyclopedia now known as *Almagest* (Arabic for "The Great System") and his *Planetary Hypothesis*, wherein he developed the more mathematical basis of his Earth-centered system of the world. In those days, "world" meant everything that we now refer to as the universe or cosmos.

Two convincing arguments were put forward by Ptolemy. The first was based on the Aristotelian argument that falling objects always moved toward the center of the world. Since any object released above a well or other deep hole always fell into those depths, it followed that the earth's center must be positioned at the center of the world. The error in this reasoning could not be understood until 1,600 years later when Sir Isaac Newton deduced a better understanding of the nature of gravitational forces.

Ptolemy's second argument was similarly hard to dispute. It rejected the notion that the earth was spinning about its polar axis in a 24-hour cycle. He reasoned that if the earth were rotating about its axis, any object launched vertically upwards would lag behind as the earth spun beneath it, and would fall to a different location. Since it fell back to the point from which it had been thrown, it must follow that Earth was immobile, which seemed self-evident. Consequently, it was difficult 1,500 years later for others to accept Galileo's correct conclusion from his studies of motion that the object thrown aloft would have the momentum given it not only by the upward thrust, but also by the lateral, rotational motion of the earth. It would simply return back to its original starting point, just as a ball dropped from a great height would fall to a spot directly beneath.

This Ptolemy was not kin to the powerful dynastic line of pharaohs known as Ptolemy. He was a commoner, a Roman citizen from the Egyptian town of Ptolemais Hermiou, from which he took his name. After his book was translated into Arabic in 827, it became available in Europe. This belief in an Earth-centered universe would then survive as the dominant worldview for almost ten centuries. It had the powerful advantage of being consistent with Biblical narratives, the teachings of Aristotle, and now the calculations of Ptolemy. It must have seemed utterly foolish for anyone to imagine that the stable Earth spun about its own polar axis or twirled through space in some annual circumference about the sun. Copernicus and his followers had to tread carefully.

Retrograde Motion of Planets

There was a troubling little problem with this Aristotelian/Ptolemaic concept. Astronomers knew a little secret that ought not be discussed in polite company: the **retrograde motion** of planets. Ordinarily, the motion of a planet across the field of stars is a steady progression from night to night. However, for three outer planets (Mars, Saturn, and Jupiter) there were times when each reversed field and moved back in the other direction against the star field. There were enough observations that astronomers could predict accurately when the next such aberration would occur.

There was no good explanation for this anomaly, so a bad explanation had to suffice. If Aristotle's concentric crystalline spheres held each planet in its position and carried each along in its circuit through space, there had to be some derivative device to account for the curious retrograde motion. Ptolemy concluded that there had to be a little grooved place in the Aristotelian crystalline spheres of these three planets, so that periodically the planet would take a little spin around this groove at the edge of its sphere. He called this an "epicycle," meaning "on the circle."

Perhaps you have enjoyed one of those rides at the state fair, where you sit in a bowl at the end of a boom. The boom moves the bowl around in a generally circular path. Every now and then the bowl goes into a spin on its short axis out at the end of the boom. Did you enjoy your epicycle ride?

Ptolemy borrowed this idea from the third-century BC mathematician Apollonius, and also Hipparchus, one of the greatest astronomers of the ancient world. So it had been hanging around for some 500 years, giving it an aura of rationality. Retrograde planetary motion was regular and precise enough to be predictable by "mathematical models," but without Aristotle's crystalline spheres, there was nothing physical to hold these objects in their epicyclical tracks. Geocentrists had to have some metaphoric model to account for retrograde motion, even if this one amounted to a "Rube Goldberg" machine out there in space, with no concern how it got there.

There was a related problem for the other two planets, Mercury and Venus. Both of these seemed to stay close to the sun, being visible either soon after dusk or just before morning. Venus, you may remember, has been poetically enshrined as the "morning star" or the "evening star," depending upon the allegorical point being made. Mercury and Venus were never observed in the midnight sky (okay, except by the few living above the Arctic Circle). At times, they arose in the east just before sunrise. At other times they declined below the western horizon soon after sunset.

Ptolemy simply invoked another epicycle mechanism to account for this. Mercury seemed to have a steadily spinning epicycle around a point that moved in a synchronous fashion with the sun. The same had to be true for Venus. This seems weird today, but was calmly accepted back then. They needed some explanation that would "save the appearances" and accommodate the belief that all those seven moving objects (sun, moon, Mercury, Venus, Mars, Saturn, and Jupiter) were orbiting around Earth.

Copernicus, lacking a better explanation, simply accepted these epicycles. He envisioned the Aristotelian spheres for his planets, including Earth, concentrically nested around the sun. Kepler's later calculations affirmed this simpler explanation without the epicyclical contortions. If Earth (our only vantage point for observations) and Mars were both revolving about the sun with Mars further away in its larger and slower orbit, most of the time Mars would be gliding along nicely and steadily against the night star field. Then when the time came for Earth, in its faster inner orbit, to pass between the sun and Mars, the faster motion of Earth would cause Mars to *APPEAR* to be moving backwards against the stars.

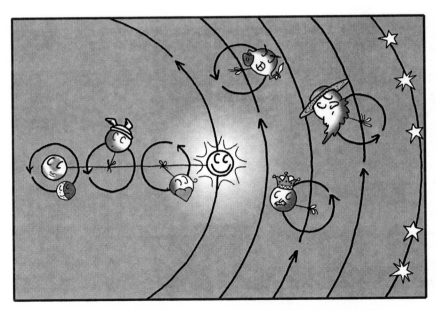

Retrograde Motion according to Ptolemy's Epicycles

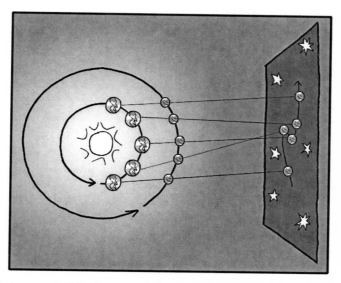

Retrograde Motion according to Copernicus and Kepler

If you enjoy sailing, you may have seen this same effect on a nearby rival sailboat against a distant background of trees onshore. If it sails in the same direction as your vessel and you are sailing faster, the other boat will appear to be going backwards against the frame of reference of more distant trees. We say we are "making trees" on the competitor.

In a late sixteenth-century exchange of correspondence on these subjects, Johannes Kepler urged Galileo to join him in an intellectual challenge to the Ptolemaic geocentric view. It was far too risky for Galileo. In Italy, he was subject to the reach of the Vatican, although Kepler had to be just as wary of Lutheran authorities. Galileo's turning point would come a decade later when his telescopic observations excited and emboldened him. By that time, Kepler was already there. Maybe Kepler was predisposed to accept the Copernican concept, having written, "it reflected the divine design of the cosmos: the sun at the center was the image of God."

Kepler had calculated the orbit of Mars (1605) from Tycho Brahe's precision measurements of its movement against the starry background. This was consistent only with an elliptical orbit with the sun at one focus of the ellipse. He published this in 1609, just as Galileo was beginning to describe what he saw through his spyglass. Kepler also pointed out that the periods of the orbits of the known planets were such that the farther a planet was from the sun, the longer it took to make a complete circuit.

Ironically, it may have been pressure from Protestants that forced the Copernican system into the Catholic courts on grounds that it contradicted the Bible to say the earth circles around the static sun. In the early sixteenth-century, the reformer Martin Luther, with Melanchthon and other Protestants, had used this "heresy" claim about Copernicanism to proselytize Catholics and urge them to convert to Protestantism. This forced Catholic clergy defensively into a similar posture.

In 1613, Galileo had been confronted by his patroness, the Grand Duchess with the Biblical narrative of Joshua commanding the sun to stand still. Galileo's apt reply may not have satisfied her, but was surely on point: "The Bible does not tell us how the heavens go, but how to go to Heaven!"

[Incidentally, there was a fascinating third cosmology developed by Tycho Brahe, the talented Danish astronomer (pages 45-49). You will be astonished. Was it disingenuous; or truly ingenious?]

Prelude to Inquisition: The Galileo Affair

A number of books have been devoted to "the crime of Galileo" and the circumstances that led him before the Inquisition. Two mutually consistent versions are *The Crime of Galileo* by Giorgio de Santillana (1955) and *The Crime of Galileo: Indictment and Abjuration of 1633* by Paul Halsall (1998). Other interpretations have been published as well. There is general agreement that this was one of the most profound contests between science and authority. Here, we can only sketch the essential ingredients.

Father Tommaso Caccini was among the Catholic prelates who took up the Protestant challenge, proving that no Protestant could outdo him in defending Scripture by condemning the Copernican heliocentrism. This cause gained favor amongst the Dominican Order. Caccini was joined by Friar Niccolo Lorini, who preached that Joshua commanded the sun to stand still (*Joshua 10:12–14*), giving Scriptural authority to the belief that the sun revolved around the fixed Earth, and not the other way around. Heresy was thus sharply defined in their view.

One can argue that Galileo should have stayed out of this ruckus. The Catholic Church had no problem with him as long as he left theology to theologians. But then he would not have been Galileo! True to form, our hero could not ignore the trap laid out before him. To a Dominican friend, he protested that the Copernican Theory did not contradict the Bible, and offered several interpretations of Scripture in support of his position. This was a tactical blunder, as it allowed Caccini to pin Galileo with the charge that he had now crossed the boundary into the theological realm. As ordered by the Council of Trent, any interpretation of the Bible was then the sole province of the reverend clergy, with the Vatican Councils as the final arbiter. Clearly, Galileo had strayed dangerously into the forbidden domain of theology.

Inquisition I

In 1616, Galileo was hauled before the Congregation of the Holy Office, a.k.a. the Inquisition, and ordered to desist from any more meddling in doctrinal matters and to limit his teaching of heliocentrism to a hypothesis, but never as Truth. The Ptolemaic concept of a geocentric planetary system was not a matter of dogma. The problem was that Galileo was attempting to interpret the Bible, which was not his province or authority. This order was applied directly to Galileo by Cardinal Bellarmino, and the Copernican text was placed on the *Index of Forbidden Books*.

Bellarmino, by the way, was among those on the Inquisition court who convicted Bruno of heresy 16 years earlier. He cautioned Galileo that, while "the appearances could be saved" by imagining the sun was at the center, one must not cite proof that it actually *is* there. Cardinal Bellarmino ordered him not to use his theories and observations to interpret the Scripture or to defend Copernicus. His later conviction was for disobeying this direct order not to propound his observations and theories as if they were the truth.

Galileo had his "friends in high places." His long-time supporter Cardinal Maffeo Barberini had become Pope Urban VIII in 1623. Later that year, Galileo published *The Assayer*, which he dedicated to the new Pope. His book began as a letter defending Galileo's contribution of improving the telescope. It then veered into a denunciation of a theory of comets published by one Orazio Grassi. Grassi had reported a determination by parallax measurements that a particular comet had ventured between the sun and the moon. Galileo disputed this on the basis of his firm belief that comets were optical illusions without mass or substance. He was wrong about that.

As an amateur astronomer, Barberini accepted the scientific arguments for the Ptolemaic Earth-centered concept, but admired Galileo's work and encouraged him to continue to pursue an understanding of celestial motion. Specifically, Urban suggested that

Galileo write a treatise on the evidence and arguments for and against both the Copernican heliocentric view and the Ptolemaic geocentric concept, without advocacy, avoiding theological notions. He could include, as a courtesy, Urban's personal ideas favoring the geocentric alternative. As a papal judgment, infallible it was not.

Galileo brought forth (1632) his monumental *Dialogue Concerning the Two Chief World Systems,* and blew his once friendly *Pax Urbana VIII* into irretrievable wreckage. As a gifted writer, Galileo structured this satirical "Dialogue" as a running, four-day debate between one eloquent character named *Salviati,* who presented the obviously superior case for Copernican heliocentrism, and an Aristotelian rival named *Simplicio,* who held the field for Ptolemaic geocentrism. A third, independent character, *Sagredo,* was deployed as an initially unbiased interlocutor of sorts. It was not lost on readers that the name *Simplicio* could mean "Simpleton"!

Mistaking his papal charge as leeway, Galileo boldly delivered by including Urban's personal pronouncements in favor of a stationary Earth at the center of the universe. Urban intended this as a way to balance the matter evenly and non-provocatively. As brilliant as Galileo was, he apparently could not see that Pope Urban's own words might not translate too respectfully via the fictional voice of the "Simpleton." He just ended up making the Pope appear mindless, which handed Galileo's opponents the clear advantage that too long had eluded them.

Inquisition II and Beyond

This time around (1633), the Inquisition was better prepared and more emphatic and blunt. Ten Cardinals-Inquisitors sat in judgment against him. Eleven leading scholars (Aristotelians all) were charged to state the accepted position of contemporary science. More emphatically than in 1616, they were unanimous as to two findings that:

1. The idea that the sun was at the center of the world and motionless was foolish, absurd, and heretical.
2. The companion idea that the earth was not the center of the world and moved around the sun and had diurnal (daily) motion about its own axis deserved censure on rational grounds and also constituted theological error.

This was basically a case of observational science being trumped by outdated natural philosophy. The latter had the advantage of being enshrined in the academies of the Church.

Three more experts were empaneled to review his *Dialogue* for error, and they did not come up short. They concluded that Galileo had not merely discussed Copernican astronomy as a hypothesis (as anyone was allowed to do), but had "taught, defended and held it to be proved as physical fact." To compound the injury, he had written it in ordinary Italian, not in scholarly Latin, allowing literate citizens anywhere to read and decide for themselves. This posed a clear risk to the faith of millions. Adding insult with rhetorical excess, those who agreed with *Simplicio* were derisively taunted as "dumb idiots and mental pygmies, hardly deserving to be called human."

To put Galileo in the proper frame of mind, he may have been taken on a private, guided tour of the dungeons. This standard practice, called *territio realis*, would acquaint the accused with their frightening array of machines and instruments of torture, without actually using them. This process had proven its value for persuading others to accept compliance with Vatican teachings. In this instance, it would have focused his mind and attention on the risks he now faced and the need for careful circumspection as well as a more submissive disposition.

On April 27, 1633, Galileo humbled himself with a contrite admission of error, confessing that "upon further review" (as today's football referee would proclaim), he had inadvertently biased the case too forcefully in favor of Copernican ideas. "I am an old man. Do with me what you will."

While his plea was surely confessional and sincere, one might read into it a bit of wiggle room, especially from someone shrewd and politic enough to have secured the approval of the necessary ecclesiastical reviewers prior to obtaining a publisher for his *Dialogue*. His voluntary statement was deemed insufficient and Galileo (after eleven weeks of trial) was brought back before this Court on June 22, 1633, to hear its sentence, which was clear, direct, unmistakable, and inescapable. He was "vehemently suspected of heresy" for holding and expressing beliefs that the sun is the center of the world, and not the earth, and that the earth moves around the sun. He was ordered to "abjure, curse and detest" these and all other errors and heresies for penitent absolution, and was sentenced to prison, with the Holy Office reserving the right of later commutation.

In simplest terms, Galileo was found to have violated Bellarmino's prohibition against advocacy. The erudite Copernican arguments of

Salviati were clearly superior to the Ptolemaic clumsiness of *Simplicio*. Having insulted His Holiness did not help at all. To make matters worse, Galileo's adversaries produced documents from the Vatican archives indicating that he had been instructed in 1616 not to teach or <u>mention</u> the two critical and heretical ideas that the sun was stationary and that the earth moved. If so, it would be far more severe than what he had understood to be an injunction to avoid <u>promoting</u> Copernicanism as truth contrary to the Bible.

In this historic confrontation with authority, Galileo chose discretion by denying and abjuring the very theses upon which his reputation rests today. Abjuration is the solemn renouncing of an alleged heresy with the intent of winning acceptance with the Church. If one later recanted the abjuring oath, the penalty was excommunication and being turned over to civil authorities for execution, usually by burning at the stake. In retrospect, it was not necessary for the advancement of science for Galileo to defy his captors and take the painful consequences. His book was already published and would carry the final verdict of history and theology, which is sufficient testimony to his transforming brilliance.

Realizing the danger that he now faced, and having conceded that his *Dialogue* was not "balanced," Galileo threw himself upon the mercies of the Holy Office. Here was a crucial moment to choose between unambiguous commitment and fatal defiance. As directed, Galileo held in his hands an unequivocal statement of abjuration, which he read before his ten Cardinals-Inquisitors who held his life in their hands. To read moving translations of these statements, see *The Crime of Galileo*, by Giorgio de Santillana.

Galileo's book was banned, but it was by then widely circulated and beyond recall. He himself was found guilty of violating a direct order to avoid theological controversy, and sentenced to prison. He never got there, as Urban arranged to commute the sentence to detention at the residence of the archbishop of Siena and later to confinement in his own home in Arcetri. Some have opined that this outcome not only enabled the Catholic Church to respond aggressively to the Protestant accusation of delinquency in defense of Scripture, but may also have saved Galileo's head from those seeking to silence him permanently.

While subjected to a full trial by the Inquisition, Galileo was never excommunicated. Rather he was found to be "vehemently suspected of heresy," and confined to house arrest for the remainder of his life. This somewhat ambiguously qualified condemnation (***guilty*** of ***suspicion*** of heresy!) remained in effect until he was restored to proper standing by Pope John Paul II, who had the case revisited in 1979. In doing so, he spoke in clear terms that reflected Galileo's own views on the subject of Biblical interpretation of science: "Research performed in a truly scientific manner can never be in contrast with faith, because both profane and religious realities have their origin in the same God."

Four years later, the Papal Commission found that Galileo should not have been condemned, which conclusion John Paul II endorsed, saying: "Ironically, Galileo was the better theologian." In 1992, John Paul II did redeem Galileo from suspicion of heresy, albeit posthumously, by having the anti-Copernican prohibition of 1616 reversed. John Paul II did not go so far as to endorse Galileo's position on the "Two Chief World Systems." After all, that would have put the Church again in the predicament of taking a position on the science. Yes, we can learn from history!

While Galileo was no fiery renegade, he could have used a modicum of diplomacy now and then. He continued his faithful allegiance to his Church, and believed that the Bible was the revealed word of God. At the same time, he knew that nature was the handiwork of God, and that we should cultivate our knowledge and understanding of it through careful observation and measurement. In this, he was far ahead of his time, and duly acknowledged now to be the founder of modern science, both for his astronomical observations and for his studies of motion and the strength of materials.

A century after his death, a legend arose that after solemnly renouncing his heliocentric belief that the earth revolves around the sun as he had been directed to do, Galileo then muttered "and yet it moves!" There is no record of anyone attesting to this, nor did Galileo later make any such boast, so it has to be taken as probably just another charming fiction, albeit true to his obstinate character. To recant abjuration was unthinkable.

Harvard scholar Stephen Greenblatt has written an engaging discourse on *De Rerum Natura* (*On the Nature of Things*), the once lost poem by Lucretius, and its influence upon the Enlightenment. In tying this loosely to Galileo, he suggests that there could have been another issue before the Inquisition: the suspicion that Galileo harbored the heretical belief in atomism, which was key in Friar Bruno's undoing. Citing the 1982 discovery in the Inquisition's archives of a document from one Cardinal-Inquisitor raising such suspicions after reading Galileo's *The Assayer*, Greenblatt seems to imply an atomism heresy against the Holy Sacraments as another problem for Galileo. Pietro Redondi has raised similar concerns. However, the fact that the referenced document was not presented or mentioned at trial indicates that it was not given any weight in the proceedings. Had it been, the outcome could have been abrupt and lethal.

Post-Script

There are many lovely sequels to this tragic affair. House arrest was initially under the care of the Archbishop of Siena and later in Galileo's own villa in Arcetri, across the river from Florence. There he discovered the distressed condition of his daughter, Virginia, a Roman Catholic nun, who had taken the name Sister Maria Celeste. She died in 1634, just four months after his long-delayed return home. Her devoted letters, supporting and encouraging him throughout his ordeal, have been immortalized in a remarkable memoir, *Galileo's Daughter*, by Dava Sobel.

Although fast approaching blindness, he devoted his remaining days to another major work on the nature of motion and the strength of materials. Entitled *Discourses and Mathematical Demonstrations Relating to Two New Sciences*, it has served as the basis for later contributions by Isaac Newton and Albert Einstein. Repeat appearances of the same characters were deployed: *Simplicio* presenting Galileo's earlier ideas, *Sagredo* with his transitional thoughts, and *Salviati* with their more sophisticated development.

Upon Galileo's death at age seventy-seven, Ferdinando II, Grand Duke of Tuscany, proposed to have him buried near his father in the Basilica di Santa Croce in Florence. This was opposed by Pope Urban VIII and others on the grounds that Galileo had been condemned for "vehement suspicion of heresy." Instead, his remains were secretly stored in a remote room, its Chapel of the Novitiate, by the friars of Santa Croce. There he reposed for ninety-five years until 1737, when the civic elite of Florence ultimately prevailed to have him moved into a monumental sarcophagus in that same Basilica di Santa Croce, in artistic style and grandeur rivaling that of Michelangelo's tomb nearby. When the old crypt was opened for the transfer, several body parts were removed as souvenirs. Among them, his middle finger was cut off, to be displayed in a defiant salute in the Museo Galileo in Florence! You might search that brilliant image on the Internet.

Astonishingly, it was discovered that there were two other corpses in there with him, and all three were reinterred together. One is known to be that of his able editor and first biographer, Vincenzo Viviani, who assisted him in his final years. The other, a younger woman, is undoubtedly that of his daughter, Sister Maria Celeste.

Chapter 3

Tycho!

One of the most intriguing and remarkable figures of early science was the incomparable Danish astronomer Tycho Brahe (1546–1601). Tycho was the Latin form of his given name Tyge. It is enough that he is regarded as the most important and productive astronomer of all time before the advent of the telescope, and without the benefit of its superior light-gathering capacity. In fascinating addition to that, he was one truly memorable character who finessed the ecclesiastical insistence that the sun moved around the immovable earth. Wait for it.

Tycho Brahe (pronounced **Tʃə-kō Brä-**hə) is sometimes depicted with or without his false nose. As a student, he got the short end of swordplay in the dark, and lost the bridge of his nose. Out of vanity, he would insert a carved, wooden plug for everyday use and a nice brass version for formal occasions. You can see and admire artistic renderings of these in the Tycho Brahe Museum in Copenhagen if you like.

Uraniborg

Young Tycho was raised by his uncle Jørgen Brahe, who had been promised a child from Tycho's parents. Uncle Jørgen died of pneumonia soon after rescuing the Danish Prince Frederick II from an icy moat, a valiant sacrifice for which the future King of Denmark would forever be grateful, providing financial sustenance for Tycho's chosen career.

While never married formally, Tycho and his lady sustained a happy common-law relationship that produced a house full of eight offspring. Such abundance required a large home, which he constructed as a combination residence, **Uraniborg**, and his observatory, **Stjerniborg**, on the island of Hven, half of which was provided for his use by King Frederick. Hven is near Elsinor Castle (famous in Shakespeare's play *Hamlet*), just off the coast across from the nearest point of Sweden. The

Brahe mansion had monumental proportions, and they lived there for twenty-one years.

After he moved to Prague, the Hven property fell apart under the acquisitive pilfering of his former neighbors, who never liked him anyway, as they considered Tycho an overbearing intruder. Today, the government and various supportive foundations are rebuilding the scientific facilities of his one-of-a-kind observatory, with reproductions of some of the giant sextants, quadrants, armillary spheres, and other oversized instruments that he designed, built, and used. After all, Tycho is considered the second most famous Dane in history. Who do you suppose might have surpassed him?

In the old center of Copenhagen, there stands today a circular tower (rather appropriately named *Rundetaarn*) that Tycho used for many of his early astronomic observations. It features a wide, helical, cobblestone ramp, without stairs, ascending 110 feet above street level like the grooves of a left-handed screw (falsely foreshadowing the right-handed helix of DNA) to a small museum and observatory at the top. Local history recounts that Czar Peter the Great of Russia rode his horse up and down this structure. The Czarina ascended in a carriage. You may walk it, as we did. Copenhagen also features the Tycho Brahe Planetarium that you would enjoy.

Tychonic Astronomy

Mechanical clocks had been somewhat improved by 1570, and Tycho had four in his observatory that ticked the seconds, so he could take the time of night from their average. Tycho designed and assembled most of his own important stargazing instruments. They were enormous in proportions and vastly superior to anything else available. Some used a type of Vernier scale, allowing measurements a hundredfold more precise than any alternative for determining angles between stars.

This enabled him to produce superior maps and a globe showing 777 most prominent stars, with precise data for predicting the positions of the five known celestial planets (Mercury, Venus, Mars, Jupiter, and Saturn).

In 1572, Tycho made careful observations of a new star that had not previously been seen. He recorded this in *De Stella Nova* (Latin for "new star"). We now know that this was a supernova 7,500 light-years away (its remnant still visible by telescope today). Five years later, he studied a comet passing through the planetary system. This led him to reject the Aristotelian notion that the planets were moved by the rotations of crystalline spheres (which would have blocked passage of the comet).

After Frederick II died, Tycho fell out of royal favor with the successor King Christian IV. He moved to Prague in 1599 as imperial astronomer to Holy Roman Emperor Rudolph II. There he retained the support services of a right fair mathematician named Johannes Kepler. Tycho permitted Kepler access only to his position tables for Mars. From these precise data, Kepler calculated the slightly elliptical orbit of the red planet. Upon Tycho's death in 1601, Kepler obtained the data on the other four planets, from which impeccable treasure he derived their precise orbits around the sun, thereby reinforcing in 1609 the heliocentric theory of Copernicus.

Geometric *Finesse*

Tycho, in his day, accepted neither the Copernican (heliocentric) nor the Ptolemaic (geocentric) model for the celestial motions. He devised an ingenious alternative that had the sun and moon orbiting around a fixed Earth, but with all other planets orbiting around the sun.

In 1616, at the very time Galileo was first ordered by the Inquisition to desist from claiming the earth moved around the sun, the Catholic hierarchy sensed that the Ptolemaic version would no longer stand against Galileo's evidence. Tycho's concept was officially and gratefully approved by the Vatican Council, as it had the virtue of being based upon a fixed, unmoving Earth. It would have made a mess of Aristotle's crystalline spheres, but was never elevated and enshrined as dogma. Privately, Tycho did not exactly believe the earth was unmoving, for he was certain that it was rotating about its own axis.

In the Tycho Brahe Planetarium in Copenhagen, there is a mechanical working model of this Tychonic planetary system hanging from the ceiling. It is a wonder to behold. In 2002, I had the great pleasure to visit there and had lunch with the Director of the Planetarium, Bjørn Franck Jørgensen and his associate. The Director shared with me a memorable and enlightening thought-experiment.

Suppose, he said, that you were larger than the solar system as we know it, and stood over it with the moon orbiting the earth, while the earth and all other planets orbit merrily around the sun. You wait with a spike and hammer until the earth comes close to where you can reach it. Then, just as it passes right before you, WHAM! You drive that symbolic spike into Earth to halt its motion. The Law of Conservation of Momentum abruptly causes the sun (with all its retinue in tow) to orbit Earth. By this clever analogy, the Copernican solar system is transposed into the Tychonic "geo-heliocentric" system, neatly sidestepping all theological controversy.

Enjoying this brilliant illustration led us to recognize that the Tychonic system is essentially the geometrical equivalent of the Copernican System, but with the spatial coordinates of Earth always defined as $x = 0$, $y = 0$, $z = 0$ for convenience. (Or, if you prefer, Earth is merely placed at the origin of spherical coordinates for mapping the Copernican solar system.) It seems the Vatican had approved what amounted to being the banned Copernican concept, with its coordinates shifted so that its geometric <u>origin</u> was at the earth—our familiar observation point. Earth was "fixed," but only by its coordinates!

Tycho Brahe died under strange circumstances in 1601, eight years before Galileo turned his spyglass to the night sky. The standard story was that he had a urinary blockage that caused excessive bladder pressure when, rather than be discourteous, he delayed getting up to relieve himself at a dinner with visiting noblemen. That led to a fatal ruptured bladder, or so the story goes, which is doubted by recent biographers and urologists alike. A urinary infection is considered more likely.

A retrospective biography of Tycho, *Heavenly Intrigue*, written by Joshua and Anne-Lee Gilder (2005), has composed a far more sinister interpretation based on the discovery of mercury in a lock of his hair. They point out that Johannes Kepler had all the elements of motive, opportunity, and the means to eliminate his mentor by poisoning him in order to gain access to all of his precise data on planetary motion. The Gilder hypothesis seems highly unlikely at a crucial time when Kepler was depending upon Tycho's endorsement as his highly placed advocate, actively encouraging Rudolph II to appoint Kepler as the Imperial Mathematician.

A more plausible explanation of the tainted tresses would have noted Tycho's exposure to mercury during the normal course of years of study of alchemy, but it adds greater intrigue to infer a more villainous plot owing to the latent tension between this pair of synergistic giants. These allegations were quelled in 2010 when the Danish government disinterred Tycho's remains and found less-than-lethal traces of mercury to be present.

Who, then, surpasses Tycho as the most famous Dane? No, it's not Prince Hamlet, the famous but fictional Shakespearean character. May we have the envelope, please? And the winner is:

Hans Christian Andersen, of course!

Chapter 4

Revelation Through Astronomy

The science of astronomy has come a very long way since Tycho Brahe and Galileo. The movement of all known galaxies (except closest ones!) away from our observation point on Earth is such that each has an apparent velocity proportional to its distance from Earth. This expansion can only be interpreted to mean that all stars in the universe began from the same point at the same moment in time, $t_U = 0$ (cf. *Genesis I*). Some have pointed out that it would require an exceptional degree of fine-tuning of a number of physical parameters. I will try to present this vital material in language comprehensible to the educated nonscientist, but with every attempt to be acceptable to the most sophisticated mathematical wizard.

"Red Shift"

Astronomer Edwin Hubble summed it up pretty well: "The history of astronomy is a history of receding horizons." Clever *double entendre* there! Ever since Galileo revealed that the wispy Milky Way was actually a mass of stars, it had long been accepted that this constituted the entirety of the universe. With the enhanced resolving power of the 100-inch Mount Wilson telescope, Hubble discovered that the numerous spiral nebulae were not gaseous clouds but remote galaxies, each made up of millions of stars. This discovery fueled excited speculation that perhaps we were not alone (see chapter 17). In the 1920s, Hubble turned his attention and his telescope to stellar distance measurements.

Meanwhile, Vesto Slipher had been working on a different front: using a prism to refract the faint light from stars to study their emission spectra. From his data, he could identify spectral lines for various chemical elements in the stars, by comparison with the refracted spectra from each of those same elements in the laboratory. His most important findings came from studying remote galaxies far beyond the Milky Way.

Fascinated, Slipher observed that all of the spectral lines from these galaxies (with the sole exception of Andromeda, the closest to us) were shifted toward longer wavelengths; that is, toward the red end of the visible spectrum—some more than others. He reasoned that the "red shift" from each galaxy was a Doppler effect, indicating that each one was moving away from his Lowell Observatory in Arizona, and thus away from Earth.

Austrian physicist Christian Doppler (1842) studied the change in pitch of sound from a moving source as it raced toward and then away from him. His interpretation was that the wavelength of sound was compressed to shorter wavelengths (higher frequency and higher audible pitch) as the source approached, and that it was stretched to longer wavelengths (lower frequency and pitch) as the source pulled away. He generalized this to all wave motion and demonstrated the same effect with waves on the surface of water. One publication applied this principle to the shifting colors of binary stars. As the twins revolve in tandem around each other, each in turn moves toward us or away, thus alternately producing red and blue shifts.

The Familiar Doppler Effect

You are familiar with the effect: a drop in pitch as a train or siren goes by or an airplane passes overhead at low altitude. This principle is utilized in Doppler radar for highway speeding and for imaging weather systems. Doppler ultrasound technology is effective for imaging the blockage of blood flow in arteries of the brain and heart.

After investigating dozens of galaxies in different directions, Slipher realized that each was moving away from Earth, for the light from each showed this "red shift." For most galaxies, the spectral shift corresponded to a very fast velocity. He could find none with a trajectory toward Earth (with the curious exception of Andromeda). Were they receding from Earth? Were Earth and our galaxy part of a mass flight from somewhere else? Was the universe expanding? This was a lot to think about.

Because Hubble had accumulated the most precise measurements of interstellar distances, he was able (1929) to compare Slipher's published data on velocities of stars with his own data on distances. The comparison was astounding. The galaxies furthest away were the ones with greatest "red shift," indicating faster speed of departure. He realized that they were more distant <u>because</u> they had receded faster.

In general, the red shift (thus velocity) was proportional to distance, a conclusion that became indisputable as Hubble and others achieved greater accuracy measuring distances. To Hubble and Belgian physicist Georges Lemaître, this evidence was startling in its cosmological significance. Extrapolating backward in time and space for each galactic light source, Lemaître projected that all "merged" with us at the same time of origin. This raised the clear and profound implication that all matter in all of the galaxies of the universe was created at the very same instant, all at the very same point in space. The entire universe was not expanding at random, but from the same original place and time. Incidentally, an observer at any other location in this expanding universe would perceive that everything else was receding directly from his own particular point in space.

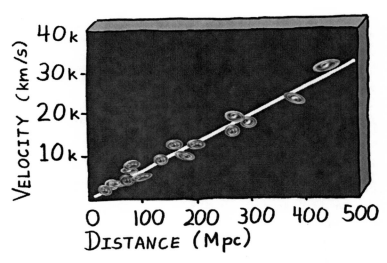

Hubble Graph of Galactic Distance v. Receding Velocity

One rival astronomer, Fred Hoyle, was not yet ready to concede this conclusion, preferring a Buddhist alternative "steady-state" universe with no beginning. Hoyle ridiculed Hubble's creation postulate as a "Big Bang" Theory. Hoyle's derision achieved ironic staying power, as the Big Bang soon became generally accepted by most astronomers (see "Serendipitous Echo" below). Modern satellite telescopes (such as "The Hubble") are adding millions of galactic distances to our star catalog. This produces a much better straight-line fit (except for the outermost reaches of space) for plotting distances against the magnitudes of red shift (velocity) of the collection of galaxies. This allows even greater precision in extrapolating the line back to the Beginning ($t_u = 0$). The most accurate measurements of velocity and distance of galaxies and star clusters fix that moment of creation at 13.7–13.8 billion years ago (**Bya**).

That was a long time ago. This is a very old universe.

This finding does pose something of a problem for many young-earth creationists who believe that the earth is only a few thousand years old. To explain away Hubble's evidence, one would have to imagine that, at the moment of creation 6,000–10,000 years ago, God placed other galaxies more than ten thousand light-years away, so that we would fall into a trap of thinking their light had traveled more than 10,000 years. But why would God do that? Was it Divine mischief intended to misdirect and confuse us, or test us? He could have just left us happily ignorant.

Such a creative creationist explanation must be modified in order to explain how we can see light from stars that are over 10,000 light-years away, if no star is older than ten thousand years. The problem can be illustrated by the familiar Andromeda Galaxy, which is 2,500,000 light-years away. If light from Andromeda has been traveling toward Earth for only 10,000 years, it would take another 2,490,000 years before we could see it. Clearly, some new understanding is in order.

One would have to imagine further that if God created the universe no more than 10,000 years ago, it was not enough merely to place most stars over a million light-years away from Earth. He also had to salt the intervening space (at least out to 10,000 light-years!) with beams of light photons headed toward Earth so that we could see them. Otherwise, all of the stars that are more than 10,000 light-years away would still be invisible.

Furthermore, at a minimum, all those streams of starlight photons would have to have been pre-positioned continuously along all intervening positions between each star and every point of Earth's orbit so that these distant stars would not blink on and off. In anticipation of radio frequency and infrared detection, there would have to be a complete spectrum of electromagnetic energy similarly foreordained.

Would it not strain our concept of an all-wise, loving Creator for them to suggest that God had placed enough photons coming here on a continuum of all intervening positions throughout space so that photons would be arriving for us to see at all times, today and tomorrow, while appearing to have emanated from each discrete star point? Surely, we are not being deceived by the revelations of astronomy.

Ironically, there would be no need for any actual stars out there . . . just streams of light photons. As Wake Forest University physicist Eric Carlson has noted: from the young-earth creationist's view, images of a distant supernova like SN1987A, 2.5 million light-years away in Andromeda, would have arrived here from a star that had never existed! How could it blow up long before it was created? Whoa!

Would it not be better to accept the best scientific evidence that this universe is approximately 13.7 billion years old, and move forward with the faith that God trusted us with that information, and wanted us to be able to discover and reveal His Truth?

Is there anything in the Bible to suggest that God is constrained in time and space, in energy and matter, in a way that would limit Him from being able to create the universe billions of years ago? Could He not arrange the order of that universe in such a way that life would appear on this planet in the fullness of time ten billion years later? What's the rush?

In fairness, the authors of Biblical creation stories in *Genesis* had no capability to measure either distances to remote galaxies (which they could neither see nor imagine) or the velocities at which they were receding from us. Such technology would not become available for another three thousand years. Most of the Old Testament originated even before the Aristotelian idea that stars were points of light on one huge crystalline sphere that spun them around the earth. That ingenious concept placed the moon, sun, and five planets on seven progressively larger spheres rotating *ad seriatim* just inside the outer star-laden sphere. When Tycho Brahe observed a comet sweeping into interplanetary space and back out again, nothing was shattered by it except his belief in Aristotle's crystalline spheres.

[Some seventeenth-century theologians concluded that Heaven must be in a ninth level out beyond the star-studded eighth sphere. To keep things in balance, they formulated nine levels of Hell down within Earth. This became the basis for the scenario described in

Dante's *Inferno* and its fabulous illustration, *Mappa dell' Inferno* by Botticelli.]

Furthermore, what if those writing early Scripture had received some visionary revelation about telescopes and the Doppler Effect, or that the universe was over 13 billion years old? How could they have interpreted that correctly to their fellows? What was a billion anyway? What was a light-year? Would anyone read or heed their scrolls?

In the Beginning . . . Pow!

Let's think a bit more about the beginning of time from what astronomers can tell us. On our cosmological clock, we can refer to this as $t_u = 0$. Hubble and his successors have demonstrated convincingly that the universe is steadily expanding and that remote galaxies are moving away from us at a velocity proportional to their distances from us (with a few nearby exceptions, like nearest neighbor Andromeda . . . see page 67 below).

[Einstein's theory of gravity predicts that space itself is expanding. Consequently, galaxies simply hold their relative position within that space, and are carried along with it. The effect is the same as if the galaxies were moving away from each other and us. Hmm. Then what about Andromeda?

When these data of position and velocity are extrapolated backward in time, all galaxies (all stars, all matter) are projected to converge at (or to have emanated from) the same point at the same instant. This point in space and time (at $t_u = 0$) can only be the moment of creation of all known and suspected matter. Referenced to today's calendar, that would have been 13.7 billion years ago (*Bya*).

Some astronomers argued that the Big Bang did not originate from a singular point, but simultaneously from throughout space. If true, there can be no edge to space. Besides, if galaxies were cast about from many points in space, wouldn't we observe just as many of them moving toward us as away from us? How could outward velocity be proportional to distance?

Come to think of it, are we certain that it all began from a single point? Could it have been "bigger than a bread box"—a large, incredibly dense and hot bread box? At the end of this chapter, you will see a simpler but less sophisticated mathematical hypothesis about the size of the universe at its beginning $t_U = 0$. Too simple for some? Perhaps just right for some!

What came before that? Science cannot tell us anything about what preceded the moment of creation. Science has no physical evidence from before $t_U = 0$. If there were any prior physical matter and energy, its structure would have been consumed in the event. It would have been obliterated. No trace could have survived for us to observe.

There is, however, some fascinating mathematical speculation about what probably happened during the first critical seconds immediately after $t_U = 0$, although there is modest evidence other than how it all turned out. The initial density of matter would have been so unimaginably great that individual atoms would have no meaning.

Quantum mechanics cannot adequately deal with this "point zero" condition, which is termed a "**singularity**," for which science has no adequate theory. The precepts of quantum mechanics do not allow any particle to be part of a space smaller than its own wavelength. All initial matter would be so compressed that it occupied the same spatial singularity, in which case there were no discrete particles. In lay terms, this untenable state might necessarily accelerate the initial rate of expansion, like the effect of a trampoline or maybe an illegal golf club!

Astrophysicists have been busy with their calculations of the initial moments of the universe in order to construct a plausible scenario for all that transpired during those miraculous first seconds. The next few pages discussing this in lay terms could still be difficult for some. Spend as much time as you can, as it will be worth your while.

When Time Began

The earliest minute would have been so momentous that its description had to be subdivided into minute fractions of a second. It all began with the **Inflationary Epoch**, which encompassed the first 10^{-32} of a second of the Big Bang. During this brief, almost instantaneous span, the velocity of expansion of the universe would have been greatly accelerated before suddenly slowing down to the present rate. Then, after $t_U = 10^{-32}$ second, the universe would have reached lower density, and some factor slowed the decompressing mass to the "normal" rate of expansion observed by Hubble.

It has been calculated that by the end of that initial Inflationary Epoch the universe had already expanded by "100 trillion-trillion (i.e., 10^{26}) times its original size." According to Einstein's General Theory of Relativity, something called "**dark energy**" would have caused the initially rapid expansion. We cannot master General Relativity in this book, but you might think of this dark energy as a kind of **negative gravity**, or some other way of describing the internal pressure of all that mass occupying insufficient space. According to mathematical models, once the universe had grown enough, its expansion slowed down to its present velocity, as if something (gravity?) had put on the brakes. Dark energy was invoked later to explain an acceleration currently observable in the deepest recesses of space.

The next segment in this fast paced expansion was another brief flash of time, called the **Electroweak Epoch**. Its duration was from the end of the Inflationary Epoch at $t_U = 10^{-32}$ second until $t_U = 10^{-12}$ second. By the end of this time, only a trillionth of that first second had yet elapsed. At the start of this fraction of a second, the universe's temperature was down, but still too incredibly hot at 10^{28} degrees Celsius. There is no good way to imagine how hot that was, but the mathematics tell us that it was now low enough for the emergence and operation of the three additional fundamental forces: the electromagnetic force and the strong and weak nuclear forces, along with gravitation.

The Next Ten Seconds after the Big Bang

While there is only mathematical speculation about that first 10^{-12} second or so of nearly infinitesimal time, it is because those conditions cannot be approached experimentally. After that, however, a good deal of evidence is being assembled to support the following probable course. In summary:

The **Quark Epoch** began at $t_U = 10^{-12}$ second (remember, that's just the first trillionth of a second!) after the Big Bang. This was the moment when fundamental particles called quarks (both matter and antimatter) acquired identity as they separated from each other, leaving vacant space between them. During this abrupt time period, the four fundamental forces would have been operating independently in their present form. The prevailing energy was still far too hot for quarks to combine into hadrons.

The **Hadron Epoch** followed at $t_U = 10^{-6}$ second (one millionth of a second) after the Big Bang, when the temperature had cooled sufficiently for **gluons** (aptly named) to bind **quarks** and form **hadrons**, the most important family of more massive particles, such as **protons** and **neutrons**. Protons have a positive charge, and neutrons are neutral, with no charge. They have very nearly the same mass. At the end of this brief moment, a lower temperature allowed anti-hadrons and the more abundant hadrons to collide and annihilate each other, leaving the excess hadrons that compose most of the remaining mass of the universe. Now we're getting somewhere, after just a millionth of a second!

By the way, it is not expected that you need to memorize all these new particles. You just need to appreciate that particle physicists have fun in their jobs. Also, you don't have to memorize these epochs comprising the first minute of creation. There will not be a test covering it in this life. It will be enough if you can get to the point to say, "wow!"

At the threshold of <u>one second</u> after you-know-what, things started to settle into something we can more easily visualize. This began the **Lepton Epoch**. Leptons are a group of low mass fundamental particles, which includes **electrons, positrons,** and **neutrinos**. As the name implies, this epoch was where they dominated, both leptons and anti-leptons, in a dynamic equilibrium. [Electrons are the essence of electricity and lightning, and the essential operators for the <u>chemical</u> properties of atoms, such as covalent bonds that define the structure of molecules.] As with hadrons, the temperature drop due to further expansion allowed mutual annihilation of anti-electrons and the more abundant electrons. Of the two, only electrons remained after this period, which extended to t_U = 10 second. For comparison, try to hold your breath that long.

You may have wondered how fortuitous it was that in the very beginning (t_U = 1 sec) the amount of matter exceeded antimatter. Had they been created in equal amounts, there would have been nothing left. With the excess of hadrons (above), leptons had to have exceeded anti-leptons, or else. Is this just another very fortunate coincidence?

The Dark Ages

After a total elapsed time of 10 seconds, the **Photon Epoch** began. With antimatter gone, hadrons and leptons had become prominent, but the most abundant particles in this expanding cauldron were photons, particles of light. The uniform density was still high enough that all the photons in the universe were absorbed by its gravity, like some vast, totally opaque plasma. For that reason, or whimsically, this might be mistaken for "**the Dark Ages**" of creation (illustrated on page 59). In the first minutes of this epoch, protons and neutrons began to form atomic nuclei of the hydrogen isotope known as **deuterium**.

[A single, lone proton is the stable nucleus of hydrogen (^1H), but one heavier isotope of hydrogen, deuterium (^2H), is also stable. The combination of one proton with one neutron forms the deuterium nucleus. A third isotope, tritium (^{3}H), with one proton and two neutrons, is unstable. Note that we use the convention of writing an element's symbol with a small whole number as a superscript prefix to connote the approximate mass of the atom relative to a proton.]

About 3 minutes into its expansion, this mixture had cooled enough (still indescribably hot, of course) that a **thermonuclear fusion** reaction combined pairs of deuterium nuclei to form helium-4 (^{4}He), which held two protons and two neutrons in each nucleus. Only the very lightest elements, hydrogen and helium, along with a little bit of lithium (^{7}Li), were produced at this time. These three lightest of all the elements were about all that could be synthesized by nuclear fusion under these conditions. Then, after another 14 minutes of vigorous expansion, the temperature would have fallen below the threshold necessary for such nuclear fusion. At this point (t_U = 17 minutes), having generated only three stable elements, elemental synthesis was suspended until the first stars began to form 150 million years later. The Photon Epoch lasted 380,000 years.

There were still no stars for the next 150 million years, and that is actually what astronomers call the "Dark Ages" of Creation. With no stars, it would be very dark.

Artist's Rendering of Dark Ages of Creation

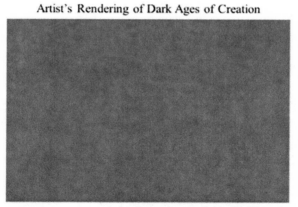

Personal art . . . Pardon the Whimsy!

Serendipitous Echo from the Big Bang

At the end of the Photon Epoch, 380,000 years after the Big Bang, everything had "cooled" down to 3,000 degrees Kelvin, the temperature below which the positively charged atomic nuclei could hold on to their negatively charged electrons to form stable atoms. This combination was highly fortuitous, and has been called "recombination."

By this time, the atoms had spread apart so that photons of light "decoupled" from the more massive atomic nuclei and were able to move through space freely without being blocked and absorbed by the denser nuclei. The universe became transparent. This aftermath of Big Bang theory led to a hopeful prediction that this decoupled remnant of light energy might be detectable somewhere out there. The prediction would have to be tested somehow. But how? There was no sign of it using optical telescopes suitable for the visible range of light or even infrared light. It surely would have cooled to lower frequencies by now.

Sometimes, like the fabled "Princes of Serendip," we just get lucky. At the Bell Laboratories in New Jersey, **Arno Penzias** and **Robert Wilson** were interested in radio astronomy and the practicalities for improved satellite communication. When they deployed a radiometer the size of a railroad boxcar, capable of detecting microwave frequencies, they found the "Lost Chord" of cosmology (1965). What they observed was a faint glow of microwave energy almost uniformly distributed from all directions. It did not vary near stars or galaxies, and so could not be attributable to such sources. It was like some ephemeral "veil of photons" that had occupied the vacuum of space since the end of the Photon Epoch, when space became transparent. At first, however, they did not realize what they had discovered.

PENZIAS, WILSON AND THE "BIG EAR"
Credit: Dayton.HQ.NASA

Their radiometer had been invented by MIT nuclear physicist **Robert Dicke**. At Princeton in 1964, his research group had begun to assemble their own radiometer for the express purpose of searching for the elusive cosmic microwave background radiation (CMBR). Dicke received an inquiry from Penzias and Wilson a few miles away asking for help. They told him their radiometer antenna at Bell Labs seemed to be slightly off zero when pointed skyward in any direction, and they were just wondering if Dicke could advise them how to get rid of this unexpected effect. It was as if outer space had a temperature of some 3 degrees above Absolute Zero. Robert Dicke immediately realized what his callers had detected. He announced to his colleagues, "Boys, we've been scooped!"

The Princeton group nobly went to meet with Penzias and Wilson, and discussed what had probably been observed, concluding that it was cosmic background radiation. Dicke confirmed their observations independently, adding a theoretical explanation in support of his rival neighbors' discovery. A great debate ensued as to whether this was indeed the cosmic signal from the dawn of creation.

Penzias and Wilson and others were able to demonstrate (a) that a graph of the variation of intensity at different observed frequencies was a precise match for what Max Planck had found for radiation as a function of temperature, and (b) that the frequency of its peak intensity was the same as that calculated for a temperature of 2.7 degrees Kelvin (i.e., 2.7 degrees above Absolute Zero). Thus, this CMBR was not generated by any light source in the last 13 billion years, but was the relic of the Photon Epoch after it had itself cooled down by expansion of the universe. Fred Hoyle's theory of a "steady state universe" could not account for it. This was truly the "echo" of the Big Bang. Penzias and Wilson serendipitously were awarded the Nobel Prize in 1978. One can only wonder why Dicke wasn't included, since the Nobel protocols do allow up to three honorees.

Additional evidence has helped strengthen the above conclusions. In theory, if there had been an Inflationary Epoch (extremely rapid expansion during the earliest micro-fraction of the very first second of time), after which gravitation caused the expansion to slow to the present rate, there should have been some "rippling" wave effect in that dense mass due to the onset of gravity. A group called BICEP2 programmed its telescope in Antarctica to examine the CMBR to see if its faint light was polarized (see Louis Pasteur at page 268). They report (2014) that it did exhibit polarized light, and that there were "swirling patterns" in the polarized light. Controversy ensued, but if confirmed, this discovery of the gravitational rippling would approach Nobel laureate dimensions. This is **BIG**.

Condensation during Expansion

In the theoretical sequelae to the Big Bang, the universe continued to expand and its structure to unfold. Gravitation, having restrained the initial burst of expansion, now began pulling hydrogen and helium particles together into clumps, and those in turn into larger and larger masses. At around 150 million years out, this aggregation had assembled masses large enough that their external gravitation would pull them into extremely massive gases that became the first stars. These were very hot giants, with enough hydrogen "fuel" to burn for a billion years. The very hottest of them would burn out in less than 100 million years.

Such enormous masses of hydrogen and helium (with inconsequential traces of lithium), estimated to have been a hundred times the mass of our sun, would be so dense and hot that they could spontaneously initiate thermonuclear reactions. Thus was ignited the new fusion process for synthesizing the next few elements in the Periodic Table: beryllium ($_4$Be), boron ($_5$B), carbon ($_6$C), nitrogen ($_7$N), and oxygen ($_8$O). These were not made during the Photon Epoch, which generated only hydrogen, helium, and the small amount of lithium ($_3$Li). Before the earliest stars, the universe was devoid of elements heavier than lithium.

Here was an important clue. While some stars have spectra from an abundance of metals like iron ($_{26}$Fe), sodium ($_{11}$Na), and calcium ($_{20}$Ca), many others have spectra of even heavier elements—the same range of elements as the earth's crust. We now know that the sources of elements heavier than iron in all of the visible galaxies of stars were the remnants of **supernova** explosions of earlier stars. We'll look at that in a moment.

The time span from 150 million to 1 billion years after the Big Bang is called the **Reionization Period**, during which the first stars were formed by gravitation. These first stars initially would have been composed of hydrogen, helium, and trace lithium. They and the early **quasars** (below) gave off such intense energy that the unattached atoms in the space around them were separated from one or more electrons and became ionized (i.e., each acquired a positive charge). Millions of stars pulled together around super-dense black holes and quasars to form galaxies. Astronomers have found that most galaxies are pulled into groups called galactic clusters and superclusters (with thousands of galaxies). The Local Supercluster, of which our Milky Way is a part, contains 47,000 galaxies. This has generated a neat debate about the homogeneity of the universe.

Quasars and Black Holes

Quasars were extremely large stars with intense light equal to the combined luminosity of some entire galaxies. More than 200,000 have been observed and catalogued. Almost all of them were formed during the early universe, and are billions of light-years away. Because they are super-bright and so very distant from Earth, astronomers were unable to detect the galaxy of which each quasar is a part until special tools like the orbiting Hubble telescope could resolve the image enough to distinguish the host galaxy. Galaxies all seem to be assembled around black holes and/or quasars: the two focal points of the enormous gravitational pull that initiated the gathering of stars into galaxies.

NASA's Jet Propulsion Laboratory has reported finding one of these early quasars 12 billion light-years away. This gigantic mass, with a black hole at its center, contains an enormous amount of water (mist and vapor), "140 trillion times all the water in the earth's oceans." The powerful thermonuclear fusion of the central mass had created enough oxygen to combine with hydrogen to form water in "galactic volumes."

While we can observe the light from these earliest stars, emitted when they were billions of light-years away, these stars no longer exist. They would have extinguished long after they emitted the light now being observed. Stars in this first wave were very large and very hot, and doomed to a limited life span of just a few hundred million years. When one had exhausted its hydrogen, it cooled down and collapsed. Enormous densities were generated thereby, which pressed atomic nuclei together, fusing them to form the heavier elements. Eventually, this gravitational process contracted the dying star to such a high density and temperature that it exploded as a **supernova**, showering the nearby stars and surrounding space with all these new, heavier elements.

The second and third waves of stars would be formed mostly from the still abundant hydrogen and helium, but they would also incorporate these new elements. Harvard astronomer Owen Gingerich has pointed out that the element Iron (Fe) is the "end point" in the evolution of normal stars. All elements heavier than iron would be synthesized only by the thermonuclear fusion reactions within a collapsing star just before it exploded as a supernova. Incidentally, a substantial amount of these heavier elements would collect into smaller objects, not large enough to form stars. These became planets and asteroids.

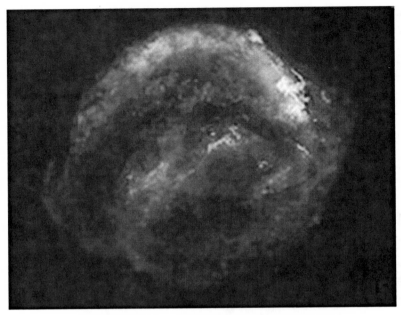

Supernova Photo, Credit: NASA

And so it came to pass that 4.5 Bya our solar system was formed with the sun and its planets, over in our corner of the Milky Way Galaxy. That event occurred when the universe was over nine billion years old, and had gone through several repetitions of supernova blasts in our fraction of space during the intervening billions of years. It would take another billion years for our planet to cool down enough and collect the right atmosphere for the first rudimentary lifeforms to appear (chapter 16).

It appears that every galaxy has a **black hole** at its center, providing the necessary centripetal (gravitational) force to hold it all together. While black holes emit no photons of light (hence their name), they can be affirmed as the necessary condition for stars observed to be swiftly orbiting around the billion-mile proximity of the galaxy's center. Such high velocity orbits indicate the need to sustain sufficient centrifugal force to avoid being pulled in and consumed. One star (named SO-2)— very close to the center of the Milky Way—orbits in just 15.5 Earth-years, separated from the galactic center some 120 times the distance between Earth and the sun. A closer, fainter star (SO-102) zips around in 11 years. The black hole's presence is shown by their acceleration (wider spaced dots in the image below) as they revolve closer to their common focal point.

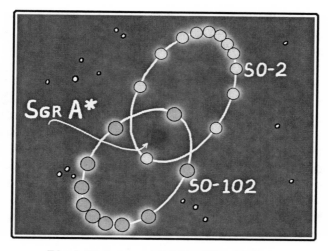

Black Hole in our Milky Way Galaxy

[Occasionally, when a large enough asteroid (say, 24 miles across) falls into a black hole, a brief flare of x-rays is observed when the rock plunges meteor-like through the surrounding dust and gas before feeding a "snack" of mass to the super-massive core. Our Milky Way Galaxy has a black hole, named **Sagittarius A*** (SGR A*, located out there between the constellations Sagittarius and Scorpio). It has a mass estimated to be 4 million times that of our sun, but does not appear to be as ravenous as some other galactic centers. It flares only once or twice a day, or so. We are fortunate to be 26,000 light-years away, out in our remote arm of the Milky Way, far beyond the "death-spiral" grasp of SGR A* and orbiting it only once every 235 million years. In case you wondered, at that rate we are in just our twentieth galactic circumnavigation since Earth and sun were created: $4.55 \times 10^9 \div 235 \times 10^6 = \mathbf{19.4}$]

More Evidence for the Big Bang

Astronomers began to wonder whether there remained any big pockets of primordial hydrogen and helium gases left over from the first 380,000 years of the Photon Epoch, the time before condensations formed stars capable of nuclear fusion. Was it possible that some of the original hydrogen and helium was still out there in large volumes that never got gathered into stars or mixed with the newer elements?

A team at the University of California at Santa Cruz reported (*Science*, November 11, 2011) finding clouds of pure hydrogen and its heavier isotope deuterium in deep space, 12 billion light-years away, and uncontaminated by other elements. They had scheduled one of the telescopes at the Keck Observatory in Hawaii to peer into several zones of dark sky, seeking evidence of a second relic left behind from the Photon Epoch. This finding would be a severe test for Big Bang cosmology. The microwave echo (above, pages 59-61) had been predicted by Dicke, George Gamow, and others, but it was discovered inadvertently by Penzias and Wilson. Here was a second prediction: that once the earliest nuclear synthesis of hydrogen and helium (and a little lithium) during the Photon Epoch had cooled and ceased production, it would be a few hundred million years before stars formed with thermonuclear furnaces capable of making the next larger elements Be, B, C, N, and O. If any quantities of pure hydrogen and helium gas survived and could be detected, uncontaminated by heavier elements, it would further substantiate the Big Bang Theory.

The trick was to know where and how to look for it. There it was, deep in the dark recesses of space behind the constellations Ursa Major (the "Big Dipper") and Leo. In their report, the UC-Santa Cruz group headed by Xavier Prochaska studied the spectrum of light that had passed through the gas. This light had originated from ancient quasars back beyond the dark clouds. It showed missing wavelengths of light, but only at those values that would be absorbed by molecular hydrogen as the light passed through the gas. It was the exclusive absorption "fingerprint" of hydrogen alone.

Their spectral absorption method was specific for **covalent bonds** in molecules, particularly diatomic hydrogen, H_2. It would not detect helium and lithium, as they do not form covalent bonds, so it does not mean He and Li were missing. It would certainly have detected any traces of carbon, nitrogen, oxygen, and other elements that form covalent bonds, and their absence was the provenance in this elegant experiment. Professor Prochaska summed it up very well: "This is a very pristine gas—exactly what the theory predicts. It's material not polluted by stars or galaxies." Brilliant!

Ironically, these clouds of pure hydrogen probably no longer exist today. The light absorption spectrum analyzed by the UCSC computers was emitted billions of years ago, and it is likely that the gas by now has been contaminated with the heavier element detritus of supernovas. Some will have been incorporated into new stars and galaxies. We won't fret over such a lost treasure of hydrogen fuel, however, even though there is still more intergalactic hydrogen and helium dispersed as gas than there is in stars. Besides, at those distances it would cost far too much time and energy to go get it (nudge, wink).

The End Is Near

The following should probably be kept away from impressionable children of tender years. I would be remiss, however, if I did not share with you a little taste of some imaginative speculation about the ultimate destiny of the universe. Will it continue along its merry way, or are there pitfalls ahead? Some predictions do not bode well for this universe. A number of these suppositions have been summarized in an Internet article "Timeline of the Big Bang" prepared under the aegis of *Wikipedia*, my initial source for these three paragraphs. None of this is likely to be accessible to any experimental proof in the next billion years, so we need not get too anxious about such irrelevancies.

One stark forecast is that eventually, after many repeated iterations of supernovas, the whole cosmos will run out of hydrogen fuel, and all stars will go dim. The universe and every part of it will continue to expand and cool down until there is no more energy. This Grand Extinction has been projected for some vague time in the next <u>100 trillion years</u>, so it is not imminent.

Another looming catastrophe supposes that the rate of expansion of the universe will slow down and gravitation will take over, causing everything to swing the other way and collapse. According to this scenario, we've only got another <u>hundred billion years</u> or so before this "Big Crunch" sets the stage for the next Big Bang in an unending cycle. It is imaginable that such a collapse could have immediately preceded our Big Bang sequence. This threat has been pretty much discredited, though. While the gravitation constant has been agreeably fine-tuned to balance things merrily for lo these first dozen billion years, the future is now guaranteed against collapse by a gradually accelerating expansion driven by that same dark energy that powered the initial Inflation Epoch.

Long before these prophecies can be fulfilled, there is another far more immediate menace approaching. Precise measurements by the Hubble Space Telescope show that Andromeda galaxy (M31) and our Milky Way galaxy are falling <u>toward</u> each other at 250,000 miles an hour. That's what happens when two galaxies are too close. Roeland van der Marel at the Space Telescope Science Institute in Baltimore calculates it will get here in just 4 billion years, since Andromeda is 2.5 million light-years away. Maybe a bit sooner if they accelerate toward closure. Then what? Most likely, there will be few collisions of stars from either galaxy, because even the nearest stars after merger would still be many light-years apart. The two disc-like galaxies will slide through each other practically untouched. Gravitational drag will eventually haul them back into one somewhat spherical system so gradually that few stars will be effected in this glancing encounter. Stars near the paths of the two black holes won't be so lucky. This is moot for us anyway, because our sun will run low on hydrogen fuel at about that time. None of these seem to be among our more urgent problems.

Carbon Isotopes

At all levels of life, from the simplest to the most complex, one chemical element is **the** enabling substance of life, without which there can be no life worthy of the name. That element is carbon (chemical symbol: $_6$C). Water is essential; carbon is quintessential. Because of its unique ability to bond to other carbon atoms in a variety of ways, as well as with atoms of hydrogen, oxygen, nitrogen, chlorine, and so forth, carbon is the molecular backbone of the organic matter that makes up all living beings. For this reason, the study of carbon compounds (chapter 14) is called **organic chemistry**. In that sense, except for its mineral and water content, all food is "organic."

Every stable carbon atom has 6 protons and 6 or 7 neutrons; thus its atomic number is 6 and its atomic mass is either 12 or 13. These **isotopes** of carbon differ only in the number of neutrons in the atomic nuclei. The most abundant of these (99% of natural carbon) is carbon-12 (or ^{12}C, using the same mass convention discussed earlier in this chapter). It has exactly 6 neutrons combined with the 6 protons in its nucleus. Carbon-13 (^{13}C, with 7 nuclear neutrons) makes up the remaining one percent. Another isotope, the unstable, and therefore radioactive, carbon-14, is formed by natural collisions of carbon with hot cosmic neutrons in the upper atmosphere. Atmospheric mixing brings trace amounts to the earth's surface, where it is incorporated into all living organisms via photosynthesis and the food chain, and in the same steady-state proportion to ^{12}C as in the atmosphere.

Since dead organisms cannot absorb any carbon, after death the moderate decay half-life (5,730 years) of carbon-14 gradually reduces the ratio of ^{14}C to ^{12}C in a precise manner. The isotope ratio can be measured by mass spectrometry, allowing the number of years since the organism's death to be calculated. That is pretty neat. It's valuable for determining the length of time since particular specimens were alive.

One of the great riddles of astrophysics is how carbon could be formed. None was produced under the energy conditions of the first 17 minutes of the universe, the earliest moments of the "Photon Epoch" long before the first generation of stars. That process converted hydrogen only into deuterium and helium plus a trace of lithium.

[Helium ($_2$He) is an inert, mono-atomic element with atomic number 2 and having a mass number 4. Helium has two stable isotopes, ^{3}He (traces) and ^{4}He (99.999%). Helium makes up 24% of the mass of the Milky Way Galaxy. It is the second-most abundant element after hydrogen (74%). All other heavier elements combined make up only 2% of the mass of this galaxy. That distribution ratio is typical of most other galaxies. Fortunately, that 2% is all we need.

Although helium was formed within the opening minutes of the Big Bang, and is continuously formed by hydrogen fusion within stars, any helium being accumulated on Earth as it was being aggregated from supernova debris would not be retained. The mass of Earth was not large enough to hold on to helium or hydrogen gas, which escaped into the upper atmosphere and beyond. We make diatomic molecular hydrogen (H_2) gas as needed, mostly as a byproduct of catalytic reforming of petroleum hydrocarbons and by electrolysis of water.

Natural helium (^{4}He) is formed within the earth by radioactive decay of unstable heavy metals like uranium and thorium. This decay emits positively charged helium nuclei, which are alpha (α) rays. Helium from this radioactive α-decay is trapped in deep rock formations and accumulates in natural gas, from which it is commercially distilled. I thought you might like to know that.]

Hoyle State

So, where <u>did</u> the carbon come from? In order to answer this question, it helps if we restate in a bit more detail what has already been mentioned briefly about supernova processes. Let's take a moment to do that.

The enigmatic English astronomer Fred Hoyle first proposed (1957) that carbon-12, along with elements like nitrogen, oxygen, and phosphorus, would have been formed in mature stars (red giants) billions of years after their birth. Hoyle had calculated that an extremely high energy state of carbon-12 (7.65 MeV, which for our purposes you need only understand to be "an extremely high energy state") was prerequisite to its synthesis from three atoms of helium-4, even though there was no physical evidence in his day. In effect, he based his belief in this "Hoyle state" of carbon upon reasoning that otherwise carbon could not have been formed, and he would not be living to think about it. This brilliant insight seems an early version of the Anthropic Principle (pages 89 ff.).

In *Magic Furnace*, Hoyle's biographer Marcus Chown called this "the most outrageous prediction" ever to arise in science. The superlative may be extravagant, though intended as a compliment, and it would certainly make one sit up and take notice. This 7.65 MeV state, Hoyle argued, was essential to carbon-based life. "Thus Hoyle was saying—and nobody had ever used logic as outrageous as this before—that the mere fact that he was alive and pondering the question of carbon, was proof the 7.65 MeV state existed."

[Footnote on the **MeV**: The term *MeV* refers to a million electron volts. One electron volt is the kinetic energy gained by a single unbound electron when accelerated by the electric potential difference of one volt. One way to put this in perspective is that 7.65 MeV is roughly $1/25^{th}$ the energy released in the nuclear fission (as in the Hiroshima atomic bomb) of each single Uranium-235 atom. However, if this description of the term MeV does not come together for you, just accept that the energy released by the fission of one U-235 atom would raise the energy of 75 helium atoms to the Hoyle state, a rather enormous amount of energy to form 25 carbon atoms: $3\ ^4He \rightarrow\ ^{12}C$.]

As it turned out, Hoyle was right about this. He and his collaborators succeeded in demonstrating the high energy Hoyle state. In 1957, they published their great contribution to the understanding of how elements larger than oxygen are synthesized in "the magic furnaces" of aging red giants, later to be scattered when they explode into smithereens. Without those supernova smithereens, which later gathered by gravitation into new stars and galaxies, we would not be here. Curiously, the Nobel Prize in 1983 was awarded to Hoyle's collaborators, but not to their iconoclastic leader Fred Hoyle (who had insulted the Nobel Committee on an unrelated matter).

Jugular Hoyle

It did not help that Hoyle's manner of argument was often blunt and offensive, albeit clever enough. He was certain, for example, that chance reaction could not generate the first mono-cellular life forms: "Belief in chemical evolution of the first cell from lifeless chemicals is equivalent to believing that a tornado could sweep through a junkyard and assemble a Boeing 747 from the materials therein." The man had style!

In a similarly picturesque jab, Hoyle thought the chance of just one functioning protein being assembled by random, natural chemical processes was as unlikely as a "solar system full of blind men solving Rubik's Cube simultaneously." In 1984, he calculated that the probability of assembling the complete set of enzymes for the simplest of single-cell organisms was one in $10^{40,000}$ (more about that in chapter 15). Since the estimated number of atoms in the known universe was a mere 1×10^{89}, he saw no chance of this synthesis happening by any random, undirected process.

This gift for skewering his opponents made so many enemies that it not only cost him the Nobel Prize, but also has made Hoyle an inviting target for his adversaries. That he indiscreetly held some rather peculiar views certainly gave his critics ammunition for ridicule and *ad hominem* attacks. His death in 2001 protects them from his counterattack.

There was one other little problem for the last fifty years. As we have seen, Hoyle's theory stipulated that carbon-12 would have been formed via a transient, high-energy level, referred to as the "Hoyle state" of carbon. He had experimental evidence to back this up, but many theorists were troubled by the fact that no mathematical formula could be devised to describe this Hoyle state. It was thought that this would take too many dedicated lifetimes for even the fastest computer technology. Not anymore!

The Hoyle problem has now been overcome by collaboration from the University of Bonn, Ruhr-Universitat Bochum, and the Jülich Center for Hadron Physics, along with physicist Dean Lee at North Carolina State University. They published (2011) a solution for an extremely complex calculation of the 7.65 MeV Hoyle state using a dedicated supercomputer and a vast array of numerical input. Amazingly, it still took their Jülich supercomputer no less than seven days to crunch the numbers.

N.C. State's Dean Lee wonders whether this is an example of a highly fortuitous outcome that carbon could be formed at all, or whether it is yet another instance in which nature is fine-tuned for three helium atoms to combine into one carbon atom at just the right energy level envisioned as the Hoyle state. Lee puts it this way:

Physicists use the term 'fine-tuning' to describe a phenomenon which requires some parameter of nature being nearly perfectly aligned. Without this near-perfect accident, the effect would not happen. The production of carbon and the Hoyle state of energy are examples of this fine-tuning.

The clear implication is that carbon did not get here by chance.

Oddly, some "young-earth" creationists have found convenient arguments from Hoyle's early writings in opposition to the Big Bang. He is a curious crutch for creationists, since his preferred steady-state cosmology was totally and intentionally contrary to the notion of any creation "in the beginning." Was it Hoyle's early way of avoiding God? His steady-state concept, furthermore, has been disproved by (a) later refinements of Hubble's measurements of distance and velocity of the expanding universe, (b) the subsequent discovery of an echo from the Big Bang, and (c) the discovery of those remote pockets of primordial molecular hydrogen gas.

In 1949, Hoyle appeared on BBC radio and coined the term "Big Bang" to demean what since then has become the prevailing theory of sudden creation out of nothing 13.7 billion years ago. Hoyle later demurred that it was merely a neutral term to help listeners understand better. One can imagine that he winked and nudged.

A few experts working in this exciting field of cosmology today prefer not to use the term "Big Bang." Georges Lemaître had to call it something, his preference was "the Hypothesis of the Primeval Atom." Maybe so, but when cosmologists wish to write for the noble purpose of enlightening the rest of us, do you think they call it "the hypothesis of the primeval atom?" If you guess No, you are correct. All of their argumentative articles on the subject are so enthralled by the brilliance of Fred Hoyle's phrase-making that they just employ the familiar title of "Big Bang," as do I.

One thing surely can be said in favor of theological acceptance of the Big Bang Theory: it does validate Scriptural teaching (Chapter 1) that the universe had its moment of creation "in the beginning."

Deflating the Inflation Epoch with Parsimony

To the average educated nonscientist, uninitiated into the wizardry of astrophysical mathematics and the Grand Unified Theory, the most difficult part of the foregoing account of Big Bang Theory is the discussion of the Inflationary Epoch. This was the explosively rapid (almost instantaneous!) expansion of the universe in its initial time from $t_U = 0$ to $t_U = 10^{-36}$ sec, after which it suddenly slowed down to today's

Hubble rate of expansion. The picture might seem counter-intuitive to you. It does to me. After all, what necessitates adding a plug-in device such as the Inflationary Epoch? Was there some fixation about starting from a point? Or something hypothetically close to it, like a few cubic millimeters? With due respect for General Relativity equations and the value and insight that scholars gain from exquisitely sophisticated mathematics, a simpler hypothesis (metaphor) might offer a more satisfying imagery for the average person.

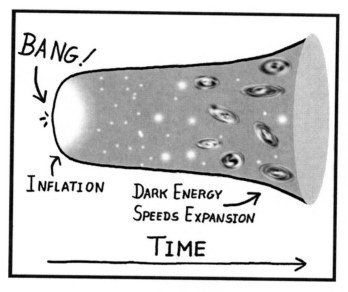

Astronomers' Depiction of Big Bang (not to scale)

Did creation really have to start from a dimensionless <u>point</u> in space and time? Is that an unnecessary figment? Was it "bigger than a bread box?" One might question whether that initial volume (at $t_U = 0$) could be smaller than the minimal volume for the total number of 10^{89} protons and neutrons (or their quark predecessors) in the universe, closely packed together. There is no evidence for or against that supposition.

Using the smallest measured dimension of a proton, its "electric charge radius," as 8.41×10^{-16} meter (*Science*, January, 2013), we calculate (below) that the most compact volume of all these closest-packed nucleons of this **proto-universe** would have a diameter on the order of 8.63×10^{11} km. That would be 536 billion miles. For reference, that is larger than the size of our solar system, out to well past Pluto and the farthest planetesimals. That's a pretty big "bread box!" Did our exploding universe begin at $t_U = 0$ with spherical 536-billion-mile dimensions? . . . Or did it achieve that condition one-trillionth of a second thereafter, after somehow expanding at a gazillion times faster than the speed of light? ? ?

Compactly Stacked Cannonballs

[Since the volume (V) of a sphere $= 4/3 \, \pi \, r^3$, where r is the radius and $\pi = 3.1416$, then the <u>volume of one proton</u> would be $4/3 \, \pi \, (8.41 \times 10^{-16})^3 = \mathbf{2.492 \times 10^{-45}} \ \mathbf{m}^3$.

Now, when any number of equal spheres are stacked in the densest, most compact arrangement, a certain amount of space is vacant between them. It was important to know how much when stacking cannonballs in old warships. It turns out that the best that can be achieved is 25.95% void and 74.05% solid. So we can apply that factor to calculate the minimum volume in cubic meters of 10^{89} close-packed protons and neutrons:

<u>Volume of the proto-universe</u>, $V_{U'} = (2.492 \times 10^{-45} \times 10^{89}) / 0.7405$ $= \mathbf{3.365 \times 10^{44}} \ \mathbf{m}^3$

From this volume of the densest arrangement of 10^{89} nucleons, we derive the radius ($r_{u'}$) of that hypothetical sphere as the <u>cube root</u> of 3/4 x $V_{u'} / \pi$

So, $r_{u'} = [(3 \times 3.365 \times 10^{44}) / (4 \times 3.1416)]^{1/3} = 4.315 \times 10^{14}$ m

Thus the radius of the hypothetical proto-universe = 4.315×10^{11} km, or
$$= \mathbf{2.68 \times 10^{11} \text{ miles.}}$$

So the diameter of the hypothetical proto-universe = **536 billion miles.**

And the radius of the hypothetical proto-universe, 268 billion miles, is 75 times the distance from the sun to planet Pluto, or out to the suspected orbit of the new, unconfirmed, **ninth planet** in our solar system. At the maximum speed of light (186,282 mi/sec) it would take 16.7 days to get there.]

This concept of 10^{89} close-packed hadrons could be consistent with several cosmological theories of cyclical universes. This idea presupposes a successive series of universes, for which the collapse of one universe leads to the bursting forth of the next, and so forth, until the gravity constant is correctly balanced by the initial expansion velocity.

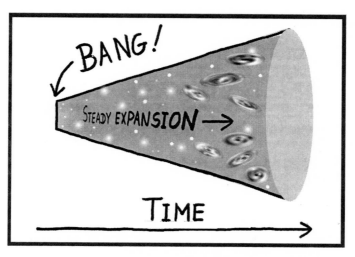

**Big Bang from Compacted Minimal Volume of All Matter
(also not to scale)**

If, however, one feels compelled (mathematically or psychologically) to believe that the Big Bang started from something finite but on the order of a <u>point</u> in space, here is a simpler interpretation. IF we assume the <u>original</u> diameter of this "point" was on the order of 10^{-11} m (one-hundredth of a nanometer!), and IF it expanded by 10^{26} times that original diameter in an instantaneous fraction of a second (page 56-57), the diameter would have grown to 10^{15} m. That last span is roughly the diameter (above) of a close-packed sphere of all those 10^{89} protons and neutrons in the universe. Until that condition, there would be no discrete particles to attract each other by gravity, because the density and temperature would be too great for any particles to exist.

For you and me (in my simplified hypothesis, which is not based on any quantum mathematical model), we might imagine the initial burst of expansion as being driven by the immense internal pressure of too much mass, intensely overheated, in too little space.

When the exploding volume of the universe reached the condition at which non-overlapping particles could emerge (quarks and gluons at 10^{-12} second, and later, hadrons at 10^{-6} to 10^{-4} seconds), that internal pressure would abate as if its "first stage rocket" had flamed out. At about this time, gravity would begin to exert attractions among the emerging discrete particles to put the brakes on—in a delicate, fine-tuned anthropic balance, of course. In this convenient but imaginary hypothesis, the initial Inflation would slow down when the mass separated into discrete particles upon which gravity only then could begin to operate.

Perhaps it is instructive here to reflect upon a brilliant allegory offered by American astronomer and self-professed agnostic **Robert Jastrow** in *God and the Astronomers*:

> *For the scientist who has lived by his faith in the power of reason, the story ends like a bad dream. He has scaled the mountains of ignorance; he is about to conquer the highest peak; as he pulls himself over the final rock, he is greeted by a band of theologians, who have been sitting there for centuries.*

Chapter 5

Revelation Through Physics

When I was a graduate student fifty-seven years ago, the understanding of the basic building blocks of matter was changing around us. Not long before that, the wave theory of light had to be taught as a separate course from the particle theory of light photons. That was because the two concepts seemed incompatible until Planck and Einstein unraveled the code to show the fundamental relationship between matter and energy. We joked about the olden days when light was taught as waves on Monday-Wednesday-Friday of the college calendar, and as particles on Tuesday-Thursday-Saturday. We studied six days per week back then. Pity.

Theory is Metaphor (and *vice versa*) in Physics and Chemistry

Physics is happening. In this chapter, we will look at some special insights that physics reveals about the most basic nature of things. Let's begin with the theory of atoms.

Many of the explanations for scientific phenomena are expressed in metaphoric language. This enables scientists to describe a theory of matter or behavior in analogical terms that are more familiar to scientists and nonscientists alike. Another advantage of metaphoric explanation is that it readily generates questions that can be tested by experiment. We can see this in the scientific explanation of atoms.

The earliest conception of atoms described them as the tiniest building blocks of all matter. The Greek philosopher Leucippus (440 BC) viewed matter as consisting of minute particles, which he called atoms, surrounded by a spatial vacuum to allow atoms to move. His student Democritus (*circa* 420 BC) was later credited by Aristotle with carrying this idea further, idealizing the atom as "the smallest indivisible unit of matter," which could not be cut into smaller pieces. Indian philosophers, such as the Jain School, had a similar concept more than a century earlier, though less publicized.

Two thousand years later, this proposition was adapted by Robert Boyle to describe chemical elements as composed of distinct atoms. John Dalton (1803) refined this by proposing that the atoms of any particular element were identical, but different from the atoms of any other element. From this insight, he could explain that interactions and combinations of atoms were the basis of chemical reactions. He pictured atoms as spherical solids, a useful working metaphor for some predictions such as the packing geometry of solid metals and salts.

The ratio of weights by which two elements combined chemically to form a compound allowed the calculation of relative **atomic weights**. In 1869, Dmitri Mendeleev was able to arrange 63 known elements into a Periodic Table, based on their increasing atomic weights and any similar reactivities. The atom was still a mysterious, hypothetical particle. This periodic order was later revised to a sequence of elements based on their **atomic number**, the number of protons in an atom of each element.

Protons were postulated when Ernest Rutherford demonstrated experimentally (1911) that the mass of an atom was concentrated in a very small central nucleus, with its electrons (discovered by J.J. Thomson in 1897) outside the nucleus defining the effective volume of the atom. Rutherford bombarded a thin sheet of gold ($_{79}Au$) with beams of alpha-rays ($_2He^{+2}$ particles). If there were no gaps in the gold atoms, the α–particles would all reflect backwards. He observed that most passed straight through, with some deflected by the positive charge of the gold nuclei, and a very few ricocheted back in various directions. From this ingenious **"gold foil"** experiment, he calculated that the mass of each gold atom must be densely concentrated in a minuscule fraction of its volume. The atom's extranuclear electrons held the nuclei far enough apart for most α-particles to shoot right through without being impeded by the low-density electron field.

In 1918, Rutherford discovered the proton. It was concluded that the number of protons would equal the number of electrons in each neutral atom, thus defining its atomic number. One problem was that for almost all then known elements, the atomic mass was approximately twice the number of protons in the nucleus, or more. Rutherford (1921) attributed the mass difference to neutral particles, which he called neutrons, having the same mass as a proton but no electrical charge. In 1932, Rutherford's young colleague James Chadwick found the experimental proof of neutrons.

Rutherford's "gold foil" experiment led Niels Bohr to devise his
Atomic Theory (1913) that the electrons of an atom circled its nucleus
in "orbitals" with discrete energy levels, which Max Planck called
quanta. The chemical reactivity of each element would be controlled by
the outermost electron orbitals alone. This "planetary" analogy helps
students visualize the concept of covalent bonds that hold atoms together
at fixed distances and angles in molecules. "Ball and Stick" models
became popular, but was that the true nature of atoms and bonds, or just
an analogical convenience?

Louis de Broglie demonstrated (1923) that electrons have a dual
nature of both particles and waves, which inspired Erwin Schrödinger
to show (1930) that an atom's electron orbitals were more effectively
interpreted by means of complex wave equations. Schrödinger depicted
the electrons as clouds occupying all the space around the atomic
nucleus, but more densely in symmetrical lobes within the Bohr orbital
dimensions. Wave equations also worked for electron pairs shared by two
or more atoms in covalent bonds to form molecules, and even accounted
for bond angles and lengths.

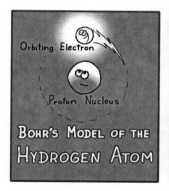

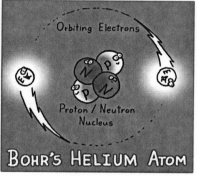

From this, you may be able to see how metaphoric analogies evolved
to help scientists describe the behavior of electrons around atoms and
molecules, as the theory advanced from simple to more sophisticated
levels of understanding. These mathematical equations and the
descriptions of "orbitals" and "clouds" are still metaphoric in character.
To follow a gifted scholar on the use of metaphor in scientific theory, you
should read *Metaphor and Myth in Science and Religion* (1976) by Earl
MacCormac.

For this work, the Nobel Prize was awarded to J.J. Thomson (1906),
Ernest Rutherford (1908 for earlier work on radiation), Niels Bohr (1922),

Louis de Broglie (1929), Erwin Schrodinger (1933), and James Chadwick (1935). Nobel laureates also honored important contributions to our theory of atoms by Marie Curie (1903 and 1911), Max Planck (1918), Albert Einstein (1921), Robert Millikan (1923), and Werner Heisenberg (1932). Sadly, Mendeleev was nominated but never honored, apparently due to an untimely rivalry with respected Nobel committeeman Svante Arrhenius.

Fundamental Particles

Niels Bohr had developed a simple and understandable concept of atomic structure, depicting an atom of any element with a nucleus consisting of protons and neutrons with almost all of the mass defined by this nucleus. There would be a flight of discrete, low-mass electrons whizzing about the space just outside the nucleus to account for all the chemical properties of acids and bases, oxidation and reduction, ionic and covalent bonding. This was soon replaced by the highly mathematical treatment of **quantum mechanics** with its much more sophisticated wave equations for the nature of atomic electrons.

A similar revolution was going on with understanding the atomic nucleus. Atoms were once considered to be the indivisible elementary particles, until it was shown that atoms consisted of smaller particles called protons, neutrons, and electrons. We now know that these in turn are composed of yet smaller particles. How did this come about?

Particle accelerators (cyclotrons) were designed and used to slam protons into atoms of various elements to see what would happen to these smallest known particles. Sometimes, the accelerated particles would imbed in the nuclei of the target atoms and form new, heavier elements. When the velocities were great enough, target atoms fractured into smaller fragments, often with a release of radiation. It was a whole new world of subatomic particle physics. The next step was the circular accelerator, patterned after the cyclotron, only vastly larger.

Hideki Yukawa had predicted (1934) from quantum mathematics that protons and neutrons were held together by binding forces carried by more basic particles, which he called **mesons**. It was still true that a simpler concept of indivisible protons, neutrons, and electrons could take us far in interpreting and predicting physical and chemical behavior of elements and their compounds. They remained convenient particles for most purposes but were no longer the ultimate building blocks of matter. The idea of smaller components seemed incomprehensible until mesons were detected experimentally (1947). For his bold prediction, Yukawa became the first Japanese Nobel laureate (1949).

Since then, physicists have predicted no less than 17 fundamental particles, of which 16 have readily been confirmed (6 quarks, 6 leptons and 4 bosons). This concept holds that protons and neutrons are made of quarks; while electrons, positrons, and other leptons are themselves fundamental particles. Bosons are more like <u>forces</u> that operate within and among quarks and leptons. A great deal of interest has focused on the sole missing 17th particle, the **Higgs Boson,** named for British physicist Peter Higgs, who predicted its existence and properties mathematically in 1964. In theory, this is the ubiquitous particle that gives all other particles their mass. Owing to its elusiveness and its importance in confirming the latest **Standard Model**, the Higgs Boson has been popularly dubbed the "God Particle." That irreverent misnomer has no theological or scientific significance. It's just what someone called it. Even so, a better understanding of how matter takes on mass would give theists a new revelation of how God ordained it to be.

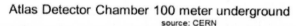

Atlas Detector Chamber 100 meter underground
source: CERN

The highest energies available for smashing atoms into such particles are possible at the Large Hadron Collider at the Center for Nuclear Energy Research (CERN) laboratory near Geneva, Switzerland. This device is an array of high powered electromagnets firing in perfectly synchronized, ultrafast sequence around the vast circumferential core of a circular 17-mile tunnel on the border between France and Switzerland.

It is designed for accelerating protons up to 0.999999991 times the speed of light if ever operated at full power. In terms of the difference between these velocities and the speed of light, **c**, we can say these particles would be accelerated to within 10^{-8} of **c**.

Their objective was to get protons going in opposite directions to collide at that velocity and smash them into fundamental particles. Once CERN researchers narrowed the possible range of accelerating energies needed for the Higgs Boson, they succeeded in finding it. In July 2012, it was announced that the Higgs boson had been generated, based on its observed effect on other particles, and its expected decay products. Work continues for determining its properties, after ramping up the power of the collider.

Higgs Boson Formation and Decay
Credit: CERN

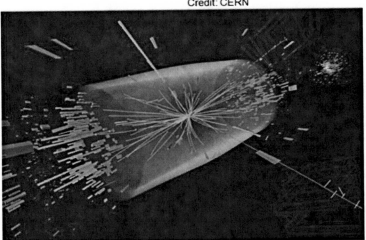

Now you have seen how theories benefit from different levels of sophistication. The 2013 Nobel Prize in Physics went to Peter Higgs and his coworker (and Holocaust survivor) François Englert.

Entropy and the Second Law of Thermodynamics

Thermodynamics is a branch of classical physics studying the energy properties of matter. It was a hot topic back in the days when steam engines were being developed. In studies of the behavior of enclosed gases as heat is added, or taken away by cooling, physicists have developed the fundamental Laws of Thermodynamics. One popular interpretation of the Second Law of Thermodynamics has invited a great deal of speculation as to what it tells us about the emergence of complicated, living organisms. Here we will see not only why the Second Law is so intriguing, but also why we should be cautious about trying to apply it to matters of faith. See what you think of it.

The **First Law of Thermodynamics** (from Rudolph Clausius, 1850) states that energy cannot be created or destroyed, but can be converted from one form into another, such as from heat to work, or from potential energy into kinetic energy. It defines a concept of Internal Energy that is increased by heat transferred in, and reduced by work transferred out. That seems intuitive enough, except it then had to be modified to accommodate the finding of nuclear physics that mass (m) can be converted into energy (E) according to Einstein's equation, $E = mc^2$.

The **Second Law of Thermodynamics** (from Sadi Carnot, 1824, as restated by Clausius, 1856) affirms that heat cannot flow spontaneously from one mass at lower temperature to another at a higher temperature. One consequence is not self-evident without a thorough study of this Second Law, but Clausius deduced that this puts a limitation on the available energy that can be transformed into work, and he called this restriction **Entropy**. Entropy can be represented as a measure of the degree of disorder within a closed system of matter. For any isolated system (into which no heat can be added and no external source of symmetry, architecture, or other orderliness can be introduced), the entropy of that system cannot decrease. It can only stay the same or increase. This inexorable increase in entropy means that the system's contents must eventually become more disorderly. We will come back to this shortly.

The **Third Law of Thermodynamics** (from Walther Nernst, 1912) states that for a perfect crystal at **absolute zero** temperature (0° Kelvin, which is -273° Centigrade) the entropy is zero: perfect order! This is a theoretical reference point, and presupposes that a system of matter cannot be cooled down to absolute zero. Other Thermodynamic Laws have been formulated, but they need not concern us at this time.

Of particular interest here is the **Second Law**, and its concomitant entropy. The mechanism through which heat can be transformed into work has a limitation whereby the entire system subject to the heat transfer process becomes more disorderly. For an isolated system with no way to add or remove external heat or introduce orderliness, the entropy of that system tends toward a maximum. Another way of saying it is that the degree of disorder will increase until there is complete disorder. In most equations of physics, time has no directional element. Entropy, however, clearly imposes a direction upon time, as this tendency within a closed system is always toward disorder, and never toward greater orderliness. The system does not go backward toward lower entropy. What does this relationship tell us about cosmology?

We must be careful here. *Order-to-Disorder* is one of those neat metaphors that helps us interpret what is going on, but is not referenced in any of the formulas that define the Second Law. There is another metaphor, preferred by Ludwig Boltzmann, relating higher entropy to a greater freedom of motion of molecules and atoms. Here's an illustration that may help. The phenomenon of temperature is conceived as the amount of molecular motion in all modes: molecules flying through space (up, down, and sideways), tumbling (yawing, pitching, and rolling) as they fly around, and vibrating internally along their covalent bonds (compressing bond lengths and angles between bonds). Heat transfer involves collisions between the hyperactive molecules of the hotter material and the more sedate molecules of the cooler object. The latter gain more vigorous motion, which we record as a rise in temperature (the colored liquid in the thermometer also has acquired more vigorous motions from the molecular collisions, and consequently expands in its thin tube—which we read as a temperature increase).

When ice melts, its water molecules gain a higher degree of freedom of motion in the liquid phase than in the crystalline solid lattice. When boiled and vaporized, the water molecules gain even greater diversity of motion, and the entropy of the system rises further. In this case, an increase in freedom of motion and the increase in random disorder both help interpret the increase in entropy.

This leads to an interesting question about entropy when applied to the cosmology of the universe and to the origin of life. How orderly was the universe at its beginning? This gets a little tricky. Think about how the early universe was described in chapter 4, in the first few minutes after the Big Bang. Upon casual consideration, the Big Bang might seem completely disorderly and chaotic at first. From that perspective, it was hours into the expansion process before a certain orderliness began to emerge as atoms formed, then discrete gases, which condensed through gravitation into stars, which later exploded as supernovae, spraying the surrounding space with new, heavier elements, which then aggregated into new stars and planets, one of which begat life. If it was gradually becoming more orderly, would that decrease in entropy violate the Second Law of Thermodynamics? How could order be introduced into the initial disorder?

Ah, but was it disorderly at $t_U = 0$? Up until what is called the Hadron Epoch, before atoms were delineated at $t_U = 10^{-6}$ second, this early universe actually had a very high degree of order in the uniformity of its compact state. In its extremely dense phase, before there were any discrete particles of matter, before nuclear and electromagnetic forces emerged, one can visualize almost perfect order within its confined space, before this exploding volume scattered. In Boltzmann's metaphor, prior to the Hadron Epoch the only freedom of motion was expansion of the undifferentiated mass, before protons and neutrons had emerged as discrete particles. When they did separate, there was a large increase in diversity of motion of particles within the expanding mass, consistent with a definite increase in entropy, as required by the Second Law.

As you can see, it is easy to get tangled up when trying to describe the effect of entropy in the universe, either in part or as a whole. It is tempting here to cite Big Bang entropy changes as evidence for belief, but not easy to win that argument.

According to either scenario, while the incipient universe continued its expansion, various elements of order transferred from some of its zones to others. For example, disorder (entropy) decreased locally as atoms formed, but increased overall as they scattered and emitted light photons. The early aggregation of matter into stars and galaxies brought zones of order, but their outward flight countered with disorder, as did every exploding supernova. Some parts gained a higher degree of order at the expense of other parts which became more disordered, so that the total entropy of the universe never decreased, thus in complete agreement with Thermodynamics.

Pope Pius XII translated this directly into the theological realm:

Through the Law of Entropy, it was recognized that the spontaneous processes of nature are always accompanied by a diminution of free and utilizable energy. In a closed material system, this conclusion must lead eventually to a cessation of processes on a macroscopic scale. This unavoidable fate, which stands out clearly from positive scientific experience, postulates eloquently the existence of a Necessary Being. ("Theology and Modern Science," 1951)

In other words, there must be <u>something</u> outside the universe that gave it a higher degree of orderliness either at $t_U = 0$, or soon after the Big Bang, bringing "order out of chaos." The *Book of Genesis* has one answer, albeit in poetic, allegorical, and theistic terms.

Meanwhile, the irreversible direction of order to disorder may be invoked without reference to entropy and the Second Law. Take as an illustration what happens to a fine porcelain cup and saucer when accidentally dropped to the floor. It definitely becomes less orderly, and no matter how many times it is repeatedly dropped, it will never return to its original form. That example has little to do with entropy and the Second Law, for there is insignificant transfer of heat. Nevertheless, the shattered teacup does reinforce the implications of entropy to the extent it helps you understand that basic metaphor.

Heisenberg's Uncertainty Principle

In classical physics, we measure the precise location of an object and its movement through space in order to devise a formula to explain and predict its behavior. For extremely small particles, however, there is a fundamental limit to the validity of such measurements. In 1927, Niels Bohr's colleague and former student Werner Heisenberg showed that very small subatomic particles like electrons are affected by the very beam of energy with which one attempts to observe them. He concluded that we can measure the position of such a particle, or we can measure its momentum of motion through space, but not both at the same time. After rationalizing this mathematically, he noted: "The more precisely the position is determined, the less precisely its momentum is known, and *vice versa*." An electron could not be treated as having any precise position and momentum as part of an atom.

This realization required a restatement of Bohr's classic depiction of the atomic model, with each electron revolving in a precise orbit at a fixed radius around its atomic nucleus. His planetary model did not fit the nature of very small particles; e.g., electrons. To go further required the development of quantum mechanics, exceedingly complex mathematics whereby the electron is described by a standing wave in which the electron simultaneously occupies all of the space around the atom, yet concentrated with the greater part of its density in a shaped volume very close to the nucleus.

For his contributions to quantum mechanics, Heisenberg received the Nobel Prize in Physics in 1932, ten years after Bohr. At the same time, the emergence of atomic physics brought inherently profound dangers, raising caution as well as specters of science phobia.

[**The Bomb:** Pierre and Marie Curie's daughter Irene, while working in the radiation laboratory of her parents, had met and later married another French assistant Frederic Joliot, fusing both of their names to Joliot-Curie. They demonstrated that it was possible to bombard various pure, stable elements with alpha particles (positively charged helium-4 ions, $^4He^{+2}$) to produce slightly heavier radioactive elements artificially by the absorption of the helium mass into the target nucleus. This justified the 1935 Nobel Prize in Chemistry being awarded jointly to the Joliot-Curies. In their Nobel Prize lecture, Frederic and Irene prophesied the inherent danger of starting a chain reaction that might generate enormous energy, attributing that to the explosion of a supernova observed by astronomers.

James Chadwick had just discovered neutrons (1932), the nuclear particles having almost the same mass as protons but lacking any electrical charge. Immediately, Italian Enrico Fermi began bombarding various elements with neutrons, using particles emitted in some radioactive decay processes, with results similar to those of the Joliot-Curies. Fermi continued to experiment with every known element of the Periodic Table up to and including the heaviest natural element, naturally radioactive uranium ($_{92}U$). Notably, the Nobel Prize in Physics went to Chadwick in 1935 and to Fermi in 1938. Clearly this was the hot topic of the decade.

Another contributor, under the guidance of Max Planck, was Lise Meitner, the second woman to earn a doctorate in physics at the University of Vienna. She became the first woman physics professor at the Kaiser Wilhelm Institute, where she worked with Otto Hahn on experiments to bombard elements with slow neutrons, converting some into heavier isotopes and elements. Although compelled to flee Nazi Germany in 1938 as persecution of Jews intensified, she continued correspondence with Hahn.

In one exchange, Meitner learned that Hahn and Fritz Strassman had detected barium ($_{56}Ba$) among the products found after neutron bombardment of uranium, but could not explain their finding since barium was a lighter element, a little over half the atomic mass of uranium. How could addition of a neutron produce a lighter element? Meitner and her nephew Otto Frisch correctly deduced that Hahn's experiment had caused the first known instance of "nuclear fission" (her original term) of the unstable uranium atom.

She later calculated that this fission produced three product neutrons for every one neutron that caused uranium to fission, which she predicted would have the potential in a larger mass of uranium to trigger an out-of-control chain reaction. This, coupled with Bohr's finding of an inordinately high energy emitted during uranium fission, led her to realize its terrifying military application. Her astonishing report had an explosive effect within and beyond the scientific community.

When the Nobel committee selected Otto Hahn for the Chemistry Prize in 1944, it chose not to include Lise Meitner, without whose acumen Hahn might never have understood what he had discovered. We may never know whether this slight was because the committee did not wish to offend Hitler, or because Hahn ungallantly discounted her contribution. Perhaps nationalist blinders led Hahn to resent Meitner's decision to leave German jurisdiction. Either way, it ranks among the most egregious oversights of the committee's distinguished history.

One trio of European scientists who had immigrated to America, Leo Szilard, Edward Teller, and Eugene Wigner, feared that respected colleagues remaining in Germany would have the same knowledge and intellectual capacity for devising an atomic bomb. They persuaded their more famous colleague Albert Einstein to write a warning to President Roosevelt, which led to the top-secret establishment of the code-named Manhattan Project in a race to produce an atomic bomb.

There is a fascinating yet ambiguous sequel to the Heisenberg and Bohr relationship. Niels Bohr, a Dane of Jewish descent, had sensed a growing antipathy within the Nazi government to scientific inquiry, especially suppressing the new physics of quantum mechanics. He found refuge in America in early 1939. Meanwhile, Werner Heisenberg had become a leader among German scientists in their new *Uran Verein* ("Uranium Club"), studying and seeking to develop nuclear fission for energy and military use. Although never anti-Semitic or a Nazi Party member, Heisenberg had accepted the nationalist expectation of inevitable German victory and supremacy. European-trained theoretical physicists in Germany and the United States equally recognized that their counterparts across the Atlantic understood the ramifications of a fission chain reaction, but neither had any knowledge of what actually was being attempted on the other continent.

When Heisenberg realized that atomic weapons held the potential for enormous destructive power, he decided to initiate secretly a moral pact among atomic scientists on both sides to forestall its development. In September 1941, even as the German *blitzkrieg* was advancing across Europe and into Russia, he made his move at great personal risk. While attending a German-sponsored conference in occupied Denmark, Heisenberg arranged to meet with his mentor privately to avoid being overheard. Apparently, the furtive nature of their clandestine conversation left each with different perceptions as to what the other was communicating. Their respective notes and memories years later reveal uncertainty (what irony!) as to who said what. Heisenberg mistakenly thought there had been a meeting of minds, from which each would seek to stall development of nuclear weapons on his respective side. Bohr suspected it was just an attempt to coopt him and his colleagues in America to abandon any threat to German ascendancy.

While some historians today are skeptical of Heisenberg's motives, it is clear that, at enormous risk for a treasonous act, Heisenberg had slipped a drawing of a German nuclear power reactor to Bohr. Even though it was not a bomb design, Bohr was alarmed and delivered it to the American atomic bomb scientists in Los Alamos. They recognized that the Germans were far along. Heisenberg may well deserve credit for facilitating the German command decision to divert resources away from the expensive uranium project. Meanwhile, America's Manhattan Project was spurred to greater urgency, achieving historic success at Los Alamos just ten weeks after Germany surrendered.]

Anthropic Coincidences and Fine-Tuning

How, then, does the development of atomic theory relate to theological revelation? A strong case for reconciliation of modern science and religion has been made by John Polkinghorne, a British mathematician, physicist, and Anglican priest who wrote *The Faith of a Physicist* in 1994. Polkinghorne presented a fascinating scientific case for a Creator based on numerous physical constants that have no inherent theoretical basis other than that they are essential for vital physics relationships to work. Examples included the four fundamental forces released very early in the Big Bang sequence:

1. the gravitational force constant,
2. the strong nuclear force constant,
3. the weak nuclear force constant, and
4. the electromagnetic force constant.

It had been noted earlier by Robert Dicke, Brandon Carter, John Barrow, Frank Tipler, Stephen Barr, and others that if any one of these had been slightly higher or lower at the burst of creation, the universe could not have developed into what we now observe. Barrow and Tipler wrote a strong exposition of the concept in *The Anthropic Cosmological Principle* (1986). The question arises whether this fine-tuning implies a theological explanation or can be explained by natural causes.

If certain of these constants were very slightly stronger or weaker, the conditions could never exist for life to emerge and evolve. We would not be here to observe life or the universe. This is a bland, brief, and inadequate summary just to introduce the idea. The fact that there are so many vital but finely tuned physical constants is known as the strong "**Anthropic Principle**," that all are precisely right for the creation of a universe and world inhabitable by a species of sentient creatures.

Dicke suggested (1961) that if the universe were only one-tenth its present age, not enough carbon, oxygen, and nitrogen would have been generated. If it were ten times its present age, there would remain no "main sequence" stars large enough to hold planetary systems. We could not be here except during the current age of the universe. That wide span of time does not constitute an anthropic coincidence, however. It's just a simple coincidence of eventually good timing.

Matters heated up at a symposium on the 500th anniversary (1973) of the birth of Copernicus, who was being honored by discussion of the so-called **Copernican Principle**. This was the popular notion that Earth has no special or central place in the universe; but is just an average planet orbiting an ordinary star, in some nondescript corner of an ordinary galaxy, in a backwater of the universe. Others called this the "**Mediocrity Principle**," which would have been more appropriate. After all, Copernicus himself believed the sun held a very special position as the fixed center of the world.

During that conference, Brandon Carter spoke in opposition to this Mediocrity Principle as promoted by others. He objected, based on a number of examples of physical constants whose values were precisely right for stars and planets to form, and for human life to emerge on this one. Others rallied to his Anthropic Principle with other examples.

Anthropic Constants and Conditions

1. Consider Newton's **Gravitational Constant**, denoted by the letter G. In mathematical formulations of processes occurring during the first few seconds of creation (according to the "Big Bang" theory), the value of G is critical, and finely balanced between two disastrous outcomes. Had the gravitational constant and the gravitational pull between masses been

slightly higher by one part in a hundred billion (1×10^{-11}), our newborn universe would have collapsed during the first second of creation. That would not have worked out for us. On the other side, had the value of G been slightly lower by one part in a million (1×10^{-6}), gravity could not have pulled the expanding hydrogen cloud into large aggregates to form stars. That would not have worked for us either.

It has been said that the gravitational constant G is finely balanced on a razor's edge of improbability. Are we lucky, or what?

Some would object on the basis of an assertion that G is fundamentally inherent to the universe and therefore not coincidental. If so, it merely requires a restatement of this example as a profound coincidence that the mass and outward velocity of the universe have just the right (finely-tuned) values to comply with the inherent gravity constant.

2. **Strong Nuclear Force** is the attraction that holds together the protons and neutrons in the nucleus of an atom, and also holds together **quarks** to form the protons and neutrons. Protons are the subatomic particles that define the fundamental chemistry of each element. Hydrogen has just one proton in its atomic nucleus. Helium has two protons, and lithium has three, beryllium four, boron five, carbon six, and so forth. The problem with this is that each proton carries a positive electrical charge, and it is well-established that like charges repel each other. Hydrogen has only one proton in its nucleus, so that is not a problem. For a heavier element with more than one proton, what holds the nucleus together? What is there to overcome the repulsions among the six protons in a carbon nucleus, or even the two protons of the helium nucleus, so that it does not burst apart?

One clue to this riddle is the **neutron**, which has almost the same mass as a proton but no electrical charge at all. Each stable atomic nucleus (except the smallest hydrogen isotope) has a number of neutrons approximately equal to the number of protons, or somewhat higher. To take carbon (C) again as an example, it has two stable isotopes, carbon-12 (also represented as ^{12}C) and carbon-13 (^{13}C). Each has 6 protons, but ^{12}C has 6 neutrons while ^{13}C has 7 neutrons. Notice that the isotopic mass number is the sum of the numbers of protons and neutrons. That number also is the relative atomic weight, since the masses of the proton and neutron are almost the same. Carbon also has an unstable isotope, carbon-14, which is therefore radioactive. Its slow decay rate is useful in "carbon-dating" the age of fossils of once living organisms.

Let's get back to that magic neutron. It has been shown that the effect of neutrons within each nucleus is to stabilize it somehow against the repulsion forces of all those protons' positive charges. There is a quantifiable exchange of energy and matter ($E = mc^2$) that lowers the internal energy of the nucleus to a level where it is stable. This is called the Strong Nuclear Force. I will spare you the theoretical details, as it involves **gluons** (aptly named!) and quarks—a subject for a more advanced treatment. The main point is that this Strong Nuclear Force (SNF) is finely balanced at just the right value. If it were somewhat weaker, no nucleus could hold more than one proton, and hydrogen would be the only possible element. If this vital SNF were somewhat stronger, a case has been made that all hydrogen atoms would have converted to helium during the early Photon Epoch of Big Bang creation (pages 58-59). With no elemental hydrogen remaining, early stars could never have turned on their thermonuclear fusion furnaces to generate heavier elements. Either way, we would not be around to figure this out.

Even if the Strong Nuclear Force were just slightly stronger, all the carbon in stars would have converted to oxygen atoms. Well, that would not work for us either. Perhaps this particular constant is precisely tuned for carbon, the singular elemental ingredient for all of us living organisms (see chapter 14). It has been noted that if it were slightly weaker, a few of the heavier elements would not be stable, with no great detriment to life.

3. **Weak Nuclear Force** is one of four fundamental forces in nature, the others being strong nuclear force, electromagnetic force, and gravity. The Weak Nuclear Force (WNF) operates over very short distances, and is involved both in radioactive decay and in hydrogen fusion in stars to convert hydrogen nuclei into deuterium and helium. Beta (β) decay is a process whereby one atomic nucleus emits a low-mass β particle, typically an electron with its -1 charge, thereby increasing the atomic number of the atom by one. For example, carbon-14 decays by beta decay to form stable nitrogen-14. The original C-14 had 6 protons and 8 neutrons, hence an atomic mass of 14 with atomic number 6. Beta decay converts one of the nuclear neutrons into a proton and an emitted electron, leaving the resulting nucleus with 7 neutrons and 7 protons. This sequence redefines the atomic number as 7, which is nitrogen (N-14), without changing the atomic mass number.

Oddly enough, nitrogen-13 (an unstable isotope with 7 protons and only 6 neutrons) also decays by beta decay, but emits a positively charged β^+ particle, a positron. This converts one proton into a neutron, decreasing the atomic number by one. The product has 6 protons and 7 neutrons, carbon-13, which is stable. The theory for how this works was formulated in the late 1960s by Sheldon Glashow, Abdus Salam, and Steven Weinberg, for which they shared the 1979 Nobel Prize in Physics. Dr. Salam was the first Muslim scientist to receive the Nobel Prize. He also led the development of atomic weapons in his native Pakistan.

It has been argued that if the Weak Nuclear Force were substantially stronger, the universe would consist of hydrogen and no other elements. All of the neutrons in the early universe would have decayed, leaving none to stabilize atomic nuclei containing multiple protons. If, however, the Weak Nuclear Force were slightly weaker, not enough neutrons would have decayed in the early going, and there would be about the same number of neutrons as protons. This could have resulted in all protons being bound up in helium-4 nuclei, with 2 protons and 2 neutrons, so there would be no hydrogen leftover to fuel any thermonuclear fusion reactions in stars.

This has been cited as yet another finely tuned example of an anthropic coincidence at work. It may not be so simple. As noted by Eric Carlson, an early universe without helium would be no worse than a temporary setback. Hydrogen would still condense into stars, making $_2$He and $_3$Li and then proceed with synthesis of higher elements. In another scenario, if WNF were just ten times stronger, there would be more helium than hydrogen—but still plenty of hydrogen—and might produce carbon-12 and oxygen-16 even faster. A shortage of neutrons would not be an insurmountable problem for stars as they begin synthesis by combining protons. That step is followed by positron emission to convert one of the protons into a neutron to make the heavier isotope of hydrogen: deuterium (^{2}H), which pairs off through several steps to make helium-4. The Weak Nuclear Force value may have considerable leeway.

4. Electromagnetic Force is the attraction or repulsion between two charged particles, and is inversely proportional to distance. Any two particles with both having positive charges (or both negative) will repel each other. Any two particles with opposite charges (one having a positive charge and the other a negative charge) will attract each other. Salt crystals have structures with all cations (with positive charges) interspersed closer to anions (with negative charges) than to nearest cations, so that net attractions are stronger than repulsions.

Fortuitously, the electromagnetic force (EMF) is 1/100th the magnitude of the strong nuclear force. Had that ratio been slightly greater, all atomic nuclei other than hydrogen would be inherently unstable and would have decayed rapidly. No number of neutrons could suffice to hold two or more protons together in a nucleus unless the strong nuclear force were correspondingly stronger. Here, it seems the 1:100 ratio of EMF to SNF could be cited as coincidence, but caution is in order. Physicists have formulated Grand Unified Theories (GUTs!) that show mathematical interrelationships by which all of these fundamental forces depend upon each other. At most, this would allow just one unified coincidence. To some, however, their GUTs tell them there is no coincidence at all: it is what it is.

5. **Matter and Antimatter.** In the beginning, theory expects, matter and antimatter should have been created as quarks and antiquarks in nearly equal abundance. It is calculated that almost immediately, at $t_u = 10^{-6}$ second, these particles would have collided and mutually annihilated each other, releasing photons of light energy. Had the abundance of each been precisely and perfectly equal, all that would have been left would be pure light photons (quite a spectacle to be seen, but with no one to see it). There must have been some excess of quarks, for here we are.

It has been estimated that for every <u>billion</u> pairs originally, there would have been <u>one</u> extra quark. Once again, we are here because of a very improbable coincidence, for the universe had 10^{89} quarks left over! That particular numerical excess, however, is not the anthropic limit, as life on Earth might well have arisen from 10^{80} quarks, or even less. We might place the lower limit at just one healthy galaxy, or 10^{77} quarks, in a universe one-trillionth the size of ours. We do not yet know (chapter 17) if the Milky Way Galaxy, or our little backwater of it, has produced more than one outgrowth of life.

6. **Speed of Light**: Physicists have developed a large number of mathematical formulas to describe the behavior and relationships of matter and energy. These are typically stated as a function of one or more variables whose dimensions are controlled by a numerical constant. One familiar example is the speed of light, symbolized by the letter "c" and having a value just over 186,000 miles per second. In metric terms, that is 300,000 kilometers per second (3×10^8 meters per second). It is a vital part of the Einstein equation for the conversion of mass and energy, $E = mc^2$, where E is energy and m is mass. Since the operative proportionality constant is c^2, the square of a very large number, it follows that conversion of a small amount of matter yields an enormous amount of energy.

The most precise value of c, the speed of light, is given as 299,792,458 meters per second. That is light's velocity through a vacuum, and is considered to be the maximum theoretical and physical value for velocity of any matter. It is also given as the speed for propagation through space of gravitation attraction between two masses. Light travels very slightly slower through other media such as water and glass. This fundamental constant also occurs in other formulas, so let's not double count it as anthropic.

7. The **Cosmological Constant** was an element of Einstein's theory of General Relativity. You may want to shield your eyes from the next couple of paragraphs, not because it is too racy, but because it is hard to reduce to simple concepts. Here goes.

In 1917, there was no Doppler evidence that the universe was expanding, so most thought it was static, neither expanding nor contracting. To counteract the force of gravity from collapsing all matter, Einstein had to adjust his General Theory of Relativity to stabilize the universe with an antigravity term, which he dubbed the Cosmological Constant. After it was established that the universe was expanding, Einstein felt he had committed his "worst blunder." His constant was resuscitated when the earth-orbiting Hubble telescope and other satellite platforms examining remote supernovas found that the expansion of the universe is not uniform, but has been accelerating again during the last couple of billion years. The only way to account for this is to concede that there is some force of energy out there within the vacuum of space that is accelerating this expansion, just as it did during the Inflation Epoch. The ready solution for acceleration was Einstein's antigravity factor, which was reborn as **dark energy**, a term for whatever is causing acceleration of expansion.

The Cosmological Constant, represents something like an energy density somehow operating within a vacuum. It was assumed in classical physics that an absolute vacuum would contain no matter, and therefore no energy. That being so, it was argued that the value of the energy density was zero. It has been shown by experiment that Einstein's Cosmological Constant has a value of 10^{-8} erg/cm^3 ("ergs per cubic centimeter"), a much smaller value than had been derived from theory. Steven Weinberg has calculated that if it were 10 times its present value (i.e., at 10^{-7}), rapid inflation would have been too fast for stars to form. In the opposite direction, some feel that if the Cosmological Constant had been smaller the universe could be friendlier to life.

It had been expected that a new mathematical model called **string theory** would bring a rational explanation for why the various force constants are what they are. Instead, string theory turns out to have multiple sets of solutions, only one of which is conducive to the known universe. Could there be multiple universes?

This Cosmological Constant had to be finely tuned to accommodate the universe as we now know it. As Carlson has suggested, the foregoing discussion makes a good case for an anthropic principle on a sliding slope: the value of this dark energy is set at a value making it POSSIBLE for life to occur, without it being EASY! This outcome must provide great comfort to the theists among us, but the debate is not yet settled.

8. **Critical Density** is yet another knife edge cited for improbability. It is the density of the universe above which gravity will pull all matter back into one incredibly enormous black hole, perhaps launching another "Big Bang." If the actual density of the universe were greater than the critical density, expansion of the universe would come to a full stop, followed by a cataclysmic collapse. As the universe expands and its total kinetic energy cools, the critical density will become gradually lower. At the same time, the actual density is decreasing due to Hubble's expansion. This leads to the question whether the critical density will decrease faster than actual density. If this happened, actual density could exceed critical density and expansion will slow to a halt, followed by collapse. It has been calculated that the density of the known universe is one-third of the critical density. If so, it will continue to expand for another few billion years. The important thing is that there is surely no danger of collapse any time soon!

"In the beginning," at barely one second after creation, according to one calculation, the density of the fledgling universe was just slightly less than the critical density: by one part in a <u>trillion</u> (1×10^{-12}). According to that calculation, had the density been even one part in a million lower, atomic particles could never have coalesced into larger masses, and no stars or planets could have formed. In the opposite direction, if at t_U = one second the density had been greater than the critical density by one part in a million, the whole business would have collapsed long ago.

As you must have guessed, this concept is basically a corollary of the Gravity Constant. To count both would therefore be double counting. It is easy to see that the critical density of a hot, expanding universe depends upon the strength of the gravitational constant. If the gravitational constant were higher, the critical density would have had a lower value.

96

In a mutually interdependent way, both were perfectly balanced for that successful first second after the "Big Bang."

9. The **Planck Constant** (h) expresses the proportionality between the energy (E) of a photon of light and its frequency (v), as $E = hv$

Since the wavelength of the light (λ, in meters per wave) is calculated as the speed of light (c, in meters per second) divided by the frequency of the light (v, in waves per second), this Planck Equation may be stated as $E = hc/\lambda$.

Louis de Broglie later showed that this relationship must apply to any particle, even a much more massive proton. This was soon confirmed experimentally. If we combine the Planck equation with the familiar Einstein equation, we get:

$E = hc/\lambda = mc^2$ Thus, $h/\lambda = mc$ and $\lambda = h/mc$

With its very small mass, an electron might have a wavelength in the visible spectrum. For a proton, with its much larger mass, the wavelength would be very short. The Planck Constant is clearly fundamental to many other factors, and consequently has to be set aside from double counting.

[The value of the Planck Constant **h** is extremely small, 6.6×10^{-34} joule seconds, and one of the smallest fundamental constants in physics. It is important in explaining that when metals are heated until they glow, only certain precisely discrete frequencies of light are emitted, not as a continuous spectrum. This was interpreted to mean that the electrons of an atom could only have precisely discrete energy levels (quanta). When a metal is heated, one or more electrons are "excited" to a vacant, higher energy level. When one of these excited electrons subsequently falls from its temporary, higher energy level to an available lower energy level, the specific wavelength (λ) of the emitted light is determined by the difference between the two energy levels (ΔE). The energy difference between the higher and lower energy levels was termed a **quantum** of energy, and the process was a "quantum leap." The next time you hear someone boast that they have achieved a "quantum leap" of some kind, you might remind them that it is one of the smallest increments of energy in theoretical physics!]

10. Various **Quantum Mechanical Constants** arise in the formulation of these complex equations of quantum mechanics. This would include the **Fine Structure Constant**, having a dimensionless value of 1/137, describing the effect of electromagnetic energy on charged particles.

Another would be Fred Hoyle's carbon resonance (discussed in chapter 4). We won't try to master this, except to say that each has a rather precise value that is free standing and not derived from anything else. Are these also highly fortuitous?

Recapitulation of Distinct Anthropic Conditions

The material summarized above suggests six dynamic "coincidences" from astrophysics (after eliminating double counting among dozens that have been proposed) that strongly support the Anthropic Principle:

- The Gravity Constant and its counterpart, the Critical Density, with a fine-tuned range of 10^{-11}
- The ratio between the Strong Nuclear Constant and the Electromagnetic Force, with a wider permissible range of 1%.
- Weak Nuclear Force, with an upper limit 10% above the known value.
- The Cosmological Constant, with a range of 10%.
- The Fine Structure Constant, with a range ± 4%.
- The Hoyle Carbon Resonance energy, with a range of ± 10%.

What, then, is the probability of all of these anthropic constants being precisely tuned at the same time? This is not an idle question.

What if each of two constants or conditions must be within a close tolerance of the perfect value and the random probability for each were one in ten thousand? The probability that two would have the right value at the same time is $1 / (10^4 \times 10^4) = 10^{-8}$. That's a probability of one in ten thousand for either one to get it right, but one in a hundred million for both at the same time. Using range estimates from the preceding paragraph, the probability of all six simultaneously being within their permissible ranges is $1 / (10^{11} \times 100 \times 10 \times 10 \times 25 \times 10) = \mathbf{1 / 2.5 \times 10^{17}}$, or one chance in **250 quadrillion**. Dicke, by the way, had calculated that the fixed ratio of the Gravity Constant to the Electromagnetic Force Constant is so fine-tuned that any divergence by more than $\mathbf{10^{-40}}$ of one without the other would be incompatible with life.

Timothy Ferris reflects on this problem in his wonderful *Coming of Age in the Milky Way*. He describes the atheist philosophy as "Genesis in a Vacuum" for **something** (matter, energy, time, and space) had to come miraculously from **nothing** (an immense, boundless, absolute vacuum). At the beginning of creation ($t_u = 0$), the entire universe might be envisioned as one incredibly massive particle with incredibly high energy. For that ultimately to work out for us to be here, Ferris calculates that, at $t_U = 10^{-35}$ second, the deviation from the critical density had to be less than one part in 10^{49}. It would take quite a stretch to think that happened by pure chance.

In other words, that improbability is so remote that it strains belief to think that it would happen just by chance. Freeman Dyson placed a refreshing interpretation on this array of fortuitous physical constants and conditions. It is as if, he said, "The universe must have known we were coming!" Francis Collins believes this is an argument in favor of a Creator, not necessarily a proof. Indeed, it is a very strong argument.

John Leslie has posed a metaphoric illustration. Just imagine, he says, that you face a firing squad with fifty rifles at ten paces aiming for your heart. The command is given and all rifles fire, but all fifty miss. Would that outcome be considered <u>lucky</u> or <u>intentional</u>? In *The Wonder of the Universe: Hints of God in Our Fine-Tuned World*, Karl Giberson offers three interpretations:

- you were very, very lucky; or
- there were an infinite number of firing squads, and you just happened to have faced the one for which all fifty rifles happened by chance to miss; or
- your firing squad was controlled by some influential ally.

Multiverses

What if there were an infinite number of universes, as in Hinduism, each with its own set of different physical constants according to string theory? This was suggested by the brilliant physicists Stephen Hawking and Richard Feynman, and endorsed by others. If so, we would expect at least one to have the right combination. If it had any sentient inhabitants, they might well be asking these very same questions. Most other universes either would have failed to condense into stars and planets or would have collapsed back to whence they came. Such speculation is not within the realm of evidentiary science. Critics might say it is closer to science fiction . . . with no plot. There is no experimental way to test this hypothesis, because there's no way to observe or measure anything about such undetectable, imaginary universes.

Yet the felicity with which sophisticated mathematics can describe intellectually satisfying alternative universes is truly deserving of the deep thought that has been given to it by some of our brightest thinkers. Max Tegmark has taken this modest accolade to the higher plane of total allegiance. He takes the success of sophisticated mathematical models as stand-alone evidence that every prediction therefrom must be accepted without observational proof. It is Tegmark's dictum (1998) that anything that is predicted by higher mathematics and not found experimentally to be false has a presumption that it exists in nature. If it arises unrefuted in mathematics, it exists without proof or direct observation in nature. Tegmark then builds a firewall around his standard of proof by saying that this theory is falsifiable. I would say it is not a theory until it has been subjected to experimental test of that falsifiability. In the business world, pro forma projections of profitable results for a future business model have often been accepted by investors or lenders on similar assurances, with unhappy consequences.

Science writer Ethan Siegel interprets cosmic inflation as a new theory that has so far made five predictions, four of which have been tested and verified. Its fifth prediction is that innumerable Big Bangs could have created multiple universes. Some could have similar chemical elements. So far none have been observed. That could mean that they do not overlap our known universe. They would seem to be "too far out," both physically and semantically! Lacking falsifiability and physical evidence, the Multiverse hypothesis of Siegel seems to be more "metaphysics" than physics. Would Galileo accept sophisticated reasoning contrary to observation?

In the classic double-slit experiment, when electrons or photons of light are passed (from left to right) through two slits as in the diagram below, interference patterns are observed on the other side. Richard Feynman has wryly noted that this is subject to many interpretations. Indeed, physicist David Deutsch has interpreted this familiar double-slit phenomenon as evidence of multiple universes.

From quantum mechanics, we find that the electron is not just a discrete particle that could only pass through one slit or the other. Its wave properties define the mass of the electron as occupying a wide range of space simultaneously, so that it passes through both slits at the same time. The two new wave fronts expanding from the slits intercept each other in such a way that a symmetrical pattern of peaks and troughs appears on the other side. The same effect is observed when light passes from one side of a wall to the other through two slits. For that matter, uniform waves of water passing through two gaps in a seawall (or the laboratory equivalent in a pan) will produce similar interference patterns. Indeed, double-slit interference was part of the proof that light photons and electrons have inherent wave properties as well as mass.

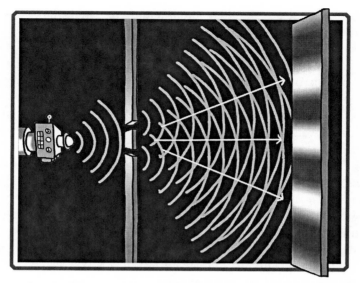

Interference Pattern from Light Passing Through Two Slits

In his modestly entitled "Theory of Everything" (1997), Deutsch contends that this works for an electron because one slit is in one universe and the other slit somehow is in a different universe. Read that again. It is these two universes that interfere and create the observed interference pattern. What we have here is a neat circular argument:

- Deutsch invokes the hypothetical premise of a one or more parallel universes, heretofore undetected, on the ground that complex mathematical models allow or predict them.
- He asserts that one slit is in one universe and <u>the other slit is in another universe,</u> despite the inconvenient fact that both slits were assembled in the same universe—namely, ours—and both were still visible in this one. Two universes? Sharing the same box?
- He concludes that the interference is evidence of the hypothetical unseen universe containing the second slit, present and clearly visible in this universe.

Some physicists concur that Deutsch has found at least one parallel universe and possibly many. I find myself on the side of those skeptical physicists who don't see the logic of his syllogism, believing (a) the double-slit interference works satisfactorily with both slits in the same universe, and (b) it is better to accept the double-slit interference simply as evidence that electrons, like photons and ocean swells, have wave properties.

The search continues. One North American group headed by Stephen Feeney (2010) reported that their examination of data from the Wilkinson Microwave Anisotropy Probe (WMAP), a project studying cosmic microwave background radiation (CMBR, pages 60-61), has revealed circularly shaped abnormalities, which they interpret as minor collisions between our universe and parallel universes billions of years ago. The Planck telescope with higher resolution did not confirm this bumping effect. Likewise, there has been no evidence that our universe has been tugged at by gravity from any neighboring, or overlapping, alternate universe.

Victor Stenger has published an Internet-accessible formula for predicting the likelihood of any hypothetical alternative universe achieving sufficient longevity for life to emerge and evolve. Stenger calls his formula *MonkeyGod* for some reason (probably not very reverently), and bases his calculations on those same four important fundamental constants: (a) the electromagnetic force, (b) the strong nuclear force, (c) the mass of the proton, and (d) the mass of the electron. By varying the value of each, his computer then generates the predicted lifetimes of stars, some of which can achieve multibillion-year life spans. Just for fun, check it out at www.talkreason.org/articles/*anthro_philo.pdf*

Admittedly, this is a game that leaves out many other important constants (gravity or critical density, weak nuclear force, neutron mass, etc.), but presents an intriguing concept that might function equally plausibly if more factors were incorporated. Clearly illustrating the point that a change in one factor can be offset by a compensating adjustment to one or more others, Stenger argues that there is no basis for ruling out a great variety of simultaneous universes. Perhaps, but neither is there anything but eager imagination (or faith?) for supposing such a multiverse. We do observe this one universe of which we are a part. It is here, and we are here. That is all we can observe and ponder from the viewpoint of science. While alternate, mathematically imaginary universes should certainly exhibit some kind of gravitational field or electromagnetic wavelengths, none has ever been observed, not even a single clue.

We should certainly note and pay attention to critics of any anthropic constants and factors—a sturdy group of scientists, some of whom are atheists, and some are theists, and some are neither. They would say that each of these constants has precisely the only value that it could have, and there is nothing special about it. The fact that we are here and can devise these mathematical relationships and constants simply means they are what they are. In that vein, philosopher Robert John Russell, in *Bridging Science and Religion,* has written that the Anthropic Principle is an ambiguous argument. Francis Collins has acknowledged the same observation, but has put forward a compelling analysis of that ambiguity.

In *The Language of God,* Collins defines that ambiguity as allowing three logical possibilities, any one (but only one) of which can be true. Paraphrasing his three possible scenarios and the essential elements of each goes as follows:

1. One can imagine there might be a multitude, even an unlimited infinity, of distinct universes, each with its own combination of these physical constants, conditions, and coincidences. With an infinite number of universes, differing in the variety of numerical values for the kinds of constants we have been discussing, at least one would have it all just right. At least one or more would have all the constants precisely balanced as we have observed to be the case in our home universe. The problem with this presumption is that there is no evidence of any universe other than our own. Zero. The only credible scientific fact about this concept is that not one alternative universe has yet been observed. To base one's cosmological philosophy on such an ephemeral poltergeist would require its own leap of faith.

2. A second possible concept is that there is only one universe, the one we inhabit and observe, and it just happened by chance to have all the right stuff since its beginning. This outcome depends upon the almost infinitesimally low probability that all of these constants would all just happen to have the only values that work. It seems to me that this philosophy might be called the "Luckiverse!" Collins concludes that this view is the least plausible of the three. The odds against are almost infinite. Those odds will seem even more remote by the time we finish chapter 17.

3. The third remaining possibility is that there is only one universe, and this is it; and that it reflects the mind, purpose and creative action of The Creator, an external and eternal power and intellect we can only partially comprehend. This position has its roots in Thomas Aquinas, who reasoned that if there was a Creation event, there had to have been a Creator. The nice thing is that a growing number of scientists have found comfort in this philosophy. For many skeptics, the jury's still out.

Perhaps a fourth scenario is missing from the above. Would an all powerful Creator of this universe have any restraining limitations against creating alternatives with different combinations of definitional constants? You may take your time thinking about all of this. With intent to be provocative, this chapter has introduced you to the concept of anthropic coincidences and conditions, which you may find encouraging or vexing, depending upon your belief system. Just wait until we get to this subject in later chapters.

[A word of caution is in order. It has been claimed that Stephen Hawking at various times contributed ably to both sides of this debate. He has written, for example, in discussing what he calls the "hot big bang model" of creation:

> *This means that the initial state of the universe must have been very carefully chosen indeed if the hot big bang model was correct right back to the beginning of time. It would be very difficult to explain why the universe should have begun in just that way, except as the act of a God who intended to create beings like us.*
>
> *A Brief History of Time* (1988)

Without doubt, that free-standing quotation implies purpose. Whether intended as a deist view, or Spinoza's concept of pantheism (that God and nature are synonymous), or simply for standing up a "straw man" argument, only Hawking can say.]

To the atheist, the universe is the most exquisite masterpiece ever constructed by nobody.
———Unknown, attributed to G.K. Chesterton

I think; therefore, multiverses exist.
———Pseudonymous, with apology to Descartes

Revelation
Through
Science

Part Two

Chapter 6

Antecedents of Evolution

Evolution is said to be <u>the</u> central organizing and unifying principle of all biology. There is no dispute about that among biologists. That is not to say there is no scientific disagreement about evolution. Indeed, there are vigorous challenges about the origins of taxonomic phyla, classes, orders, and families of organisms, if not about species and genera. However, these arguments will likely be resolved by modifying the fine elements of Darwin's brilliant insights. Whatever comes of this scholarly debate will retain the essentials of random variation of heritable traits with natural selection. Ongoing research may solve the riddles of the unique and sudden Cambrian Explosion of new phyla, whether evolution of species and genera generated enough variation to spin off new families and orders (or *vice versa*). We may discover how the first prokaryotic life ever emerged from a mixture of chemicals, and much later evolved into eukaryotes with amazingly complex cell nuclei. These topics are for later chapters.

One could make the case in modern biology that DNA (with its life-defining code, and how that is replicated for cell division and reproduction, or transcribed from genes to RNA, and then translated to the derived code sequence of amino acids) is itself truly the "organizing and unifying principle" of biology (a conclusion to be examined in chapter 15). The previously unknown mechanism by which variation and transmission of heritable traits occurs has been solved by molecular biology. The source of variation is now attributable to unrepaired misalignments of the DNA code. Natural selection remains undefiled. Darwin is confirmed. Evolution stands.

In this short chapter, we will review the antecedents of Darwin's concepts of evolution. What were natural philosophers thinking at the time about the rich variety of plant and animal structure? Descriptive biology was sending numerous clues that had fertile eighteenth-century minds searching for answers to the riddle of life. In geology, some held fast to the concept of **Catastrophism**, believing that the earth and its composition and inhabitants were formed in sudden bursts of change within the relatively short timeframe of six thousand years or so (chapter 11). Others challenged this idea, preferring a better rationale in **Uniformitarianism**: the belief that all earlier changes and processes of the earth were the same processes observed around us today: earthquakes, volcanic eruptions, ice fractures, erosion, and the like (chapter 12). These latter mechanisms were either very slow or very rare, and would require a much older Earth to gradually achieve its present form. There was this tolerant difference of opinion among scholars as well as the lay public about the nature of the earth's structure.

As to the origins of living organisms, the most commonly held belief was **Essentialism**, the idea that each species had its own essential features that were fixed and unchangeable. This had origins in Plato's *Theory of Forms*, in which he reasoned that the Creator had made all of the physical forms based upon a limited number of essences. Given the new surge of scientific discoveries of geologists, archaeologists, and biologists, many intellectual discussions of the eighteenth century were churning with competing creative speculations about the complexities of teeming life forms, and how they might have originated.

The contrary notion of evolution from a single universal ancestor was expressed in theistic imagery, interestingly enough, by Erasmus Darwin (1795), a physician and the grandfather of Charles Darwin. He put forth the prophetic notion that all life had a common ancestor, which he envisioned as a "filament of life." Most of the writings of Erasmus Darwin were poetic in style. In today's light, his most important book was a scientific text titled *Zoönomia* (1796). Among other topics, here Dr. Darwin launched a novel idea about the evolution of species. In one remarkably bold and prophetic passage he wrote:

> *Perhaps millions of ages before the commencement of the history of mankind,*
> *Would it be too bold to imagine that all warm-blooded animals*
> *Have arisen from one living filament,*
> *Which the great First Cause endued with animality,*
> *With the power of acquiring new parts, attended with new propensities,*
> *Directed by irritations, sensations, volitions and associations, and*
> *Thus possessing the faculty of continuing to improve by its own inherent activity,*

And of delivering down those improvements by generation to its
posterity,
World without end!

Grandfather Erasmus would surely have been familiar with the supposition of his contemporary G.L.L. Buffon that all varieties of cat species had a common ancestor, and the radical opinion of James Burnett that humans were descended from lower primates. Grandson Charles could not have been unaware of family discussions of this topic. This thought was not original with Dr. Darwin, except in its poetic mode of expression. Ancient Greek philosophers had devoted deep reflection to the possibility of land animals' emergence from ancestral water species. Whatever support this idea enjoyed in the late eighteenth century soon gave way to a theory that seemed more plausible at the time: the inheritance of acquired traits.

Lamarckian Transformation

The theory propounded by Jean-Baptiste Lamarck in 1801 expressed what would become the Victorian ideal of evolution. Simply stated, when an organism is confronted with an ecological opportunity or stress, it gradually adapts to that environmental challenge by some structural or behavioral change. The adaptation might be either a gain of some capability or feature, or the loss of another. Once the organism succeeds in this adaptation, its newly acquired trait can be transmitted to future generations. A similar concept was part of Tao philosophy of ancient China: that no species is static and unchanging, but constantly evolves new structure and behavior to suit the conditions around it.

The most frequently cited example is the long neck of the giraffe. Lamarck presumed that the early giraffe cohort continually attempted to stretch for tastier food on higher branches. After a time, the stretching caused the sinews and bones to become elongated, a result that was then inherited by offspring whose necks started out somewhat longer, and who then mimicked the pattern and continued the quest for higher and higher hanging food . . . and longer necks!

Unlike Darwin's random variation, Lamarckian adaptation has a purposeful and repetitive action as its initiating element. In the modern, molecular version of Darwinian evolution, each variation is the result of some change in or damage to the DNA coding sequence. This special biomolecular mechanism has lofted Darwin's explanation far beyond its original basis, and far beyond Lamarck's.

In his early beliefs, Charles Darwin did not reject Lamarckian transformationism, for he had no reason to do so at the time. He even put forth an idea of a microscopic **pangene** (from the Greek: *pan genesis*, for "overall origin") that somehow carried information about the particular characteristics of its original cell as the pangene traveled throughout the body of its organism. He had no idea how to test that hypothesis, as there was in those days no clue about the intricacies of molecular structure and function of DNA within cells. Furthermore, his respect for the advocate of the then-prevailing theory of evolution would not be surprising, since young Darwin's studies had been under the learned tutelage of Robert Edward Grant, a British anatomist who subscribed to Lamarck's views on transformationism.

Lamarck also promoted the corollary belief that if an animal did not use a particular organ it would deteriorate or atrophy over generations and become trivialized in future descendants. To this category might then be assigned such anachronisms as the human appendix, mammalian male nipples, and the partial loss of human body hair and skin pigmentation in some varieties. The converse of this was the belief that vigorous exercise of a part of the body would cause it to grow in size or proficiency. Hmm!

It is amusing to suppose that some anatomical contribution from the opportunistic mechanism of Lamarckian adaptation could cause humans a few generations hence to grow thinner, more nimble thumbs, better suited for working the small keyboards of pocket telephones, with all their wizardry and applications. However, any such expectation will likely be preempted by voice-activated technologies (or perhaps thought-activated?), leaving our heirs with thick, maladroit thumbs.

Before we dismiss Lamarck, there has been some modest renewal of scientific interest in his transformational adaptation in recent years. It is in the nature of science that one must not abandon and disregard earlier concepts, even if they have been largely superseded by apparently better theories. Consider the emerging biological field of **epigenetics** (the Greek prefix *epi-* means "on top of"). Is there some process "on top of" genetics?

If the gene expression in a particular segment of DNA is deactivated or suppressed by some external factor, without changing the sequence of nucleotide pairs in the DNA, the study of that cause and effect is epigenetics. Such an acquired modification has been found to be transmitted to successive generations in some experimental cases. Such has been the explanation for a behavioral change in the foraging patterns of chickens subjected to starvation. This stress may have led to partial methylation of gene sites, a blocking effect which could then have been transmitted to later generations. Another theory is that the stress may have caused a change in the way the DNA or RNA and its derived protein is enfolded within the germ cell. An awkward twist here and there might well occlude and diminish some gene functions (see pages 299 ff.).

A similar finding was shown in the inheritance of obesity among daughters of male rats exposed to a diet rich in fats. Their DNA sequence was unchanged, but certain gene expressions were modulated in a way that the acquired trait could be inherited by offspring. It is also in the nature of controversy-oriented science that these experiments will in turn be subjected to intense challenges. That is what scientists do.

It is a tribute to Darwin's Theory that this is still a very rich field for research, and we can safely expect more investigations to explore this complex subject of heritable characteristics. Now, before we move on to other wonders, let's take another brief "flashback" to the dawn of the idea of evolution.

Antecedents of the Antecedents

The thought that different species could share a common ancestry did not originate with the European Enlightenment. Many ancient philosophers in Greece, Rome, and China discussed the concept without reference to any particular evidence. For example, Chinese Taoists as early as the fourth century BC thought that any particular species might develop significant differentiating traits due to the influence of different environments, a concept that would presage Lamarck. At about that same time, Aristotle wrote about a relative Scale of Nature as a "chain of being," which ranked as higher life forms those organisms with superior vitality and abilities.

With all this churning of ideas about the causes and origins of the abundance of plant and animal species, some philosophers came to different views as to the role—or for that matter, the necessity—of a supernatural Creator as the First Cause of the natural order. Those who held no belief in any supernatural Creator were more likely to need some natural explanation, while their theistic colleagues were intellectually comfortable with or without such exercises. Among early Greeks, Empedocles (430 BC) saw no need for any supernatural organizing agent to make things happen. Aristotle did not accept this, nor did Plato, who wrote reverentially of a Demiurge, a benign Deity who created everything and made changes as needed.

Some early Christian theologians readily accepted the "Creation" texts of the Old Testament as to their literal meaning. Others interpreted them as allegorical in meaning and style. More than a thousand years before the rise of modern science, St. Augustine (in *City of God*, 426 AD) was one of the first to urge caution, especially with regard to the opening chapters of *Genesis* and their depiction of creation. He believed that living plants and animals had a "potentiality" for perfection and were gradually "transformed slowly over time," in a pious foreshadowing of evolution.

St. Augustine believed on theological grounds that creation was not spread over a sequence of six days but was one singular, cohesive, and instantaneous act. The concept of time was considered an attribute of the physical world, and therefore not a precedent or relevant to its creation. He understood the few-thousand-year chronology of the Old Testament, but wrote that *Genesis* was about the relationship between God and creation. In his chapter on "The Literal Interpretation of Genesis," St. Augustine said that one must not insist upon the literal interpretation of a text if it conflicts with what is evident from our God-given reason and experience. Referring specifically to the six-day sequence of *Genesis I*, he wrote:

What kind of days these were is extremely difficult, or perhaps impossible for us to conceive, and how much more to say.

Augustine had been born (354 AD) in what is now Algeria, part of Roman Africa at the time. With the Roman Empire in serious decline, he had sought wisdom and understanding in the Manichaean religion, which was prominent around much of the world in his day. As something of a composite of Buddhism, Zoroastrianism, and Christianity, Manichaeism posed a growing threat to each, and consequently was subject to persecution on all fronts. Turning from that to a Neo-Platonic philosophy, Augustine was converted to Christianity and baptized in 387. He was ordained to the priesthood, and rose to become Bishop of Hippo (present-day Adana, Algeria). Owing to the brilliance and volume of his preserved sermons and other writings (principally his autobiographical *Confessions*, his multi-volume *City of God*, and his influential *On the Trinity*), St. Augustine has become a beacon of faith and practice throughout Christianity.

Augustine's theistic view of natural processes, and his recognition that the allegorical and poetic truths of the Bible must not always be taken in a strictly literal interpretation, were elevated to a higher plane of reasoning nine centuries later by Thomas Aquinas. The latter believed that we can improve our understanding of God's handiwork by observing and pondering the structure and behavior of nature. In his view, it was not scripturally mandated that such efforts be suspended if they led us to different conclusions from the authors of *Genesis I* and *II*. Without question, those Holy Scribes of *Genesis* were divinely inspired, but God's inspiration should be just as surely at work in the minds of Aquinas's thoughtful contemporaries (and perhaps many of ours).

What do these examples say to us today? You and I may reach similar or different conclusions on many subjects. Nevertheless, it should be comforting to know that if we come to believe that the "Creation" story of *Genesis I* was divinely taught and inspired, and that its style was poetic or allegorical rather than a technical record of six 24-hour days, we will be in good company with St. Augustine and Thomas Aquinas.

Chapter 7

Charles Darwin (1806-1882:
The Theory of Evolution

Science and Religion struggled to reach a mutual reconciliation with regard to Galileo's daring assertion that direct observation of the planets could disprove and supplant the established geocentric model of the planetary system, as envisaged by Ptolemy. The Roman Catholic Church at first accepted Tycho Brahe's clever dodge (chapter 3) of having only the moon and sun orbit the central earth, with all other planets orbiting around the sun. Eventually the clamor quieted down, and for about two and a quarter centuries all was quiet on the cosmological front.

A lot of churning was going on, especially in geology and its new field of paleontology (chapter 12). Questions were being raised about the possible age of this earth. The rising debate was vigorous but inconclusive, and nothing to get really upset about. And yet, this long era of *Pax Scientia* was about to be shaken as never before.

The Voyage of HMS *Beagle*

Can you imagine the intense, conflicting emotions that young Charles Darwin faced, weighing the choice before him? Having coordinated his early scholastic studies in anticipation of the Anglican priesthood, he had also found great appeal in his encounters with science, especially biology and geology. Through the intercession of his uncle, he now had a rare and coveted opportunity to travel the world as ship's naturalist aboard the HMS *Beagle*. He couldn't resist, embarking in 1831 under the watchful command of Capt. Robert FitzRoy. How this came to pass is a wonderful sea story.

Following Admiral Nelson's celebrated victory over the combined French and Spanish fleets at Trafalgar (1804), Great Britain's naval power was soon deployed to secure trade routes around the globe. One major assignment was the interdiction of piracy and the slave trade, but a third naval objective was the charting of sea routes and harbors, especially among the newly liberated, former colonies of Spain and Portugal in South America. The *Beagle* was commissioned expressly for this service in 1820.

By the time young Darwin embarked on his soon-to-be historic voyage, the Hydrographic Service had enjoyed sound scientific leadership under the overall command of Capt. Francis Beaufort. It was this same Beaufort who had devised the so-called Beaufort Scale for estimating wind velocity from the appearance of the water surface and, if inshore, its action on trees and flags.

Beagle's first survey trip (1826–1830) had been to the southern coasts of South America. Upon the tragic suicide of Captain Stokes, Lt. Robert FitzRoy assumed command and brought all hands safely back to England, along with four young natives from Tierra del Fuego (one of whom soon perished after a smallpox vaccination). FitzRoy, newly commissioned as Captain of the *Beagle*, was anxious to resume his surveys, and to return the three surviving Fuegans to their homeland as Christian missionaries and as directors of a proposed naval provisioning station.

Captain Beaufort, seeing merit in FitzRoy's request that a naturalist be added to the ship's complement, contacted friends at Cambridge for recommendations and volunteers. After several qualified gentlemen demurred, the opportunity was extended to young Darwin by his Cambridge professors George Peacock and John Henslow. Somewhat protectively at first, Darwin's father objected, realizing this could well divert his son permanently from his preparation for the gentler duties of a clergyman. Charles was supported by his uncle (and future father-in-law) Josiah Wedgwood II, whose reputation as purveyor of finest porcelain persists today. Father Darwin relented, and Charles set out for Plymouth to pursue the adventurous position.

Fortune continued its benediction upon Darwin's *rendezvous* with destiny, for just one hour before he met with Capt. FitzRoy, another young gentleman who had just been offered the job had turned it down. FitzRoy believed he could discern the character of a person by the appearances of his features, and thought Darwin's nose was a sign of weakness and lack of determination. With amusement, Darwin wrote to a friend that "my nose had spoken falsely."

Aboard ship, Darwin was assigned the aft-most cabin, which doubled as the chart room. His home for the next five years was a mere 9 feet by 11 feet of total floor space with no more than 5 feet of headroom. Center cabin was filled by the 4' x 6' chart table, above which swung young Darwin's hammock.

There were a series of delays, owing to repair of extensive rot about the decks and fittings of the *Beagle* before its historic voyage finally could get underway. Darwin used the time to assemble a kit of scientific equipment and books. Notable among his 14 volumes were Alexander von Humboldt's "Personal Narrative" of his travels in South America, and Charles Lyell's *Principles of Geology, Vol. I.* This young man was ready for destiny's call. The first two attempted departures were driven back into harbor by fierce gale-force headwinds. At last, on December 27, 1831, the *Beagle* cleared Plymouth Sound and sailed into history. It was recorded that our young hero was one very seasick naturalist!

Bon Voyage!

Stopping at the Cape Verde Islands early into the voyage, Darwin took the opportunity to examine compacted layers of seashells in cliffs 30 feet above sea level. This was far more exciting than the filtered plankton he had hauled aboard thus far. It was even more thrilling when they reached South America, where he found an abundance of rare birds, beetles, and other species, which he sent with his careful drawings of them back to his mentor in Cambridge, Professor Henslow. Among these was his most important find to that date, an extinct, sloth-like *Megatherium* fossil exposed in the face of a cliff.

Almost a full year after departing England, the voyage finally arrived at Tierra del Fuego, where the three Fuegans were returned to their native home along with an eager British missionary. This gentleman soon found that his properties had been dispossessed by the friendly natives, who valued them more highly than his evangelistic zeal. He prevailed upon Captain FitzRoy to be taken back aboard. We can suppose that he was taught a new trade: reefing and furling the mains'l in a blow. Then again, he may have jumped to another ship headed for home.

Another year and a half were occupied with surveying and charting the coastal waters from Montevideo to the Falklands. While exploring the frigid glacial bays in the vicinity of Cape Horn, the crew almost lost their lifeboats and any hope of returning to the *Beagle*. A large iceberg calved from the nearby glacier, sending a wall of water straight for the landing party. It would have swept their small boats away had it not been for the alert Mr. Darwin. For his courage and fortitude, Captain FitzRoy named the place Darwin Bay and the nearby prominence, Mt. Darwin.

Completing the turn without incident by way of the Straits of Magellan, *Beagle* made safe harbor at Valparaiso for repairs. This was a special objective for Darwin, who had persuaded his father to outfit him for an Andean expedition. His opportunistic side excursion took Darwin away from his shipmates for the greater part of seven months ashore. His trek endowed him with quite a few valuable samples, plus the frightful experience of an earthquake up close and personal, as we say. From this encounter, Darwin gained a unique understanding of the geological impacts of this phenomenon. He saw its effect of lifting oyster beds five feet higher, demonstrating support for Lyell's **uniformitarian** theories (see page 196).

This historic voyage, originally commissioned as a coastal survey, came close to ending ignominiously. While Darwin was ashore hiking the Andes, Captain FitzRoy had begun to have serious doubts about the accuracy of some of the survey data collected back along the southeast coast of this continent. He was about ready to sail back around the Horn to complete the assignment. So overcome with this imagined inadequacy, he exhibited suicidal tendencies and resigned his command. Fortunately, intervention by other officers calmed FitzRoy and persuaded him to reign in his self-doubt and continue as though nothing untoward had happened.

Shipboard life was becoming more stressful for young Darwin. He was obliged to serve as his captain's intellectual and dining companion, but their minds were sailing on different tacks. FitzRoy was overbearing in matters of politics and religion, with firm traditional views that clashed with Darwin's more open-minded approach. Still, it was not prudent to challenge or defy someone who by nautical law held absolute authority at sea. Nevertheless, Rules of the Sea did not intrude upon Darwin's mind or cloud his thinking. It may be that his thoughts were sharpened by the peculiar circumstances of his daily protocols. Gould has opined that Fitzroy's doctrinaire attitude may well have been a catapult for Darwin's flights of theoretical creativity, and that this so troubled Fitzroy in his later years that he ultimately followed through with his earlier suicidal intention.

Galápagos Treasures

Beagle sailed as far north as Lima, then set a westward course for the Galápagos Islands, which framed their horizon on September 15, 1835.

They made for shore, where their intrepid naturalist would make some of his most compelling discoveries. As a budding geologist, he was excited about studying volcanic activity around the Pacific. He had also assured Professor Henslow that he would collect any interesting plants and animals, hopeful that some unique specimens might have escaped the notice of previous visiting naturalists.

Barely five weeks were spent among these islands with their numerous volcanoes. These and similar geologic wonders on other Pacific islands would lead Darwin to publish one of his first theories. He reasoned that the nearly circular atolls around some islands could have been the result of volcanic eruptions forming a circular rim. If this rim were to subside slowly enough, he reasoned, it would allow the gradual build-up of the encircling reef structures. He had already studied and accepted Charles Lyell's theory from the geologic evidence that the earth had been slowly, steadily changing its shape over many millions of years. His observation, too, would tend to confirm Lyell.

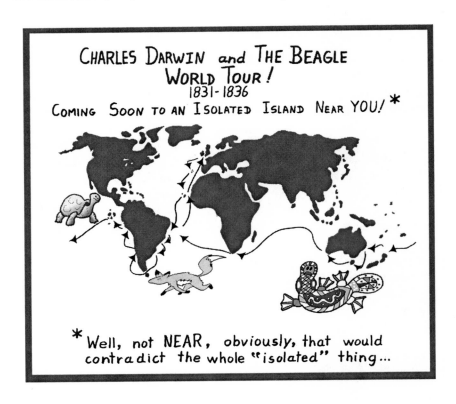

Darwin found more layers of fossil seashells imbedded in exposed hillsides well above sea level. These remains could not have been deposited by lava flows, thus proving that at least part of the Galápagos was formed by upheaval from the ocean floor. His contribution to understanding geologic time was significant, but it was his collection of unusual flora and fauna specimens that would displace all other ideas about the formation and interrelation of species. It would take another 24 years to bring all of this to fruition.

There was no sudden flash of discovery, however. No earth-shaking "Aha!" moment burst into Darwin's imagination. It would take years of quiet reflection to solve this puzzle of the auspicious progression of life. Even so, Darwin knew immediately that he had found something important.

These islands were home to an abundance of tortoises, one of which was added live to his collection. From the English Vice-Governor, he learned that the Galápagos natives could tell which island each tortoise came from by visual inspection—just by the shape of their shells. Darwin had earlier recorded a conversation with a Falklands native that the fox endemic to West Falkland was smaller than the East Falkland fox. Later, this would become an important clue to some kind of ancestral relationship, with differences preserved by the geographic isolation of each family venue.

More clues were seen in the strikingly different beaks and subdued plumage coloration of the Galápagos finches. Darwin's finches were a special case, because he had misidentified them to be different genera of mockingbirds, finches, wrens, and other birds. It was not until after his return home that he was corrected by John Gould, a friend who was an expert ornithologist. Darwin now began to sense that this was telling him something important, but its essence still escaped him.

[Beaks were selected for the available island food, with the original South American seed eater in the center, and

119

from the top, clockwise: a finch with a twig "tool," an
insect catcher, leaf cutter, grub digger, and nut cracker.]

Throughout most of this five-year voyage, Darwin still accepted
the prevailing view of Lyell regarding the permanence of species. His
was the belief that, while Earth's mantle was ever so slowly changing,
every known species was fixed and unchanging, with each created
separately. However, the accumulating evidence had begun to raise
doubts. In the Falklands (foxes), Patagonia (mussels), Galápagos (finches
and tortoises), he was finding evidence that species displayed a variety
of distinguishing features, depending upon some degree of isolation of
families over many generations. Eventually, this compelled him to the
conclusion that changes were taking place by some natural process.

The crucial connection came to him while completing his notebook,
undisturbed during the next westerly Pacific leg of the expedition. He
recognized that each island was home to its own typical variety of bird,
and he began to suspect that each might be a localized species. By
then, Galápagos was well astern and beyond his reach for additional
observations and specimens. With Gould's help years later, it became
clear that he had seven different <u>species</u> from the finch genus, one of
which was identical with a South American finch. This meant that
different species had emerged on each island, and that there was no
fixity or permanence of a species.

Galápagos had been a rich source of specimens (especially beetles,
birds, and a barnacle), but more clues would be needed before the puzzle
could be solved. But before leaving this "world unto itself," an unrelated
phenomenon deserves mention. In his notes, Darwin made the briefest
reference to a "comet." This was surely a sighting of Halley's Comet, whose
nearest approach to Earth coincided with the Beagle's anchorage among
the Galápagos. The Almanac in Darwin's kit predicted the visitation of this
celestial eminence, which would have been visible to the unaided eye.

Beagle sailed west to Tahiti, making landfall after four weeks at sea.
After brief stops there and at New Zealand, there followed several stops
along the Australian coast, including its large southeastern island of
Tasmania (February 5, 1836). Darwin had read about the kangaroo and
platypus and other odd animals endemic to Australia, but now saw them
with his own eyes in their natural habitat. In his journal, he noted the
similarities and differences between marsupial and placental mammals.
It gave him a lot to ponder.

Rendezvous with Herschel

Seven months remained until this epic circumnavigation would bring *Beagle* home to England, but one more intervening port of call is worth mention. There had been a few islands to chart and explore in the Indian Ocean. When the vessel rounded the African Cape of Good Hope, and set anchor at Cape Town, Darwin (now a ripe 27 years of age) was feted by the local scientific community, who informed him that he was now famous. Professor Henslow had published some of his letters in one volume, and it had created quite a stir in Europe.

Among his South African hosts was Sir John Herschel, the most esteemed astronomer of that time. Darwin felt duly honored to be received by such a dignitary. The two spent several conversations comparing deep thoughts about the concept of evolution, an interesting idea that had been circulating, albeit without any clear explanation as to how it might work. One can only imagine how this must have sharpened Darwin's mind and built confidence in the majestic but impertinent presumption that he might be able to resolve a profound question that had attracted the world's most brilliant philosophers for more than two thousand years!

It is noteworthy that Herschel did not agree with Lyell about the fixity and permanence of species. If Earth's land forms were slowly evolving, he wondered whether the same might be true for its inhabitant organisms. The eminent astronomer confided to Darwin his reckoning that Earth was much older than Lyell thought: "many thousands of millions of years" old.

The final leg of this great adventure, northward along the west coast of Africa, would take almost four months. This allowed our hero plenty of time to reorganize his notes and drawings, and begin the process of drafting his reflections about what had caused the generation of so many vastly (or even slightly) different species, possessing such similarities that seemed to express to him that there was some kind of ancestral relationship that had previously eluded the world's greatest minds. It also gave him time to ponder that such a departure from accepted doctrine would not be well received by many biologists, let alone theologians and the general public.

In due time (October 2, 1836), *Beagle* and her crew finally returned to home port and the welcome embrace of family. With the help of his growing host of admiring scientists, including his former teachers, Darwin was able to make considerable progress in the characterization and cataloging of his unique collection of specimens. He began the publication of a series of books on *Zoology of the Voyage of HMS Beagle*. Each volume quickly sold out, with the next eagerly awaited. Not one word about his speculations on the origin of species was hinted in this authoritative and profitable compendium. Darwin was the toast of London society.

Domestic Darwin

In 1839, Charles married his first cousin Emma Wedgwood. They had ten children, seven of whom survived to adulthood. He had symptoms of nausea and anemia, but his father and other physicians could assign no diagnosis, and no therapy. He and Emma withdrew London social life and made their home in a more rural setting. There in the village of Down, he quietly continued to prepare manuscripts for publication, and finish characterization of his thousands of specimens. His finances were sustained by the publication of his next book *The Structure and Distribution of Coral Reefs*, and a related text on volcanic islands.

During this time, Darwin's strange illness grew more complex, with an assortment of more than two dozen distinct symptoms that defied diagnosis. Fatigue from these incessant disorders had driven the move from the social frenzy of London to the relative solitude of Down. Finding no traditional medical relief, from 1849 until 1863 Darwin turned to a succession of practitioners of an unorthodox treatment called hydrotherapy. From various accounts, this can best be described as a regimen of profuse sweating, induced by heat lamps, followed by a brisk massage with cold, damp towels. This calls to mind the Scandinavian sport of dashing from a sauna into a frigid lake. In addition, walking and dietary discipline were required and were probably beneficial. The discipline of exercise did provide temporary relief.

That Darwin seemed to gain some relief from this regimen has led some to speculate that psychosomatic maladies were involved. In recent years, several medical papers have appeared suggesting that the unusually great quantity of symptoms could indicate a simultaneous combination of some of a dozen possible diseases. It is not suggested anywhere that Darwin could possibly have endured all these maladies at once. As for all of the speculation, modern medical experts are not at all settled upon a consensus diagnosis. Requests to examine tissue samples from his remains have been denied. Irrespective of the diagnosis, it may well be that Darwin's nausea and anemia led him to a more reclusive life under the gentle ministrations of his wife Emma, allowing him the valuable time for reflection and concentration so vital for his writing.

Reluctant Radical

It was the quiet before the storm. All he could manage as to evolution was to revise his notes on the subject. During the period 1842–1844, he did write an outline of his thinking and drafted a manuscript of 189 pages. What a tragedy if Darwin's caution had postponed publication of his most profound idea until he no longer had the physical capacity to publish anything! It was one thing to entertain the masses with stories of high adventure at sea and colored sketches of hundreds of unfamiliar, even weird, creatures that he had observed across the broad reaches of the Pacific. It was quite another to drop a blockbuster on the established doctrines of science . . . and religion!

Well, there was this one other small thing: the barnacle. Darwin had not written anything on this part of his collection. It occurred to him that before he could risk his reputation by thrusting his concept of natural selection upon an unprepared public, it would strengthen his case to be established as the expert on something. Besides, he had become close with Joseph Hooker, the prominent botanist, who encouraged this niche pursuit of scholarly preeminence. Whatever the motivation, Darwin vigorously set out (1846) to claim the barnacle as his domain: to become the world's foremost expert on the lowly barnacle. How hard could that be? No one else cared to claim precedence. He borrowed specimens from any and all who would respond. For eight years, Darwin studied barnacles from every angle and magnification.

When he had a question, Hooker was there to help. This led to such a level of mutual confidence in 1847 that Darwin finally revealed to Hooker what he had been up to, and asked him to read a copy of his 1844 outline on the origin of species. Hooker returned the compliment by giving a fairly constructive critique of what Darwin had written. Hooker was not yet ready to accept such a drastic departure from accepted thinking, but proved his mettle as a friend and confidant.

In April 1850, Darwin's nine-year-old daughter Annie died rather suddenly while being treated by one of Darwin's hydrotherapists. This was an unbearable shock, both to Darwin's health and to his faith. His faith may not have had sufficient nurture during the years since he had abandoned the path toward seminary and shipped out aboard the *Beagle*. He lacked vital resources for coping with the age-old torment as to why bad things happen to good people. In any case, his physical health deteriorated and his spiritual health turned to agnosticism, a term coined later by his zoologist friend T.H. Huxley.

Throughout these setbacks, Darwin took some solace in working to complete his writing. He had added Huxley and Charles Lyell to his special cadre of close confidants. Each held some skepticism about whether his ideas would stand up in the court of peers, but each encouraged Darwin to press forward. Lyell went so far as to urge immediate publication, lest he be preempted. Again, Darwin declined, as it had become his firm conviction that he had to anticipate and cover every possible argument and question with thoroughness. He knew that rough seas would attend the launching of this vessel, and was determined that there must be no vulnerability about its hull, rigging, or canvas.

Alfred Russel Wallace

In 1858, Darwin received a letter from a young colleague, **Alfred Russel Wallace**, which enclosed Wallace's draft manuscript on the mechanism of natural selection for prioritizing the variation of traits among species. It was astonishingly close to Darwin's concept in all major respects, if not as thorough. This posed a professional ethical dilemma for Darwin. Should he seize the initiative and bypass Wallace in order to claim truthfully that he had first possession of the idea? He had impeccable witnesses to vouch for him. Or should he yield to Wallace for the first volley, and then bring out his own broadside as the definitive manifesto?

As narrated by Sean Carroll in his splendid account, *Into the Jungle*, Wallace had spent four years in the Amazon among its tributaries, and had assembled a remarkable collection of specimens, samples of which he had forwarded to agents for sale to eager museums and collectors. The bulk of his collection was lost in 1852 when his ship caught fire and had to be abandoned without baggage and specimens before it sank, leaving him and his fellow survivors adrift for ten days. Wallace overcame this dispiriting calamity, and rallied himself to continue his collecting. This time around, he chose the vast group of islands then known as the Malay Archipelago.

Wallace found that if he drew a line on the map between Borneo and Sulawesi, and extended it southward through the narrow Lombok Strait between Bali and Lombok, this imaginary line would separate certain distinctive animal groups on each side. On the west of Wallace's Line, tigers, rhinoceros, various monkeys, and woodpeckers were abundant. None of these were found just east of this boundary line. Instead, there was a distinctive collection of unusual animals, such as kangaroos, lemurs, various small marsupials, and cockatoos, none of which were known west of Wallace's Line. From this and other observations, Wallace devised a theory remarkably similar to Darwin's. Who, then, should be first to publish?

Cool heads prevailed. Lyell and Hooker proposed having both theses presented at the Linnaean Society. Wallace's paper would be presented first, then Darwin's abridged version, by Lyell and Hooker as surrogates. Wallace was delighted to have what he considered near-equal billing with the famous and popular Darwin. Wallace accepted that Darwin had been at this quest for over two decades. At the event, an unexpected thing happened. The first public exposure of this fantastic idea was received politely, stirring neither excitement nor outrage. No, but torches had been lit. Within another year, in 1859, Darwin finally published his long-deferred opus, *On the Origin of Species by Natural Selection, or the Preservation of Favored Races in the Struggle for Life*. The first printing sold out in one day.

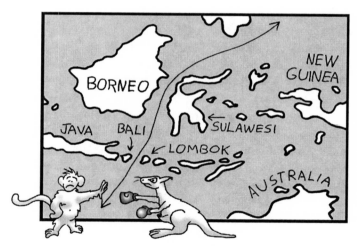

Wallace Line through Lombok Strait, Indonesia

Carroll also presents an important footnote to this history in describing the contributions of a third colleague, **Henry Walter Bates**, who spent eleven years collecting biological specimens in Brazil's Amazon Basin. Bates had briefly collaborated with Wallace before the latter departed on his ill-fated voyage home. While Bates did not reach the conclusions of Darwin and Wallace, his collections added valuable strength to the foundation for their novel explanation of the varieties and similarities among species.

It was Bates who recognized and wrote about the phenomenon of **mimicry,** whereby some creatures survive by appearing to be something dangerous or bad-tasting. One example was a caterpillar with markings that resembled a snake's head. Bates noticed that in regions inhabited by certain butterflies whose natural defense was emitting a foul odor, other butterflies had survived simply by having acquired similar markings that would dissuade predators, without the pungent bouquet.

Evolution: Darwin's Illuminating Theory

You may certainly supplement what I am about to say by reviewing the treatment of Darwin's Theory in a modern biology text. Here is presented one chemist's simplified version of the essentials of what Darwin proposed. It can be summarized in three statements.

1. **All living organisms are related by ancestry**. Differences in structure and function are the result of small changes accumulated gradually over millions of years. Darwin called this "**descent with modification**." He had absorbed this idea of common ancestry from his grandfather Erasmus Darwin. This breakthrough concept was developed more thoroughly in his companion book, *The Descent of Man*. For many lay readers, this descent with modification was radicalized into the uncomfortable idea that humans descended from apes. This alone created an enormous backlash of rejection on many fronts. It did not cause as much furor on the scientific front, because that was not what Darwin said. What he actually proposed was that our human species had evolved from the same ancient ancestor as did apes. That might not be any less of a strain to the human psyche, but at least one could say that humans descended much farther than did the chimpanzee. Terry Pratchett opines that Darwin could have saved himself and us a lot of grief had he only substituted the verb "ascended!" I wouldn't bet on it.

2. **Variations in structure and behavior occur in an unexpected fashion, and may be transmitted to future generations**. Such variations can confer either an advantage or a disadvantage. The variation may be a change in one aspect of appearance or size of some part of the anatomy. It might enhance the function of another part. A few such modifications will engender a

new <u>variety</u> of the parent species, while a sufficient number of changes will produce a new species, especially if reproductively insulated from earlier species. Darwin did not have a clear idea as to any mechanism that produced these variations. We now know it is the result of changes in the DNA code.

3. **The factor that favored the eventual preference of one variant in a particular trait rather than another was the relative efficacy of each. Darwin and Wallace each called this process "natural selection."** It might involve any modest advantage in the ability to find food, reproduce offspring, or defend itself and its fledgling family from natural predators—or its prowess as predator. Advantages prevail. If the new characteristic or feature provided a significant advantage, it would displace weaker traits within a few generations. On the other hand, if the new trait carried a clear disadvantage, it would probably disappear after a few generations, or might even carry the species into extinction. Darwin offered numerous illustrations of such extinct species from the fossil record.

Darwin's thinking was influenced (1838) by the writing of Thomas Malthus on the principle that population growth is controlled by the available means of subsistence. Darwin's reasoning began from the observation that species generally produce an excess of offspring, which must compete for limited resources. According to Malthusian principles, not all can survive. This means that any traits that confer an advantage in the competition for subsistence would favor survival and likely be inherited and become dominant.

One example was the specialization among Darwin's finches. While visiting the Galápagos Islands, Darwin believed that he had observed and collected many genera of birds. When he returned to England, and had his specimens examined by John Gould, it was determined that he actually had found new species of finch. Realizing that he had observed exclusively one distinct species on each island convinced him that this was strong evidence for his theory. Each species had features of plumage and talons and beaks that had become isolated on each island's habitat. A family of modest coloration, his finches differed mainly in the size and shape of their beaks, conferring suitability for the available diet of seeds, leaves, insects, etc. indigenous to each island.

Darwin had no ready concept of what caused variations in size, shape, color, or function. We shall soon consider the effect of changes in the coded sequence of nucleotide pairs within the DNA structure (chapters 14 and 15), for modern Neo-Darwinism has clearly correlated mutation with DNA code changes. In his mind, this process just happened; it had no direction or purpose. If humans had evolved from some extinct ancestor, he did not consider this an improvement other than which heritable traits were most suitable for adaptation to the prevailing environment. Humans were not higher on his ranking of animals; they were simply fit.

On the Origin of Species soon became controversial within the realm of science, and the most distinguished biologists were divided for or against its acceptance. There was no section devoted to humans, and the word "evolution" was not used. The closest Darwin came to that hot button was to use the word "evolved" near the end. In contemporary parlance of his time, "to evolve" meant to unfold.

Darwin himself acknowledged a number of potential objections to natural selection, and included many in his book. He was particularly alert to the fact that there was no fossil specimen that could be designated as that early common ancestor. One had to proceed with caution until that "Missing Link" was found. Well, today there are dozens of no-longer-missing links, with more being discovered every year (see chapters 8 and 12). First, there was the discovery of "Lucy," the early African hominid that came down from the tree canopy 3.7 million years ago. Then there was long-tailed "Ida," among the first primates from 47 million years ago. Other possible ancestral mammals had made a timely but endangered first appearance, well before the disappearance of the last of the dinosaurs, against which these furry forebears survived mainly by evasion in the treetops.

Upon my recent first reading *On the Origin of Species*, the great patience with which Darwin approaches his climactic revelation was palpable. In anticipation of the critical intensity he was certain to face, Darwin began his discussion indirectly. He invoked the recognition among those familiar with breeding livestock and domesticated pets (his own favorite was pigeons): that human selection of the better and best plant seeds and breeding animals can lead to substantial and profitable improvements in the stock. From that introductory stage, he advanced cautiously to the description of other artificial variations that were familiar to knowledgeable readers. Only after establishing a secure beachhead for breeder selection did he then reveal and commit to his central thesis: the parallel concept of natural selection.

It certainly appears in retrospect that Darwin deemed it advantageous to draw vital parallels between artificial selection and natural selection before raising an inevitably contentious controversy among his fellow naturalists. He could then hope for some to be more open-minded for his comparison of (a) the natural struggle for existence among and between species and their varieties in competition for limited supplies of food and water, avoidance of predators, sexual attraction, and climate change; versus (b) the advantages for preferred varieties when artificial selection by breeders guides the outcome.

Next, Darwin more boldly asserted his conclusion that natural selection has superior results to artificial selection because it has the tremendous advantage of the vastness of time for natural selection to entrench the best variety, which then defines the species. Darwin was careful not to get too far off base into the question of the origin of families, orders, phyla, etc., the wider classifications of plant and animal taxonomy. His basic arguments apply to observations of species of the same genus. In *Descent of Man*, of course, he would go much deeper.

His friend Herbert Spencer coined the phrase "survival of the fittest." To Darwin this term implied no superiority of competitive strength or ferocity, but rather the advantage of providing the best "fitness" for the overall environment. The rabbit might not overpower any adversary in a predatory encounter, but its fertility and facility of evasive tactics gave it a favored edge for survival in a hostile environment. All of that is exciting, but what Darwin mainly had in mind was competition for the available food, water, and mate. Tennyson's memorable phrase, "Nature, red in tooth and claw," has often been associated with natural selection, but has more to do with the bestial behavior of carnivorous predators than with the natural selection of the fittest as more broadly conceived by Charles Darwin.

A Little Help from His Friends

It must be noted that while Darwin's Theory of Evolution was becoming controversial in scientific and theological circles, its most inflammatory impacts arose from several more radical derivative ideas conjured up by his friends. Darwin's scientific contributions alone would deserve to be debated and challenged, as should all scientific notions, for that is how science works. In evolution, there was certainly enough departure from accepted thinking to generate serious popular and religious debate, but Darwin suffered from the special help of his friends, who added heat-seeking embellishments. Two of these distinguished gentlemen have modern biographies characterizing each as a "**polymath**" (someone expert in multiple fields). This laudatory term could apply to many sixteenth- and seventeenth-century scientists who contributed to the founding and development of so many emerging disciplines. Thereafter, it remained the Renaissance ideal standard for the well-rounded, broadly educated person.

Herbert Spencer

The Wikipedia biography of Herbert Spencer states:
"As a polymath, he contributed to a wide range of subjects, including ethics, religion, anthropology, economics, political theory, philosophy, biology, sociology and psychology."

Herbert Spencer was among the most highly regarded and influential English philosophers of the nineteenth century. In a biology text he authored (1864), Spencer coined the term "survival of the fittest" to describe Darwin's concept of natural selection in biological evolution. As a biologist, sociologist, and political thinker, he carried evolution far beyond Darwin's biological framework into sociology and ethics, and even the development of the physical universe. Spencer had considered ideas about evolution before Darwin. He was ready to adopt Darwin's explanation of natural selection, while preferring Lamarck's mechanism of variation driven by adaptation rather than Darwin's unspecified random process. Most notably, he believed in a sort of Lamarckian evolution of human social structures from lower levels of complexity to higher levels as a consequence of striving.

Spencer figured out that if the relative dominance of living organisms could depend upon what he called "the survival of the fittest," the same should be expected for businesses and other social organizations. The ablest and most resourceful would rise to the top. The inept would fall in any competition. Undoubtedly, that seemed self-evident. Elements of this line of thinking held a special cachet among advocates of *laissez faire* economics and mercantilism. Besides, if rival nations or corporations could be totally defeated and annihilated, would that not gain for society the benefits of superior organizations? He felt that nation states would fade away as society evolved beyond such encumbrances. This would lead to the emergence of "the perfect man in the perfect society."

In many respects, Spencer would be viewed today as a libertarian anarchist. Carrying his ideas to their logical conclusion, Spencer openly opposed what we call a "safety net" of social programs administered or funded by governments. His argument was that natural selection should be allowed to work its cleansing power on weaker elements of society.

Governmental interventions of support were altruistic, but contravened the fundamental, perfecting principle of natural selection. He was quite serious. He and those who shared his philosophy were very clear in the view that European stock was superior, while those of the colonies and other nations and cultures were decidedly inferior. This was not in any way attributable to Charles Darwin. As already noted, he did not regard evolution as having any higher purpose or direction, and he applied the concept strictly to plant and animal species and not to organizations. The transposition of a biological principle to a military or mercantile empire was foreign to him.

Spencer's bold extension of evolution was to become widely popular in the early twentieth century. Some have speculated that it was a key organizing principle of the German High Command during the First World War (1914–1917), an intriguing notion but hard to verify. His views were known to be openly popular among Austrian political leaders, who recognized that "survival of the fittest" required a nation to be well-armed and trained. For debate purposes, it is enough to see that Spencer's Social Darwinism has handed anti-Darwin antagonists a fearsome weapon for discrediting evolution. This is unfair to Darwin, who clearly had nothing to do with this corruption of his theory.

Francis Galton

The friendly website www.galton.com describes Francis Galton as:
"Victorian polymath: geographer, meteorologist, tropical explorer, founder of differential psychology, inventor of fingerprint identification, pioneer of statistical correlation and regression, convinced hereditarian, eugenicist, proto-geneticist, half-cousin of Charles Darwin and best-selling author."

As a kinsman of Charles Darwin, Francis Galton therefore would be privy to the discussion around the Darwin family hearth of Charles's novel interpretation. He bought into the idea that nature would select for the more advantageous traits of structure and behavior. The only problem, in Galton's view, was the inordinate slowness of natural selection. It wasted too much time and needed a boost. Galton and other eugenicists proposed that it was desirable to help nature make the best selections without delay. This was a truly radical notion, and has generated a great deal of mischief (as well as problems for Darwin by transference). While Darwin dissociated himself from these distortions of natural selection, his critics didn't shy from trying to attach them falsely to his reputation.

Galton conceived the first weather map, developed the science of psychometrics for quantifying mental abilities, and devised the forensic technique for fingerprinting. He was adamantly persuaded that intelligence was hereditary, and was the first to consider studies of identical twins to show the influence of heredity in order to differentiate "nature and nurture," as he put it (1875). Recent research at the University of Minnesota, *Study of Twins Reared Apart*, has connected a substantial contribution of heredity to intelligence and other behavioral traits.

It was Galton who founded the subject of eugenics (from the Greek for "well-born"). In its purest form, eugenics is the study of how to guide and improve human heredity. Eugenics has been called "the self-direction of human evolution." Many leaders in the early twentieth century endorsed its selective promotion of desirable traits to achieve perfection of humankind, just as in animal husbandry.

In practice as a social movement, however, it has been applied for what were once considered "progressive" but now discredited purposes of limiting reproduction of those with "undesirable" traits, particularly in Sweden, Brazil, Belgium, and Canada, as well as in the United States. The U.S. Supreme Court upheld Virginia's compulsory sterilization law by an 8:1 decision in *Buck v. Bell* (1927), a decision that guided the entire United States for another four decades. Writing for the progressive majority, Justice Oliver Wendell Holmes Jr. declared:

It is better for all the world if, instead of waiting to execute degenerate offspring for crime, or to let them starve for their imbecility, society can prevent those who are manifestly unfit from continuing their kind. The principle that sustains compulsory vaccination is broad enough to cover cutting the Fallopian tubes.

This extension of Galton's ideal greatly magnified the controversy, leading to what many considered a wealth of potential advantages, but also the most despicably interventionist sociopolitical policies. To their credit, neither Galton nor Darwin advocated any such governmental control and "social engineering" in these matters. Others were eager enough to do so.

In its most putrid manifestation, it went beyond sterilization to become part of Adolph Hitler's abhorrent justification for extermination of entire classes of people, most notably the European Jews. Spencer's "Social Darwinism" perverted organizational thinking during the First

World War, while Galton's version would inspire the worst horrors of Adolph Hitler's "Final Solution" and the Holocaust of the Second World War. When held to account during the Nuremberg War Trials in 1948, Nazi officials cited Justice Holmes's majority opinion in their defense, albeit unsuccessfully.

This author has had some tangential experience with one aftermath to the practice of eugenic sterilization. As a novice county commissioner in Mecklenburg County, North Carolina, I had taken office just as our County Health Department was about to move away from an earlier policy of sterilization to prevent poor and disabled women from bearing any more unwanted children. Welfare Director Wallace Kuralt came to us in 1967–8 to request local funding to provide these women free contraceptives instead. Oral contraceptives had been approved by the FDA for use in America in 1960, but were still controversial and not generally available at first, or affordable for unmarried women. Commissioners were relieved to be able to provide this new, more humane alternative.

The foregoing discussion was not intended to discredit the scientific merit of Spencer or Galton. The problem was in applying such concepts to public policy, which evolved into something distasteful and horrifying. Essentially, Galton's tangent of social Darwinism was not much different from the hobby of breeding pigeons, which had become quite popular among European gentry, notably including Charles Darwin.

Thomas Henry Huxley: The Evolution of Conflict

It is inescapable that Darwin's work has turned the world upside down as profoundly as did that of Galileo 250 years earlier. In contrast with the approach of that brilliant and assertive Italian genius, Darwin was cautious and mild-mannered, to the point that he reserved publication of his greatest contribution for 23 years. Only then did he publish his theory regarding the origin of species, and only because otherwise he was about to be preempted by another enterprising naturalist, Alfred Russel Wallace.

It is important to note that both Darwin (initially) and Galileo were steadfast Christians, although Darwin lost confidence in his religious faith in later years. Various biographers have sought explanations for his drift into agnosticism, some attributing this to remorse over the death of his daughter Anne. It may be that the harsh ecclesiastical reception of many to the implications of his Theory of Evolution also helped drive him further from the Church of his youth.

As I have read these accounts, the thing that jumped out at me was the disservice to Darwin and his science by so many of his friends and associates, who were opportunistic in using evolution for their own ends. Prominent among them at the time was his friend and confidant, the eminent naturalist T.H. Huxley. Huxley became a staunch advocate of Darwin's evolution all across the European continent, designating himself no less than "Darwin's Bulldog." Doggedly effective he certainly was.

Huxley had found in evolution the framework for his own personal belief system. Huxley coined the term "agnostic" (as in *a-gnostic*, denoting the lack of knowledge of God). It was not the mild-mannered, gentlemanly Darwin, but bold Huxley who sought to drive evolution wedge-like into all contemporary discussion of religion and science. This became the sure adversarial advantage not only for experimental biology, but also for others' advocacy of atheism. As the ensuing philosophical debates churned around the world, his followers, not Darwin, seized science as a hammer for relentlessly propagandizing atheism on behalf of evolution, and *vice versa*.

It may have been a strategic error that defenders of the faith chose to pour all their vilification on Darwin. His contribution was strictly to interpret the observations and discoveries of science, while it was Huxley who first applied it as a vigorous battering ram upon the citadels of religion. Challenging authority had become the popular stance among upper intelligentsia of the mid-nineteenth century. But why target Darwin? Was it because Huxley was exceptionally skilled in the tricks of debate, while Darwin was more reticent, and therefore more easily and safely reviled and attacked? Was it because Darwin presented the more vulnerable surrogate target?

Huxley took center stage in one historic confrontation with Bishop Samuel Wilberforce at a session of the British Association in Oxford in 1860. This was the same Wilberforce who in Parliament successfully championed the abolition of slavery, but in this arena he was outgunned by Huxley. At first, Huxley had been reluctant to confront the issue in front of this nonscientific audience, but it was his only available venue.

The opening statement from Wilberforce was a model of scholarly decorum, avoiding theological dogma, relying on the prevailing scientific view of the time. His argument was compelling that the biological record (at least in 1860) revealed no example of one species converting into another, a difficulty Darwin himself had acknowledged.

Wilberforce emphasized many examples that supported the fixity of each species, and the inability of hybrids to reproduce. He could truthfully claim that the greatest names in the contemporary annals of science stood in opposition to Darwin's proposal, with the understandable exceptions of Huxley and Hooker. The latter singularly had come out publicly for Darwin during the third day's action in Oxford.

Huxley countered that Darwin's theory was the best available explanation for abundance of species and their anatomical similarities in both the fossil record and contemporary observation. He made some headway against Wilberforce's appeal to the preponderance of authorities, but most historians of that year called it at best a draw.

The most memorable and climactic moment of this three-day rhetorical combat came when Wilberforce lost his cool, chiding Huxley as to whether it was from his grandfather or his grandmother that he claimed his descent from a monkey? With perfect timing and a flair for oratorical effect, Huxley's response was devastating. He was not ashamed to have a monkey for his ancestor; but would be ashamed to be related to a man who used his great gifts to obscure the truth. Another unattested version of this exchange has it that Huxley's withering retort came out: "I would rather be descended from an ape than a bishop!" Huxley later disclaimed this attribution. Each man was faulted editorially for such an unsportsmanlike exchange, although clearly Wilberforce started it.

Quo Vadis?

Where do we go from here? Darwin's Theory of Evolution proved to be as controversial as it was brilliant and productive. It is often said to be THE organizing and unifying principle of biology, and for good reason. It has been tested and sustained by generations of research, from paleontology to comparative anatomy, to genetics, to cell biology, and most profoundly by the molecular biology of DNA. Elucidation of the genome of humans and comparison of its sequences with those of other species, genera, and families connects us to all living organisms, indicating sequels of common ancestry. We will examine this in more depth in later chapters.

Some choose to interpret this as blasphemous heresy, because their faith rests upon literal interpretation of the preferred translations of the Old Testament. From this point of view, anything from science that seems to contradict even the most poetic and allegorical texts of Scripture must be rejected. They have yielded their strict position once before, having had to accept that the sun, not the earth, is the center of our system of planets. They will not readily yield again.

Others of us prefer to interpret the same scientific evidence as modern revelation of the creative glory of God, revealed to us through the unique intellectual powers that He has provided for us to acquire. Even the most elaborate and sophisticated instruments that scientists have conceived and assembled stand as testimony to the empowering role of intelligence to which humans have evolved, as though this were foreordained by a benevolent and loving Creator. Of these two views, cannot different minds find different conclusions as to which is more faithful to God's love for us?

Chapter 8

Descent of *Homo sapiens*

Unde Venimus? From Whence Came We?

The evolution of humans and apes from some common ancestor had
been cautiously presented in *Origin of Species*. It was enough to stir up
a storm of protest and debate in scientific circles as well as theological.
Here was a bold departure from what almost everyone believed, and an
easy target for ridicule and innuendo. The fierce debate soon subsided
in intensity, but may well have stirred Darwin's determination to follow
through with a more definitive and logically unequivocal restatement
of the point. He was also disappointed that Wallace had retreated from
advocating <u>human</u> evolution, hedging the position that the human brain
was too complex and superior to have evolved slowly.

    Descent of Man was published as a two-volume edition in 1871. The
full title was *The Descent of Man, and Selection in Relation to Sex*. No,
Darwin did not indulge ribald fantasies. The subtitle emphasized his new
theory that natural selection not only favored those heritable changes
that improve access to food and water or territorial adaptation, but also
those that enhance sexual attraction or reproductive efficiency. In part,
this was intended to counter an argument that the beauty of male birds'
plumage had no apparent usefulness and, therefore, presented evidence
of design by a divine aesthete.

    Darwin cited many examples in which some distinguishing physical
appearance of one male gave it an advantage for wooing potential mates,
resulting in more descendants. The peacock's tail feathers were probably
an encumbrance in the act of mating, but adduced more opportunities
for the most stunning male. Having the most imposing size of a rack
of antlers would confer the same benefit to male deer and elk. These
traits, being heritable, would gradually and inevitably prevail in later
generations.

By the politically correct standards of some today, Darwin may have overstepped when he generalized to humans the discriminating observation that male traits appealed to females. Numerous socioeconomic and religious factors had contributed to a subordinate status for most women, but *Descent of Man* emphasized sexual attraction as well as the male role in selecting tools and weapons. This earned Darwin a swift rebuke from one Antoinette Blackwell in a foreshadowing of today's feminist movement. I digress.

Jurassic Mother

Humans belong to a group of animals known technically as *Eutheria*, more familiarly called placental mammals. These are mammals that carry their fetal offspring internally to term (i.e., until live birth) within the mother's uterus, nourished and protected by an embryonic membrane known as the placenta. This is nothing to get excited about, as I just want to place in perspective our subclass of animals known as placental mammals. There are roughly 4,000 species of placental mammals, mostly rodents and bats, but also including whales and porpoises, elephants and wildebeests, horses and cows, sheep and goats, dogs and cats, apes and humans.

In recent decades, studies of DNA similarities and differences, especially chromosome rearrangements, led to a prediction that we placental mammals must have diverged from nonplacental mammals and marsupials (which deploy a placental membrane only briefly) approximately 160 million years ago. It would have been a dangerous time for any warm-blooded creatures during the era dominated by dinosaurs until their beneficent extinction 65 million years ago. Until recently, the oldest placental mammalian fossil was in deposits laid down 125 million years ago (*Mya*) in Liaoning Province of China. Named *Eomaia sinensis* ("Earth Mother from China"), this furry little creature was only 4 inches long and weighed less than an ounce. Its discovery focused hopeful paleontologists upon any geological formations from a few million years earlier.

In 2011, a Chinese research group led by Luo Zhe-Xi reported finding a fossilized small, shrew-like placental mammal in 160 Mya formations, early in the Jurassic period. Named *Juramaia sinensis*, or "Jurassic Mother from China," this is the oldest known fossil of a placental mammal. It is said to be well adapted for life in tree tops, far above carnivorous dinosaurs. This could suggest that the vaunted marsupial/placental divergence may have occurred somewhat before 160 Mya. And the search goes on.

Another odd creature from this period is worth a bit of attention. *Multituberculata* were a burrowing herbivorous order of mammals that first appeared about 155 Mya, foraged among the dinosaurs, and survived until 35 Mya, well past the latter's extinction. Distinct from both placental and marsupial mammals, multituberculates evolved as many as 200 species in a burst of evolution 85 Mya. They were eventually displaced by true rodents.

Primates and Hominins: The Last Common Ancestor

A number of important pieces for our paleontological family tree have been discovered in the fossil record. Furthermore, chromosomal comparisons suggest that apes separated from humans (and vice versa) roughly 5–6 million years ago. As we shall examine more closely, there are at least 14 distinct species of the *hominin* subfamily that preceded our *Homo sapiens* clan, all of which have become extinct, leaving us as the only surviving *hominin* species. The earliest species of our genus *Homo* appeared in the fossil record 2.3 Mya, called *Homo habilis* (the "handy man"). Preceding that, the most important fossil finds in our lineage were the *Australopithecus* genus, and before that the *Ardipithecus* genus. These presumptive ancestral figures were the first to descend occasionally from the trees, with skeletal features typical of, and suited for, upright bipedal (two-footed) locomotion.

Within taxonomic categories, gorillas, monkeys, and humans all belong to the *primate* order and *hominid* family. Humans are the only remnant of the *hominin* subfamily. It is at this level of classification that we diverge from apes. Recognition of this genetic <u>proximity</u> was obvious upon early taxonomic evaluation, based solely on anatomical particulars. It has become even more evident with the mapping of DNA sequences and their chromosomal placements (see pages 283-285).

What is notably distinctive is the genomic similarity between humans and chimpanzees. One study had estimated that 98.5% of the genetic code is identical across these two species, finding that only 450 or so human genes differ from those of the chimpanzee genome. More recently, Matthew Hahn *et al* of Indiana University (2006) compared 22,000 genes of chimpanzees and humans, designating 1,418 genes (6.45%) missing from one or the other genome. This infers a genomic commonality of **93.5%**, and implies some close evolutionary relationship, as in a not-too-remote mutual ancestor.

In some respects, chimpanzees demonstrate behavioral traits that immediately suggest imagined similarities with humans. Numerous studies have quantified the intelligence of chimpanzees. The findings so far emphasize that, uniquely among nonhuman species, chimpanzees laugh and socialize and are able to make and use simple tools. There has been some correlation in the recognition of language, but this appears to be limited to mimicry, with no originality on the monkey's part, and no expression of thought patterns. A curious facility for memorizing number patterns has been observed. The hand of the chimpanzee is very similar to ours, but with so little brain-power devoted to it, its manual capabilities are rather limited. Our chimp is no *Homo sapiens.*

"Lucy in the Sky with Diamonds"

For a century and a half after Darwin, common ancestry was purely speculative, and readily disputed and ridiculed. Where was the "Missing Link," about which Darwin himself had recognized a potential vulnerability for his theory? In recent decades this core question has begun to be answered with multiple links.

A remarkable find in Ethiopia (Donald Johanson and Thomas Gray, 1974) shows a significant fossil intermediary between humans and apes. With the taxonomic name *Australopithecus afarensis*, this little female was popularly dubbed "Lucy." That nickname stuck because the favorite song played repeatedly by the young workers at the excavation site was the Beatles' classic, "Lucy in the Sky with Diamonds." About 40% of the skeleton was intact, enough to show she would have been 3.5 feet tall, weighing in at about 60 pounds—a young adult. Particularly intriguing was the fact that the ratio of her humerus (upper-arm bone) to her femur (upper-leg bone) was halfway between that of humans versus apes.

The configuration of Lucy's leg and knee cap indicate that she was able to walk upright, balancing on one leg at a time, and her pelvis and spinal curvature were adapted for an upright posture. Interestingly, she also had features associated with tree-climbing, with a shoulder structure like that of a gorilla. Lucy was not totally apelike, nor was she yet fully human. Her small brain cavity indicates that expansion of cranial volume probably did not precede (and facilitate) bipedal walking.

[You can see a three-dimensional display of the CT-scan image of her jaw on the Internet at: www.wired.com/wiredscience/2009/02/lucy
Just be careful to type that as "wired," not "weird."]

Radiologic dating of the deposits in which Lucy was found shows that she lived 3.2 million years ago. As paleontologists continued to scour this region of Ethiopia, another amazing discovery was uncovered in 2006: a more complete fossil infant of the same species as Lucy. This specimen has been called "Lucy's Baby," although it was preserved in deposits a hundred thousand years before Lucy. Was *Australopithecus afarensis* an early departure in the line of humans' divergence from apes? Or was she a separate and distinct evolutionary line that faded into extinction without begetting a successor? Specimens of another species, *Australopithecus africanus*, are said to show a more likely direct lineage to humans.

Ardi

Another important find in this unfolding fossil drama came from another dig in Ethiopia. From sedimentary rock 4.4 million years old (thus a million years <u>before</u> Lucy or Lucy's Baby), Tim White *et al* (1994) found a partial fossil skeleton of a possible predecessor of Lucy's, taxonomically named *Ardipithecus ramidus* (nicknamed "Ardi"). This different first name indicates White's belief that this was a different genus from Lucy, although similar in a good many evolutionary respects. White does not contend that Ardi was a direct ancestor of Lucy or of humans. She might be just our "long-lost cousin."

The skull is apelike in most respects, but has distinctive features indicating that it rested atop the spinal column, and did not extend out in front of its spine in the manner of dogs, cats, and other quadrupeds. Since that initial discovery, nine different specimens of *Ardipithecus ramidus* have been found, providing a greater wealth of data about this early primate species. From measurements of pelvic and limb features, as well as its prehensile big toe, it was concluded that this species was able to walk on two feet and climb trees with agility using hands and feet.

Tugenensis to *Sediba*

There are two possible ancestral candidates from an even earlier time. *Orrorin tugenensis* (meaning "first man, found in Tugen region" of Kenya) was recovered from a 6 Mya formation, having features associated with both bipedal walking and tree climbing. Not enough skull fragments have been obtained to allow estimates of cranial capacity, and there is no evidence of any use of tools or fire. Claims of direct ancestry are suspect until more evidence can be accumulated.

Even before that, *Sahelanthropus tchadensis* is believed to have roamed the Sahel region of what is now Chad. Discovered in 2001 by Michel Brunet of France, this species had smaller canine teeth and walked upright. The position of its *foramen magnum* (the spinal cord entry into the base of the skull) indicates that the head was mounted above the erect shoulders and spine. Fossilized 7 to 6 Mya, it lived at about the time (8–5 Mya) when DNA evidence projects that humans diverged from apes. This possible Link may need more data before it can be assigned to the human or ape line, or antecedent to both.

Moving forward in time from Ardi and then Lucy, another very interesting fossil, *Australopithecus sediba*, was found in South Africa in deposits that are 1.9 million years old. Studies of four partial skeletons reveal the important feature of having opposable thumbs, which could be suitable for manipulating tools. There is another skeletal distinction associated with humans: the angle from the lateral femoral head (outer hip bone) through the center of the knee joint and down to the center of the ankle is not a straight line, but is bent such that the knees are set inward slightly toward each other. So are yours, by the way, which is the very point of mentioning it. This is the ideal for walking on two legs, and is normal for human knees. It allows the weight to be borne more steadily in a bipedal stride, minimizing side-to-side waddle.

Quadrupedal animals (walking on "all fours") do not have this slight inward knee displacement since their gait balances on two limbs at a time. For quadrupeds, there is a straight line from the distal (outer) femoral head (hipbone) through the center of the knee to the center of the ankle. There are indications *Au. sediba's* gait was rather pigeon-toed.

Lee Berger, the South African discoverer of *Au. sediba*, suggests that this species could be a precursor ancestor of our genus *Homo*, perhaps a transitional species between *Australopithecus africanus* and the first humanoid, *Homo habilis*. There is one problem. For four-legged mammals, the length of the forward legs is almost the same as the hind legs. For two-legged humans, our arms are significantly shorter than our legs. *Au. sediba* fails this test, with arms nearly as long as the legs. This should not discourage us, as it is not presumed that numerous features evolved simultaneously. In time, the discovery of more transitional missing links should eventually clear up these questions.

Hominin evolution from *Australopithecus africanus* to *Homo sapiens* proceeded through at least seven distinct (and extinct) species, with at least another fifteen tangential and extinct "cousins" that do not appear to be part of our direct lineage.

Brain Size

Comparison of the skulls of successive species of humanoids shows a definite, recent trend of expansion of the frontal region. Data in the following table show the gradual but distinct enlargement of the cranial capacity across the succession of the genus *Homo*, following the previously settled brain volume of the *Australopithecus* genus. From this sequence, it can be seen that expansion of brain size began about two million years ago.

TABLE 7. A CHRONOLOGY OF CRANIAL EXPANSION

TIME SPAN	GENUS AND SPECIES	CRANIAL CAPACITY	MALE AVG. HEIGHT
7–6 Mya	*Sahelanthropus tchadensis*	360 cc	3'–4.5'
6 Mya	*Orrorin tugenensis*	partial specimens	4'-5'
4.5–4.3 Mya	*Ardipithecus ramidus*	300–350 cc	4'
3.9–3Mya	*Australopithecus afarensis*	400–500 cc	4'
3.0–2.0 Mya	*Australopithecus africanus*	428–625 cc	4'
2.6–1.2 Mya	*Australopithecus boisei*	500–550 cc	4'3"
2.5–0.8 Mya	*Australopithecus robustus*	550 cc	4'
1.9 Mya	*Australopithecus sediba*	>450 cc	4'3"
(3–1 Mya?)	*Homo naledi*	560 cc	5'
2.3–1.7 Mya	*Homo habilis*	600–750 cc	4'3"
1.6–0.3 Mya	*Homo erectus*	800–1200 cc	5'
600–300 Kya	*Homo heidelbergensis*	1100–1400 cc	5'4"
300–125 Kya	*Homo rhodesiensis*	1230 cc	5'4"
250–35 Kya	*Homo neanderthalensis*	1200–1800 cc	5'6"
200 Kya ...	*Homo sapiens*	1350 cc	5'–7'

An earlier attempt to explain this progression in cranial capacity suggested that it resulted from coping with several Ice Ages. The flaw in that concept is obvious, as the same cranial expansion did not occur among other animals facing the same cold: they just put on more bulk. A more plausible explanation has been offered by Francis Collins in *The Language of God*. He cites a gene MYH-16 that up-regulates the strength of the jaw muscles in primates. In humans, unique among mammals and primates, this gene is mutated so that the human jaw muscle is not nearly as powerful. This singular "defect" in the genome of our genus *Homo* would reduce the compression force from the jaw muscles upon the frontal skull where they are anchored, allowing gradual evolutionary expansion of the brain cavity.

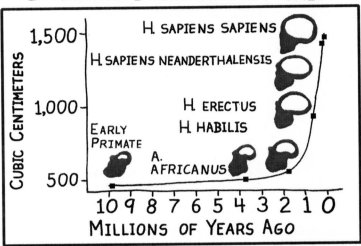

Survival of our ancestral species with weaker jaw muscles may also have been favored by the timely advent of cooked food among *H. erectus* and *H. neanderthalensis*. This breakthrough certainly introduced a bit of flavor to life.

Out of Africa

Most of the early discoveries of human-like fossil remains were found in Africa. This led to a supposition that the first humans (*Homo sapiens*) had originated in Africa. Questions had to be asked whether these findings were confined to Africa because (a) that's the only place where the first humans originated, or (b) because Africa just had more undisturbed sites that were conducive at the time for fossilization processes to preserve the specimens and their artifacts. As more evidence accumulates, the exclusively African origin is becoming increasingly more certain.

Homo habilis was discovered 50 years ago in Tanzania by Louis Leakey, son of famed Richard and Mary Leakey. This find was given a name connoting "handyman" because of its apparent early affinity for stone tools. *H. habilis* was also the first to make use of fire. This is the earliest known humanoid or **hominin**, and could be the first link to descend from Lucy's family of *Australopithecus afarensis* and *Au. sediba* to the genus *Homo* and us humans. We may assume this until someone finds a better intermediary. Museum models made from *H. habilis* fossils show apelike facial features. With long forearms and bipedal legs, this appears to be a true diverging link distinguishing *hominins* from apes.

[Hold the presses! Just as we were on the very brink of closure for publication, there came an astonishing announcement of a quite auspicious discovery of a possibly new fossil species of *hominin*. At the bottom of a South African cave, accessible only through a very narrow chute, the slenderest members of Lee Berger's team spelunked into the lower cavern and recovered bones, teeth, and artifacts of over a dozen nearly intact specimens and parts of hundreds more. Named *Homo naledi* (*naledi* being the local Sotho word for "star"), it shows aspects of apelike climbing ability, transitional dental structure, legs longer than its arms, human-like feet, and a cranial capacity that is said to be comparable to the *Australopithecus* genus of 2–3 million years ago. Is *H. naledi* a key link in our ancestral lineage, or just another long-lost cousin? It is a mystery how this community of hominins came to be there, with no evidence of food or tools. The working hypothesis is that they were intentionally placed there in a crude but sanitary disposal of the dead. Would that indicate a more recent existence, coincident with the early Neanderthals? The exact radioisotopic time of these specimens has yet to be reported. Berger has willingly invited criticism from others—a certain inevitability anyway. It is noted that this discovery comes 50 years after Louis Leakey's discovery of *Homo habilis*.]

One crucial ancestral species was the *Homo ergaster*, whose fossil remains have only been found in Africa, and who occupied an important *hominin* position from 2.0 to 1.4 Mya. *Ergaster* developed language skills, and was succeeded by two *hominin* branches, *Homo erectus* (both "Java Man" and "Peking Man," which roamed across Asia), and its larger European cousin *Homo heidelbergensis*; either or both of which could be our ancestor. *H. heidelbergensis* was the first known to practice sanitary burial of the dead, while *H. erectus* was an early cave-dwelling hunter, and was adept at managing fire and stone tools. Some 300–400 thousand years ago, it had figured out the advantages of cooking its food, which improved its digestion and reduced the amount of time devoted to eating.

Homo erectus also had a phenomenal capacity for endurance running. In his fascinating book *Born to Run*, Christopher McDougal ponders the riddle of how *Homo erectus* could have subsisted on a diet of meat for his calories, fat, and protein, while he lived and foraged at a time that preceded arrows and spearheads by at least a million years. The solution devised by McDougal is that our ancestral *H. erectus* had the ability unmatched among animals to sustain a steady trot for many miles without stopping. This gave him the unique ability to keep tracking after deer, antelopes, and similar game, chasing them on foot until they became overheated and oxygen-depleted, and could run no further.

The rival *hominin* line *Homo neanderthalensis*, while superior in some physical respects, could not come close to matching this singular ability. Our Neanderthal cousins were a different breed, strong and cunning, able to surround their slow-ambling prey (bison, bear, or elk) in a canyon ambush and kill it with sharpened wooden poles, but could never run after swifter animals. They, too, adapted methods for cooking meat in shallow earthen ovens, cared for their sick, buried their dead, wore jewelry and may have developed rudimentary language and musical skills. Overall, they were quite successful until they became extinct some 30,000 years ago.

Were they outwitted by *Homo sapiens*? Probably not. McDougal reasons that the end of the Ice Age gave way to global warming, which replaced forest cover with drier grasslands. This new climate would have been more conducive for antelope herds rather than elk, and Neanderthals starved to death. The advantage of great muscular strength had given *Homo neanderthalensis* a definite edge in the cool forests and canyons, but sapped their endurance when ambient temperatures rose above 90° F.

Somewhere in the evolutionary chain, our ancestral line acquired this unequaled physiological trait of fast-jogging, which some among our species can still demonstrate in marathons and other distance-running competitions. McDougal has a citation of the fabled Tarahumara tribe of Copper Canyon, Mexico. While infant mortality is extremely high for these indigenous people, the adult males possess remarkable stamina for distance running. There are websites devoted to their exploits of being able to run for days without stopping. Could it be that these people carry remnant genes of *Homo erectus* in our day?

There may have been an intermediate subspecies between *Homo ergaster* and *Homo heidelbergensis,* based on a collection of bone and jaw fragments and rudimentary tools found in Europe (Spain and England). This specimen has appropriately (maybe prematurely?) been named *Homo antecessor.* Some experts consider this to be just another European variety of *H. heidelbergensis.* Nevertheless, these are important finds of the first European colonization by close precursors of humans 1.2 million to 800,000 years ago. Perhaps *Homo antecessor* was the transitional predecessor of *Homo rhodesiensis,* a vital crossroads species. Occupying Africa, Asia, and Europe from 600,000 to 300,000 years ago, *H. rhodesiensis* is thought by some to be the common ancestor for both humans and Neanderthals. Other experts assign that special distinction to *Homo heidelbergensis.*

Anatomical comparisons of skull specimens found in Romania (2006) have suggested that *H. sapiens* and *H. neanderthalensis* may have interbred to some extent before the stronger but stamina-challenged (and perhaps even mentally less nimble) Neanderthals were displaced and became extinct as late as 30,000 years ago. Meanwhile, there has been some progress toward decoding the DNA of a 38,000-year-old Neanderthal discovered in Croatia. This led to a tentative conclusion that Neanderthal DNA was 99.5% identical to that of humans due to common ancestry. The leader of this project, Edward Rubin of the Lawrence Berkeley National Laboratory, believes the two rival species began to evolve from a common ancestor 700,000 years ago, completing the divergence 500,000 years later. Yet another team from Harvard and the Max Planck Institute cite evidence that humans from Eurasia carry more pieces of DNA from the Neanderthal genome than do modern Africans, suggesting interbreeding. There's a healthy dispute about this, so stay tuned.

The picture after that is beginning to fill in. Fossil evidence places the first known *Homo sapiens* in East Africa some 200,000 years ago. Small tribes of these hunters gradually migrated into other parts of the African continent in search of food. It has long been understood that approximately 50,000–75,000 years ago a major migration of humans moved up and out of Africa to as far away as Southeast Asia and some adjoining islands. They found successful survival conditions in India and Australia.

It has been reported that DNA evidence from a lock of hair indicates that Australian Aborigines are the surviving descendants from this first wave of migrants. Now (*Nature* 2015), a team from the Chinese Academy of Sciences has reported finding fossil teeth of *Homo sapiens* in a cave in southern China locked in a stalagmite 80,000 years old. Whether that was a separate migration or an advanced guard remains to be seen.

Roughly 45,000 years ago, there was a second wave of emigration out of Africa and the Mideast. Some of these wandered northwest into Europe and are the ancestors of modern Europeans. Others moved northeast into China. These latter humans undoubtedly encountered and interbred with descendants of the first wave of migrants who had settled in Southeast Asia. These first- and second-wave migrants were the ancestors of most Asians today. Some of these people were able 15,000 to 30,000 years ago to cross over into North America via a Russo-Alaskan land bridge.

This continues to be an active and exciting field of study, with new discoveries reported every few months. Not all will stand up to normal scrutiny by scientific peers, but this keen activity offers a huge potential for finding more prehuman "missing links." There are also a large number of branches on our family tree that are not in our direct line of descent. For example, in 2008 a Siberian cave yielded a partial fossil skeleton 40,000 years old. That is about the limit for much DNA to still be intact, so it was fortunate that the research team could map this genome using material taken from its little finger. What they found was that the DNA of this "distant cousin" was significantly different from both modern humans and fossil Neanderthals. They estimate that its last common ancestor with us and/or Neanderthals would have been a million years ago.

It is interesting to ponder the fact that early humans appeared and evolved only within the continent of Africa. There is no evidence as yet that anything like intelligent humankind originated and emerged from any other place. What does that mean? Were we just lucky? This curious fact of our antecedents clearly adds pressure on paleontologists to search for other sites of human origin. It also spotlights the question of whether intelligent life could readily evolve on other suitable planets (chapter 17) if it was unable to evolve on other suitable continents right here on Earth.

Hobbits

Yet another curiosity is a unique and extinct species known as *Homo floresiensis*, which has been found only on Flores Island in Indonesia, just east of Wallace's demarcation line where it passes through Lombok

Strait (see p. 124-125). First discovered in 2003, this creature had dwarf proportions (standing about three feet tall) and a small brain, and yet appears to have mastered the art of making stone tools. In today's fascination with motion picture characters, it is unavoidable that *H. floresiensis* would be nicknamed the "Hobbit of Flores." The original specimens suggested an existence spanning from 75,000 to 13,000 years ago, although recent dating of the site indicates that this little fellow may have been extinct by 60,000 years ago. Local tradition, however, favors likely encounters of surviving individuals with the first humans to migrate to the surrounding islands, no earlier than 11,000 years ago. Indonesian lore is rich with references to "Ebu Gogo," a tribe of diminutive fellows that walked with an odd gait and whose "speech" was unintelligible. This apparent conflict awaits further fossil evidence.

One enigmatic question about the Flores Hobbit is whether it descended from *Homo erectus*, the only early hominid to occupy this part of Asia. One theory suggests that its size diminished in evolutionary response to its inadequate food resource. Some experts contend that would have involved too profound a shrinkage in body and skull size, and they prefer the idea that it evolved from a smaller *hominin* ancestor. Yet others favor that this is just a rare example of an isolated clan of *Homo erectus* people that had an inherited thyroid malfunction that stunted their growth (cretinism). This whole debate may never be resolved until DNA can be retrieved from a specimen, especially if they can get mitochondrial DNA.

A Disturbing Criticism

In 1880, fossil remains having strong similarities with modern humans were found near Castenedolo, Italy. The strange thing is that these were found in sandy clay, said to be from the Pliocene period, which was 3 to 4 million years ago. This anomaly was seized by creationist writers to cast doubt on the more commonly accepted evolutionary sequence (above) that *Homo sapiens* first appeared some 200,000 years ago. Other examples are the Olmo (Italy) skull, from Pleistocene strata, and bones found by miners in Calaveras County, California. Ironically, young-earth creationists can take little comfort in 3-million-year-old fossils.

The Castenedolo bones were subjected to radioisotopic dating in 1929, indicating that they were merely a <u>few thousand</u> years old. Radiocarbon techniques employed at that time are open to some criticism that inadequate care could have allowed these samples to become contaminated with dust of more recent "vintage." If so, a falsely higher carbon-14 ratio would have been measured, resulting in a calculated date more recent than the actual age of the clean specimens.

More careful radiocarbon analysis repeated in 1969 pins their age at 25,000 years, indicating that these were more recent (Holocene) burials in older Pliocene clay. The Olmo skull was found to be somewhat older at 75,000 years (the Stone Age). Therefore, neither of these examples refutes the accepted 200,000-year existence of *Homo sapiens*, a conclusion now acknowledged by Intelligent Design websites. As for the Calaveras skull, it turned out to be from another state, planted in the mine as a hoax, which was satirically memorialized in jest by Bret Harte's poem "To the Pliocene Skull." For fun, look it up!

This dispute has been discussed from the creationist perspective in *Forbidden Archaeology* by Michael Cremo and Richard Thompson, and by others. Their argument deserved to be addressed (and promptly was) by paleontologists, whose specialty is the fossil record. Notably, Cremo and Thompson pay little attention to the most compelling case for evolution based upon comparisons of DNA in the genomes of similar and different living species.

Genetics of Race

It is believed that *Homo sapiens* emerged from a single origin in East Africa. After migrating to other continents, isolation from their origins allowed distinct racial varieties to evolve. Geneticists have pursued the basis for racial characteristics with considerable interest. What they have found shows little difference between human races insofar as DNA gene sequences are concerned. That may seem counterintuitive, but we have to work with the evidence that's there.

For perspective, genomic studies of individuals have shown that from one human to another of the same sex, there may be some variation among up to forty to fifty genes. That is on average 46 (0.2%) of the 23,000 human genes. Stated another way, we can say that 99.8% of genes are the same among all humans. Of these 46 or so differences, some 40 or so are variations within the same race, while only six (15% of the total variation) differ from one race to another. At most, then, transracial variation affects 0.03% of the human genome. Clearly, genetic studies don't show clear racial borders.

Race is a term of convenience based mostly upon skin color, although an anthropologist might identify other features such as eyelids, nose, and hair, for example, and a propensity for certain diseases. Some of these attributes are not exclusively distributed within one race alone, although sometimes there is higher frequency of clustering in one race than another. One theory is that it is based more on kinship or self-identification with an ethnic or cultural group or country of origin, but that would seem to be as much a sociopolitical theory as a biological one. Or it may turn out to be **epigenetic** in origin (see page 110).

Recapitulation

Charles Darwin acknowledged his concerns that the linkage between apes and humans was not evident in contemporaneous species or in the fossil record. For many decades thereafter, this "Missing Link" idea was cited as negative evidence against his theory of evolution. Recent decades have been kind to him, as paleontologists have discovered at least seven distinct "links" plus another three to four possible ancestors and many more non-lineal "cousins." Consequently, this issue no longer supports criticism of Darwin, but adds anatomical support along with evidence from DNA similarities. Darwin's main concern for his theory has been transformed into validation. The former liability has become his asset.

Chapter 9

The Scopes "Monkey Trial"

Dayton, Tennessee, 1925

In February 1925, the State Legislature of Tennessee passed what became known as the Butler Law. This made it unlawful in Tennessee "to teach any theory that denies the story of Divine Creation as taught by the Bible and to teach instead that man has descended from a lower order of animals." One could not lawfully teach evolution of apes or pigeons even if there was no mention of common ancestry with humans. Much of today's debate about evolution was shaped by one truly amazing historical incident in Dayton, Tennessee, in the hot summer of 1925. In the first trial in American jurisprudence to be carried live on a radio broadcast (WGN Chicago), a young teacher named John Thomas Scopes was convicted of teaching evolution, violating the Butler Law.

The Scopes trial achieved great national interest when the famously controversial social reformer and three-time presidential candidate William Jennings Bryan joined the prosecution team. Bryan had been a national leader in the early 1920s movement to get states to prohibit the teaching of evolution. He was matched in celebrity and eloquence when the American Civil Liberties Union (ACLU) brought in the famous trial lawyer Clarence Darrow to bolster the defense. Even today, some consider it to be America's "Trial of the Century."

Inherit the Wind

This bizarre story has been told most powerfully in the 1955 dramatization *Inherit the Wind* by playwrights Jerome Lawrence and Robert Edwin Lee. Having read the play several times, and having seen a number of good productions, I thought I had a good idea of what had transpired in rural Tennessee ten years before I was born. That was before I read a more engaging review of both the trial and its fictional dramatization in Stephen Jay Gould's *Rocks of Ages*, which you will want to read. That led me to seek a better comprehension of issues of cosmology.

Inherit the Wind was a great commercial and sociopolitical success. Written at the time of Senator Joseph McCarthy (R-Wisconsin) and his efforts to scour Communists, real and suspected, from public life, the play is a brilliant metaphor for what was going on in Washington, DC. Rather than a direct depiction of the contemporary characters and themes, the play substitutes another story from thirty years earlier and with a more rural setting. It evokes the human interest of ordinary folk caught up in powerful forces beyond their control, with the added dimension of a famous clash of opposing legal titans.

The play is about the trial of one Bertram T. Cates (standing in for the real John Scopes), a young teacher and coach who had violated state law by teaching evolution. Cates is the understated hero, while the concentration of theatrical passion is reserved for the roles of Henry Drummond (standing in for Clarence Darrow) and Matthew Harrison Brady (literary surrogate for William Jennings Bryan).

The Broadway run was long, following a premiere in Dallas with local actors. When it was staged in New York, the key roles featured actors of exceptional talent and reputation, with Paul Muni as Henry Drummond and Ed Begley Sr. as Matthew Brady, with Tony Randall as the Baltimore reporter E.K. Hornbeck (mirroring the great epitheticist H.L. Mencken of the *Baltimore Sun*). The characters were so vivid that four motion picture versions have been produced. A stage revival was launched in 2007 starring Christopher Plummer as Darrow, followed by another in 2009 with Kevin Spacey in that coveted role. It would be hard to imagine a more distinguished cast than graced these four movies:

Table 9. Casts of Characters in Motion Pictures, *Inherit the Wind*

	(Clarence Darrow)	(Wm. Jennings Bryan)	(H.L. Mencken)
Year	Henry Drummond	Matthew Brady	E.K. Hornbeck
1960	Spencer Tracy	Frederick March	Gene Kelly
1965	Melvyn Douglas	Ed Begley Sr.	Murray Hamilton
1988	Jason Robards	Kirk Douglas	Darren McGavin
1999	Jack Lemmon	George C. Scott	Beau Bridges

[Other notables deserve mention. In the 1960 movie version, Bertram Cates (Scopes) was portrayed by young Dick York, who achieved

his most successful role in the popular television comedy series
Bewitched. In the same film, the role of Judge Coffey (representing
the real Judge Raulston) was played by Harry Morgan, who later had
considerable TV success as Colonel Potter in *M*A*S*H.*]

On another dimension, it was the Butler Law that was on trial.
One must allow for a degree of literary license, and there are plenty of
departures in the flow of a well-told story. This does not detract from
the power of the message and its challenge against attempts at thought
control. Indeed, Lawrence and Lee had just the right disclaimer: "It's not
about science versus religion. It's about the right to think."

The Trial

In contrast with the unrelenting seriousness of the play, the real Scopes
trial had its share of farcical elements. John Scopes was a football and
track coach at Rhea County High School, who taught physics, math, and
chemistry, with no particular expertise in biology. As a substitute for the
regular biology teacher (about three months after the Butler Law was
passed), Scopes apparently made no more than a passing reference to the
section on evolution in the back of the textbook in case any student cared
to check it out. Whether that violated the law, it gave the appearance of
it. Ironically, during the early phase of the trial, Scopes was obliged to go
and round up two young students and persuade them that it would be all
right to testify as witnesses against him.

That anecdote may seem weird enough until you realize that the
whole thing was a civic stunt dreamed up in Robinson's drugstore
by several town promoters desperate for a little action to draw more
attention and visitors to quiet little Dayton, Tennessee. The reputed
leader was a man named George Rappleyea, a local coal mine operator
who instigated the ruse and recruited young Scopes to be their star
scapegoat. Others among the "drugstore conspirators" were:
(a) Frank Robinson (owner of the drugstore and Chairman of the
School Board),
(b) Walter White (Superintendent of Rhea County Schools and one
of two adult witnesses for the prosecution),
(c) Attorney Herbert Hicks and his brother Sue Hicks, whose name
may have inspired the Johnny Cash ballad "A Boy Named Sue"
(both would join the prosecution),
(d) a local judge, and

(e) three other attorneys (all of whom would serve as volunteer assistant prosecutors).

There had been a news story in the *Chattanooga Daily Times* that the American Civil Liberties Union (ACLU) was looking for a test case among the few southern states that had adopted such laws. Rappleyea wrote to invite them to come to Dayton, which the ACLU accepted by return telegram, agreeing to cover the costs of the defense. It was quickly arranged to have Scopes indicted, and the trial was set for July 10, 1925. Scopes and his lawyer met with ACLU officials in New York City, and the defense was worked out. Things were moving fast. There was no intention to prove Scopes was innocent, by the way, because the only clear way to test the constitutionality of the law was for the accused to be found guilty . . . which, technically of course, and by intent, he was.

In keeping with the town's unabashed excitement, first Bryan and then Darrow were feted with separate banquets in their respective honors. It was noted that in the first gala Scopes was seated right beside Bryan. Imagine the youthful admiration for the famous gentleman from Salem, Illinois, where young Scopes had attended high school. Bryan needled Scopes for supposedly laughing during Bryan's speech at Scopes's graduation. The man had either a keen memory or a keen wit—probably both!

With a few more preliminaries out of the way, the trial began July 10 and ran until July 21. In many respects, it was as heated as that summer's cauldron through which it simmered. In due course, Scopes was convicted by a jury of true believers. It had its full share of fireworks, as Clarence Darrow fought hard and eloquently, seeming to lose track of the ACLU's need for a test case to end in a conviction, so that it could be appealed. Reporters and some historians credit Darrow with humiliating his old nemesis William Jennings Bryan, but that is not so clear from a reading of the transcript, which you may examine for yourself on the Internet (search "Scopes trial transcript").

Circuit Judge John T. Raulston did not allow the jury to hear scientific testimony from eight attending biology experts, since this was simply a trial whether Scopes had taught evolution in violation of Tennessee law, which he had. His Honor was technically correct, as Charles Darwin was not on trial; Scopes was. The judge did allow their written scientific testimony into the record, to be available in case of a likely appeal.

In a brilliant courtroom tactic, Darrow then called Bryan to the stand as an expert witness on the Bible, an honor that Bryan's vanity could not decline. With agnostic zeal, Darrow put the Bible on trial, and for that cause, Bryan rose nobly to its defense. This great scene was played out under the elms outdoors after Judge Raulston decided it was so stifling in the Court House that all the handheld fans provided by local funeral homes could not bring relief. Legend has it that the gawking gallery had swollen that day to around 5,000 souls.

Darrow had prepared thoroughly for this "Duel in the Shade," and caught Bryan off guard. Darrow repeatedly hammered Bryan about the *Genesis* accounts of the Garden of Eden, the serpent, the flood, Jonah and the whale, plus Joshua commanding the sun to halt, and every miracle mentioned in the Bible. Unprepared for so many stealthy specifics, Bryan deflected as best he could.

Over and over, Bryan was pressed to get him to advocate that *Genesis I* meant that the earth was created, provisioned, and populated in "six 24-hour days." Bryan would not fall for it, repeating that he had a pretty good understanding that the earth was much older than 6,000 years, but that he personally had not tried to calculate how old. When Darrow pounded Bryan over Creation's date of 4004 BC as footnoted in some Bibles (see chapter 11 below), Bryan parried that it was Darrow alone who had spoken that date and that Holy Scripture did not say that, as to which he was quite accurate.

As the hot afternoon wore on, the prosecution team several times tried vainly to intervene with Judge Raulston to halt the questioning, but Bryan himself prevailed for it to continue. Apparently, Bryan believed that he was doing just fine, thank you, and that he would have his turn to question Darrow. This vain expectation never came to pass.

In one exchange about the age of the earth, the following banter illustrates that Bryan's responses were at times whimsical, if not always sufficiently circumspect, since the immediate audience (if not the reporters) was on his side that day in Dayton:

Darrow (about the age of the earth):   "What do you think?"
Bryan: "I don't think about things that I don't think about."
Darrow: "Do you think about things you do think about?"
Bryan: "Well, sometimes."

Whether you laughed with Bryan or laughed at him might depend upon your point of view, historically and philosophically.

Mencken, for his part, kept the readership back in Baltimore reassured about the relative inferiority of these backwoods yokels by means of a steady flow of acerbic diatribes hawked as journalism. You can search "Scopes trial Mencken" and read more of his daily columns for fun, but let me insert here a couple of his barbs for illustration:

July 14 (the third day). *The net effect of Clarence Darrow's great speech yesterday seems to be preciously the same as if he had bawled it up a rainspout in the interior of Afghanistan. That is, locally . . . upon the so-called minds of these fundamentalists of upland Tennessee. It rose like a wind and ended like a flourish of bugles. The very judge on the bench, toward the end of it, began to look uneasy. But the morons in the audience, when it was over, simply hissed it."*

July 18. *All that remains of the great cause of the State of Tennessee against the infidel Scopes is the formal business of bumping off the defendant. There may be some legal jousting on Monday and some gaudy oratory on Tuesday, but the main battle is over, with Genesis completely triumphant. Judge Raulston finished the benign business yesterday morning by leaping with soft judicial hosannas into the arms of the prosecution. The sole commentary of the sardonic Darrow consisted of bringing down a metaphoric custard pie upon the occiput of the learned jurist: "I hope," said the latter nervously, "that counsel intends no reflection upon this court."*

Darrow hunched his shoulders and looked out the window dreamily. "Your honor," he said, "is, of course, entitled to hope."

Darrow has lost this case. It was lost long before he came to Dayton. But it seems to me that he has nevertheless performed a great public service by fighting it to a finish and in a perfectly serious way. Let no one mistake it for comedy, farcical though it may be in all its details. It serves notice on the country that Neanderthal man is organizing in these forlorn backwaters of the land, led by a fanatic, rid of sense and devoid of conscience. Tennessee, challenging him too timorously and too late, now sees its courts converted into camp meetings and its Bill of Rights made a mock of by its sworn officers of the law. There are other states that should look to their arsenals before the Hun is at their gates.

That should give you the flavor of it. To Mencken, and to many historians, William Jennings Bryan was the national buffoon, a sideshow clown treating the yokels to a display of foolishness. Mencken might have added the court's response to the quip above. According to the trial transcript Darrow actually said: "Well, Your Honor has the right to hope!" For Judge Raulston fired back: "I have the right to do something else!" Darrow was held in contempt until he later apologized.

Reprise

These were the last days of a once great orator (he died a week after the trial, not on its last day as in *Inherit the Wind*). The Great Commoner had been a two-term Congressman from Nebraska, 41st U.S. Secretary of State under President Woodrow Wilson, three-time candidate for President of the United States, devout Presbyterian, and a Democrat. Bryan had rallied the nation against the gold standard with his famous "Cross of Gold" speech, and was a champion of women's suffrage. Here is what he said in closing his rousing speech to the 1896 Democratic National Convention in Chicago: "You shall not press down upon the brow of labor this Crown of Thorns; you shall not crucify mankind upon this Cross of Gold!" It was reported that Bryan finished this rhetorical image standing with a flourish, his arms spread as upon a cross, whereupon the hushed audience leapt up in a rapture of wild ecstasy.

Bryan had written that his main objection to the teaching of evolution arose from its derivative eugenic policies of forced sterilization and abandonment of the infirm (see "Francis Galton," page 131). The 1920s churned with efforts to legislate such practices, then in vogue among Scandinavian countries with which American progressives were so enamored, against opposition by equally fervent traditionalists and populists like Bryan.

In closing for the defense, Darrow outwitted the prosecution by waiving his right to a closing speech, and asked counter-intuitively for a "guilty" verdict, as the ACLU had intended all along. Under Tennessee law, this waiver also had the effect of foreclosing any opportunity for Bryan to showcase his prepared closing remarks.

As a constitutional test case, *Scopes* never proved anything. Judge Raulston apparently had neglected to refresh on Tennessee's State Constitution, which provided that only a jury could levy a fine greater than $50. Dutifully, he had fined Scopes $100, the minimum required by the Butler Law. The Constitution took precedence over any law, a convenient technicality that let the State Supreme Court off the hook. Contending that it had no power to correct the fine, the Supreme Court of Tennessee declared that Scopes was no longer guilty. As the defendant in the meantime had moved on to Chicago to study engineering, the court directed that the matter be dropped (*nolle prosequi*).

The word went out quietly to leave the ban against teaching evolution in the law, but go easy on enforcement. This still left an intimidating climate for textbook publishers, who expediently began to take the safer course of omitting any reference to evolution. While the most significant courtroom trial of the twentieth century did not settle anything, that definitive judgment day would not be long in coming. Both Louisiana and Arkansas had similar prohibitions against teaching evolution. We will take a look at those cases in chapter 18. For now, we can let John Thomas Scopes rest his case.

Chapter 10

Evolution of Dissent with Moderation

From the moment Darwin's new interpretation was made public (1859), the scientific debate over it was vigorous. In the minds of most contemporary biologists, the adaptive mechanism of Lamarck was well established and superior to Darwin's idea of natural selection. T.H. Huxley raised Darwin's Theory as an irreligious icon. Others surpassed him in using it to promote atheism against the religious establishment. Although an agnostic, to use his own term, Huxley must have noted that his advocacy of Darwin's Theory gave comfort to atheists. They would accept more readily the sanctuary of a godless explanation of this great question. Others were offended by all this, and fought against evolution in order to counteract the atheists.

As additional support for evolution continued to accumulate, entrenching descent with modification, sorted by natural selection, as THE scientific explanation for how all species sprang from ancient common ancestry, some on both opposing sides took the position that evolution and atheism were one and the same. Atheism's bottom line was very simple: If one accepts evolution (and the implication that every phenomenon has a natural, mechanistic explanation), one need not and, therefore, should not believe in God. This was their ultimate logical syllogism: evolution just happens naturally; therefore, there is no need for supernatural intrusion.

At least, that's what an atheist could assert with confidence at a time when relatively little was known about the molecular complexity of matter and especially of all living beings. One who respects science must acknowledge that similarities of anatomical parts and shapes, textures, and colors clearly infer an inherited connection between and among different species. Throughout the last century—indeed, until recently—it seemed to some that each discovery about the nature and structures of life meant one less need for God as an explanation. Today, ironically, the more we discover about the breathtaking complexity of the universe and living systems, the more we are led to consider some guiding principle or purpose.

Questions regarding **teleology** (purpose) are not accessible via experimental science. This limitation does not diminish their importance.

The debate did not go well for defenders of the young-earth faith. Atheism's initial advantage solidified as support for evolution accumulated, answering more and more questions. That advantage was largely conceded by the creationism movement when it adopted the same punch line, only stated in reverse: If one believes in God, they said, one cannot believe in evolution. By equating the scientific theory of evolution with atheism, anti-theists had attacked religion. Creationists chose to counterattack science by similarly equating evolution with atheism. In so doing, they unwittingly undermined their own credibility. *To equate evolution with atheism mistakenly abandons evolution to be the intellectual asset of atheism.*

Evolution is *just* a Theory

Creationist's strategy was to demean evolution as nothing more than a mere *theory*. Scientists are offended when those who reject Darwin's Theory of Evolution protest that "it is only a theory!" That's an uninformed attempt to impugn the dignity of the concept by implying that it has little substance, has never been proven, and has nothing to do with truth as we know it (or something like that). By false inference, if an explanation is no more than a theory, there should be little or no reason to give it any respect or credence.

Such semantic puffery demonstrates that those who make such a claim have inadequate, if any, acquaintance with science, its methods and principles, and what it is that research scientists do in their day jobs. Introductory textbooks in science present the orthodox algorithm known as **the Scientific Method**, which can be described as follows:

- From many reproducible observations, one conceives an explanation for the behaviors or processes that have been observed. This may be stated in metaphoric terms, or mathematical formula, or imagery, and is called the **hypothesis**. The original hypothesis gains added stature if it leads to a large number of useful, testable predictions. Others can attempt to duplicate these observations or refine them, which may serve to clarify or modify the hypothesis. If the reported experimental observations cannot be replicated by others, the hypothesis likely will be discredited or remain a conjecture or an assumption.

- For the hypothesis to stand, it must be falsifiable, *i.e.*, susceptible to experiments designed to test its predictions and conclusions. These experiments have special value if any possible outcome has potential to disprove or cast doubt on the hypothesis. To be taken seriously, the hypothesis must also have utility or important consequences.
- If numerous experiments fail to contradict or disprove the hypothesis (other than to make modest adjustments in its basic concept), and it survives all attempts to reject it, it then becomes elevated to the distinction of being accepted and promoted as a **theory**.

That is about as high as you can get in any science: to devise an explanatory hypothesis that is useful and falsifiable, and then to have it survive numerous tests to become accepted as a theory. If the original hypothesis does not stir the most fertile minds in science to devise ways to test it, the lofty status of theory may be elusive. It is vital that the hypothesis be able to generate ideas for useful devices or products or processes; in short, that it have utility. Without utility, it could be ignored. Darwin's original hypothesis challenged the established order. It would have to survive decades of intense experimental challenges from contemporary biologists all over the world, many of whom were staunch Lamarckians. Accordingly, it is among the most established and important theories in modern science. It is THE organizing principle of modern biology, as mass and energy are to physics, and covalence is to organic chemistry.

We must acknowledge here that Darwin's original evidence was an accumulation of descriptive observations that led by **inductive reasoning** to his generalizing hypothesis for the origin of species. Quite often, initial conclusions from descriptive biology, fossil paleontology, and observational astronomy are not readily amenable to designed laboratory experiments.

While that logic limits the provenance of hypotheses when based solely on inductive generalizations, any such shortcoming may be overcome by a massive accumulation of supporting evidence. Furthermore, once the hypothesis can be subjected to a search for predicted phenomena, the deductive elements of the Scientific Method can provide the ultimate test of falsifiability. We saw that in the successful search for an echo from the Big Bang, as well as astronomers' detection of uncontaminated, primordial hydrogen, which confirmed a key prediction of Big Bang mathematics (see pages 60 and 66). So it is with evolution theory. Modern research on DNA similarities of the genomes of humans and growing numbers of species provides compelling evidence (see below and chapter 15) of a high degree of Darwinian common ancestry that cannot be ignored or wished away.

A theory becomes established as an explanation of numerous observations once it has prevailed over numerous attempts to disprove it. It represents the zenith of scientific understanding. It is the very best that scientists can do. As a basic principle of science, like gravity, evolution is not in doubt. Is it subject to refinement? Yes, of course. Is its scientific foundation vulnerable? Not likely.

Refining the Paradigm

Even an established theory is continually subject to new challenges. Some of these challenges may lead to improvements in the basic theory. Even if unable to disprove it, these experiments may reveal fresh insights that can help to clarify and expand the original. This is certainly true for Darwin's Theory of Evolution and the origin of species.

During his lifetime, Darwin had no clear idea what caused random variations. He could only describe the great variety and similarity between and within species, and derive his mechanism of natural selection as the driver to explain what he and others had observed. He even acknowledged shortcomings in his understanding, thereby inviting objection and criticism. He was apparently unfamiliar with the limited circulation of papers about the laws of inherited traits by the little known Moravian biologist Gregor Mendel (1868), who codified the term "genes."

A century later, when biologists began to understand an association between DNA and heritable characteristics, a more modernized version of Darwin's theory began to unfold. Oswald Avery showed that DNA, not protein, was the transfer agent for genetic inheritance (1944). There was not yet any theory of how DNA could carry out that function. In one of the great breakthroughs of modern science, the molecular structure of DNA was elucidated by James Watson and Francis Crick (1953). They developed the theory that all DNA had a molecular structure consisting of a double helix of alternating phosphate and a sugar, spanned internally by pairs of four nucleotide bases whose sequential order encodes unimaginably vast genetic information. The sugar is deoxyribose; hence the full name, deoxyribo-nucleic acid (DNA).

A key step in solving this puzzle was the finding that in the DNA of any species the molecular abundances of two of the four nucleotides, **guanine** (G) and **cytosine** (C), were always identical, and the molecular abundances of **adenine** (A) and **thymine** (T) were always the same as each other but different from guanine and cytosine. This clearly indicated some profoundly distinctive correspondence, a one-to-one molecular ratio for each of these two pairs. In each case, one was a specific **purine**, A or G, and the other a **pyrimidine**, C or T (see pages 267 and 285). Watson and Crick noted that the geometrical dimensions of each of the four nucleotides were such that a bridge between guanine and cytosine (G:C) spanned exactly the same spatial distance as that between adenine and thymine (A:T). No other pairing of the four (or any other pair of nucleotides) would bridge the exact distance across the space-gap between the two intertwining helical coils.

The helical nature of DNA had occurred to Watson, but he needed evidence. When Maurice Wilkins showed him an x-ray diffraction image of DNA taken by Rosalind Franklin of Kings College London, Watson concurred with Franklin's recognition that it had a geometrical pattern typical of helical structures. It is quite amazing that they were able to deduce this structure without the benefit of modern x-ray crystallography, a more sophisticated technology that clearly confirms their double-helix model of DNA's structure in great visual detail.

[Historical Footnote: In 1968, Watson, Crick, and Wilkins were awarded the Nobel Prize for this singular discovery. The vital contributions of Oswald Avery and Rosalind Franklin could not be honored by the Nobel committee, since both were deceased by the time of the award, and the Nobel indenture precludes posthumous honorees.]

A causative relationship has been found between specific diseases and alterations in the sequence of nucleotide pairs in DNA. The coded aspect of this highly complex cipher has become apparent. Furthermore, a part of the DNA code associated with one gene is transcribed onto RNA, which then controls the biosynthesis of protein, so that the code sequence of the protein is defined by that of the DNA. With this understanding of the structure and role of DNA, Darwin's Theory was elevated above any further challenge. It now has the loftiest possible importance because it is rich with predictive capacity and medical utility, and has extended Darwin's idea far beyond a mere generalization of anatomical distinctions and similarities. It has gained a molecular basis that cannot be disputed, as we shall see in chapter 15.

Plan B: Intelligent Design

Undeterred by their failure to prohibit the teaching of evolution (chapter 9), some ardent creationists devised a new legislative strategy. This time they would appeal to the popular ideals of balance and fair play. They proposed that young-earth creationism be taught alongside and as a scientific alternative to evolution. Their internalized justification for this position arose from the belief that evolution is atheism—which it is NOT. For public consumption, they asserted their official position that creationism is science—which it is NOT.

When this "equal time" approach also failed to pass constitutional muster (see pages 355-356), their next ploy was to promote **Intelligent Design** as a scientific field of study. Anything explained by Darwin's evolution would be interpreted instead as the result of divine intervention. As with creationism, the fundamental ingredients of this belief system are that (a) each species is fixed and unchanged, and the result of one specific act of creation; (b) the earth and the universe are only 6,000–10,000 years old; and (c) fossil deposits were divinely placed there for misdirection. Some ID advocates, however, sidestep (b) the "young earth" element.

Ted Peters and Martinez Hewlett have collaborated on an excellent book, *Can You Believe in God and Evolution?* Their unequivocal answer is an emphatic "YES." They point out the danger of imposing on young minds a choice between science and religion: either they will abandon science or abandon religion. Neither course is healthy. The choice can be traumatizing.

These two thoughtful authors share with young-earth advocates of creationism and intelligent design a strong opposition to the teaching of atheism in our schools, and applaud them for leading that opposition. At the same time, Peters and Hewlett are concerned that this worthy cause is being undermined by an indefensible tactic of the young-earth activists: misrepresenting creationism as the moral equivalent of science. You will find many fine insights in their book, which is a well-written introduction to this subject for the non-technical reader.

In politics, I have often wished that those whose philosophy I share, could have been the first to deploy (and thereby "own" the meaning of) some particularly clever phrase that others had already expropriated for a different meaning. Here I will simply use as my example the phrase "intelligent design." I believe that the universe and the earth, as well as the great variety of life on Earth, all had to be part of some intentional purpose for which the Almighty created us. The point is that the phrase "intelligent design" had already been taken by those who believe the earth is just 6,000 to 10,000 years old, and that Darwin's theory of evolution is wrong.

If I, or any fellow theistic scientists with similar beliefs, had been first to publish ideas about "intelligent design," our view would have given the phrase a different meaning than the one in circulation today, more respectful of the Scientific Method and its findings. For one thing, we would insist that evolution as it is understood by scientists is part of that divine design, not its antithesis. For another, we would accept the best scientific evidence that the universe is 13.7 billion years old and that the earth was formed 4.5 billion years ago. We would develop this concept to celebrate that, in the fullness of time, our Creator God endowed us with analytical minds and the ingenuity to construct sophisticated instruments so that we might observe, describe, quantify, and understand His creation.

Revelation through science does not dishonor our Creator, but adds to our understanding of His majesty and love for us. But I cannot take for myself the imprimatur of "intelligent design," or endorse it, because it has already been characterized to mean something different and antithetical to science. Those who were first to use this term have declared it to mean a young earth with fixed species of plants and animals, all created in their present form with no gradual variation in DNA coding and without natural selection. They have annexed it as a rejection of science. When it presents a false interpretation of the fossil record by construction of scenes showing humans sharing life among dinosaurs, it is entertaining but nonscientific nonsense. When it pretends that 6–10 thousand years ago God placed fossils in various shale deposits and photons arriving from remote stars to mislead and confuse us, it is anti-conscience.

That is not to say that evolution is a perfectly understood explanation of all biological complexity. It is nevertheless the best explanation science can give us. What we now know about the similarities and differences in DNA sequences of separate species, whether anatomically similar or different, compels acceptance that Darwin's theory as amended by these findings is irrefutable as to the origins of species. When it comes to the origins of taxonomic families and phyla of plants and animals, however, it does seem that more research will be needed to sort it all out. Molecular changes in the nucleotide code sequences in DNA are sufficient to account for mutations in species and how a new genus might arise. Reproduction is facile when the mutant parent and the second, perhaps unaffected, parent have the same chromosomes. But to get from one common ancestor to a different class, order, or family requires reproduction often involving different numbers of chromosomes, which is more difficult to explain.

Reconciliation

With the close of the twentieth century and the dawn of the twenty-first, the philosophical pendulum may have begun to swing back toward a mutually accommodative relationship between science and religion. Many scientists are discovering the importance of purpose and faith in their daily lives. They realize that the Scientific Method cannot address many of the most vital questions of <u>why</u> we are here, the meaning and purpose of life, and the ubiquitous moral imperative. In recent decades, a number of contemporary scientists have stated their belief that science in general and evolution in particular show us God's way. The modern theory of evolution is their best scientific understanding of how God ordained the origin of species. Science is no longer an impediment to their religious faith and practice.

Unlike the creationist movement, with its perceived need to denounce evolution in order to oppose atheism, this new breed of scientists is finding God in <u>all</u> that science reveals about nature. There are many prominent scientists today who make philosophic allowance for both. Science cannot reach back before the instant of creation of this universe; there are a number of crucial physical parameters that would seem to be fortuitously tuned for intelligent life on Earth; and the molecular complexity of living organisms has emerged mainly in spurts since Earth's surface cooled. This (and more) is all based on science. Either you believe this all happened by improbable chance, or you believe it followed a divine purpose, or you don't know.

At the same time that more scientists are expressing a new, mutual compatibility between science and religion, contemporary Christian ministers are presenting sermons and leading discussions of the growing reconciliation between these alternative quests for truth. They are inviting scientists who profess religious commitment to present their ideas and insights about faith and science within the order of worship, and as part of the church school program. That's how this book got started.

Anthropic Coincidences Revisited

Recognition of anthropic physical constants (fine-tuned to beget and sustain life) has led many scientists to accept that life has purpose. They see that the primordial universe was physically and chemically attuned very precisely for the emergence of life, culminating thus far in an intelligent, self-aware species. This topic was introduced in chapter 5. It deserves mention here, because *the concept of more than a half-dozen physical constants and conditions, each independently and simultaneously so finely tuned, is part of a series of wonders in modern science that clearly reclaim it from being any exclusively provincial domain of atheism.*

Essentially, what we have is this: if any one of these constants were out of its actual value by a small fraction, we would not be here. We are here, so how is it that numerous constants are so precisely tuned for us? Some even go so far as to cite this as proof of a Divine Creator. Others are a bit more cautious about that, but nevertheless view it as rather strong evidence. For those of atheistic persuasion, it is a new challenge.

In chemistry also, there are a number of unique curiosities that are extraordinary. Among these are the complexities of molecular structures of large organic compounds that abound in nature. The ease with which they are synthesized in plant and animal cells is in sharp contrast to the extreme difficulty of synthesizing them in the best equipped organic chemistry laboratory. Yet they are essential for complex life and its evolution.

Another is the chemical property known as the **hydrogen bond**. Best exemplified in liquid and solid water, the hydrogen bond is weaker than a covalent bond, but stronger than the electrostatic attraction of a polarized covalent bond. Most importantly, it has strict geometric requirements that cause the solid phase of water, which we call "ice," to be less dense than the liquid phase so that the solid form (ice) floats on its liquid form (water). With almost every other substance, the solid is denser than the liquid and sinks to the bottom. In chapter 14, we will see how this curiosity works, and how vitally significant it is, especially in DNA and proteins.

Asymmetry and Chirality

There is another phenomenon in chemistry that is little known outside the ranks of organic chemistry students. It is not that we are priestly in our subject field, but that we are required to visualize asymmetric molecular structures, and deal with their architecture in three dimensions. Suffice it to say at this point: many a carbon compound exists in two mirror image structures that are chemically identical in all other respects. For convenience and familiarity, we refer to them as left-handed and right-handed structures so that students can begin to grasp this important dichotomy of organic molecular structure called **chirality** (from the Greek word for "hand").

The key for you to take away at this point is that when we synthesize chiral compounds from simpler symmetrical molecules in the laboratory, we always get exactly equal amounts of left-handed and right-handed forms. There is never the slightest bias for one or the other unless we introduce some asymmetric starting material or catalyst. Yet in nature, there are many naturally occurring organic structures that are found exclusively as one preferred three-dimensional configuration, with none of its mirror image.

Proteins, for example, are polymeric chains of amino acids. What could be more complex yet vital in life processes? The smallest amino acid, glycine, is symmetrical, but all other amino acids are asymmetric (existing as two nonsuperimposable mirror images). When we synthesize any one of these in the laboratory, we always get precisely equal amounts of each configuration. In every plant or animal protein chain, however, almost all of these amino acids are left-handed. Only a trace of them is right-handed, and for reasons that prove the rule. Natural carbohydrates, on the other hand, are all right-handed without exception. So the causality questions arise: why is that? How did that happen? We will examine these chiral properties in chapters 14 and 15. There we will see the organic relationship of proteins and sugars to the right-handed helical structure of RNA and DNA.

Perhaps this introduction can give you a sense of the awe one experiences upon realizing that of two equally probable mirror-image forms of a chemical compound, only one occurs naturally in living plants and animals. This astonishing exclusivity is special. It is an enigmatic riddle with profound cosmological meaning. Did some purposeful Power beyond the scope of science fortuitously arrange for such an exclusive asymmetric bias for DNA and RNA? Did some random collision of molecules produce one incredibly improbable but fortuitous result? Which of these alternatives requires the greater "leap of faith?"

How else can there be an absolute and exclusive natural preference for one chiral form of every carbohydrate, for all DNA and RNA, and for the amino acids in all natural proteins, and for hundreds of other molecular structures? This question has challenged many talented and creative scientists to seek a mechanistic, testable answer (chapter 16). That is what the best scientists do: they take on the most difficult puzzles. They may find the answer to the riddle. If and when they do, we may nevertheless regard this peculiarly exclusive and ubiquitous asymmetric singularity as part of the accumulating evidence pointing us to our Creator.

The God of the Gaps Syllogism

In 1877, shortly before Darwin died, a Scottish evangelist named Henry Drummond (cf. page 153) cautioned against relying on things that science could not explain as proof of supernatural intervention. Chemist C.A. Coulson called this phenomenon the "God of the Gaps" in his book *Science and Christian Belief.* He pointed out that there was a grave risk in trying to prove the existence of God by the contemporary gaps in scientific knowledge. For, as science subsequently fills in those gaps, one's faith in God would be relegated to fewer and smaller gaps.

Today, one might well counter with the observation that the more science explains, the more it raises new questions. It could certainly be argued that there is no shortage of major gaps in our understanding of matter, energy, and the structures and processes of life. The more we discover and know, the more gaps we find in our knowledge. We must still recognize the wisdom in what Drummond and Coulson have said. What if a specific and substantial scientific gap should become a basis for many believers to hold as proof of God? Would it not become the focus of intensified efforts to find a scientific explanation? If achieved, that could have drastic consequences for those whose belief system depended upon such a crutch. Besides, does it glorify God to confine Him to what we don't yet understand? Should we believe God incapable of increasing the variety of life via alterations in the molecular code of DNA? Is a 13.7-billion-year span of creation beyond the One who is above time and space?

This problem was addressed most poignantly by the heroic German Lutheran pastor Dietrich Bonhoeffer. Bonhoeffer had studied theology under Reinhold Niebuhr in America, and held strong views on social reform that led him to speak out against the Nazi movement in general and Adolph Hitler in particular. This brought him into trouble enough, but also into a pastoral relationship with others who thought that Hitler must be removed.

Most incriminatingly, Bonhoeffer's name was among the papers of some of the military officers who plotted the assassination of Hitler and were caught when their effort failed. This became known as the "Valkyrie Conspiracy," dramatized in a motion picture by that name, starring Tom Cruise. For whatever reason, the movie did not mention Bonhoeffer. At the same time, neither did it mention the known involvement of Field Marshall Gen. Erwin Rommel, Germany's celebrated "Desert Fox" tank commander who had fought Gen. George Patton and Field Marshall Montgomery all over North Africa and Europe. Probing more deeply into Bonhoeffer's letters and other primary sources, Eric Metaxas (in *Bonhoeffer: Pastor, Martyr, Prophet, Spy*) has concluded that the young pastor was more engaged in courageous activism than previously thought.

In a letter written shortly before his death, Bonhoeffer, in response to a question received from a friend, wrote: "We find God in what we know, not in what we don't know." This makes the whole case in the most positive way. Tragically, Bonhoeffer was executed by his captors two weeks before American soldiers liberated his prison camp.

Macroevolution *versus* Microevolution

There is one theoretical controversy among evolutionary biologists that some have considered a fundamentally unexplainable gap, although once again caution must be our watchword. This has to do with what is termed **macroevolution,** or evolution at higher taxonomic levels than those more modest variations observed within a genus or species. Macroevolution would apply to variations creating new families, orders, classes or phyla; while **microevolution** covers all changes <u>within</u> a species and possibly a genus. The latter mutations have at times been observed both experimentally and in nature. Examples have been cited:

1. Gradual color changes in moths,
2. Variation in spots of guppies swimming over sand or over gravel,
3. Bacteria acquiring resistance to antibiotics, and
4. Fruit flies with white eyes instead of the normal red eyes.

Such evidence has mainly been obtained from species with short lives and rapid reproduction. It further substantiates the theory of evolution insofar as it produces changes within a species in a span of time short enough for a practical experiment. An accumulation of microevolutionary variations might lead to a new species. In this way, in different geographical regions, varieties of *Homo erectus* could likely evolve into *Homo neanderthalensis*, and later *Homo erectus* could branch into *Homo sapiens*. Among biologists, there is no disagreement about it. Microevolution has been thoroughly documented.

It is a different story when it comes to macroevolution, which has very rarely been observed either experimentally or actively occurring in nature. Not one example can be cited for a laboratory transformation into a new order, class, or phylum. The fossil record shows no clear transitional form that leads to a new body type (phylum), class or order. This is important because many new phyla appeared very suddenly during the Cambrian Explosion, with no evidence of any gradually evolving intermediary. (For more on this puzzling paleo-biological event, see pages 200 ff.) The fossil record has many dozens of examples of abrupt "punctuational" changes to new body plans, but only a few gradual transformations to new families.

On the one hand, some purists believe that the same kinds of variations that lead to evolution of a new species could accumulate over a long time span, until a new class or order resulted. Critics ask: where is the evidence? Where is the intermediate form leading to a conversion from earlier invertebrate animals to vertebrates? It is believed that birds evolved from small dinosaurs. One undisputed transitional form, *Archaeopteryx*, was discovered in 1861, two years after *Origin of Species* was published. It was documented and promoted vigorously by T.H. Huxley as proof of evolution. A number of birdlike features (hollow bones, wishbones, feathers, long arms) are now known to characterize raptors and other carnivores. Modern taxonomy classifies birds as a different class (*Aves*) from *Archaeopteryx*, but J.A. Gautier (1986) classifies some birds as *Coelurosauria*, lightweight, hollow-boned predators, the same suborder as *Archaeopteryx*.

The nearest thing to a major change observed in the laboratory is the experimental finding that certain flies with two wings can evolve into flies with four wings, which would clearly be of a different genus.

Perhaps the best example of a macroevolutionary transformation would be the sequence whereby dry-land ancestors of porpoises and whales returned to aquatic life. The genomes of whales are remarkably similar to various even-toed (hooved) species, such as hippos, sheep, deer, and cows. All these are of the same taxonomic order, *Artiodactyls*, which means *even-toed*. They also have similar digestive systems. They differ taxonomically at the subordinate level of families. Fossil evidence reveals a series of seven candidate intermediate *Artiodactyl* forms. The transformation began 60 million years ago (Mya) with the small pig-like forest animal, the *Indohyus*. Within a few million years, a number of clearly amphibious variants were deposited in the fossil record. Within 10 million years overall, there was a gradual and complete progression to fully submersible but air-breathing whales (50 Mya). If confirmed, this would be a clear evolution of new families at numerous stages.

There is a current thought that there might be a punctuational event in which a new taxonomic family or order arises via what is termed "whole genome duplication." This has been studied extensively for plant evolution. The origin of single-cell eukaryotes from prokaryotes would also require some type of whole genome duplication. Even so, it is hard to see how that could explain the proliferation of new body forms exclusively during the brief time of the Cambrian Explosion. A great deal of work remains.

Meanwhile, those who have developed the so-called Modern Synthesis of Darwin's Theory contend that the gradual accumulation of many micromutations over millions of years could lead to macroevolutionary change. As a best possible explanation for the disappointing scarcity of intermediate forms, they offer speculation that there may be fossil deposits that have not yet been discovered or opened by paleontologists, and that eventually they will be found. Perhaps so. Until then, there is little to support such a rationale. In fact, the fossil record is rather abundant. It includes many new soft-shale deposits with numerous examples leading to a new genus or species, as within the whale **family**, but none transitioning to a new **order** or **class**.

And Still Today

As philosophical descendants of Thomas Aquinas, most theologians today are able to reconcile the discoveries of science with the fundamental tenets of religion. As the Catholic Church wrapped up its reinvestigation into the case of Galileo in 1981, Pope John Paul II delivered an encompassing statement about the compatibility of these two domains of truth:

> *The Bible itself speaks to us of the origin of the universe and its makeup, not in order to provide us with a scientific treatise, but in order to state the correct relationships of man with God and with the universe. Sacred Scripture wishes simply to declare that the world was created by God, and in order to teach this truth it expresses itself in terms of the cosmology in use at the time of the writer. The*

Sacred Book likewise wishes to tell men that the world was not created as the seat of the gods, as was taught by other cosmogonies and cosmologies, but was rather created for the service of man and the glory of God. Any other teaching about the origin and makeup of the universe is alien to the intentions of the Bible, which does not wish to teach how heaven was made but how to go to heaven.

That final clause of the above passage is clearly respectful of Galileo's terse aphorism: "The Bible does not tell us how the heavens go, but how to go to heaven!"

A similar, contemporary commentary is found in a 2004 manifesto circulated as "The Clergy Letter." Signed by thousands of Christian priests and pastors, it proclaimed:

We the undersigned, Christian clergy from many different traditions, believe that the timeless truths of the Bible and the discoveries of modern science may comfortably coexist. We believe that the theory of evolution is a foundational scientific truth, one that has stood up to rigorous scrutiny and upon which much of human knowledge and achievement rests. To reject this truth or to treat it as "one theory among others," is to deliberately embrace scientific ignorance and transmit such ignorance to our children. We believe that among God's good gifts are human minds capable of critical thought and that the failure to fully employ this gift is a rejection of the will of our creator.

From the scientific side, the late, great evolutionary geologist Stephen Jay Gould, a self-proclaimed agnostic, devoted one of his brilliant books on cosmological origins, *Rocks of Ages*, to promotion of his own philosophical concept of Non-Overlapping Magisteria (NOMA). He believed that science and religion were separate realms of truth, neither of which had the capability for dominion over the other's sphere of inquiry and understanding. This is essentially the viewpoint of benign neutrality in "The Clergy Letter" and that of John Paul II.

A quite different, less passive approach is that taken by Francis Collins in his book, *The Language of God: Evidence for Belief.* As the former head of the NIH Human Genome Project, Collins presents a clear understanding of the complexity and function of the DNA code, to which he attaches his brilliant metaphor of divine language. Of equal importance and inspiration to the rest of us, Collins shares his personal conversion from atheism to evangelical Christianity. For this, he relied not upon scientific evidence, but upon the exemplary inspiration of C.S. Lewis, whose own autobiography described a similar path of auto-conversion. This personal disclosure led some in Congress to raise a futile objection against his nomination by President Barack Obama to become Director of the National Institutes of Health, a position he holds with distinction.

Rather than take the simpler approach of separating science and religion into different camps with a wall of separation between them (Gould's NOMA), Collins has joined a fresh tide of scientists who base their reputations and spiritual lives on the insight that science and religion are not merely compatible after all, but complementary one with the other.

First Cause

One of the tenets of Aristotle's philosophy was the concept of a **First Cause**, or Prime Mover: the "unmoved mover who moves." This is generally interpreted as a "Supreme Being" or God who causes everything without being caused by anything else. This was further developed by Thomas Aquinas as his Argument from Design. Every aspect of everything must have a cause: that which caused it to be and to have attributes of structure, position, and momentum. Science can explore the immediately preceding cause(s), or what Aristotle termed the **"effective cause"** of change, but cannot approach the question of a First Cause.

The question of a First Cause has arisen nevertheless in many scientific issues. As science grew during the nineteenth century, it was accepted that science could not ask or answer questions about ultimate causes, or about the **teleology** (i.e., purpose) of natural phenomena. We cannot avoid the subject, because too many lines of evidence and theory have pointed to intimations of a First Cause. One must be careful, however, not to attribute one's perception of purpose to science, for purpose is not subject to experimental falsification or validation.

As Hubble's "Big Bang" has become widely accepted in astronomy, there followed the question of what preceded it. What was its First Cause? Science cannot frame an experiment to answer that question. There is no evidence remaining from before that moment that could give any scientific clue about its Prime Mover. Stephen Hawking (*A Brief History of Time*, 1988) has pointed out that time moves forward and not backward, with three illustrations, here paraphrased: (a) the thermodynamic "arrow of time," **(entropy)** inexorably trending toward disorder in any closed system; (b) the psychological arrow of time, whereby we can remember the past but not the future (to which is added that we can affect the future but not the past); and (c) the cosmological arrow of time: the universe has been expanding since its beginning, and never contracting. All three point in the same direction. As for the third example, time has no meaning before $t_U = 0$, at the instant of the Big Bang. Could something ever precede $t_U = 0$? Hawking thinks not, but that conclusion may be a mathematical convenience.

Physicists and astronomers have compiled a growing list of **anthropic coincidences** (see pages 89 ff.), so finely tuned for our existence that they appear to be evidence that we did not get here by random chance or without intention. The structures of ice and of many vital organic compounds (chapters 14 and 15) pose further evidence that life could not emerge by chance. Some would add to this what they call irreducible complexity of the eye and other organs, while others look at an incredibly vast complexity of all organs and biological functions. Most theistic scientists would caution that while these revelations of nature may be viewed as evidence consistent with faith, they are not proof of the existence of God. One must be wary of getting into the trap of the "God of the Gaps" syllogism.

Circumspect Reflection

Here I must take a moment of personal circumspection. As I began my literary research for this work, I was preconditioned to "profile" all intelligent-design advocates as a bunch of religious zealots determined to foist their religious views on an unsuspecting public. After all, among the earliest instigators of this movement, many did resort to political strategies to advance their literal *Biblical* views against evolution. Their primary motivation was to counteract atheism, but their immediate impact was to bring ridicule and scorn upon themselves.

At the same time, a small but growing number of scientists have begun to assert their view that Darwin's theory is inadequate; a work-in-progress. They, too, have been vigorously denounced, to put it mildly. These are not theologians, but research biologists who began their careers as Darwinists and sort of "fell from grace." Some have become leaders of the intelligent-design movement. Others are just dissenting scientists.

I had naturally wanted to get a better understanding of the scientific "heresy" of intelligent design, so that I could be alert and forewarned against it. As I read both sides in the debate that had raged across the Internet for the last dozen years, it dawned on me that the most strident use of sharply *ad hominem* attacks against the opposition was being launched not from the ID side, but from aggressive Darwinists. Disreputable motives were attributed to dissenting scientists, as though they were nothing but a front for religious fundamentalism. It was easy to lob that volley without recourse, equating fellow biologists with those seeking to legislate the teaching of young-earth intelligent design as an alternative to evolution.

Encountering this style of rhetorical combat made me more than a little uneasy, for I had seen enough of that guilt-by-association tactic during my political days. It had been too easy to decry and disparage the position of anyone who actually took such a stealth approach advocating "equal time" for creationism. It became equally easy to use the same derogatory labels to discredit anyone who criticized any tenet of Darwin, especially in its modern, molecular version. I even encountered such bullying from an anonymous reviewer of an earlier draft of this book!

I must confess that this did give me pause. I had seen this same pattern of personal rebuke to demean one's adversaries in politics, especially in the vigorous politics of academia. Once Keynesian economics took hold as the majority view in related academic departments, suspected conservatives were too often marginalized, excluded from appointments, or denied tenure. Even in institutions that had defended "academic freedom" for alleged faculty Marxists, there did not seem to be the same tolerance of conservative thinkers and academicians. Although so many fine institutions have promoted the lofty purpose of diversity, that ideal of inclusion was extended for almost every imaginable attribute; but not so much for conservative values, speakers, and teachers. It would be my hope that, with all their devotion to inclusion of every cultural, ethnic, and social minority, our colleges and universities would be just as open to a diversity of political philosophy for the enlightenment of their students. Contemporary academia should welcome ideological diversity. Not even a dialectic Marxist would try to achieve synthesis without both thesis and antithesis.

Let Not Your Heart Be Troubled

Having said all that, I am not convinced by the arguments of intelligent design that Darwin's theory is in error and must be replaced. For one thing, they have nothing with which to replace it. As Thomas Fowler has noted in his book *The Evolution Controversy*, critics have raised some good questions, which Darwin's defenders should welcome the opportunity to answer. Isn't that exchange supposed to be good for science? For example, some have raised cogent problems with the slow evolution of the eye (see pages 217-222). This objection has stimulated sound, rational answers.

Another interesting problem the ID writers cite is the slow evolution of the whip-like flagellum that provides forward motion to certain bacteria, requiring the assembly of dozens of specific proteins before it could work. To their credit, the Darwinists have made a good show explaining how both of these examples might have evolved by descent with modification. At the same time, they would probably admit that there is a lot of room for improvement in their mechanistic explanations. Give the ID fellows some credit for raising these challenges. Darwin himself acknowledged and predicted some of them. I intend to raise some more in later chapters.

We need not fear scientists who raise questions about Darwin's theory as it presently stands, with all its compelling molecular brilliance. It is still THE organizing and unifying principle of modern biology, especially for species and genera. If there are things it cannot yet explain, don't neglect that little word "yet." Besides, the more challenges there are being raised, the more there are new directions for research to resolve them. That, after all, is part of the utility of the Scientific Method for a good theory: that it generates a great deal of productive discovery.

More recently the issue has focused on the Cambrian Explosion, that brief episode of geologic time over a half billion years ago, when so many anatomically complex organisms suddenly appeared. It has been stated that before this period the relative degree of animal complexity was limited to lots of microbes, worms, sponges, and jellyfish. Then in swift succession, some four dozen or so new taxonomic phyla appeared with unprecedented body plans, and made their mark in soft-shale deposits in what are now Utah, China, and Australia.

All of this transpired in the short geologic span of something like 10 to 15 million years, which surely seems rather abrupt for any gradual Darwinian process lacking intermediates. Thereafter, about half of them, along with the ubiquitous trilobite, became extinct in the next few hundred million years. What is yet more astonishing, since the Cambrian Explosion of new phyla, not one more new phylum has arisen on the paleontological scene during the intervening 500 million years. Did this creative process just pop and stop?

What are we to make of this? Darwin had sketched a famous *pro forma* drawing of a "Tree of Life" for the possible ancestral relationships between animals. It showed a trunk with limbs that divided into branches, which sprouted twigs. If you were to draw up a sketch representing the Cambrian Explosion, it would look more like a four-legged candelabra with a few dozen or so candles (half of them truncated). You might depict a picket fence with all four bases rising from pedestals to 535 million years ago, and half with their staves' tops haphazardly broken off before they reached today.

This brief burst of activity is not consistent with gradualistic evolution. Genomic data compel us to accept that there is kinship from one phylum to another, but that does not yet fully reveal a transformational mechanism for the *origin of phyla, classes, and orders.* In a panel discussion on "What is Life" at Arizona State University (2011), the consensus view of common descent from a single universally shared ancestor was rocked by one uncommon dissent. Corporate genomicist Craig Venter objected that at least one bacterial organism, *Mycoplasmas* (submicroscopic with no membrane), processes the protein-forming code of messenger-RNA quite differently. It is a gram-positive bacterial phylum with limited diversity. Several dozen species are infectious to mammals. Does that mean there was a second "prime ancestor" that just never got far off the ground evolution-wise? Little more has been said about that report.

What began as a politically driven movement to oppose the teaching of evolution in the public schools has now been overtaken by a lively debate among scientists whether science (or at least some aspects) can be interpreted in metaphysical terms of purpose, direction, and First Causes. Harvard astronomer Owen Gingerich has enlightened this discussion, not from the viewpoint of intelligent design but as a theistic scientist. Writing in *God's Universe*, he questions "whether random mutations can generate the incredible amount of information content required to produce even the simplest of cells, and whether even the great antiquity of the universe could make this possible." His answer:

Here science, dealing with extremely low probabilities balanced against vast numbers of opportunities is frankly on shaky turf.

In some corners, the temper of the confrontations over intelligent design has become more respectful, although Darwinists understandably remain warily on guard. Some of the more polite debates have been over philosophic differences regarding what is called "specified complexity," a feature of biological systems that is distinct from inorganic systems. An instructive pair of essays by William Dembski for the ID side versus Howard Van Till for the Darwinists has been preserved for us on the

Internet since 2003. Dembski advances arguments for cosmic teleology. Van Till counterpunches with effective images of cosmic roulette.

In one exchange, Van Till launched a clever flight of rhetoric to taunt the intelligent-design advocates. He reached back to nineteenth-century theologian William Paley's metaphor that if you found a clock in the field, you knew that it had to have been designed by someone. Van Till suggested that since the known world is defective, the Clockwork Creator must have made mistakes, and had to rewind and reset the clock. Dembski retorted by posing a different metaphor of creation being a musical instrument that works best when the Creator plays it. As you can see, these exchanges can reach into the realm of **metaphysical** semantics.

The time for Reconciliation is at hand. Thanks to the intellectual leadership of so many emerging theistic scientists, there remains no persuasive argument compelling anyone to choose between religion and science. We may choose <u>both</u>. The more I have read literary contributions by these prominent theistic scientists, the more I have accepted the realization that science has become a modern expression of Divine Revelation.

Revelation Through Science

Part Three

Chapter 11

The Age of the Earth

"The poor world is almost six thousand years old."
———Rosalind to Orlando: Shakespeare, "As You Like It" (1599)

Cruising Under Sail

Our family loves to sail. Our cruising sailboat, a 1979 Alajuela 33 (a cutter-rigged double-ender with moderately full keel) has plied most of the East Coast cruising grounds. We named her *Genesis*, as this was our originating experience voyaging into the wilderness on our own. The dinghy was named *Exodus*. Not content to stop there, we named the galley "Les Victuals," the head was "Numbers" for obvious reasons, and the engine compartment: "Diesel-Room." This memorialized the entire *Pentateuch*, albeit with inadequate creativity for *Deuteronomy*.

We enjoyed many overnight runs into the Atlantic and back, sailing up and down the coast, including a memorable Christmas cruise to the Bahamas. Homeward bound in the spring, we caught a nor'easter in the Gulf Stream. Fatigued from that storm, we resorted to the old seafaring maneuver of "heaving to," with our small jib backed to windward, a double-reefed mainsail secured to leeward, and the rudder locked away, hard to windward. In ten seconds she settle into equilibrium, gently lifting before softly settling as 10–12 foot swells slid beneath us. That reprieve allowed us the luxury of a two-watch system, with three hours sleep sandwiched between three-hour watch periods on deck. There's not much to do while hove-to, dragging that big keel sideways all night. Still, someone had to keep an eye out for steamship traffic. We couldn't rely on them seeing us in a storm-tossed sea-lane.

Our one foray at racing under sail was in the 1980 "Great Ocean Race," once around the Delmarva Peninsula, with the main rule being to keep land to starboard. Thrice becalmed among giant zombie mosquitos, we were among those contestants who did not finish in the allotted time. For that and other reasons, my zeal for "racing" expired.

In 1981, we had organized a fine group of wind sailors, Members of Congress and other U.S. Capitol employees, to form our cruising flotilla officially known as "Capitol Ships" (Gilbert and Sullivan aficionados will understand). Well, I was honored to be its founding commodore. This mighty Armada explored and laid claim to many fine anchorages on the Chesapeake Bay. Those first to arrive would set firm anchors, and later vessels would "raft up" alongside. Our favorite cruising/rafting grounds were Baltimore's Inner Harbor, St. Michaels, Oxford with its many fine Choptank River bays, Smith Island, and Solomons Island. The annual highlight was Labor Day at Crisfield, with its Crab Derby and the Skipjack races near Deal Island. Twice we attended Smith Island's annual softball game between the "Geezers" and the "Codgers," happy to be invited to operate their scoreboard.

After we moved to Raleigh, North Carolina, *Genesis* enjoyed new moorings and dockages in Manteo, Beaufort (pronounced **Bō**-fərt in North Carolina), Swan Point (near US Marine Corps Camp LeJeune) and Wrightsville Beach near Wilmington. We had easy access to the Atlantic, and also enjoyed cruising the Pamlico and Albemarle Sounds, which have ambience and cruising grounds similar to those of the Chesapeake Bay. Many excursions involved passages through the Intra-Coastal Waterway (ICW) and other canals.

Navigating the ICW required strict attention lest you drift out of the channel onto a sandbar. Like road rallies for sports cars, it also favored a sense of timing in order to minimize waiting while bridge tenders stop road traffic and clear the bridge for boats to motor through. This typically generated quite a lot of marine radio chatter, as boat captains exchanged information about anchorages and marinas ahead, swapped with those coming from the opposite direction. There were also exchanges with the bridge tenders, who had distinctive styles and attitudes. An apocryphal story was told of one occasion when an impatient sailor moving south for the winter radioed brusquely to the lady tending the bridge: "Does this bridge open on demand?" Back came her best "sweet tea" reply: "No, Captain; but it will open on <u>request</u>!"

Whale of a Tale in Hobuken

On one memorable cruise in 1982, as was our custom we motored into a cut known locally as the Hobuken Canal. Hobuken, North Carolina, is where (according to legend) "why the chicken crossed the road" was just to show the 'possum *it could be done*! ("Bu-doomp---boomp!") We stopped just before the swing bridge to top off fuel and supplies at R.E. Mayo Company, which provided net repair services for the local fishing fleet and doubled as the friendly local marina/grocery. This had become a favorite waypoint for us. On this occasion, we were surprised and curious to find a monstrous skeletal whale head standing right outside the store. Such an exhibit was totally unexpected in this isolated venue, over forty miles from the Atlantic.

Overcome by curiosity, I inquired of the store owner as to how a whale head came to be there. He politely and somewhat proudly replied that local fishermen had picked it off the bottom of the Pamlico Sound with their net, and deposited it with him until they could decide what to do with it—while having their net repaired.

Now, I knew that this area, and indeed all of "Down East" coastal North Carolina, would have been submerged under the ocean during earlier geologic periods. To demonstrate my scientific background and objectivity, I had to remark to the small group of locals gathered there: "Wow! That whale must have lived and died there millions of years ago!" Not one of the locals seemed impressed. It got real quiet. After a brief, uncomfortable pause, one of the men calmly corrected me: "No, sir," he explained, "we reckon she couldn't have been there more'n six thousand years!"

One could almost hear the ominous strains of "Duelin' Banjos" (*dantle-lank-dank-dank-dank-dank . . . dank . . . dank!*), that great bluegrass hymn, written by North Carolina's own Arthur Smith and made famous (without prior permission) in the popular motion picture "Deliverance." No, I did not stand my ground and debate the age of the earth with these fine gentlemen. I knew what I knew, part of which was that they knew what they knew, and this debate was not winnable. It was foregone . . . as was I!

At the time, you see, I was a practicing politician and this area was not a Republican stronghold by any means. There was no advantage in stirring up the opposition. If there had been one favorable vote in Hobuken, I did not want to forfeit it! Discretion, as they say, is the better part of valor. I retired to my boat valorous, bemused, and wiser.

The Age of the Earth

How old is the earth? This is a very serious question for many people. How old is the sun? How old is the universe? Some philosophers have held that the earth was infinitely old, and had always been here. Others interpreted evidence to show it had to be millions of years old. Today, the best scientific evidence places the age of the earth at 4,540,000,000 years old. That's 4.54 billion years old (4.54×10^9), within a margin of error of a few million years. The best estimate of the age of the sun is slightly greater, at 4.56 billion years. We have evidence (chapter 4) that the universe is 13.7 billion years old, and that it was all created at once, in one profound burst of energy and matter called "The Big Bang."

Equally fascinating is the history of how Biblical scholarship of a much earlier day concluded that the earth is only some 6,000 years old. What a huge discrepancy between these two conclusions! Is it a very young 6.02×10^3 years . . . or is it a very old 4.54×10^9? Here we have a fundamental conflict between the scientific evidence that confirms a very old Earth, and the Biblically based belief of "young-earth creationists." How did we get into such a mess? Who stirred this up in the first place? Is this disagreement really necessary? Is there no reasonable solution that can accommodate these disparate views? Stay with me, dear reader, for a riveting historical narrative awaits.

The King James Version

Among your collection of Holy Bibles, you are fortunate if there is an early edition of the *King James Version*, the most revered translation of the Bible in the English-speaking world. First published in 1611, it was the product of the collaboration of fifty-four of the most eminent biblical scholars in Great Britain. It has a special standing because of the high literary excellence of its soaring and memorable Elizabethan phrasing and the high standard of its scholarship. Four centuries later, with many new versions offering more modern, even "politically correct" revisions, the *King James Bible* holds an enduring place of honor.

If you have an older edition, turn to the powerful and gripping opening passage of *Genesis*. "In the beginning God created the heavens and the earth." Here, in these ten words, stands the bold and stirring claim of the origin of all that there is (chapter 2). It affirms that there was a singular moment of Creation, and that before that moment there was God. The succeeding verses then proceed to describe the emergence of sun and stars, of waters and land, and of plants and animals, culminating in the appearance of our primal human ancestors, Adam and Eve.

This is a wonderful and remarkable story. Attributed to the patriarchal Moses, and undoubtedly involving literary contributions of other venerable scribes, this account of creation stands out among several somewhat conflicting versions in the Old Testament. It asserts clearly that the earth did not always exist as such, but was created "in the beginning." Now, look more closely. See the footnote right beside the phrase "In the beginning . . ." which leads you to the median margin. Wait for it! There it is: "**BC 4004.**" Is that Scripture or footnote commentary? Does the Holy Bible tell us that the earth is 6,020 years old? Is that what the Bible says? Well, not exactly.

I have two different editions of the *King James Bible*. The older printing from 1909 by the Oxford University Press is the *Schofield Reference Bible*, edited by C.F. Schofield. It has the date "BC 4004" at *Genesis 1:1*, and lists other momentous dates for the Flood (BC 2349), the destruction of Sodom and Gomorrah (BC 1898), and BC 1689 for the death of patriarchal Joseph, and so forth. It does not show "BC 4004" or any of the other dates as any part of the original or translated <u>text</u> of *Genesis*. Those are merely seventeenth century scholarly footnotes added in the margin of the majestic *King James Version*. Could this refute science? What are we to make of it?

I also have a later version, published as the *New King James Version*. This revision was undertaken by Thomas Nelson Publishers of Nashville in 1975, and published in 1984. Nelson was the American successor to the British firm that had first published the *English Revised Version* of 1885, the *American Standard Version* (1901) and the *Revised Standard Version* (1952). This *New King James Version* has no mention of the date of creation or of any of those historic events in *Genesis*, allowing the narrative to stand on its own as written and translated.

Nevertheless, there is a strong view among many Christians who believe in the absolute inerrancy of Scripture (and its footnotes), that the Heavens and Earth were created in six calendar days in the year BC 4004. Others blur the precision to approximately 10,000 years ago. In fairness to their position, we need to pause a moment to understand how this date came to be placed in the *King James Bible*, as it was never part of any original text. Throughout the last two millennia, many scholars have tried to calculate the age of Earth and the physical universe. With each attempt, the best available evidence was used. Before the advent of spectroscopic astronomy, geology/paleontology, radiometric dating, and the like, there was not much physical evidence to work with. Therefore, for lack of other metrics, one had to rely on the narrative records such as are found in Judaic documents that were incorporated into the Holy Bible, along with ancient Sumerian and Babylonian texts. For a thorough review of this development, you are referred to Martin Anstey: "The Romance of Bible Chronology" (London, 1913), accessible on the Internet.

The trail goes far back into antiquity. There had been numerous legends and written accounts of the descendants of the first man (Adam in Jewish texts, or Alorus in Babylonian versions) and about the kings before The Deluge. These provided partial chronologies, but did not attempt to fix a date of creation. Egyptian chronologies had been compiled, as well as those of the Medes and Persians. For records of the latter empires, we are indebted to the brilliant astronomer/astrologer/geographer/mathematician named **Ptolemy**, acknowledged as the founder of the study of geography, and the author of the Ptolemaic (Geocentric) System of Astronomy (see pages 33-34).

One must be careful to differentiate the various eminences named Ptolemy, for this was the name of one entire dynasty of kings of Egypt beginning in 323 BC, following the death of Alexander the Great. This Ptolemaic line included Queen Cleopatra. Ptolemy the astronomer/etc. (AD 70–161) was not of this family, but was a Roman citizen of Greek descent from the Egyptian town of Ptolemais Hermiou on the west bank of the Nile. This Ptolemy compiled a thorough chronology of the kings of Israel. From Babylonian records of astronomical events, he fixed the date of Nebuchadnezzar's death at 562 BC, which helped later scholars to reconcile records that included this event. Ptolemy refined other estimates using references to ancient eclipses.

Two other contributors during the early third century were Theophilus of Antioch and Julius Africanus. Each developed a system of chronology allocating reasonable numbers of years between successive "begats" and kingdoms. Theophilus was the first to reckon a specific year of creation, which he fixed at 5509 BC. Africanus derived Adam's appearance to be in 5500 BC, so something of this order became ingrained in contemporary third-century thinking.

This brings us up to the fourth century and the First Council of Nicaea (325 AD), which gave us the Nicene Creed. This historic conclave was commissioned by Roman Emperor Constantine, whose conversion to his mother's Christianity heralded a new day of tolerance for long-persecuted Christians. The Council's charge was to identify and purge heretical movements, so that there could be greater consensus as to what one should believe about Jesus Christ. One of its vexing tasks was to deal with the heresy of Arius. Arianism was the anti-Trinitarian belief that Jesus was a created human being and not of the substance of God.

Among those attending this Council of Nicaea was Eusebius of Caesarea, a respected scholar and *the* church historian of his day, but also suspected of harboring Arian beliefs and tendencies. This Eusebius, Bishop of Caesarea (AD 263–339), was Constantine's biographer, and at the Emperor's direction in AD 322 had prepared and delivered fifty Bibles to the young churches in Constantinople. In so doing, Eusebius was one of a dozen or so scholars of the second through the fourth centuries who attempted to catalog the acceptable Christian texts. This eventually led to the Synod at Rome (AD 382) resolving this contentious issue of inclusion and exclusion by bringing canonical closure with twenty-seven books of the New Testament, eliminating another nineteen.

These twenty-seven were recognized by the Holy See and published in Latin as the *Vulgate Bible* (AD 384), translated by St. Jerome. This entire matter was formally reconsidered, along with many other questions of organizational and moral reform, at the Council of Trent in 1546. Finally, these twenty-seven books were canonized as the collective articles of faith to which all must conform, and opposition to which was *anathema* (i.e., ecclesiastically accursed).

Eusebius was especially innovative in constructing chronological tables of great events. He compiled genealogies of twenty-one generations from Adam's firstborn to the deportation of the Jews. This particular event was crucial, as it completed the chronological sequence to the date of the death of Nebuchadnezzar, which Ptolemy had fixed to be 562 BC.

Eusebius cautions the reader with this admonition: "no one, like some have done, should believe that he is calculating dates with full accuracy, and be deceived in that way." This disclaimer did not, however, detract from the general conclusion that the days of the earth were numbered. In today's more scientific regimen, we must respect that this was the best scholarship of his day, if not of ours. Just as Ptolemy's geocentric model of the planetary system stood the test of many challenges for almost 1,500 years until Galileo, these early computations by Ptolemy, Josephus, Theophilus, Africanus, and Eusebius met every test until the advent of modern technology.

The work of Eusebius was examined by eminent mathematicians of the Enlightenment period, such as Johannes Kepler (1615) and Isaac Newton (1707), each of whom offered useful refinements. Kepler corrected certain dates of astronomical events, and computed that the date of creation was 3992 BC. Newton filled in gaps from the Greek period, concluding that the date of creation as 4000 BC, a number that excited an outbreak of millennialist speculation. This date was also said to be the preference of Martin Luther almost two centuries earlier. It was a question of compelling interest to the greatest minds of the day.

During this latter span of time, two highly regarded theologians applied their separate interpretations to this profound question. Dr.

John Lightfoot (1642) and Archbishop James Ussher (1650) were well-acquainted with the chronological methods that placed the date of creation within the range of reasonable time spans by adding up recorded successions of families and kingdoms. Ussher was a specialist on the known history of the Persians, Greeks, and Romans, and his range of expertise covered the Old Testament, astronomy, and ancient calendars. He had collected an impressively massive library for these fields. If any scholar was adequately prepared to wrap up this debate, it was Ussher. His work was preempted in time and "precision," if not in influence, by the calculations of Dr. Lightfoot that "Man (was) created by the Trinity . . . at nine of the clock in the morning." He later added in a sermon that this event occurred at equinox in 3929 BC.

Ussher was far more thorough in his work. From the consensus of scholarly chronologies, he accepted that creation was in the near vicinity of 4000 BC. He also held the belief that Earth's time was defined by thousand-year epochs, or millennia. Since King Herod died in 4 BC in our current calendar, Jesus Christ was born no later than 4 BC. It was also believed that Solomon's Temple was completed in 1004 BC. These key milestones led Ussher to the nearest millennial year: 4004 BC.

The rest was easy. The Jewish calendar began in autumn, and the apple with which Eve was tempted would have been available in that season. So Ussher determined that the momentous first day of creation had to have been the first Sunday after the autumnal equinox, and concluded this had occurred on the evening preceding Sunday, October 23, and thus on October 22, 4004 BC. It did not trouble him that there could not be an autumnal equinox before the sun was created. One need not be distracted by trifles.

It was in 1650 that Archbishop Ussher asserted this age of the earth. After fifty years without challenge, it became sufficiently accepted that it appeared in the margin of *Lloyd's Bible*, published in 1701. Soon thereafter, it was adopted in the *King James Bible*. As the first *King James* edition was published in 1611, there was no marginal reference to 4004 BC for its first ninety years, until which time it followed the historical precedent of *Lloyd's Bible*.

Today's student should recognize that this was a product of the best formulation possible in that day, using the best available evidence. It incorporated some element of science, as in calibrating historically recorded eclipses, in order to pinpoint human events that had been "tagged" by such observations. It took a century after Ussher's projection before new fields of science began to raise doubts. The question now is whether Ussher's calculation should stand against the accumulated evidence of today's science.

[For a better account of this point, see online Stephen Jay Gould: "Fall in the House of Ussher," a clever wordplay on the short story by Edgar Allan Poe.]

Geologic Time

To some, the earth itself was showing its age. Especially in England, the clues were evident to miners digging for coal, engineers moving earth for canals and roads or setting foundations for large structures, surveyors mapping boundaries, and others who found seashells on their property far from the coast. What to make of this was not so evident.

James Hutton (1780) came to the conclusion that the peculiar form and character of some rock faces indicated that they had been thrust up from deeper underground and even from underwater. He was the first to interpret this as requiring a much greater span of time for sediment to be deposited, then buckled upward by forces he could only imagine, and ultimately to be eroded by thousands of years of the normal processes of erosion by frost and rainstorm runoff. He supposed that the action of earthquakes and volcanoes could cause the upheaval. To Hutton, the earth must have been here forever, with no beginning. Charles Lyell, William Smith, and others added important geological discoveries, as did Charles Darwin himself aboard HMS *Beagle*.

Scholars in other fields were impressed by the geologists' reasoning, and some devised elaborate experiments to deduce the age of the earth.

Earth Is Not Ageless, but Very Aged

During this same timeframe, in 1779, French naturalist Comte du Buffon devoted his studies to the rate of cooling of small, solid spheres composed of materials much like the known crust of the earth. Extrapolating to a sphere the size of the earth led him to estimate that the earth was at least 75,000 years old. Clearly, something had to give.

William Thomson, knighted **Lord Kelvin** (meaning "ship's friend") in 1866 for his vital contribution to laying the first Trans-Atlantic telegraph cable, had studied many effects of temperature, especially of gases and solids, revising the First and Second Laws of Thermodynamics. From his own measurements of the rate of cooling of large, solid metal spheres, Kelvin extrapolated his results to the size of the earth. From experiments on relatively miniature surrogate spheres, he estimated in 1862 that the age of the earth was in the range of 20 million to 40 million years.

Kelvin's research is far from the best evidence available to us today, but even then required that the earth had to be much older than some thought at the time (or even today, for that matter!). Kelvin had no knowledge of the heating effect of radioactive minerals within the earth, nor was there any understanding of the convection of heat within the earth's core outward toward its surface. This introduced a considerable error into his calculations.

In debates against "Darwin's Bulldog" T.H. Huxley, Kelvin argued that 40 million years was not nearly long enough for evolution to get very far. Huxley countered with the assertion that the earth was ageless, and had been right here forever. Both were wrong, but no one at that time could disprove either. During those debates, Kelvin conceded that the earth could be a lot older, but only if there were some unimagined internal source of energy. We now know that within subsurface rock formations radioactive decay amply provides for that heat effect quite naturally.

Three dozen years later, a new method for measuring the age of rocks was introduced (1905) by the celebrated physicist Ernest Rutherford. He demonstrated that the half-life for decay of a radioactive element was independent of its chemical form, regardless of temperature and pressure. By 1940, mass spectrometry had become the established technique for measuring more precisely the ratio of radioactive elements and their decay products in a sample. By comparing (a) the steadily declining ratio of uranium-238 to its daughter lead-206 and (b) the ratio of uranium-235 to its daughter lead-207, physicists began to close in on the age of many minerals found on or near the earth's surface. Then, in 1956, C.C. Patterson reported radiometric dating of one fragment of an asteroid that fell 50,000 years ago at Canyon Diablo Crater, Arizona. He calculated its age to be 4.55 billion years ($\pm$ 1.5%). The astronauts of the *Apollo 15* moon landing brought back several rock samples that have been subjected to radiometric dating. One of these, dubbed "The Genesis Rock," is 4.5 billion years old.

Most rocks on the earth's surface do not show such advanced age. Rocks in Greenland are 3.9 billion years old, and the oldest strata of the Grand Canyon are only 1.9 billion years old. Most show even less aging. This discrepancy is due to the remixing of mineral composition by the fluid dynamics of stratification processes and tectonic shifts. This does not refute the date of the oldest rocks, so we need not spend any more time here on this interesting subject of fluid dynamics.

In the intervening years, analysis of a growing number of meteorites has placed their ages in the 50-million-year range from 4.53 billion to 4.58 billion years. This finding has led some to speculate that this may have been the span of time from the supernova explosion that formed a solar nebula that preceded us 4.58 billion years ago until gravitation aggregated it to coalesce into the sun and planets of our solar system. The earth would have been formed during this same period of time; hence, it is believed that it is 4.54 billion years old. Does it surprise you that the sun and Earth are not nearly as old as the universe? How can that be? We'll get to that.

Where Does This Leave Us?

Understanding Earth's age has taken a long pathway, with earlier scientific methods reaching conclusions ranging from tens of millions to billions of years. Before there was scientific evidence, genealogical studies led to the conclusion that all was created some 6,000 years ago. There is no scientific evidence today that the earth is that young. Some believe that there was never any creation *per se* and that the universe has always existed, but there is no scientific evidence for that either.

From the best science, we know that the earth was formed four and a half billion years ago. One may choose to disbelieve this, as many have done. One may believe that planet Earth is 6,020 years old or 10,000 years old, but not on the basis of science.

If some of our neighbors find that their belief in God is strengthened by an insistence that the ancient Creation text of the first chapter of *Genesis* is measured in 24 hour days, I would not quarrel with their religious convictions. It is enough to say that their view on this has nothing to do with science. They simply choose to believe that God told us all He wanted us to know and to believe on this subject at the time the earliest text of the Old Testament was first written down. My view is that the Creation stories in *Genesis* were based upon the best understanding achievable at the time.

Some would protest that all of the evidence of an older earth was placed there to confuse us, misdirect us, and test our faith. Such an approach requires a belief that God does not want us to discover an improved understanding of His handiwork in nature. This has neither a biblical nor a scientific basis. It comes close to a concept of a whimsical or mischievous divine attitude. The most serious defect in taking this approach is that it gives atheists the high ground of rationality, and opens religion to ridicule.

Should we believe that a loving and all-powerful God created a world full of pranks and misinformation and, like the Wizard of Oz, intends for us to remain confused and ignorant about it, never to look behind the curtain? Or should we believe in a loving and all-powerful and trusting God who established an orderly universe, and was pleased to arrange for us to have the intelligence to figure it out?

Revelation in Our Time

Anyone who believes in God and understands science should be able to accept the best scientific evidence that this earth is four and a half billion years old, and that the universe was created nine billion years before that. Neither scientific fact should shake or confuse our faith any more than knowing that the earth revolves around the sun and not the other way around, as once was supposed. The evidence should strengthen our belief by providing a clearer understanding of how the God of the Ages, unconstrained by time, ordained the creation of the earth so long ago. For the theistic scientist, through the revelations of modern science, there should be a clearer understanding of God's actual timetable and processes for the creation of the earth and universe.

Once again, we return to the insight that science has evolved to the point of being a modern revelation of what happened, where, when and how. Science does not ask or answer _why_ anything happened; just what, where, when, and how. There is no good reason that a religious person cannot accept this fundamental value of science. There is no good reason that a religious person cannot accept that God gave us the intellectual capacity and curiosity, along with the eventual ability to develop powerful technologies for observation, and intended us to use them to unravel nature's secrets. There is no good reason for anyone to deny that God can and does speak to us today through discoveries of science, among other languages.

And there is no good reason for a devout scientist to yield to those on either side who contend that science disproves the Bible, or _vice versa_. Science does not prove or disprove religious belief in God, and does not dishonor God. Any human endeavor that reveals an understanding of God's creation cannot dishonor God or His creation. At the same time, I believe that God does not require us to dishonor science.

The theistic scientist can, with a clear conscience, thank God for the revelations of Holy Scripture and the revelations of science.

Chapter 12

Revelation Through Geology and Paleontology

So much of what we know about the age and other characteristics of the earth has come to us from the earth science of geology, aided by some special techniques of physics and chemistry. It was geologists (1780) who first raised the notion that the earth was much older than was generally believed. They observed that rock formations that had been fractured by excavations or earthquakes revealed fossil remains and imprints of creatures not otherwise known to have inhabited the earth.

The same fractured rocks showed patterns that indicated great lengths of time for sediment to be compacted, overturned, and over-deposited with new sediment. This led others to try to decipher experimentally how long it would take for Earth's crust to cool.

This set the stage for geology's bridge to Charles Darwin. Charles Lyell was a Scottish lawyer and a respected geologist. His *Principles of Geology* (1830) spread James Hutton's idea that slow geologic processes observed today are the same processes that shaped the earth's surface features in the remote past. "The present," Lyell wrote, "is the key to the past." From his reflection on the geologic evidence, Lyell pointed out that there appeared to be repetitive sequences to these disruptive cycles.

When young Charles Darwin was about to embark on his voyage aboard HMS *Beagle*, he received a copy of Lyell's first volume from its commander, Capt. Robert FitzRoy, whom Lyell had asked to look for unusual boulders and other formations during the voyage. As we have seen (chapter 7), Darwin was greatly influenced by Lyell's idea of slow, gradual geological processes as he later began formulating his own theory of slow, gradual biological processes. The immediate payback for Lyell was Darwin's rational explanation of the formation of Pacific atolls by the slowly subsiding dormant volcanoes at their core. Here was vital new evidence of uniformitarian gradualism.

Uniformitarianism

By the eighteenth century, the industrial revolution had begun to generate a vast amount of serious information that the earth was far more complex than previously imagined. Road building, canal digging, mining, and other such invasive explorations had turned up puzzling tracks and images of fossil residues that suggested a much older earth. Added to this was the clearer recognition that the subsurface was somehow formed into a sequence of rock strata with patterns that repeated those seen at other locations.

This led geologists at the "turn of the century" (1780 to 1830) to question the prevailing idea that the earth was then only 5,800 years old, very stable, and subject only to occasional catastrophic events, like Noah's Flood. This **"catastrophism"** scenario was challenged by the view that the earth's crust is constantly changing, as it adjusts slowly to internal pressures and temperatures and displacements, as well as by the gradual but steady impact of erosion; all requiring a much longer period of time. This belief was called **"uniformitarianism."**

Geologists in particular came to accept this uniformitarian, or gradualist, concept that the changes we observe today provide the best understanding of changes that took place far in the past. This was the insight of James Hutton, a prominent Scottish physician, landowner, and naturalist, well-connected within the Scottish Enlightenment, and a close friend of economic theorist and moral philosopher Adam Smith. Hutton is regarded today as "the father of modern geology."

In 1785, Hutton noted that features of some mountainside rock faces indicated that they had been thrust upward from within the earth, some even from the ocean floor. He discovered that some rock formations contained fish fossils and seashells. He found several formations that had granite inclusions, as if the granite had been molten when it penetrated the host rock. He examined a cliff having nearly vertical strata with obvious rippling, which he interpreted as having been laid down horizontally as compressed sediment on the ocean floor, and then tilted upward much later. Hutton concluded that this required numerous cycles of sedimentary deposits on the ocean floor, subsequently forced up and out of the ocean, there to be slowly eroded or folded back beneath the sea again, and then to be overlaid with fresh deposits. This required an enormously greater span of time than the conventional 6,000 years or so. Indeed, Hutton wrote, ". . . this world has neither a beginning nor an end." Eventually that supposition of an ageless earth had to yield to scientific challenge as well.

Hutton believed that ancient volcanic activity and earthquakes were the driving forces behind these repetitive cycles, and reasoned that the center of the earth must be extremely hot and molten. Hutton concluded that the forces and processes observed in his day were the same forces and processes that had caused the folding of Earth's stratified surface in the distant past. Within the ranks of religious adherents, Hutton's concept was accepted by many as being the best understanding of how God had ordained it.

Charles Lyell extended this to reason that major changes in the earth's surface are the cumulative result of numerous changes over vast intervals of time. Lyell was born in 1797, the year that James Hutton died. It was Lyell who promoted the popularity of Hutton's uniformitarianism, confronting the prevailing doctrine that all irregular land formations were the result of Noah's Flood.

Within this context, British surveyor William Smith (1790) examined sheer walls in mines and canals, finding there a predictable continuity that extended laterally over considerable distances. After recording his findings of strata with similar fossils and other features all across England, Smith published (1799) the first geologic map showing colors to represent the location of related strata. In 1815, he completed his geologic map of England, Scotland, and Wales with this same color-coding of rock strata.

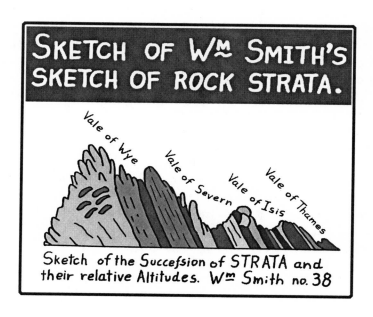

SKETCH OF Wᵐ SMITH'S SKETCH OF ROCK STRATA.

Vale of Wye
Vale of Severn
Vale of Isis
Vale of Thames

Sketch of the Succeſsion of STRATA and their relative Altitudes. Wᵐ Smith no. 38

It was Smith who first recognized that separate rock strata that contain the same assortment of fossils must be the same approximate age. Tragically for Smith, his original maps were plagiarized, and sold at lower prices. This bankrupted Smith and drove him into debtors' prison, where he languished two years with his property forfeited. In later years, a patron helped him restore his due reputation.

Radioactivity Half-Life

Eventually, methods based upon the strictly timed half-life of radioactive decay guided geologists to a precise calculation that the earth is 4.54 billion years old. The story of how we know the age of the earth is told in chapter 11, and it is a fascinating one. For the purposes of this chapter, one related discussion is appropriate. This has to do with the role of uranium. Uranium is element number 92, which means that each atom has exactly 92 protons in its nucleus. In order to provide the binding force necessary to hold 92 positively charged protons so closely together, the nucleus also contains an even larger number of neutrons. In nature, uranium ore deposits contain two isotopes, both of which are unstable, exhibiting slow radioactive decay.

The more abundant uranium-238 has 92 protons and 146 neutrons; while uranium-235 (the fissionable ingredient of nuclear reactors and atomic bombs) also has 92 protons but 143 neutrons. In natural deposits, the U-238 **isotope** makes up 99.3% of the total, with U-235 at 0.7%, and trace amounts of U-234. Each is radioactive, with a long half-life, which is the span of time for exactly half of the material to decay, unaffected by temperature or its chemical condition. For U-238, the half-life is 4.47 billion years, yet another highly fortuitous, possibly anthropic circumstance, being almost the same as the known age of the earth. Consequently, only half of its original abundance has decayed thus far.

Uranium radiation is the major factor that has heated the interior of the earth, extending the period during which its surface temperature would be suitable for warm-blooded animal life such as ours. Had U-238 had a longer half-life, it would not heat the earth's mantle enough to generate convection, and might leave the biosphere too cold. If the half-life of U-238 had been shorter, most of it by now would be depleted by decay, leaving too little heat for us. Either way, we would have missed our main chance—if this is all just about chance.

Ancient Paleontology

A great deal of exciting (and sometimes controversial) evidence of prehistoric life has been obtained by paleontological studies of fossils. We regard Georges Cuvier as the founder of modern paleontology. That will be reviewed in a moment. We should not be surprised, however, that fossils were being uncovered, treasured, and even revered by ancient Egyptians, Greeks, and Romans three thousand years ago. They inspired a great deal of mythology.

Adrienne Mayor has written *The First Fossil Hunters*, an absorbing account of fossil discoveries and collections during these early civilizations, and how they were interpreted at the time. Fossil bones of elephants or mastodons were mistaken for relics of colossal mythical heroes, such as Ajax, Pelops, Orestes, Orion, and Achilles; as well as legendary Titans and other hostile giants. Greek victory in the Trojan Wars came only after the bone believed to be the shoulder blade of Pelops was brought to Troy, as foretold by a captured Trojan seer.

The Scythian legend of the fabulous winged griffin appears to have been based upon fossil remains of the extinct dinosaur *protoceratops*. Even the Homeric figure of the gigantic one-eyed Cyclops had its likely origins when sailors exploring caves among uninhabited islands found huge skulls of endemic dwarf elephants with oversized nasal openings. Myths about centaurs, Amazons, multi-headed Cerberus, and Chinese dragons arose from similar misinterpretations of fossil discoveries.

Caricature of Mythical Cyclops and Dwarf Elephant Skull

Modern paleontology has come a long way! As seen in earlier chapters, its practitioners have discovered fossil evidence of the earliest organisms to inhabit the earth, and determined their chronology. A number of candidate fossils have been catalogued that are now believed to be the "Missing Links" between the first mammalian species and us humans (chapter 8). We can now turn to their single most astonishing discovery, the implications from which made even Charles Darwin pause.

Cambrian Explosion and Aftershock

Cambrian Explosion refers to a relatively brief geologic time period from 542 million years ago (542 Mya) to 525 Mya, during which most animal phyla, at least four dozen (some estimate twice that number), first made their concurrent appearance on Earth when it was 7/8ths its present age. Whole **body plans** (phyla) arose for the first time. Can you guess how many new body plans have emerged since that time? The correct answer is: <u>none</u> . . . zero: not one new phylum in the last half billion years.

That brief flash of geologic time is another of those profound singularities of natural history. Some Darwinian purists contend that there could have been more body plans formed earlier, undetectable because they were simply too soft and small to be fossilized. There are, however, rich deposits in China that have preserved very small, soft fossils, including sponges in various stages of cell division, but no new body types.

To put this in perspective, after the earth was formed 4.5 billion years ago, it took the first billion years to cool down enough to accumulate and hold onto an atmosphere and bodies of water conducive to the ingredients of life. The oldest fossil evidence of simple single-cell bacteria and blue-green algae is from that time (3.5 Bya). This was long before cells developed a nucleus. For the next two billion years, that was about it: bacteria continued to proliferate unchallenged. At about 1.4 Bya, unicellular protozoa (amoebae and paramecia) appeared with the first cell nuclei containing DNA.

Meanwhile, the mantle of the earth was still churning a bit from thermal convection and the shifting and crunching of tectonic plates. During that fracturing of early continents, roughly 1.8 Bya, a rare, easily eroded type of granite was exposed to the weathering forces. It began to release into the oceans various metallic elements that are necessary components of certain metal-binding proteins believed to be associated with evolution of multi-cellular organisms. John Parnell and his group at the University of Aberdeen in Scotland have found (2012) that these atypical granite sources were rich in copper, molybdenum, and zinc, and had first begun to pierce Earth's surface 1.8-1.3 Bya, which covers the period when multi-cellular life evolved.

Everything settled down a bit geophysically at one billion years ago, when the multitude of land masses formed into one singular supercontinent called **Rodinia**, balancing astride the equator. Four hundred million years later, another drastic change commenced. That massive supercontinent began to fracture into eight continents, roughly foreshadowing what we have today, but all covered by glacial ice extending to near the equator. It was not a very friendly place for life unless you were a bacterium or protozoan. You might like to search the Internet about this "**Snowball Earth!**"

Then, according to the fossil evidence from 600 million years ago, at the end of the Pre-Cambrian Era, Earth began to show some serious signs of life. Glaciers were in retreat and new lifeforms gradually began to flourish across the planet, but mostly in what we would consider rudimentary forms, like sponges, jellyfish, segmented worms, and soft-bodied precursors of arthropods. It is remarkable that the early progress in origins of life can be traced from these ancient fossil deposits, yet it was limited to very few animal phyla. Here is what is known about five body plans believed to have emerged immediately before the Cambrian Explosion:

- **Cnidaria** (the initial C is silent!) may have been the earliest animal with multiple organs, but notably lacking respiratory, digestive, and nervous systems. Cnidarian fossils include jellyfish imprints that have been found on soft shale from 700 Mya. Some argue whether they were free-swimming or attached. This phylum branched into anemones and corals during the span of the Cambrian Explosion.
- **Porifera** lack digestive, circulatory, and nervous systems. Except for brief periods of migratory motion, they are attached to sea bottoms. In this Late Pre-Cambrian Period, they were represented solely by sponges, found in soft-shale deposits from as early as 580 Mya in South China.
- **Annelids** had simpler body plans, featuring tubular structures with little or no appendages. You will recognize this in today's varieties of segmented round worms and leeches. The oldest undisputed annelid fossil is from 518 Mya, but there are much

earlier indications from wormlike tracks in the mud. An older, pre-Cambrian fossil reported to be annelid is believed by some to be an arthropod.

Two other phyla might have antecedents in the Late Pre-Cambrian:

- **Brachiopods** are marine animals with symmetrical seashells, each half shell being the mirror image of the other. While some fossils may have predated the Cambrian period, they were abundant during and afterwards. Brachiopods did quite well until they were decimated in the Permian mass extinction 251 Mya that terminated 90% of all living species. Only a few hundred live species remain.
- **Arthropods** were the most complex and diversified creatures of that geologic period, mainly varieties of trilobites. Arthropods were dominant then, and make up 4/5ths of all species today. This is truly a remarkably prodigious clan. "Arthropods" means "jointed feet or limbs," anatomical traits that define a great variety of invertebrate species, genera, families, classes, and orders. Pre-Cambrian arthropods were limited to soft-shell types. Most now have protective exo-skeletons (shells), and all have segmented bodies. Among the more familiar types today are:
  - Ants
  - Flies
  - Spiders
  - Scorpions
  - Beetles
  - Butterflies
  - Crabs
  - Cockroaches

[Aside: When geneticist J.B.S. Haldane was asked what biology can tell us about God, he offered a memorable response: "God has an inordinate fondness for beetles!" With some 400 thousand species of beetles, that's over half of the 750,000 arthropod species and about a third of **all** catalogued species, plant and animal.]

Then, after 70 million years of slow changes producing new species among a few early phyla, all of a sudden things began to erupt with the emergence of dozens of new body plans, most having unprecedented complexity. Many of these new phyla soon became extinct. Roughly three dozen animal phyla remain. Phyla that were soft and immobile, or generated a low diversity of species, were especially vulnerable to extinction. Those that survived had the advantage of favorable traits and facile speciation.

It is amazing enough that this sudden eruption of new phyla occurred as the Cambrian Era opened. Compared to that, it is astounding that no new phyla have ever appeared since then. Whatever explanation one might offer to explain the surge of new body plans, its true test will be to account for the more abrupt halt. If the rush of new phyla was in response to cooperative tendencies that cells had developed as jellyfish and sponges, which seems reasonable, why did the magic cease after a few million years?

It has been noted that the emergence of rudimentary plants about 1 Bya would inject the seas with the oxygen required for animal respiration to work. That would be a necessary precursor for animal origination during the early Cambrian Period almost a half billion years after plants, but would not account for the lack of any new phyla since then. Somewhat contrary to the timeline of this premise, an international effort led by Donald Canfield at the University of Southern Denmark has reported oxygen weathering of rocks a billion years before plant photosynthesis, which leads them to conclude that sufficient oxygen was not the only "trigger" condition for higher animal forms. Quentin Crowley's group at Trinity College Dublin has found similar geologic evidence of oxygen atmospheres 3.0 Bya, from as yet unknown sources.

**Few Body Forms Appeared Before the Cambrian Explosion
Not One New Phylum Since Then**

Guy Narbonne at Queen's University in Kingston, Canada has fossil evidence (2014) that the proliferation of new body forms was hastened dynamically by the emergence of evolution's first predators, triggered perhaps by a brief spike of oxygen. Aggressive, new phyla, such as worms with teeth, could swiftly eradicate those that lacked facile mobility. Rachel Wood of the University of Edinburgh has studied one fossil, *Cloudina*, that may have been the first animal to grow a hard crown, and to cluster in tight groups like the shields of Roman legions. Survival suddenly took on a new meaning, requiring the adaptation of speed or defensive crusts. Any novel advances in evasion or hard exoskeletons were in turn met by superior predatory traits of agility and/ or powerful teeth and grappling extremities in a desperate evolutionary race. Natural selection can explain the winners; but what accounts for the hasty escalation of unprecedented body forms if not predation?

How, then, do we account for the post-Cambrian moratorium on new phyla? Could it be the same evolution of so many predators? It would certainly menace a fledgling phylum to have so many threats feasting on its progeny before it could establish a sufficiently wide base of dozens of families and hundreds of species.

Craniata

Let's turn now to the first known species of the Chordate phylum to which we belong. This small, presumed antecedent of ours, *Haikouella lanceolata*, has been found in great abundance in Chinese shale deposits from the latter part of the early Cambrian period (525 Mya). That was the main geologic period during which the number of phyla decreased, indicating that it was still a dangerous time to appear on the scene, increasing the probability of extinction.

Haikouella was **craniate**, meaning that it had evolved a blunt head with an incipient brain. What it lacked was vertebra and an endoskeleton. This means that the head and a spinal nerve cord evolved before the backbone, the reverse order from some Darwinists' expectations. The development of mineralized spinal structure evolved 30 million years later. Incidentally, this little fellow clearly had teeth, albeit for grinding, not biting. Even so, it was a nice advantage.

There are conflicting hypotheses for the evolution of intelligence and cognition: (a) that it is highly internally controlled for inevitable emergence, versus (b) that it is highly externally contingent and therefore very rare in the universe. Is human cognition (a) inevitable, or (b) a fluke? Advocates on each side contend that *Haikouella* supports their view. Strict Darwinists favor (a) slow, gradualistic processes based on random variation, and would expect the earliest chordates to have more muscle development and not much cranial capacity until much later in the lineage. Others expected the first chordates to be headless and pointed at both ends, like the *amphioxus*, which came along millions of years later. Fred Heeren gives a good account of this in an article in *Evolution and Cognition* (2003): "Was the First Craniate on the Road to Cognition?"

There is as yet no indication as to what the immediate pre-Cambrian predecessor of *Haikouella* might have been. Its sudden appearance supports the theory of **saltation**, Stephen Jay Gould's idea that macroevolution occurred in sudden spurts of activity. Darwin, however, proposed that new taxonomic groups would gradually and steadily evolve over long time spans, diagrammed like a tree with ever proliferating limbs, branches, and twigs. The Cambrian Explosion clearly indicates that the great majority of body plans burst onto the scene at about the same brief geologic time. Thereafter, new classes, orders, and families emerged, filling out the picture. As noted previously, the appropriate evolutionary diagram would look less like a tree and more like a picket fence, with a few staves broken off (or perhaps a truncated candelabrum).

As one consequence of this defining moment in the fossil record, as Ukrainian geneticist Theodosius Dobzhansky (a Russian Orthodox Christian) has pointed out, the number of phyla, classes, and orders are fewer today than 500 Mya, but the number of species has expanded to ten times greater than then. Apparently, any new phylum was highly favored if it could generate a rapid proliferation of variant species, giving it more paths to adapt and survive. If subsequent microevolution is not agile and facile, macroevolution's immediate lineage could be doomed to failure.

Bottoms-Up!

To a large degree, the Cambrian anomaly highlights a theoretical dispute between "bottom-up" Darwinists versus developmentalists who favor a "top-down" theory of evolution. The bottom-up theory of evolution follows an extremely slow but steady variation from one species to another and then another, with more and more differences accumulating until one group separates as a new *genus*, comprising a collection of species that exhibit certain features that are distinctly different from the species of all other genera. This process continues imperceptibly slowly until there is such a wide variation of traits within a genus that there evolve two or more groups of taxonomic families. This gradual diversification grinds forward until there are sufficient distinctions of structure that we can classify orders, later followed by classes of organisms. Finally, after many hundreds of millions of years or so, these classes will have evolved into major new body types, which we call phyla. Charted over a vast expanse of time, we would expect to see evolving:

Species à Genus à Family à Order à Class à Phylum.

That's bottom-up! As Thomas Fowler has pointed out for Darwinian bottom-up theory, diversity of species precedes disparity of body forms (phyla).

The top-down evolution alternative would have as its first step the emergence of each body type (phylum), which then diversifies into enough different major traits that can be classified taxonomically as classes, each of which then diversifies into orders, and so forth. According to Fowler, the top-down process then would expect:

Phylum à Classes à Orders à Families à Genera à Species.

Chen Jun-Yuan, the Chinese paleontologist (Nanjing University) who discovered little *Haikouella* and the oldest jellyfish fossils, is among the top-down group. He interprets the fossil record to mean that something other than random accidents is driving life. This contradicts the bottom-up corollary to the Principle of Mediocrity, which is the idea that there's nothing special about us, our planet, our sun, or even our galaxy. If we simply exemplify the ordinary norm, whatever led to our species will lead other planets to evolve intelligent species whenever the temperature and size are just right. That mediocrity principle is now being challenged vigorously.

Chen contends there was no gradual build out of more and more varied anatomies, but a sudden unprecedented and unrepeated burst of new body forms. All evolution could do after that was vital and diversifying, but marginal in comparison. It is hard to ignore the implication that the Cambrian Explosion was yet another anthropic cosmic success story. It is not likely to be easily replicated on another planet any more than it was here. Without the appearance and survival of craniated *Haikouella*, there is little likelihood that any cognitive intelligence could ever have evolved. That does not follow from any Mediocrity Principle. To the contrary, it is rather exceptional.

There are few theories of importance that are more solidly established than evolution. That does not exempt it from vigorous scientific probing or attempts to revise or disprove some part of it, for that is the nature of science. "Top-down" evolution means that the outcome is driven by something other than Malthusian competition. Evolution theory itself may be evolving. Chen Jun-Yuan has offered us an interesting perspective:

"In America you can criticize the government, but not Darwin; in China we can criticize Darwin, but not the government."

Touché! In America, there is political correctness; in China, there is political correction. Chen argues that Darwin's theory needs to be revised to account for the sudden emergence of so many new phyla, some short-lived, during the Cambrian Explosion, 540 Mya. This is not a theological debate, but a purely scientific one. Some zealots worry that the anti-Darwin forces will use this as a sign of confusion within science. No, it is just a healthy rumble among friends and colleagues!

There is ample evidence for each direction, which pits thesis against antithesis. Perhaps there is a combination of both. One synthesis might start with a burgeoning of bottom-up diversification of species from the few most ancient organisms. This would progress as the first single cell species evolved into other unicellular species until something disrupted this pattern, causing rudimentary multicellular forms to appear. The Cambrian Explosion was the sudden eruption of dozens of new phyla, almost all at once. Then each of these diversified into classes, orders, families and so on, eventually into multitudes of species. If not proficient at speciation, a phylum might collapse in extinction through attrition.

Whether this or any other imaginary sequence can satisfy the intellectual need for an orderly process, it is a difficult challenge to explain the burgeoning of new phyla during the brief span of the Cambrian Explosion. Chen wonders how we could ever get here by classical or neo-Darwinian principles. There is no evidence of any accumulation of families into orders, orders into classes, all leading up to the sudden swarm of new phyla with unprecedented body forms. Would this happen by chance? After all, the most successful organisms at handling natural selection have always been bacteria. More complex life seems less capable of adaptation.

New Zealand's Michael Denton feels that the body plans of new phyla that first appeared at the beginning of the Cambrian Explosion were somehow built into the earlier cells since the beginning of life. He and his team are working on the complex folding patterns of proteins (chapter 15). All proteins are made from different combinations of the same 22 amino acids. It turns out they are not randomly folded willy-nilly, but exhibit a few discrete three-dimensional patterns. It is as if there were folding laws that regulated the shape of proteins. Instead of unlimited ways of folding in all random directions, there are but a few precise ways as defined by certain families of configurations. He sees these folding patterns being determined by a physical law, not by natural selection. This is important research, and may well be leading us to more anthropic evidence.

The Giant Step: Out of the Water

As evolution has become more widely accepted, along with its implications of universal connectivity of all living organisms through common ancestry, it has led us to interesting and unavoidable conjecture. For example, there has been speculation as to how the first land vertebrate might have emerged from its former aquatic habitat. Was that first transition at some deep ocean's shore, or was it from a stagnant, oxygen-depleted, fresh-water swamp? Arthropods had successfully crawled out 100 million years earlier, but what about the first vertebrates? Mammals more likely would evolve from land-based vertebrates, not from beetles or insects.

There are known examples of fish that can waddle on their fins on the lake bottom, and a few that can even crawl up out of the lake for a brief time. They must return soon in order for their gills to function properly. One Asian species, the Walking Catfish, can crawl on its long pectoral fins for great distances, and has adapted an auxiliary breathing function for extracting oxygen from air. Amphibians such as frogs and salamanders begin life underwater as tadpoles before adulthood launches them onto land. These creatures have piqued our imaginations as to how animal life emerged from the depths.

Adding intrigue, a team led by Neil Shubin has reported (2004) a fascinating discovery, described in his book *Your Inner Fish*. Shubin at the University of Chicago, Edward Daeschler of Drexel Institute, and Farish Jenkins Jr. of Harvard University have uncovered a grouping of fossil remains of an ancient fish, which they named *Tiktaalik roseae*. The taxonomic name for its <u>genus</u> honors the Canadian Arctic region of its excavation, and that of its <u>species</u> salutes their anonymous benefactress. This remarkable fish had evolved its pectoral fins into appendages with elbow joints and the intricate bones of wrists and rudimentary "hands." It also had a neck and a flattened head with predatory sharp teeth. All of this might conjure up the features of an alligator, except for its tail and gills.

Could this fill one very special "missing link" at the strategically vital interface for survival fitness both in water and on land? Its 375-million-year "age" is right in between previously characterized fossil fish and four-legged tetrapods of the Devonian Period. Shubin coined the term "fishapod" for this innovation: a tetrapod that swims and depends upon gills for oxygen extraction from water.

Future finds of similar fossils may show other transitional features, but this one is enough to give us pause. For one thing, the development of its pelvic region supports the idea that the shift to mobile aft appendages began in fish like *Tiktaalik*, contradicting the prevailing theory that a "four-wheel-drive" among vertebrates arose only as a means of locomotion on land. The pelvic component was among the team's original specimens, but was not recognized until they completed the painstaking reduction of one large slab, as reported by this team in 2014. The Shubin group has filmed evidence that the contemporary African lungfish has similar pelvic development, which it uses to "walk" when submerged down on the lake bottom.

Oldest Fossils

One major trail of paleontological research has been to pin down the oldest fossil, for this would place a milestone in the vicinity of the earliest **abiogenesis** of life from non-life. It would mark the timeframe when Earth had cooled enough for life to arise and survive. One group led by David Wacey (University of Western Australia) and Martin Brasier (Oxford University) appears to have hit the "pay dirt" digging around an ancient beach in Australia. Samples taken from 3.4-billion-year-old sedimentary rock have been found to contain clusters of single-cell organisms. These samples are claimed to meet the standards that had been expected for meeting the definition of "life," to wit:

1. Each is a single-cell organism with cell walls, and similar in size to the others.
2. These individual cells are found grouped in clusters.
3. There is evidence of cellular metabolism.

The last indicator is particularly interesting. The timeframe of 3.4 Bya is well before continents formed, at a time when there were only small volcanic islands. This was long before the appearance of plants with a capability through photosynthesis to replace atmospheric carbon dioxide with oxygen. These cells could not metabolize oxygen, and had to get their energy from sulfur and its compounds from deep oceanic thermal vents.

Abundance of Species

Have you ever wondered just how many species of organisms there are out there, competing with us and each other for habitat and survival? No? Well, as you might suspect, there are quite a lot of different kinds of animals, and maybe not so many species of plants. Estimates vary by several orders of magnitude. The best guess so far comes from a taxonomic partnership from the University of Hawaii and Dalhousie University in Canada. Their total calculated number is 8,700,000 (±1 million). That is not particularly precise, but for starters does give us at least a rough order of magnitude.

Not counting microbes and viruses (*Prokaryota*, having no cell nucleus), the most complex **domain** of living organisms is called *Eukaryota*, from the Greek for "good nut." This domain is defined by having a cellular membrane enclosing a cellular nucleus and other structures. Hence the name. It includes all animals, plants, and fungi.

Lest we mistake this for the dominant domain of lifeforms, it must be recognized that microbe cells are vastly more abundant in nature than cells of *Eukaryotes*. *Prokaryotes* make up half of the entire biomass of the planet. Even within your human body, the number of prokaryotic bacterial cells far outnumbers the count of your own human cells by a factor of ten by early estimates. That may be a bit exaggerated, as a collaboration by the Weizmann Institute of Rehovoth, Israel, and the Hospital for Sick Children in Toronto, Canada, have issued a preliminary note that a tighter ratio is more like 1.3 to 1. They say it is 40 trillion bacteria and 30 trillion human cells, not counting viruses. Either way, multi-trillions inhabit the gut, to assist digestion. How lucky is that?

Until recently, all organisms lacking a cellular nucleus, i.e., those that were not *eukaryotic*, could be lumped together as *prokaryotic*. That simplification has begun to fall apart. *Bacteria* and *Archaea*, both of which lack a cellular nucleus, are now considered to be two separate domains of *Prokaryota*. *Archaea* have only recently been designated a new, third domain. Its organisms were formerly classified as bacteria, but have distinct features, and are typically found in extreme environments, such as volcanic thermal vents on the ocean floor and acid drainage from mines. They are not yet easy to classify as to species. The authors estimate that as much as 86% of the potential *Eukaryotic* species have yet to be discovered, and that it would take 480 more years to complete the catalogue.

Table #12-A. Abundance of *Eukaryotic* Species among Five Kingdoms

Kingdom	Predicted Species	Catalogued Species	Fraction Known	Missing
Animals	7,770,000	953,000	12%	88%
Plants	298,000	216,000	72%	28%
Fungi	611,000	43,000	7%	93%
Protozoa	36,000	8,000	22%	78%
Chromista (a)	27,500	13,000	47%	53%
TOTAL	8,742,500	1,233,000	14%	86%

Table #12-B. Abundance of Species in *Prokaryotic* Domains

Domain	Predicted Species	Catalogued Species	Fraction Known	Missing
Archaea	455	502	**110%**	-
Bacteria	9,700	10,300	**106%**	-

Within the Domain of *Eukaryota*, the most numerous species are in the animal kingdom. The preceding table from the Hawaii/Dalhousie data shows their present estimates of the number of species predicted for each kingdom, compared with the number known and catalogued. Protozoa are single-cell organisms with animal-like behavior, such as mobility, while *Chromista* are brown algae, diatoms, and water molds. These same authors later returned to add comparable data on the *Prokaryotic* Domains. Judging from the *Prokaryotic* fractions identified, perhaps their predictive algorithm is overdue for a refresher.

One of their concerns on this frontier is that something like one-third of this number of species may be near extinction, and most could disappear before they can be observed and catalogued—before we even know they are here. Does that imply that we do not know the full extent of our own life-support system and could be in danger of losing vital elements of it before we even know it's there? Laws have been enacted in hopes of preserving endangered species from extinction at our hands. How can they now be implemented to protect unknown species? Or should they?

History of Extinction

More species (by a factor of 100) have already become <u>extinct</u> than currently <u>exist</u>. Extinction, after all, is a normal process whereby the formerly "fittest" become "unfit" and die off, while alternative species survive. If evolution works that way to weed out the less than fittest, can we expect to do much about it? Will the next mass extinction come from global warming—or the next Ice Age—or another asteroid? Or is "survival of the fittest" continuously cleaning out the gene pool?

At least nine mass extinctions have been recorded, with five major events. The first major extinction came at the end of the Ordovician period 434 Mya, followed by another at the end of the Devonian period 374 Mya. In each instance, more than half of all genera were eliminated, and reef production halted for a million years. The end of the Permian period 251 Mya was marked by the most extensive extinction event Earth has ever experienced. During its compact span of 200,000 years, a convulsion of volcanic activity acidified the oceans and consumed much of the atmospheric oxygen, resulting in 96% of marine life and 70% of land-based forms became extinct. Coral reef building ceased for 10 million years.

The fourth mass extinction fell at the end of the Triassic period 201 Mya, terminating half of all ocean-dwelling invertebrates and three-fourths of land-based quadrupeds. According to Paul Olsen at Columbia University, this resulted from another massive volcanic eruption that split apart the gigantic ***Pangaea*** continent that had girdled Earth since the early Cambrian period, creating the Atlantic Ocean. Small dinosaurs were just beginning to gain a toehold, and this late Triassic eruption acidified the waters and quickly eliminated the giant crocodiles and squid that dominated land and sea. No longer held in check by rival predators, dinosaurs took over and began their reign of terror.

Dinosaurs Never Dined on Humans (or *Vice Versa*)

The fifth mass extinction event ended the dominance of dinosaurs. These terrifying predators and their herbivorous relatives first appeared 225 million years ago late in the Triassic Period. After 160 million years marauding on every continent, they quite suddenly disappeared from the subsequent fossil record at the end of the Cretaceous Period. It was lights out for them 65 Mya when a giant asteroid some six miles in diameter fell near today's village of Chicxulub in the Yucatan Peninsula of Mexico.

The resulting chain reaction of numerous massive volcanic eruptions, earthquakes, and tsunami waves obliterated much of the habitable surface, and kicked up a cloud of dust that blocked out the sun for centuries. Growing seasons for vegetation were so diminished that all species of dinosaurs and many other animals became extinct from starvation. But for this transformational climate change, vulnerable mammals would still be small and hiding in the tops of trees. Natural Selection would not have selected for our ancestors, and we wouldn't be here. Instead they survived. This has earmarks of yet another anthropic advantage of good timing.

There has been speculation that the Chicxulub asteroid may have been followed elsewhere by one or more additional large meteorites. The first would have stunned the flora and fauna of the world, and the second and third would have finished off most of them. Such a devastating combination would have left a second or third layer of debris on the ocean floor. However, an array of recent core samples is consistent with only a single profoundly catastrophic event. More likely contributors to an unstable climate were the cyclical swings of average temperature by 20° C every 10,000 years or so. Evidence for this effect has turned up in deep-drilled cores in the Song Liao Basin of northeastern China. Such a severe climate shock would have endangered dinosaurs and other species well before the Chicxulub asteroid delivered the knock-out blow.

Nevertheless, if you want to see life-size figures depicting humans frolicking impossibly with these monsters, you can visit the **Creation Museum** in Petersburg, Kentucky, near Cincinnati. There you will see some amazing and memorable fantasies of dinosaurs peaceably coexisting with humans. Your children may ride a model of a triceratops. It won't gore or bore them. There was a similar museum near San Diego, California, but it closed. Another attraction is the **Creation Evidence Museum** at Glen Rose, Texas. Here you can look at what are said to be footprints and handprints in Cretaceous Rock, and one of a human sandal stomping a couple of trilobites. All of this "evidence" has been discredited, but that doesn't mean you can't have a nice melodramatic holiday excursion.

Never to be outdone in the competition for tourists, New York City has constructed a scale model of the largest known fossil snake: *Titanoboa cerejonensis*, a giant constrictor that lived in Colombia 60 Mya (shortly after the extinction of dinosaurs). This robust robotic monstrosity with its breathtaking (get it?) hydraulic movements is based on fossil fragments indicating that it grew to 50 feet long and 3 feet in diameter, and weighed a ton. This attraction is not displayed writhing about with humanoids, but you might be able to pet it, if you dare! Other digs around that same Colombian open-pit coal mine have also turned up giant fossils of fresh-water turtles over six feet long and several monstrous crocodiles. Their colossal fights for survival must have been truly earth-shaking!

The Next Major Extinction

Biologist Stuart Pimm of Duke University believes that we are on the verge of creating the sixth major extinction, this time due to disruptive behavior of humans. If so, this would be the first mass extinction attributable solely to one species. Pimm and Clinton Jenkins of the Institute for Ecological Research in Brazil have studied the rate of extinctions per million species. They estimate the current annual rate at over 100 per million species, while just before humans appeared the extinction rate was less than 1 per million. It can reasonably be presumed that our unique proclivities for excessive hunting and fishing, clearing land for farms and cities and highways, and burning fossil fuels for electricity generation would certainly impact the viable habitat for many species.

If no other factors can be identified, it leads to their conclusion that we humans have increased extinction events by almost a thousand-fold. A more recent study by Gerardo Ceballos, Paul Ehrlich, and colleagues (*ScienceAdvances*, June, 2015) estimates the rate more conservatively at a hundred times the background rate for vertebrates. Either way, it certainly warrants some attention to how we might place limitations on the advance of our civilization. Should we restrict economic development in undeveloped countries—or just eliminate all economic advantages in developed countries? Should we shut down electricity generating capacity everywhere—or only in advanced economies, or restrict it in poorer regions? Should personal use of carbonaceous fuel be rationed? These geopolitical questions may be impossible to resolve in a pluralistic world.

Are these fears overstated? Would 100 extinctions per million species per year produce the equivalent of another major mass extinction like the previous five? If that rate continued uninterrupted for a hundred years, the combined extinctions would be ten thousand per million, which is a whopping one percent—but not close to the 50–85% effects of past major extinctions. Still, if unabated for ten thousand years . . .?

If there's good news, it is that we may still have time.

The bad news? We may not.

Chronology of Life

In summary, there is quite a lot that we know about the main line sequence of our common ancestry. We have evidence of unicellular life beginning 3.5 Bya. There followed a slow, rarely eventful descent with variation accumulating more microbial forms until 2.1 Bya, when the first unicells acquired a nucleus. This was a major breakthrough, followed in time by another: the novelty of sexual reproduction. For the first time, the necessity for mixing genes from two parents became an opportunity for diversifying at a much higher velocity than ever before. A few multi-cellular organisms from 1.6 Bya were still simple, and introduced little other innovation. A billion years later, the action accelerated with five major examples of complex organisms (jellyfish, sponges, worms, seashells, and most dynamic of all, trilobites) with specialized body parts. Somehow, this array triggered a breakout of dozens of new and vastly different body forms, one of which (*Haikouella*) may have been our first chordate example.

It took a few hundred million years for the brutal Jurassic competition, which Tennyson characterized as "nature, red in tooth and claw," to run its course. Sometimes it was "dog eat dog." Sometimes it was the other way around. Eventually this was quelled by the Chicxulub asteroid. A few shrew-like mammals survived the terror by staying above the fray, including the first ancestral placental mammal. By 47 Mya, there appeared the first primate ("Ida," page 128), from which descended a series of genera, gradually adapting a bipedal gait. One such genus suffered a genetic defect in its jaw muscle, which allowed an unprecedented expansion of cranial capacity and brain function. And here we are.

Keep in mind that a lot more is known about the "Descent of Man" from Lucy (*Australopithecus afarensis*, see pages 140-148) to humans (*Homo sapiens*) than we can even guess about the first primordial abiogenesis, or what triggered the Cambrian Explosion—or halted it.

You may want to study in greater depth the fossil record that has been highlighted here. One useful chronology was published by Timothy Ferris in his thoughtful *Coming of Age in the Milky Way*, which includes fascinating entries from anthropology discoveries of *Homo sapiens* communities of the last 15 thousand years. You can search several other, extensive lists on the Internet. You will find that there remain today a number of significant gaps, which Darwin himself called "missing links," . . . but not nearly as many as there were just five decades ago.

Chapter 13

Revelation Through Biology

For most of the last 155 years, the overriding dispute between those who uphold a literal interpretation of the Bible, and scientists who follow a deductive method for interpreting nature has involved the fundamental biological principle of evolution. Ever since Huxley and others asserted Darwin's random variation and natural selection as needing no divine intervention, evolution has become the prime target for fundamentalist Christians in America. Independent of that controversy, and perhaps eclipsed by it, there has emerged a range of objections raised by scientists, based solely upon scientific criteria. At times the two critiques have merged, but they arise from distinctly different arguments.

This chapter is devoted to the scientific issues and what they contribute to the theological side. As disclaimed earlier, a comprehensive survey of biology would require an entire volume. Here we will examine a few topics that bear upon the issues in dispute. Let's begin with two fascinating controversies before we look at fundamentals.

Seeing Eye to Eye (Irreducible Complexity)

Evolution's critics often and vigorously have cited the eye as an organ that could not be produced by natural selection. They raise the critical problem of having it evolve through a series of steps, the earliest of which would afford no advantage for survival. There was nothing irrational about the argument, for Darwin himself had recognized what a problematic stretch this was for his theory. Even so, he was confident that eventually fossil and live animal specimens would provide a resolution of this problem.

On the face of it, the complex structure of the eye would seem to be a logical weakness of evolution. What possible advantage could there be for a species to have a partial eyeball with no retina at the back to sort out the light patterns? How could an organism benefit from a lens and optic nerve, while lacking light-sensitive tissue? How can dozens of different eye types arise from a common ancestor?

This is called the problem of **irreducible complexity**. A system like the eye during an early evolutionary stage should not be selected for fitness if any of its key components were missing. No matter how sophisticated each might be, a lens, an iris, a pupil, a retina, an optic nerve alone would be useless, conferring no advantage. Therefore, the complex eye could not just evolve over any time span. Well, it did.

I am inclined to credit advocates of Intelligent Design for focusing (get it?) our attention on the eye. They put the spotlight on an area that has benefited from the resulting research intensity. Once the gauntlet had been thrown down citing the eye as the greatest challenge for evolutionists, dozens of doctoral theses had to follow. The results have been "eye opening" indeed. From different directions, evidence has accumulated revealing rather clearly how the eye could evolve, and did, at least partway. Enough gaps remain that opportunities abound for future research projects.

Relevant evidence has come from both the famous Burgess Shale in the Canadian Rockies and the rich Australian fossil site at the Emu Bay Shale deposit on Kangaroo Island. These treasure troves cover much of the Cambrian Period, presenting a great deal of crucial information about the "Cambrian Explosion" 535 ($\pm$ 10) million years ago, when so many body forms (phyla) made their very first appearance. With such an abundance of fossil evidence at hand, supporting evidence from existing species soon followed. What emerges from this is a proposed sequence for structural development of eyes that cannot be dismissed.

The Eyes Have It

1. First, the skin developed one or more light-sensitive spots, whose photochemical response was relayed by a convenient nerve. Such a feature is evident today on the flatworm **planarian**, a little fellow with a pair of photo-responsive skin stains near its front end. Was that a lucky site? These spots have no directional quality, but would enhance the organism's circadian adaptation to night and day. It also could trigger a survival response moving the half-inch planarian away from light.
2. It would not be difficult for some random change to produce a surface depression or dent around that light-sensitive spot. If so, it would provide some protection for the spot, and give some

directional sense to its light response function. Such an "eye pit" has been observed on fossils of Cambrian snails.

3. If the pit became deeper, with the photo-receptive recessed tissue well down behind the narrow opening, this could become a small aperture for light, like a pinhole camera, projecting a reversed image on the light-sensitive area. This feature is found in the **nautilus**, whose functional "eye" has no cornea or lens.

4. It would be considerably more problematic for that photosensitive area to evolve into a more complex tissue like a retina, but suppose it did. That would be one giant leap for evolution. Andrew Parker has suggested that the early advantages of the light-processing tissue at any stage would surely have set off what he adroitly calls an "arms race" among both predator and prey. We may not be lucky enough to find evidence of this, because soft tissue rarely makes an imprint during fossilization the way skeletal bone does. It would be worth the search.

It seems that evolution followed several different pathways at this stage. Vertebrates and cephalopods ended up with different outcomes for the retinal structure at the back of the eye. In the vertebrate eye (such as yours and mine), the optic nerve ends are attached in front of the retina. This is an awkward design feature, in that the optic nerve must penetrate back through the retina, causing a "blind spot."

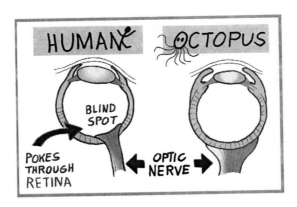

You can "see" the effect of the blind spot with an old parlor trick. On a plain piece of paper, draw an X and a prominent dot about two inches to the right of the X. Cover your left eye and look directly and only at the X.

Lean closer to the X, and watch the dot disappear. As you continue even closer toward the X, the dot will reappear. You have just moved the image of the dot onto and through the blind spot. Or you can exercise on this:

MAKE THE SCARY MONSTER DISAPPEAR! CLOSE YOUR RIGHT EYE. NOW HOLD THE BOOK ABOUT 1 FOOT AWAY AND STARE AT 👁 ABOVE WITH YOUR LEFT EYE. GET THE DISTANCE RIGHT, AND, HURRAH, NO MORE MONSTER!

Blind Spot Test for Left Eye

Cephalopods do not have this "defect." Their nerve ends are behind the retinal tissue, so that the optic nerve can exit the eye gracefully without having to disrupt any part of the retina. Consequently, there is no blind spot. Regrettably, I do not have a good parlor trick for this. Well, you could try the above trick with your right eye closed and the left eye approaching the little monster, just to see the non-effect on the right side. Just kidding!

Cephalopods, by the way, are the taxonomic **class** of invertebrate animals that have muscular tentacles and eject ink to confuse their prey. They include the octopus, squid, cuttlefish, and one form that still retains a shell, the nautilus. While the human eye, with its blind spot, is not as well designed in that respect as the squid eye, it works for us.

5. Moving right along, one more evolutionary step was needed for the process to end well. There had to be some way to complete the front of this device with a cornea, iris, and lens. Was there some lucky DNA mutation? Some have suggested a remnant of tissue left over from shedding skin the way snakes do. That might work for snakes, but seems more like a Lamarckian adaptation (chapter 6). There also had to be a way for some sort

of little convex pouch of liquid to be formed as a predecessor for the lens. This step could use a little more research attention.

It does seem to me that this could have evolved just as well if the formation of lens and cornea came <u>before</u> the modification of the light-sensitive tissue into a more complex retina. The resulting sharper pattern of focused light at the back of the eye would have magnified (!) any advantage from developing a retina.

In the case of mammals, the result was two coordinated eyes, each with a single lens. In some animal classes, especially insects, each eye has multiple lenses, sometimes at the end of stalks. Would we have been better off with the multi-lens arrangement? Also, it is puzzling how that photo-sensitive depression begat a stalk!

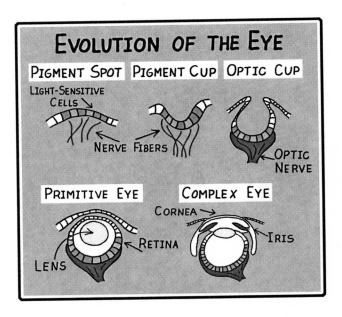

Special Honors in the category of eyes goes to an underwater predator *Anomalocaris canadensis* ("weird Canadian shrimp"), an abundant Burgess Shale fossil from 505 million years ago, with compound eyes on two stalks. It is taxonomically related to the *Arthropod* phylum of invertebrates with jointed limbs, which includes butterflies, scorpions, insects like houseflies, crabs, and 400,000 beetles. With 750,000 catalogued species, *Arthropods* make up 80% of all known animal species.

Microscopic imaging of the shale surface upon which an *Anomalocaris* specimen got imprinted shows clear details of one eye pod that was about an inch in diameter. It had some 8,000 microlenses per stalk 16,000 in all. No other animal living or extinct equals that. From particular features of the eye, specialists can tell that its visual acuity favored a successful predator. It also featured a pair of stubby arms for hugging its prey against its round, toothy mouth. Fossil specimens of its likely prey, such as trilobites, have been found with bite marks of *Anomalocaris* teeth. A typical body size was about the length and girth of a man's leg. We can be glad this character is extinct, although some might find it every bit as endearing as a shark.

One difficulty with this explanation is that many eye forms appeared suddenly (in geologic time) during the Cambrian Explosion. This is when most body forms arose between 545 million years ago (545 Mya) and 525 Mya (pages 200 ff.). There is no fossil record of slow evolution of eyes over the half-billion-year reign of rudimentary animal forms that preceded the Cambrian Period. The few pre-Cambrian animal phyla had no eyes and no need for them, as there were no predators to be avoided and nutrition was abundantly available on the ocean floor. Then in the course of the next 10–20 million years, dozens of new body plans (phyla) emerged, a few of them sporting camera-like eyes. That would seem to be very sudden for such a degree of overall sophistication. Even more abruptly, the earliest fossil evidence of eyes was deposited 540 Mya. Perhaps Parker's idea of an arms race between increasingly more aggressive predators and more elusive prey really did move things along in a lightning flash of transformation. Or was something "coincidental" going on? Ernst Mayr has noted that the evolution of eyesight occurred independently more than forty separate times.

Among the unusual eyes of Cambrian animals were the compound eyes (with rigid crystalline lenses) of the arthropod class of trilobite, with its many orders and 17,000 species dating from 521 Mya until all were lost in the Permian Extinction (251 Mya) after a good long run.

Dan-Eric Nilsson and Susanne Pelger (Lund University, Sweden, 1994) have studied the time that it might take for a seven-stage evolution from a flat, light-sensitive patch of skin to a camera-style eye. They calculated that it would require no more than 364,000 years, provided that the sequence of variation followed the shortest possible path, with each step providing an advantage for natural selection. These assumptions led Victor Torley (in www.uncommondescent.com, an intelligent-design website, 2013) to object that Nilsson and Pelger had postulated unintentionally an "intelligently guided" pathway. In fairness to Nilsson and Pelger, their intention was to calculate the fastest route for eye evolution as a starting point for the ensuing debates. For example, Torley cites the doctoral thesis of physicist Dov Rhodes (2007), which expanded the Nilsson concept to include divergent paths, concluding that it would take the barest minimum of 1.8 million years and a more plausible span of 18 million years for the random evolution of the eye. These speculations neatly approximate the 10–20 million years available within the span of the Cambrian Explosion.

It is interesting that in the six weeks following the appearance of Torley's article it had generated 176 responses; some respectfully critical, some harshly critical. None of this debate is subject to peer review, however, but illustrates the hot modern climate for philosophical dispute.

Once again, molecular biology adds confirmation. Genomic studies confirm that multiple genetic factors for the eye are similar in all eyed species of animals. What do you think of all this? Is it miraculous that our eye is a truly wonderful instrument, even if not the world's best? Admittedly, it is suboptimal in comparison with the eye of an eagle and other predatory birds, or maybe squids. To that, one wag has said: "A suboptimal eye is better than no eye at all."

Meanwhile, it seems it was not enough for some just to defend Darwin with good, strong evidence that not even the eye was too complex for evolution. They also had to impugn those who dared to raise the issue of "irreducible complexity." Citing divergent evolutionary pathways and the existence of quite a few defects, some taunting antitheists have mockingly suggested that a respectable intelligent designer ought not to have made such mistakes. Let them have their laughs while they can.

The Coliform Whip

A similar challenge for Darwinian evolution has been raised in an entirely different and less familiar example. The ubiquitous intestinal bacterium *Escherichia coli* sports a neat little whip-like **flagellum** that helps propel it on its appointed rounds. Mounted aft, this device does not swim with a side-to-side motion like a water snake or fish, but spins more like the propeller of an outboard motor. Comparing speeds with the swift cheetah on the relative scale of body length traversed per second crowns *E. coli* as the champion:

- *Escherichia coli* can achieve sixty body lengths per second;
- A cheetah's maximum speed is 25 body lengths per second;

- Our fastest humans can sprint approximately 5 body lengths (30 feet) per second; and while we're at it,
- And how about a 180-mph Formula One race car? At 16.5-feet long, it tops 16 body lengths per second. [180 x 5280 / (60 x 60 x 16.5) = 16]

Is that awesome or what? Because this motion is definitely complex, requiring the coordinated guidance of fifty different proteins, the claim of irreducible complexity must again be considered. This has been a really hot issue for those on the intelligent design side, pressing Darwin's disciples to devote quality time and creativity to a solution.

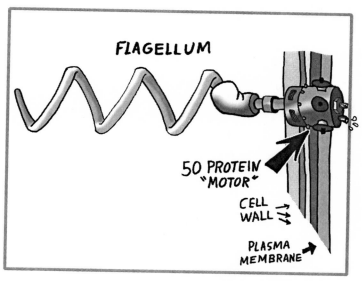

Coliform Whip with Fifty-Protein "Motor"

The Darwinian problem here is how fifty coordinated proteins could have been assembled the first time around. We know that messenger-RNA controls the production of proteins, and that the sequence of amino acids in a protein is determined by the sequence of the various combinations of four nucleotides in the RNA molecule. Each amino acid is coded by a specific triplet of these nucleotides (pages 295-298). Moreover, it is certain that the DNA code of each gene of an organism is **transcribed** into that of its messenger RNA, which, in turn, is **translated** to control the expression of just the right proteins for each function. Thus, the evolutionary variation in the proteins of any species can only result from changes in its DNA sequence of nucleotide pairs.

This puzzle has three solutions; each with inherent difficulties:

(a) If all 50 genes associated with the flagellum of *E. coli* were programmed into the DNA at about the same time, this would produce the twirling dervish and confer an immediate advantage of agile mobility to the first species to get this right. It would dominate subsequent generations of *Escherichia*. The fundamental problem with this scenario is the high improbability that the multiple DNA variations could occur all within a short time span. This would be the equivalent of fifty consecutive grand-slam homeruns, contravening the Darwinian concept of <u>slow</u> modifications. Here, the <u>mechanism</u> is problematic. Michael Behe likened this to the uselessness of a mousetrap with one of its five parts missing. His was a clever argument until Ken Miller's dazzling retort (in Solution c below).

One-Step Assembly of Complex Function

(b) If the requisite fifty proteins were programmed one at a time over a long time span, this would be more in keeping with Darwin's theory, allowing each change to be favored by natural selection. This would take a very long time to get each protein precisely right until the proper configuration of fifty proteins was ready and in place. The problem with this is the need for undirected natural selection to favor and confer an advantage at each step in order for every change in turn to be selected for. If any one of the fifty modifications were to produce less than the "fittest" variety in any generation, the evolutionary chain could not be sustained. Here, <u>natural selection</u> is problematic.

(c) The solution *du jour* is that subsets of genes produce smaller subgroups of proteins, each with a simpler but useful free-standing function of its own, providing an intervening advantage to the organism. Incorporated with other subsets later into a more complex system affording a greater advantage, the composite set would be selected for future offspring. As for the flagellum, it might have been preceded by a subgroup of ten proteins that control formation of ports that permit excretion of toxins into a host. Ken Miller of Brown University has a fascinating argument to support this concept, for which he devises working mousetraps with fewer pieces, including a two-part mousetrap that functions first as a tie-clip. Search the Internet for "Ken Miller lecture mousetrap."

Assembly of Complex Function from Functioning Intermediates

For a while there, the intelligent-design advocates seemed to have the upper hand, but the Darwinians fought back vigorously. Regrettably, some quarrels were punctuated by unkind *ad hominem* arguments against anyone believing in ID, and reputations were maligned. The quality of debate improved a bit when William Dembski calculated a vanishingly low probability for an assumption like (a) above: that all fifty proteins had to be assembled simultaneously. This produced a polite but vigorous denial by Howard Van Till, one of our able and fair-minded surrogates for Darwin. He chided Dembski for not considering the slower Darwinian path (b) above: with each protein being modified one by one, employing small changes from preexisting proteins. Would a similar calculation based on the Darwinian path (b) likely have a very low probability also? And what about path (c)? Someone else can do those calculations.

After a lot of heat, the Darwin agents formulated a reasonable scenario based on (c) the fragmented, articulated process. They contend that these proteins were not built from scratch, but by minor modifications of existing proteins already on hand, as Miller had surmised. Next, they point out that not all fifty proteins are equally vital to get the first flagellum twirling. If just a few can survive for a few generations, their fledgling flagella just might be able to produce a clumsy but effective motion. After all, awkward motility is better than no motility at all. That might be a huge advantage for natural selection's favor, buying time for more fortuitous modifications in the remaining proteins to smooth its stroke until it finalized the efficient little "outboard motor" we see today. There remain abundant opportunities for future research to try to improve or disprove any step of that assumption. After all, isn't that what the Scientific Method is about? That's the way it should be. Science and Darwin will be better off, in my opinion, if scientists on opposing sides agree to treat each other respectfully, publish their countervailing arguments, and test them experimentally.

It occurs to me as an interested spectator that one more observation needs to be put on the table. If the predecessor sans flagellum of *E. coli* grew a functioning little whip via a series of DNA changes modifying one protein at a time, or via a combination of previously unrelated intermediate subsets, would this not indicate a high degree of purpose in the overall process? Science cannot ask and answer questions about purpose and direction. Science figures out how, not why. Even so, that does not foreclose teleology; it just rules out looking for it scientifically.

If a multi-stage scenario (b or c, above) is correct, there does seem to be a directional quality: to get from A to B to C for one intermediate function; and independently from M to N to O for another; and so forth—and ultimately to the goal of the flagellum's entire coordinated alphabet. Even if we agree that the half dozen or so key proteins would require only a few minor modifications, any coding mutations able to change the sequences of nucleotide pairs in the DNA could produce wrong sequences far more often than the correct sequence. Information Theory tells us that random changes tend to degrade the message.

Some of us will feel more comfortable with an assumption that this elaborate process seems to have followed some purpose. That view seems more plausible than assuming it was all a random series of unrelated accidents, which is every bit as great a "leap of faith." For that matter, even Ken Miller's ingenious two-piece mousetrap required of him a high degree of purposeful assembly. Hmmm?

Specified Complexity

A slightly different alternative framework for this confounding issue has been put forth by Paul Davies in *The Fifth Miracle*, which Dembski has endorsed. It's called **Specified Complexity**, a special feature of biological systems not seen in inorganic systems. Specified Complexity is both complex and specified. According to Davies, the complexity of life is not always mysterious in every respect, but what he calls "tightly specified complexity" is undoubtedly mysterious. Their illustration is worth pondering:

1. In computer algorithms, a repetitive sequence of bits (1.1.1.1.1.1.1.1...1) is obviously <u>specified</u> but <u>not complex</u>.
2. A random sequence of bits (1.0.0.0.1.1.0.1.1.1.0.1.0.1.0.0...0), on the other hand, is <u>not specified</u>, as it has no discernible pattern, but is surely <u>complex</u>.
3. A sequence of bits produced by a formula (for example, a Fibonacci series or a progression of prime numbers) is <u>specified</u> by its equation and definitely <u>complex</u>.

Dembski and Davies say that a phenomenon found to have specified complexity (case 3, above) indicates metaphysical design. For those who reject any notion of metaphysics or design, or any teleological First Cause, the dismissive response is that descent with modification and natural selection can always account for it. But can it?

In our chapters on astronomy, biology, chemistry, geology, and physics, we encounter disagreements that cannot easily be dismissed out of hand. In each case, there is some counterargument, yet not always absolutely conclusive. Some ambiguity might be expected in any debate whether natural causes can ultimately explain every fact of life.

Chromosome Function

Turning now to the fundamentals of chromosomes, the human adult has 100 trillion cells (1×10^{14}, or if you prefer: 1E+14), with over 200 different kinds of cells. Each cell has within its nucleus a complete complement of the individual's DNA, distributed among one or more sets of chromosomes. However, different kinds of cells in different organs and tissues utilize different aspects of the coded information. Each cell employs the sequences of some genes but not of others. Cells select certain protein-coding genes to make a variety of vital protein catalysts called enzymes. Some regulate the generation of antibodies and other immune agents, while others control growth of anatomical features, like lungs, skeletal bones, hair, fingernails, and the like. Yet others supply the enzymes for digestion and metabolism. One out of every six controls for some inherited disease.

One principal function of chromosomes is the transfer of genetic information during cell division, so that the new cells have the same DNA sequence as the precursor cell had before division. Long before the role of DNA was understood, microscopes enabled cell biologists to observe chromosome features during progressive stages of mitotic cell division. We will consider that vital process a few pages below.

Chromosomes: Their Role in Evolution

Here's something to ponder. We know that chromosomes come in pairs, one from the mother and one from the father. We humans have 46 chromosomes in 23 chromosome pairs. With the exception of the X and Y chromosomes, the other 44 consist of 22 pairs of similar chromosomes (**autosomes**), each pair offering alternative expression of traits such as color of hair and eyes, set of jaw, susceptibility to genetic disorders, and so forth.

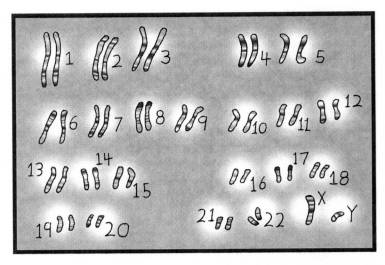

46 Human Chromosomes in 22 Autosome Pairs plus X and Y

Each animal species has its own **karyotype**, its distinctive even number of chromosomes. Dogs are mammals too, and they have 78 chromosomes (in 39 pairs), as do coyotes, jackals, or wolves, all of which are within the same genus *Canis*. The hyena has only 40, which is closer to cats, which have 38. Dogs clearly descended from wolves, but there is a little uncertainty as to when. The active domestication and breeding of dogs over the last thousand years has obscured the DNA evidence as to when they diverged. The estimates range from 20,000 to 36,000 years ago, which may be attributable to divergence at different times on different continents. One theory was that early hunter-humans tamed wolves to catch prey, each side learning to accept its symbiotic role and tolerate the other. Eventually, that interdependence might have selected a wolf-dog suitable for domestication, allowing humans to train them as pets and guardians.

Cara Canem

Ah, but now there's an exciting new explanation. Erik Axelsson at Uppsala University in Sweden has studied the genomes of dogs and wolves, finding some intriguing differences in DNA sequences. Of special interest, wolves (*Canis lupus lupus*) have only two genes that produced **amylase** enzymes that assist digestion of large carbohydrates like starches. Consequently, their diet had little use for corn, wheat, rice, and potatoes.

Dogs (*Canis lupus familiaris*), however, have some 30 such enzymes, enhancing their dietary flexibility for starches. When *Homo sapiens* emerged from forest hunting grounds and began to cluster in tribes to share basic agriculture tasks (11,000-12,000 years ago), dogs and wolves were still a hostile threat. That changed, Axelsson says, as humans began to pile their vegetable scraps just outside their settlements. This refuse was of no interest to amylase-challenged wolves, but dogs had different tastes. Furtively at first, then boldly, they scavenged for free lunches. Could this not select for a respectfully tolerant canine attitude toward humankind?

[Thus, the divergent evolution of dogs' starch metabolism could have preceded the art of domestication, which in turn favored evolution of socialization between humans and dogs. Duke University evolutionary anthropologist Brian Hare believes it goes even deeper, as examined in his *The Genius of Dogs*. Hare founded the Duke Canine Cognition Center to study the special ability of dogs to learn spoken and unspoken communication from humans. He suspects that co-evolution of humans and dogs favors interdependencies of various kinds. Dogs can learn to fetch according to verbal commands and the owner's point of gaze. Some service dogs have the ability to sense dangerous levels of blood sugar in humans and other physiological imbalances. What other pet can stare into your eyes in such a satisfying way? That simple gift raises levels of blood **oxytocin** (a mammalian enzyme associated with childbirth, lactation, and romantic bonding: "the love hormone") in both species. Have we evolved the ability to control dogs, or *vice versa*?]

Consistent with the amylase hypothesis, while the oldest dog fossil goes back 33,000 years in Siberia, the oldest <u>domesticated</u> dog fossil is 12,000 years old: a pup buried alongside its master in what is now Israel. Humans, by the way, are also blessed with the amylase producing genes, in some ways superior to dogs. Only humans have amylase enzymes in their saliva, which may be why we chew our food more, in contrast to dogs, who "still wolf it down" (to quote a clever phrase from reporter David Brown of the *Washington Post*, January 2013). "Man's Best Friend" has undergone artificial selection by a thousand years of controlled breeding. Meanwhile, we still have no idea why dogs stick their heads out the car window!

Here's a bigger puzzle for us to solve: Are all mammals related by ancestry? Was there a single ancestral species from which all mammals descended? Evolution theory postulates that all mammals descended from a single, first mammalian species. That would include whales (before their ancestral order returned to the oceans), elephants, leopards and other big cats, wolves, apes, and us humans. Yet, how can evolution go from a single species with a particular number of chromosome pairs to a new species (of a new family, order, or class) with a different number of chromosome pairs? How can evolution bring forth a new order if any intervening variant offspring has a different karyotype than its predecessor? Wouldn't that present a serious problem for bisexual reproduction? Just saying.

We cannot ignore this if we accept abundant DNA evidence that all living species descended from a common ancestor, even allowing for Venter's *Mycoplasma* exception (see page 179). Most species have a different number of chromosomes from whatever number that ancient precursor had. It is inescapable. So, how could evolution change the number of chromosomes in order to produce each new taxonomic order, such as carnivores or cetaceans (whales)— or primates (our order)? How could a species with its particular number of chromosomes produce offspring with a different number of chromosomes? Can evidence of chromosome splitting and fusion answer this complex riddle?

Take the example of a hypothetical species with 34 chromosomes (17 pairs), and some cellular damage causes one female to have 36 (18 pairs). Where will she find that necessary male with 18 chromosome pairs with which to mate and start a new species? If she is the only chromosomal variant, how can she reproduce? If there is only one male with the same altered number of chromosomes, what is the likelihood they can find each other at the right time? Will her split chromosome release a unique sex-attractant pheromone during rutting season that only he can detect? Would dozens in a pack of the species be altered nearly simultaneously?

This would not be a problem for an organism that has asexual methods of reproduction. For the first billion years or so, before sex appeared in the fossil record, asexual microbes and spores could reproduce by cell division, without needing a mate. Does that suggest **parthenogenesis** (asexual reproduction) as a possible fallback mechanism for each transition from one class, order, or family to another? Hold that thought until page 251.

Mitosis in Cell Division

Before we can understand reproduction at the cellular level, we must first grasp simple cell division. For cells that have a nucleus (**eukaryotic** cells), the cellular life cycle involves distinct stages that are preliminary to cell division. Each cell contains all of the DNA fragments along with their accompanying protein in a rather amorphous material called **chromatin**. As cell division is initiated, these diffused DNA fragments assemble with their proteins in formations of more orderly aggregates called chromosomes, which are visible under the microscope.

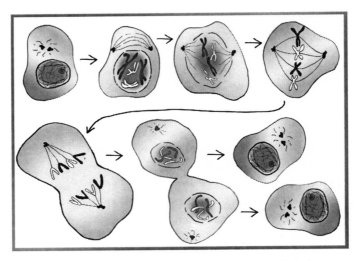

Detailed Pictogram of Cell Division (Mitosis)

The process whereby a cell actually splits into two identical "daughter" cells is called **cytokinesis**. The step just before that is **mitosis.** The other stages are essential for cell division to succeed: (a) normal cell growth, (b) DNA synthesis and replication, and (c) rapid cell growth, accumulating cytoplasm, protein, and organelles in preparation for mitosis and cytokinesis to form two new cells.

Following normal cell growth, the key step is replication of the cell's DNA. Each DNA double-helix is "unzipped" into two separate strands by the action of protein enzymes called **helicases**. As each free single strand is released and separated, specialized **polymerase** enzymes "read" its code and attach the matching nucleotides, each consisting of phosphate ions, deoxyribose, and the specific purine (adenine or guanine) or pyrimidine (thymine or cytosine) base correlated to the original template in that strand. In this way, the new strand is synthesized to complete a newly constructed double-helix, identical to the original. Meanwhile, the other released original strand of the unzipped DNA acquires its requisite nucleotides similarly via polymerase-assisted assembly of a second new, double-helix daughter DNA. The cell now has two complete, identical sets of DNA, perfectly replicated. The accompanying cartoon of DNA replication may help us to visualize a vital part this process, to which we will return in chapter 15.

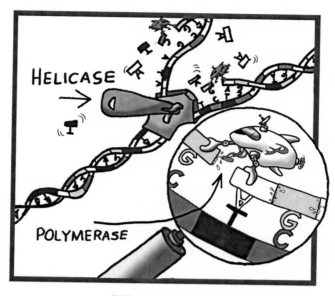

DNA REPLICATION

In a microscope view of a properly stained thin layer of tissue, some cells may be observed in each condition, collectively exhibiting all the phases of mitosis. In some cells the chromosomes are not yet evident. This soon changes dramatically. Once the cell has grown sufficiently in preparation, mitosis is observed to proceed in a regular order of a few descriptive phases, which I will simplify:

(a) The chromatin begins to coil more tightly and bulk up, appearing as shorter, thicker chromosomal structures (DNA replication having already occurred);

(b) These chromosomes begin to move, lining up along the cell's "equatorial" line;

(c) The chromosomes separate into paired sister chromosomes with one identical sister on each side of the cell equator; and

(d) The two sets of chromosomes are pulled as if by intracellular threads into identical groups on each side, and a new membrane separates the two sets of chromosomes.

(e) The cell is now ready for cytokinetic division. A constriction around the cell's equator comes between the two sets of chromosomes, and this proceeds to cleave the cell into two daughter cells, each with half of a complete set of chromosomes.

These chromosomes then repeat the DNA replication so that each daughter cell will have the same full complement of chromosome pairs. Once cell division is complete, the chromosomes pull a partial disappearing act, dispersing as smaller components of each new cell's chromatin. This whole process is awesome, and could hardly be imagined without direct observation. In the cycle of life, older cells will die off, only to be replaced by repetitive cytokinesis to keep the overall tissue healthy. Around and around and around it goes.

Each new chromosome is almost always a perfect replica in every respect of its predecessor chromosome, so that as any cell divides into two new cells each has the same DNA information in the same number of chromosomes as before, each identical to the original. Dozens of environmental impacts (oxidation, methylation, hydrolysis, radiation, heat, etc.) can alter any rung of the precisely coded DNA sequence. If an error occurs and is not repaired by the polymerase or other repair enzymes, it could cause cell death (**apoptosis**) or uncontrolled growth (cancer) or, rarely, a successful evolutionary mutation. Discovery of many of these vital repair mechanisms by Tomas Lindahl at the Francis Crick Institute, Aziz Sancar at the University of North Carolina at Chapel Hill, and Paul Modrich at Duke University won for them the 2015 Nobel Prize in Chemistry.

Sterile Hybrid Species: Mules' Odd Chromosomes

Centuries ago, those engaged in animal husbandry wanted to see if they could crossbreed a horse with a donkey. It worked up to a point. They got a mule, but one odd thing we know about mules is that they are infertile, and cannot reproduce any offspring. The horse (*Equus caballus*) has 64 chromosomes (32 pairs), while the donkey (*Equus asinus*) has 62 (31 pairs). They are different species of the same genus. When they produce a hybrid mule, it has the average number of 63 chromosomes, an odd number, and cannot reproduce. This clearly indicates that the horse and donkey evolved from a common ancestor, given the compatibility of their chromosomes to allow induced cross-breeding.

A similar hybrid has been found by crossing a domestic cat having the typical feline count of 36 chromosomes with an ocelot having 38. This cross-breeding produced a cat-like creature with 37 chromosomes. Here again the male of the litter was said to be sterile. From these two examples, it would not appear to be efficacious for evolution to depend upon gradual accretion of small increments in the number of chromosomes, one or two at a time, in order to develop a new genus or family from variations in one species. In yet another example, the gibbon, with 44 chromosomes, can be crossed with the siamang (50 chromosomes) to yield an infertile hybrid with an equally hybrid name: **siabon**. Beyond these few examples, this field of research is not all that fertile, so to speak, other than to provide a clue as to the significance of chromosomes in reproduction.

Meiosis in Reproduction

What is the role of chromosomes in reproduction? Before scientists understood the structure and genetic function of DNA, Hunt Morgan (1916) at Columbia University developed the theoretical breakthrough for the hereditary role of chromosomes. He studied mainly fruitflies (*Drosophila melanogaster*) because they were cheap, reproduced rapidly, and had a short life cycle. It also simplified matters that the fruitfly has only 8 chromosomes (in four pairs). When he studied mutations, Morgan discovered that there were only four groups of mutations, corresponding to the four pairs of chromosomes. For this work he was awarded the Nobel Prize in 1933.

The situation is now known to be exceedingly more complex. The process for reproductive cell division is called **meiosis**. In females this meiosis is the **oogenesis** process preparing the egg cell, or **oocyte**, while in males it is the **spermatogenesis** process preparing the sperm cell, or **spermatocyte**. Each of these meiotic cell divisions involves the formation of a **gamete**, a reproductive cell that is the male partner's small and mobile spermatocyte, or the female's oocyte, which is immobile and 100,000 times larger. Each gamete has half of each pair of chromosomes of its predecessor.

In reproduction, the meiotic process differs from mitosis in that it shuffles the DNA code of both parents. Upon fertilization of the ovum by the sperm, each new cell in the embryo has mixed pairs of chromosomes, with one chromosome of each pair deriving from the father and the other from the mother. The normal outcome for eukaryotes in a sexual process for reproduction is to combine one set of chromosomes from each parent. For humans, with 46 chromosomes, 23 (including the female chromosome X) come from the mother and 23 (one of which is either the male chromosome Y or a female chromosome X') come from the father. The mother has no Y chromosomes to contribute. If the father donates his Y chromosome, the offspring will be a male with an XY pair. If the father contributes his X' chromosome, the offspring will be female with an XX' pair.

The X and Y chromosomes determine the sex of the offspring. All other chromosomes are called **autosomes**. Every human thus will have 44 **autosomes**, 22 from the father and 22 from the mother, to make 22 pairs. Every male will also have an X chromosome from his mother and a Y chromosome from his father. Every female will have no Y chromosome, but two X chromosomes, one X from her mother and one X′ from her father. Any change in the code of nucleotide pairs within the DNA of a gamete may be carried to future generations.

In an effort (above) to simplify the meiosis process, we will examine only what happens to just the larger X (female) and smaller Y (male) chromosomes in the diagram of meiosis of the cell from the <u>male</u> parent prior to fertilization of the female oocyte. The first two steps are similar to mitosis, as (in Step I) the sex-determinant chromosomes (X and Y) begin to form replicating XX and YY chromosomes joined at the centromere. When that cell divides (Step II) into two intermediate cells, one cell will contain only the XX joined pair, and the other will contain only the YY joined pair. In the final process (Step III), the intermediate cell with the XX pair separates the pair and divides, generating two oocyte cells, each with only one X chromosome (in addition to one of each of the 22 autosomes, <u>not shown</u>).

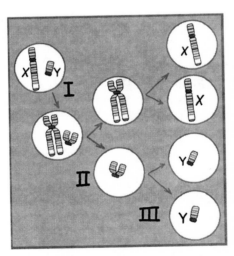

MEIOSIS SIMPLIFIED (Really!)

In the same way, the intermediate cell with the YY conjoined pair separates the pair and divides into two spermatocyte cells, each with only one Y chromosome (in addition to one of each of the 22 autosomes). Each of the four daughter cells is said to be **haploid**, meaning it has only half the number of each chromosome as did its precursor male parent cell. For the fertilized cell there are $2^{46} = 7 \times 10^{13}$ possible combinations of all 46 chromosomes. Yes, you really are one in 70 trillion!

Most mutations are neutral and quite harmless. If they occur in some non-functional part of the gamete's DNA sequence, there is simply no consequent effect. Even if some particular coding sequence is damaged, the cell has repair mechanisms that can realign the correct inherited sequence. This mechanism is not foolproof, however, and will from time to time fail to make the needed correction. Such failure leads to the new mutation being transmitted to subsequent generations. If a feature is superior, better suited to the environment, then this trait soon becomes prevalent and dominant in subsequent generations. If inferior and unfit for the prevailing environment, the hereditary trait is probably lost in a few generations. For humans, these difficulties may be ameliorated by modern medical practice.

The problem is more severe when explaining the emergence of a different taxonomic order or family. What we are learning about the genomes of many different species is that the number of chromosome pairs in each species within a family is definitive and may have some similarities with other species in the same family. The family to which humans (46 chromosomes) belong includes gorillas, chimpanzees, bonobos, and orangutans (all with 48). Species of one family will likely have little or no correspondence to the varied numbers of chromosome pairs within most other families. Capuchin and rhesus monkeys are in different families, and have 54 and 42 chromosomes respectively. Bison, cows, and goats have 60, deer have 68 or 70; while bears have 74; and wolves, coyotes, and dogs have 78. How then can the cellular aspect of reproduction work for a new family or order to evolve? The process of whole genome duplication (below) may provide a partial answer.

Evolution of Chromosomes

Biologists recognize two methods by which the chromosome numbers can change during evolution. One method is **polyploidy** and the other is **chromosome fusion**. You may skip ahead if this is too technical, but it's worth a try. First, there's the curious nomenclature.

Ploidy is the term geneticists use to indicate the <u>number of sets</u> of chromosomes. Species whose cells have two sets of all chromosomes are said to be **diploid**, and thus have one pair of each chromosome. Diploidy is the normal arrangement for most animals and all mammals, including us humans. A species with three sets of all chromosomes is triploid, and so forth: tetraploid for four sets of chromosomes, pentaploid for five sets. All examples with three or more are generalized as **polyploid**. If a species has all of its genome in one set of chromosomes, it is called **monoploid**. The **gamete** (sperm or egg cell) is called **haploid**, meaning it has half the number of full sets of chromosomes of its parent organism. In the case of humans (diploid), each haploid gamete (sperm or egg) is therefore monoploid, with 23 unpaired chromosomes.

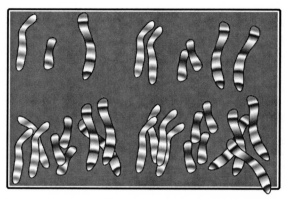

Monoploid, Diploid . . . Polyploid Chromosomes

Among plants, it is not unusual to have three or more sets of each chromosome (polyploidy). If such a species has an even number of sets of the same chromosome, it can produce gametes with one or more complete working sets of chromosome pairs, capable of reproduction. With an odd number of sets, sexual reproduction succeeds only in self-pollinating plants. This mechanism accounts for seedless watermelons. By crossing one watermelon carrying two sets of chromosomes (diploid) with another watermelon having four sets (tetraploid), the resulting seed produces a triploid hybrid plant with three sets of chromosomes. It is infertile and generates seedless watermelons.

A rather curious case is the honeybee. The female is diploid with 32 chromosomes in 16 pairs. The male arises from unfertilized eggs and is monoploid, having only one set of 16 chromosomes. It can provide spermatozoa to the queen bee, but is otherwise of little use to the hive, where female bees do most of the work.

In a tetraploid plant, there are two pairs of every gene. If mutation occurs in one pair of genes, it does not cause cell death, because the other pair is still available to carry out the normal function of the gene. If this mutation is beneficial, it might survive over evolutionary time as a new diploid, increasing the number of different chromosomes.

This mode of increasing the number of chromosomes works nicely for plants, among which it is not unusual to have three or more sets of the same chromosome. This is rare among animals, but has been reported in some birds, lizards, frogs, and insects. In these cases, the parent would be infertile via bisexual methods, and it is thought that reproduction might involve **parthenogenesis** (see below, p. 251). Mammals are almost always diploid, very rarely polyploid, so this mechanism cannot account for evolutionary increases in chromosomes among mammalian orders and families.

Chromosome Fusion

In chromosome fusion, two chromosomes become joined end to end to form one long chromosome. This mechanism would cause an evolutionary <u>decrease</u> in the number of chromosomes. In most eukaryotic organisms, each chromosome has a single **centromere** (next page), with genetic data coded in the shorter or longer arm on either side, with a sacrificial protective tip called a **telomere** at each end. If the centromere is near the middle of two arms of nearly equal length, it is called **metacentric**. If the centromere is off center, with arms of different lengths, it is either **submetacentric** or **acrocentric** with most of the genetic code in the longer arm. In cases where the centromere is at the end of the chromosome, it is said to be **telocentric**.

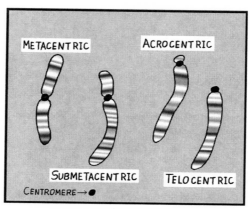

Centromere Positions in Chromosomes

Monkey's Uncle

Let's look at a couple of examples. Chimpanzee chromosomes are almost identical to humans. One significant difference is that humans (*Homo sapiens*) have 23 pairs of chromosomes and chimpanzees (*Pan troglodyte*) have 24 pairs. Of these, 22 pairs of chromosomes in each species are almost a perfect match. Remarkably, two small and unique chromosome pairs of the chimp have structures that are extremely close to what would result if the pair of human chromosomes-2 were cut in two. At one time such a split was the prevailing mechanistic assumption. More likely, the common ancestor carried the two smaller chromosomes, which coupled to form human chromosome-2, probably by fusion of two acrocentric chromosomes, but which survive distinctly unfused in the chimpanzee.

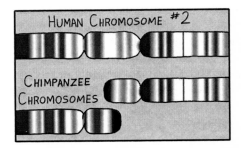

**Comparison of Human Chromosome-2 with Similarly
Banded Chimpanzee Chromosomes 2-p and 2-q**

In a structural metaphor, the tips of the telomeres at the end of the short arm of each chromosome were clipped off, and the two nearly complete fragments joined at their fractured ends. This formed a single chromosome with two centromeres, with all of the genetic information of the original arms still intact and retained. The twin centromeric structures from the two parent chromosomes are evident near the center of human chromosome-2. The offspring carrying the 24 chromosome pairs became the genus *Pan*, and those carrying the 23 chromosome pairs became the genus *Homo*. Unclear is how the first individuals of the new genus could find mates with similar karyotype. Otherwise, how could the new variant genus procreate?

One other mode of acrocentric fusion is known for **muntjac**, the "barking" deer of South Asia. The long arm of one acrocentric chromosome is broken off at its centromere, and bonded onto the long end of another acrocentric chromosome. There are a dozen species of this genus, some of which are specific to a particular island of Indonesia. The smallest species is just 25 pounds when mature, and the largest grows to 110 pounds. One distinctive feature is that the males have long, tusk-like upper canine teeth that are useful for fighting. Fossils have been recovered from 35-million-year-old deposits, making this the oldest known genus of the deer family. The muntjac seems to have taken advantage of this extended lineage, for it has accumulated numerous chromosomes that appear to have been formed by acrocentric fusion.

Some references assume that the number of chromosomes might be increased by a third process of **fission**, by which it is thought that one chromosome fractures in the center of the centromere to form two smaller chromosomes. That would be awkward. Of the two resulting fragments, only one would have the original centromere with one arm attached, and neither would have a protective telomere where the cleavage occurred. In chapter 15 we will see why telomeres are crucial for survival.

John Wilkins has proposed that the strategic alignment of DNA is not determined by the "large-scale chromosomal structure," but by small local sequences. Perhaps this accounts for the surprising finding by Nevo *et al.* (1994) of interbreeding among species of blind Turkish mole rats with slightly different chromosome numbers (karyotypes). Would that get around the chromosomal barrier? Why not in other genera?

While there are some interesting theories of evolutionary mechanisms for increasing or decreasing the number of chromosomes, this is a complex subject that is not fully resolved. This does not mean that evolution is a flawed concept. It just means that we are far from a complete understanding of certain aspects. As in other sectors of science, it seems that the more we understand in greater depth, the more we find that we don't understand. Fortunately, that leaves us with unending opportunities for research projects. It also leaves many with a growing sense that the natural world holds way too many mysteries to be explained solely by random chance.

Fibonacci Strikes Again

After that workout, maybe it's time for a recess to have some fun. Let me introduce a Scottish biologist named **D'Arcy Wentworth Thompson** (1860–1948), a leading structuralist: a pioneering mathematical biologist. In his important book *On Growth and Form* (1917), Thompson did not reject Darwin's evolution, but contended that there was a lot more going on. He observed that there are numerous physical traits of living organisms that have nothing to do with natural selection, but that are more dependent on mathematical relationships and mechanical physics. Thompson made no attempt to explain any of this, and no one else has succeeded in doing so.

One example was his observation that the spiral patterns of seashells and mammalian horns and certain plants (e.g., cacti and the successive angles of leaf and flower stems) have numerical correlations that for some reason fit Fibonacci numbers. The Fibonacci sequence, studied by the Italian mathematician Leonardo Pisano (whose nickname was Fibonacci) is an artificially derived pattern in which each number is the sum of the preceding two (1, 1, 2, 3, 5, 8, 13, 21, 34, 55, 89, 144, 233 . . . and so on).

Fibonacci sequences have been found in odd places, from symmetry of the puzzle known as Pascal's Triangle, to fluctuations in stock prices, to the first digit in the size of national and city populations. Not all examples are frivolous. Gary Meisner runs an engaging website (www.goldennumber.net) on the subject filled with examples. It is uncanny how often such numerical curiosities crop up in nature and elsewhere. "Uncanny," however, may not necessarily be compelling. See what you think about the following.

The ratio of any two adjacent Fibonacci numbers approaches 1.618034, as the numbers get progressively larger. Among ancient Greek philosophers, architects, and artists this was considered to be the "Golden Ratio," aka the "Golden Mean," for designing figures, statues, or structures with the most pleasing dimensions. This is the ratio, for example, of the length of either long side of the Parthenon to the width of its face. This ratio is derived by a formula based on the two lengths X and Y in the following figure.

For this figure, the Golden Ratio φ can be stated verbally:

The ratio φ of the total length (X + Y) to the longer section (X) is equal to the ratio of the longer section (X) to the shorter section (Y).

When restated algebraically,

$$(X + Y) / X = X / Y = \varphi \qquad \text{or}$$
$$X^2 = XY + Y^2$$

Let Y = 1, as the reference base for the ratio, and we get: $X^2 = X + 1$

The algebraic solution of this equation is: X = 1.618034

Thus, the general solution of the Golden Ratio is X = 1.618034Y
So the Golden Ratio, φ = X / Y = **1.618034**
Why would the ancients considered the most pleasing ratio in art or architecture to be 1.618034:1?
If you enjoy numbers, the <u>reciprocal</u> is unique and may not surprise you, as
1 / 1.618034 = 0.618034
Thus, **1 / φ = 0.618034** ! ! !

In other words,   Y = X / 1.618034 = 0.618034X

Here is one familiar example. If you inscribe a five-pointed star within and to the corners of a regular pentagon, the ratio of any side of the star (its longest possible line, endpoint-to-endpoint) to a side of the pentagon is what? The answer is the Golden Ratio φ (Greek letter phi), in which the ratio of φ to 1 equals 1.618034:1, which thus defines the dimensions of the ordinary five-pointed starfish!

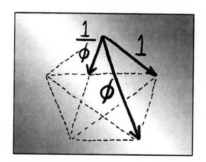

Golden Ratio of Five-Pointed Star Inscribed in a Pentagon

Examples of Fibonacci numbers abound in nature. The expanding curvature of the nautilus shell is a familiar instance. Less well-known: the average ratio of the length of successive human finger and hand bones is **2:3:5:8**. It applies differently to thumbs, whose three bone length ratios are the initial "digits" of the Fibonacci series: **1:1:2**. It has been pointed out that the number of leaves and flower petals of various plants often is one of the Fibonacci integers: 2, 3, 5, 8, 13, and so forth. The four-leaf clover is accordingly rare. However, as I write this, I can look out my window at a lovely proliferation of North Carolina's state flower, the Dogwood with its symbolic, cruciform, four-petal, white blossom.

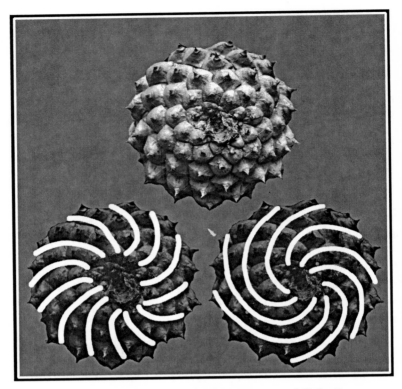

Pine Cone with overlapping Fibonacci Spirals

The typical number of petals of the familiar daisy blossom is a solid Fibonacci 34 (although some daisies have 55 petals!). Far more astonishing is the pattern within the center core of the flower. This contains numerous tiny florets in a singular geometry with one floret at each intersection of 21 logarithmic spirals turning counterclockwise crossing 34 similar but clockwise spirals. There is a similar pattern of florets in the face of the sunflower. In another curious example, the seed pods of pine cones and pineapples are arranged so that they form a pattern of 5 curves going one way around the surface and 8 in the other. For larger pine cones there are patterns of 8 and 13 curves.

We will get to the structure and vital function of DNA in later chapters, but here's an astonishing coincidence to ponder. The fundamental geometry of DNA has two coaxial helices, spiraling together like a right-handed screw. When measured by x-ray crystallography, the repeating unit is 34 Ångstrom (Å) long and 21 Å wide. An Ångstrom is an old unit of length equal to 1×10^{-10} meter, or 1/10 of the modern nanometer (1nm = 10^{-9} m). The two helical spirals are held together so that one is pushed up somewhat against the other. One way to visualize this is that helix A is closer to helix B on the left of A than to the part of helix B ahead of A. This forms a larger groove alternating with a smaller groove. Wait for the punch-line—for the distance span of the gap of the major groove is 21 Ångstrom, and the minor groove is 13 Ångstrom. Note that the span of the major groove is identical to DNA's width. What a coincidence! What? A Fibonacci coincidence?

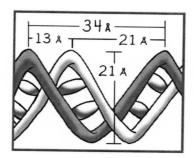

Major Dimensions of DNA have Fibonacci Ratios

One could argue that there is some anthropic fine-tuning involved here, for it is certainly an example of <u>highly</u> **specified complexity** (page 227 above). Had the DNA dimensions first been reported not in Ångstroms but in the nanometric ratio of 3.4:2.1, we might have missed the Fibonacci ratio. However, 3.4:2.1 is exactly the same ratio as 34:21. Is there some natural basis for this strange numerical ideal to be so prevalent in nature, or is it pure coincidence? Does natural selection favor some relative advantage in consecutive Fibonacci numbers? Or is this merely the most efficient pattern for spiral packing? Or is it a function of tetrahedral covalent bonds of carbon chemistry (chapter 14)? My thought is that we subconsciously admire the beauty of the Golden Ratio in art simply because, for whatever reason, it is built into all DNA, ours and daisies' petals and pinecones' seedpods, as well as our finger bones!

It has been noted that some flowers exhibit a different series, with 4, 7, or 11 petals. This is simply the pattern of the similar Lucas Series. It fudges the issue by starting with 2 preceding 1, <u>thereafter</u> following the rule that the value of each number is the sum of its two preceding numbers. This works for some flowers, as it leads to a different set of integers: 2, 1, 3, 4, 7, 11, 18, 29, 47, 76, 123, 199, 322, etc. . . . Even in this Lucas Series, larger consecutive numbers have ratios close to the Golden Ratio. Obviously, this opens up innumerable series with different initial values, which makes the number of petals less instructive than the ratio of adjacent numbers.

On a much larger scale, the spiral curvature of the arms of hurricanes and even galaxies are said to be close to Fibonacci-derived spirals. Is there some meaning to this? Is the Fibonacci sequence itself some kind of natural law? Does it reveal purpose? There is a school of stock-market analysis based on perceived Fibonacci patterns, but it has never served a profitable investment miracle for me.

Thompson was also observant enough to note that the shape of a jelly fish has a curious resemblance to a splash of a droplet of one liquid into another viscous fluid. He demonstrated that the shape of an egg was determined by mathematical considerations. Such observations led him to conclude that aside from most attributes that fit Darwin's evolution theory, a surprising variety of shapes and forms of organisms is due to such mundane factors as the densest way to pack small spheres, and the influence of mathematical relationships—factors that do not arise from random variation.

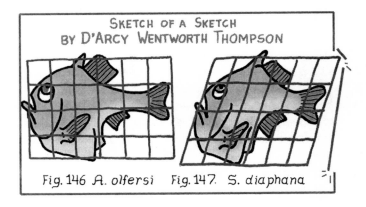

SKETCH OF A SKETCH
BY D'ARCY WENTWORTH THOMPSON

Fig. 146 A. olfersi   Fig. 147. S. diaphana

In an unrelated oddity, Thompson showed that in some cases a drawing of one species superimposed on a graph matrix can be transformed into a drawing of a related but different species by uniform distortion of the graph coordinates. In one example, he could stretch or bend the coordinates of a drawing of one fish to produce a drawing of an entirely different genus. He demonstrated the same graphic shearing on a drawing of the skull profile of Homo sapiens, resulting in a skull profile that looks a lot like an ape.

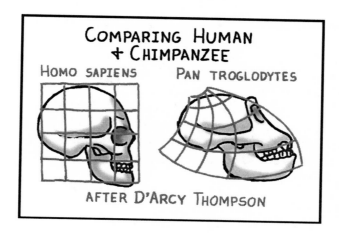

From reflection upon wonders such as these, one might well ponder whether everything in biology can be explained by random variation. Some preceding examples arguably appear to exhibit some degree of **specified complexity**. While Darwin's theory on the origin of species is indisputably established as <u>the</u> unifying, organizing principle of biology, especially as now understood to depend upon molecular changes in DNA, it may be that it is not the <u>only</u> organizing principle. There is a lot more here than can be conformed solely to one theory.

Biological Curiosities

One might well marvel at the early developments and discoveries of biology. It was a bold departure to begin to describe the inner relationships and workings of the anatomy, especially of humans. It is still a special rite of initiation for the young medical student to dissect a cadaver, a lesson that has dual value: (a) for immediate understanding of the body, as well as (b) for honing a vital surgical skill. Even today, there are countless wonders that have been revealed from basic and comparative anatomy.

For one thing, there is a great deal of structural similarity between species of a given genus and of all the various taxonomic families of an order, such as primates. It was a detailed comparison of similarities and variations in anatomical structures that enabled Charles Darwin to unravel his principle of descent with modification.

His Theory of Evolution withstood many critical assaults from scientific rivals. Once the structure of DNA unveiled profound correlations between specific coding areas and distinct physical traits, features, and diseases, coupled with comparisons of the genomes of different but related species, the original theory was elevated to firmly incontrovertible status. Even with this great contribution of molecular biology, the wonders of gross anatomy can still amaze us.

Suppose we begin with the human heart. Here we have a rather soft, boneless lump of myocardial muscle about as big as your fist, weighing in at only 10 ounces. This beauty delivers 100,000 pulses a day, pumping 2,000 gallons of viscous fluid through your 60,000 miles of capillary resistance. That takes 50 beats per gallon of flow, or a cool 2.56 ounces of flow per beat. [1 gal = 128 oz.]

The architectural brilliance of this design (there's that word again!) is stunning. There are two stacked chambers and associated valves on the right side to pump blood through the lungs so it can load up on oxygen, and two similar chambers with valves on the left side to push the oxygenated fluid out into the rest of the body (even into the tissues of the heart itself) to deliver that oxygen for energy and vitality. Each feature reveals great complexity and precise function. According to eminent heart surgeon Francis Robicsek, the particular turbulence of blood flow through the sinus of Valsalva, which gently closes the aortic valve from above with perfect timing, was first described by an anatomist named Leonardo da Vinci, the celebrated artist, engineer, and incomparable polymath genius.

One of the most surprising details about the heart structure is that it has no motor nerves to coordinate its complex rhythm. Say again! You have probably realized that it requires no conscious thought to make your heart flex or relax. It does all that on its own initiative. There are hormones and enzymes that signal the need for a faster or slower pulse rate depending upon the body's oxygen requirements, the need to expel excess carbon dioxide, and any psychological need for fight or flight, but that's another story. It still takes no thought to turn on the heartbeat or accelerate it.

Consider this illustration: when a section of tissue from the heart muscle (myocardium) is dissociated into individual cells, a sample of them can be observed under the microscope making quick, rhythmic twitching motions. As long as each cell is separate and not touching any other cell, each has its own steady beat, albeit out of step with any other cell. But if any two or more touch each other, their quick little twitching movements become synchronized. They signal each other and beat together. It would be interesting to devise a mechanism for how this response could evolve by chance natural selection. Friend, this is more complex than a tiny flagellum.

It would not work well for the entire heart to have a single simultaneous beat however, for then the left and right auricles and ventricles all would expand (and also compress) at the same time, and the pump would fail. There has to be a well-coordinated sequence, like a four-cylinder engine. As a key feature, signals are not transmitted all at once through each part of the heart, but some are diverted or delayed before transmission according to a very precise pattern. No nerves are involved. It's all in the electrical capacitance of the myocardium cells, specifically attenuated depending upon location. It works every time. The pancreas, liver, and kidneys have their own oddities.

Gross Anatomical Peculiarities

Examples of fortuitous architecture abound in comparative anatomy:

1. Flounders have two eyes on the same side of the skull. In infancy, the two eyes begin on opposite sides of the head, but one of them migrates to join the other on the side which ends up on top. Does this strange but tasty fish flop on its side on the bottom because its two eyes are on the same side? Or did one eye migrate around to the other side in a Lamarckian adaptation in order to get out of the mud? Can evolution explain that? It is likely that someone will solve this riddle, yet it does seem purposeful.

2. Giraffes and ostriches have unusually long necks, as did some dinosaurs. Herons, egrets, emus, and camels also have this feature, but less dramatic. What is the natural explanation for this? Before Darwin, Lamarck thought the giraffe grew a longer neck by stretching to reach higher leaves. To Darwin the long neck is an aberration that natural selection saw fit to survive. Giraffes are very stately in their movements except when they have to spread their front legs so their head can get low enough to eat grass. The ostrich, however, is anything but stately and graceful, but did you notice its "bedroom eyes"? Each eye is larger than its brain, by the way.

3. Many larger animals have prominent ears. The function of hearing should be more effective and sensitive over a wider range of frequencies if the ear canal were flared somewhat like a trumpet. This is often the case. Did this acoustic shape evolve from some quirky, random variation? Would larger herbivorous animals' survival have been handicapped with ear canals of uniform diameter? Some evolved the

ability to turn their ears forward or backward to help locate prey or predators. I'll bet you can't. Did you ever notice that your hearing can differentiate sharp reports in close succession better than your eyes can differentiate equally timed flashes of light?

At the base of your ear tube, the ear drum is pressed up against an inordinately complex structure of the smallest bones in the human body: the hammer, anvil, and stirrup. These amplify sound vibration into the inner ear and its sensory nerves, like built-in hearing aids. This raises a question whether random variation ever tested different shapes of the inner ear and its counter-intuitive architecture. Does that stretch the standard logic of variation with natural selection?

4. How many legs does it take? Snakes make do with none. Birds have two. Mammals generally have four; although primates use two (hands) for something useful other than locomotion. Insects have six and spiders have eight. All are coordinated for forward motion, and sometimes backward. What about crabs? Check your next crab leg dinner and notice that they have ten legs, including claws. Oddly enough, when in or out of water, they prefer to "crab" along sideways. Then there are centipedes and millipedes.

Crabs are a major component of the crustacean subphylum of the arthropod phylum. They have two eyes on the ends of stalks, plus antennae. Some have adapted to life on land. In isolation from other river habitats, one unique variety of crab has adapted to the peculiar environment of the ancient sewers of Rome: the venerable Cloaca Maxima (built around 600 BC). Rob Dunn of North Carolina State University suggests this new species evolved over the last two thousand years via a distinctly different mating season than other crabs have.

5. Is your appendix a useless, vestigial remnant left behind by evolutionary change? An international team (Heather Smith, William Parker, Sanet Kotzé, and Michel Laurin; 2013) has catalogued the diets of 361 species of mammals, only 50 of which have an appendix. These are distributed quite randomly across 130 or so taxonomic families, leading to their conclusion that the appendix feature had evolved independently at least 32 times. In general, there was little or no correlation with a change in diet. William Parker's group at Duke University Medical Center had earlier reported (2007) that the humble appendix is actually a handy reservoir for useful intestinal bacteria, providing a reserve supply for repopulating the gut after a severe bout of diarrhea. Clever evolution!

6. The digestive process of the alimentary canal has its own special chemistry: with proton pump cells in the stomach to generate hydrochloric acid for digestion, while the intestines are alkaline (slightly basic) for better nutrient absorption. That requires special cells in the duodenum portal to generate bicarbonate to neutralize the stomach acid and keep it out of the alkaline intestines. Could that be another curious case of <u>alimentary</u> fine-tuning?

7. There is yet another puzzling complexity in the knee, which is managed differently in various mammals. In humans, the knee is a major load-bearing joint that allows limited forward and backward motion, but much greater restriction of lateral motion, side to side. This pattern is controlled by a complicated arrangement of ligaments connecting from bone to bone.

For example, there are two ligaments running in between the femur's lower surface and where it rests upon the tibia's upper surface. The anterior cruciate ligament (ACL) connects the lower posterior (rear) surface of the femur (thigh bone) to the upper anterior (front) part of the tibia (shin bone). This prevents the femur from sliding backward and off of the top rear of the tibia. We frequently read about football players exceeding the tensile limits of this ligament, tearing it by hyperextension. The other direction is restricted by the posterior cruciate ligament (PCL). Its function is to prevent the tibia from sliding off the back of the lower femur. This is less common, but can occur when one falls forward onto a bended knee, striking the front of the upper tibia, as once befell my brother Dr. Bubba.

Add to these the medial collateral ligament (MCL) and the lateral collateral ligament (LCL), which hold the lower femur to the upper tibia and fibula (smaller calf bone), so that they cannot normally bend sideways. Again we have seen sports injuries in which the MCL is torn, with career-ending consequences. Then, in between the lower surface of the femur and the upper surface of the tibia there is cartilage padding known as the meniscus. This is subject to arthritic damage, but works fine during the years of evolutionary interest (i.e., reproductive years).

Parthenogenesis, Anyone?

Parthenogenesis (from the Greek for "virgin birth") is a process of reproduction without fertilization by a male. The ovum forms an embryo without benefit of male sperm. As odd as this might seem from our ordinary experience, it is not unusual for plant reproduction, and even some small animal species, such as insects and rotifers (a microscopic class of fresh water plankton), some bees and scorpions. There have also been reported cases of asexual reproduction of certain birds, Komodo dragons and other reptiles, and hammerhead sharks, plus a slowly growing list of others. In many cases, this happens only when very few males are available. The female progeny resume normal bisexual reproduction once males become plentiful. The question arises whether this might provide a path forward when there are drastic chromosome mutations to be proliferated.

This subject takes us into strange territory. If parthenogenesis is ruled out, then what heterosexual mechanism is there to proliferate a mutant new species from a single variant individual to a sustainable number of progeny? This does not mean that it did not or could not happen. It just means that we don't know how it could ever succeed at the subcellular and molecular mechanistic level. A particular problem with asexual reproduction in diploid animals is that there is no useful mixing of the coding for epigenetic markers (page 110) in the resulting DNA. As with cloning of mammals, multiple defects arise, which could become inbred within a few generations of parthenogenesis. If it worked, would males be expendable?

If you wish to follow research in this field, search the Internet for "karyotype evolution." To find the number, type, and size of chromosomes of other species, search for the common, ordinary name of the plant or animal with the word "karyotype." The **karyotype** of an organism is its total number of chromosomes. Biologists have yet to frame a satisfactory meiotic mechanism for how evolution can proceed heritably following a substantial change in karyotype, which must have been prodigious during the Cambrian explosion. The problem is not with natural selection, but with fertility.

A lot is known about chromosomes. We know how chromosome pairing works in normal cell division. We know how chromosome pairing works in normal reproduction. Less understood is how evolution could change the karyotype, and thereby evolve a new taxonomic genus or family. Could asexual parthenogenesis be the answer? Stay tuned.

Recapitulation

From this review of a number of curiosities in biology, we can make this observation with a high degree of confidence:

Over the last half billion years, evolution has been extremely busy!

From a brief look at a dozen or so examples, most of which sprang forth rather suddenly during the Cambrian Explosion (in addition to thousands more that would be required), it is clear that there were an enormous number of design challenges to be overcome by random variation with natural selection. It does not mean that a fortuitous sequence of unguided mutations could not be construed by experts to account for almost every anatomical feature and physiological function that could be discussed. Some do question its adequacy to account for the sudden proliferation of phyla in the Cambrian Explosion. Eyes and flagella could plausibly evolve in a geologic blink of twenty million years, but for more than six dozen new phyla to evolve would require too many thousands of variant features to assemble concurrently.

The problem is chromosome function. Perhaps evolutionary biologists will sort out the theoretical solutions for reproduction after a change in karyotype (the number of chromosomes) in one or more generations of descent. Until then, let's remember that Darwin's theory, enabled by coding errors in DNA, works amazingly well for natural explanations of the origin of species. One may choose to believe that nothing more is needed to explain all of the complexities of life.

At the same time, polite dissenters should not be derided as obtuse *troglodytes* if they believe that a mere twenty million years is too short for the limitless labyrinth of trial-and-error mutations needed before so great a multiplicity of favored changes could evolve in the early Cambrian. If you disagree with that last sentence, wait until the next two or three chapters, where we get deeper into the molecular structure of life. There you will see some improbabilities so stark that evolution's processes alone might never be able to overcome all of them in any span of time. After that, I will owe you a round of entertainment about the prospects of life on other planets (chapter 17), and what politicians think of science (chapter 18).

Chapter 14

Revelation Through Organic Chemistry

❖ *Asymmetry (Chirality) of Carbon Compounds*

There have been many books on science and religion written by physicists, astronomers, geologists, biologists, philosophers, and theologians. Chemists have contributed relatively little since C.A. Coulson's elegant and insightful *Science and Christian Belief* (1955). You are about to discover that there are indeed examples of curiosities and revelations from this scientific discipline that will fascinate you as well.

For one thing, what is it with all these carbon compounds? What's so important about carbon? To begin with, **organic chemistry** is the study of carbon compounds. Carbon, it turns out, is a very special and vitally important element, mainly because of its unequalled ability to form many different kinds of complex and useful compounds. It can share **covalent** bonds to other carbon atoms, as well as to hydrogen, nitrogen, oxygen, chlorine, sulfur, and other elements in a nearly bewildering array of stable molecular structures. Carbon can form single or double bonds to oxygen atoms, and can form single, double, or even triple covalent bonds to nitrogen or other carbon atoms.

Other than ubiquitous and vital water, H_2O, and the inorganic chemicals in bones and teeth, no other molecular compound lacking carbon is an essential part of the structure and driving force of living organisms. Carbon alone, in compounds so numerous and diversely complex, is involved in all the structures and functions of all living organisms, so that carbon may rightfully be considered **the** quintessential element of life.

For a thorough understanding of this complexity, you may enroll in any organic chemistry class at a nearby community college. You may consult a textbook; but it is not necessary, for you need not become a master of carbon compounds at this point. I will introduce a few useful concepts to help you visualize this material. For some readers, this may prove to be difficult as we do not often think in three-dimensional terms, but I pledge my best efforts to take you far enough to leave you in awe.

What Do Proteins Do All Day?

Proteins are vital components of all living cells. They are naturally occurring **polymers** of chains of amino acid units: **R–CH(NH$_2$)COOH**. This formula is a way of showing on one line four different groups attached to the carbon on its left. The four groups are –R, –H, –NH$_2$, and –CO$_2$H. In a protein, each amino acid is bonded to the next by removal of the hydroxyl (–OH) unit from its carboxyl group (–COOH) and a hydrogen atom (–H) from the amino group (–NH$_2$) of the next, to form a **peptide** bond, plus a molecule of water (H$_2$O). Examine the polypeptide chain of three amino acids shown in two-dimensional formulas below.

Repetitive addition of a sequence of amino acids in the laboratory forms a longer polymer called a polypeptide. Naturally occurring polypeptides in living cells are called proteins. The sequence of amino acids in each protein is not random, but has a very precisely defined order, ultimately derived from DNA's code. The physiological function of each particular protein is defined by its unique sequence of these different amino acids and by the essential way it is folded onto itself. Some are **enzymes**; others are **hormones**.

Each individual amino acid differs in molecular structure from other amino acids in the part of its structure represented by the $-$**R** side chain in the formula **R$-$CH(NH$_2$)CO$_2$H**. This $-$R portion of the amino acid formula represents a variety of structures, with varying numbers and arrangements of carbon atoms. To repeat, these protein-forming amino acids have the side chain $-$R and the amino group ($-$NH$_2$) attached at the carbon next (*alpha*) to the carboxylic acid ($-$CO$_2$H) group. This position is called the *alpha* (α) position, and we say that these are *alpha* (α) amino acids. With the single exception of glycine (H$_2$NCH$_2$CO$_2$H), all other α-amino acids have four different groups attached to the α-carbon.

For the simplest amino acid, **glycine,** the side group $-$R is just a second hydrogen atom ($-$H). If the $-$R is a methyl group ($-$CH$_3$), the amino acid is **alanine.** If the side chain $-$R is an isopropyl group $-$CH(CH$_3$)$_2$, the amino acid is **valine.** If the methyl side chain of alanine has a benzene ring (phenyl) attached in place of one of the three methyl hydrogen atoms ($-$CH$_2$C$_6$H$_5$), the amino acid is **phenylalanine.** In **cysteine,** the $-$R substituent is $-$CH$_2$SH. Memorization is not required. There are a very large number of possibilities, yet only 22 are found in the structure of natural proteins in all living organisms. That alone is quite amazing.

Of these 22 proteinogenic amino acids (including the 20 that are selectively incorporated into proteins by the direction of cellular RNA via a process called **translation**), 9 of them are now regarded as essential amino acids. This term means that the human body is unable to synthesize them from other compounds in our cells, and they must be obtained from the protein in our diet. Two amino acids have been shown to be altered enzymatically after the protein is constructed, by the chemical modification of a suitable amino acid previously placed in the protein's sequence.

For more information about proteins and amino acids, you may consult any textbook of organic chemistry. Or you might search them in the Internet. There are many brief articles in Wikipedia, for example, as well as some developed by other academic experts. Reading these, you will find some interesting ways of representing the structures of proteins, as well as the 20 different protein-forming amino acids.

Adding to the special importance of proteins to living organisms are the **catalytic** properties of many special proteins called **enzymes.** Enzymes are beneficial in facilitating chemical processes in digestion and metabolism, aiding the immune function, wound closure, the replication of DNA in cell division, and synthesis of carbohydrates and other proteins. The complexity of enzymes and other proteins is due not only to the coded sequence of amino acid units in the polymer chain, but also to the precise way in which they are rolled and folded upon themselves. This often positions some particular active site deep within a rescess, into which only the intended chemical or cell structure can gain access. Consequently, only that favored substance can reach the active site and undergo the reaction that is specifically promoted there. This requirement of a unique way in which the affected substance fits into the surface of the enzyme was described by Emil Fischer as the "lock-and-key" mechanism, for which he received the 1902 Nobel Prize in Chemistry.

One great breakthrough in the understanding of the importance of DNA was the finding that the sequential order of these various amino acids in a given protein is determined and controlled by the DNA code (more directly by messenger-RNA). A small part of the DNA sequence (gene) is coded for and controls the amino acid sequence in each specific protein. Other genes with unique sequences of base pairs will control the amino acid sequence of other proteins. These sections of DNA are called "protein-expressing genes." The selection of each amino acid is associated with a sequence of three nucleotide base pairs. The sequential order of these base-pair triplets (transcribed from DNA to RNA) thus predetermines the sequence of amino acids in each of our 23,000 proteins. We will return to proteins (pages 295-298) and how their assembly is guided by messenger-RNA.

Chlorophyll and Hemoglobin

There are so many kinds of large organic compounds that are very difficult to synthesize in the laboratory, but are manufactured naturally in cells, where they are essential for life. Here we will consider just a couple. If I had titled this section "Porphyrins," it might have scared you off! That's why I used a more familiar label. **Both chlorophyll** and **heme** (the active part of hemoglobin), have large and distinctive flat ring organic structures called **porphyrin**. Hemoglobin is a bizarre structure consisting of four heme porphyrin molecules, each coupled with an even more complex protein, **globin**. It may intrigue you to know that heme has a molecular geometry very similar to chlorophyll. Does that seem curious? Just a coincidence?

First, the plant kingdom evolved a useful mechanism for absorbing carbon dioxide (CO_2) from the air. From CO_2 and H_2O, it

257

photosynthesizes various sugars and other carbohydrates, including the cellulose that gives larger plants their rigidity and resilience. The essential catalytic agent for this biosynthesis is chlorophyll (see below). Nothing else can replace it.

[Here we must use and apologize for the chemist's shorthand device for simplifying complex molecular formulas by leaving out the symbol C for almost every carbon atom. As with these porphyrin molecules, there is a carbon atom at each juncture of two or more straight lines (representing covalent bonds), and sometimes at the tip of any straight line. Other atoms (like O, N, Cl, etc.) are shown in their known position, with the exception of hydrogen atoms (H). The number of covalent bonds (lines) to any carbon atom, subtracted from 4 (carbon's maximum **valence**), tells us the number of H atoms, if any, attached to that carbon, although not shown. Chemists use this simplification to keep the forest from being obscured by the trees. If my "simplification" doesn't work for you, please forgive us and take it in stride.]

VITAL PORPHYRIN RING STRUCTURES

CHLOROPHYLL   HEME

Later, as oxygen (O_2), the byproduct of photosynthesis, began to accumulate in the oceans and atmosphere, the animal kingdom could utilize this oxygen to oxidize its reserves of fat and carbohydrates, thereby to fuel the movements that distinguish animals. Animals relied upon a similar porphyrin chemical for the essential process of absorbing and transporting oxygen to the cells. This became the heme of hemoglobin. The striking similarity of molecular architecture is inescapable. The porphyrin ring structure is also found in vitamin B-12 in some animals.

In chlorophyll, the metal ion at the center is magnesium (Mg^{2+}), in heme and in myoglobin it is iron (Fe^{2+}), and in vitamin B-12 it is cobalt (Co^{2+}). Is this an amazing coincidence or what? Despite the unusual similarity between heme, B-12, and chlorophyll, their functions are quite distinct. Vitamin B-12 is essential for normal brain function and blood cell regulation, and has a role in the biosynthesis of DNA.

A Little Hematology

The chemical constituents of blood are well known. The fluid medium is called plasma, and its function is to facilitate the flow of some fairly large and specialized cells. There are erythrocytes (red cells) and leukocytes (white cells). The white corpuscles have five major types and are part of your amazingly complex immune system, which we will consider on page 302. For now, let's consider the red blood cells, which contain and transport hemoglobin. Their job is to bind with oxygen molecules (O_2) just firmly enough to hold them during blood flow, yet loosely enough to be able to release some to meet the needs of the destination tissues.

Delivering O_2 is the function of hemoglobin for all vertebrate animals (except one strange family of fishes called **icefish**) and for some invertebrates. Speaking of icefish, it is known that because of a gene defect they don't make any hemoglobin. Somehow they have survived by living in cold water where the dissolved O_2 is much more concentrated.

Hemoglobin consists of a precisely arrayed **heme** porphyrin imbedded in **globin** (a protein). The function of globin is to facilitate the passage of heme into the beneficiary cell walls. The globin protein differs slightly from one species to another. The heme also has eight different arrangements around its perimeter. All heme has an assembly of four pentagonal rings (called pyrroles) joined by suitable $-CH=$ bridges at the corners, holding the four internal nitrogen atoms at precise distances apart. This allows them to bond to a central ferrous iron cation (Fe^{2+}) and hold it in place where it can gently attach O_2 molecules. This elaborate chemical structure of heme was revealed initially by methods using wet chemical reactions, but later confirmed by x-ray crystallography in 1959. This achievement won the 1962 Nobel Prize for Max Perutz and John Kendrew.

Upon contact of molecular oxygen with the lungs, where the pH is slightly basic, the O_2 molecule bonds weakly to the Fe^{2+} centerpiece and goes with its flow. When it arrives at tissue sites where the pH is more acidic, the oxygen is released. Incidentally, upon exposure to either cyanide ions or carbon monoxide, those toxins bond very firmly to hemoglobin's iron, displacing oxygen. Too often, the result is death by asphyxiation.

We might reflect upon the fact that iron has just the right properties for carrying oxygen in the arterial blood: bonding neither too strongly nor too weakly. At the same time, the concentration of oxygen in the atmosphere seems to be another complementary anthropic predisposition for life. Oxygen makes up 21% of the air we breathe. This is concentrated enough to work nicely in our lungs, to bond with the iron in heme, but not high enough to carry combustion out of control with so many combustibles around.

This raises an important point. Because of its precise and complex molecular structure, it is possible but extremely difficult to synthesize heme in the laboratory, even with specialized apparatus and an array of specialized chemicals. Each of its four pentagonal pyrrole rings has to be properly positioned at just the right corner. The sequence cannot be interchanged, although some peripheral attachments may vary. Then there's the protein component. Yet your liver and bone marrow put all this together with the greatest of ease all the time. How cool is that?

Another puzzle is the mechanism by which the first plants could ever organized the synthesis of chlorophyll. Laboratory synthesis of two types of chlorophyll has been achieved in an exhaustive and concentrated effort by a Harvard team led by Robert Burns Woodward. For this and other syntheses of dozens of complex natural products (strychnine, cholesterol, cortisone, et al), Woodward was awarded the Nobel Prize in chemistry in 1965. In contrast with the extreme difficulty of synthesizing chlorophyll in the most sophisticated laboratory, chlorophyll biosynthesis is an efficient, routine process for green plants. They use special protein enzymes that do it in every leaf. Where did the first chlorophyll come from—or those enzymes? No chemical laboratory could ever make such complex molecules from a random mixture of thousands of impure reagents. Were those requisite plant enzymes assembled by chance, or trial and error? How many variant proto-plants failed before the first one got it right?

Before chlorophyll, blue-green cyanobacteria managed photosynthesis without it, and generated most of the early oceanic and atmospheric oxygen. That's another puzzle. Today, 30% of atmospheric oxygen comes from this oceanic source.

While pondering how (or if) animals ever evolved from plants, the question arises how and whether the porphyrin structure of plant chlorophyll was transformed into heme in animals. Or were they biosynthesized by different pathways? Porphyrins have been detected in trace amounts in petroleum, which is consistent with the origin of petroleum from ancient compressed plant deposits. However, there is no detectible fossil evidence of intact chlorophyll (or heme, for that matter).

After animals emerged and had been around a long time, certain phyla and classes were able to evolve blood-circulating vascular systems. That must have been quite lucky and timely! The question literally flies out: where or how did those first blood-circulating organisms get ahold of hemoglobin? Was it sitting around dormant, just waiting for its casting call? Did biosynthesis of hemoglobin precede vascularization, or *vice versa*?

The natural enzymatic biosyntheses of chlorophyll in plants and heme in animals are known to have the same initial steps, diverging only after introduction of the metal ion. Once the plant enzymes incorporate the magnesium, the subsequent processes produce chlorophyll. Once the animal enzymes introduce iron, the subsequent processes lead to heme. That delineation of subsequent steps could not be caused by the particular metal ion, but by whether the organism already had enzymes of a green plant or those of a red-blooded animal.

From a chemist's perspective, there is no way the selected metal ion could influence the structural arrangement around the perimeter of chlorophyll or heme. Even if we fully mapped the series of enzymatic processes for assembling these molecules, it would be quite a project to develop that sequence of steps from scratch. If ancestral microbes that evolved into green plants (or animals) contained some special enzymes capable of such magic, where did they come from? What was their previous function? Did the code sequence of DNA that determines the specific sequence of amino acids in one enzyme sort out its pattern simultaneously with that for all the other enzymes, or one at a time? Or in clusters that had different functions originally? Really? We just keep finding more questions than answers—fortunately for future research.

Hydrogen Bonds

Here is a simpler enigma. Water is one ubiquitous substance, so familiar yet so vital in the cycle of life. In its liquid form, it is the principal component of oceans, lakes, and rivers; and an essential part of us. In its gaseous form, it is a minor component of air, but can reach concentrations high enough to condense into clouds, which bring us some shade and the beatitude of rain. In its solid form, it can be sheets or blocks of ice, or its structure can be as delicate as snowflakes. These characteristics are familiar to everyone.

What is less well known, but a distinctive and unique feature of the liquid and solid forms of water, is the special attraction exhibited between individual molecules of water. Water molecules (H_2O, or as it is sometimes represented, H–O–H) have one oxygen atom covalently bonded to two hydrogen atoms. The geometry is not linear but angular, with an arc of 104.5° between the two O–H covalent bonds. Water has no net electrical charge, but like many other molecules is electrically dipolar, with a partial negative charge in the vicinity of the oxygen atom and a partial positive charge in the vicinity of each hydrogen atom. Polar molecules can orient relative to each other so that the slightly positive side of one attracts the slightly negative side of the other.

[One way of looking at this is to imagine the shared pair of electrons being pulled closer to the oxygen end of each covalent bond, and thus away from the hydrogen. That associates a higher electron density around the oxygen atom, producing a partial negative charge (δ-), since electrons are negative. The hydrogen atom on the other end of the bond has the shared electrons pulled away from it, so that the positive charge of the hydrogen nucleus is not quite counterbalanced by the shared electrons. Consequently, the hydrogen end of each bond has a partial positive charge (δ+). To some extent, this polarity is typical of covalent bonds between any element on the right-hand side of the Periodic Table (chlorine, oxygen, nitrogen, etc.) and an element to its left or below it on the Periodic Table. Those elements on the upper right-hand side (but not the far-right noble gases, helium, neon, etc.) are said to have greater **electronegativity**, meaning they have greater affinity for the electrons shared in covalent bonds with atoms of other elements. It might help if you familiarize yourself with the Periodic Table on the Internet.]

Typically, the stronger this attraction is between electrically dipolar molecules, the higher the temperature of the freezing point and the boiling point of a substance. Think of rising temperature as an increase in molecular vibrations and lateral velocity as the molecules absorb more and more heat by vibrating, moving, spinning, bouncing faster. For mercury (Hg) in a thermometer, as more heat is absorbed by the atoms of liquid mercury, the movement and vibration of each atom increases. Each atom requires more volume for this action as it absorbs more heat. This causes a slight expansion of the liquid mercury and its rise in the thermometer's narrow column, which we "read" as a higher temperature.

A solid will not melt into its liquid form until a higher temperature (thus, greater molecular vibration) is reached, sufficient to overcome the attractions between atoms, ions, or polarized molecules, and break up the solid lattice into the more free-flowing liquid. The greater the polar attraction, the higher the melting point, which is also called the freezing point. The same explanation works for the boiling point. Higher temperature is required to overcome the attractions between polarized molecules in a liquid in order to separate the denser liquid phase of the substance into its less dense gas phase. Again, the greater the electrical polarity, the higher will be the boiling point.

Compare the boiling points of a series of volatile liquids, each series being the hydrides of a column of elements in the Periodic Table. Periodic column 4 consists of the elements carbon, silicon, germanium, tin (Sn), and lead (Pb). A graph of boiling points of their hydrides shows a consistent pattern, right to left, of lower molecular weights having lower boiling point temperatures, typical of almost all molecular substances.

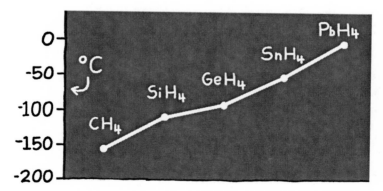

Boiling Points of Hydrides of the Carbon Periodic Family

In contrast with such normal regularity, look at the boiling points for hydrides of elements in periodic columns 5, 6, and 7. For column 6, there is the normal progression of lower boiling points for lower molecular weights of H_2Te, H_2Se, and H_2S. Then, however, there is a dramatic anomaly for water (H_2O), which has a much higher boiling point than any of its periodic family hydrides. This is evidence of a special intermolecular attraction called hydrogen bonding. There are similar, if less pronounced, anomalies for the boiling points of ammonia (NH_3) and hydrogen fluoride in comparison with normal behavior for the other hydrides of their periodic families.

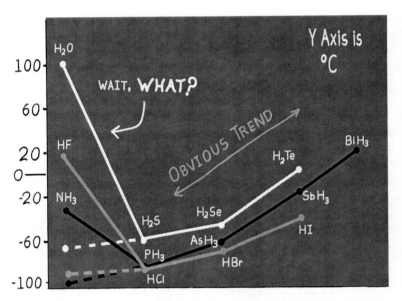

Boiling Points of Hydrides of Other Periodic Families

Now, I want you to bear with me for another few pages, because we are about to reveal a very special feature of the O–H covalent bond. If you can digest the next few paragraphs, I promise it will be well worth your while. Here we go.

The hydrogen atom is unusually small in comparison with atoms of all other covalently bonded elements. Atoms of all other elements have additional electrons that are not part of the covalent bond, but are there to balance the positive charge of the nucleus. In the singular case of hydrogen, there are **no** electrons other than the shared pair in its polarized covalent bond. So the space needed for a hydrogen atom is very small and it can approach much more closely to the oxygen atom of another water molecule. This brings the weak negative (δ-) and positive (δ+) partial charges into closer proximity so that the attraction is greatly enhanced. This rare property is called the "**Hydrogen Bond.**" It's not nearly as strong as a covalent bond or the electrical attraction of ionic salts, but it is significantly stronger than the dipolar attractions between any other molecules.

Moreover, the most stable orientation of one water molecule to another is an arrangement with each hydrogen atom directly in line between its own oxygen and the oxygen atom of another molecule. This requires all of the H_2O molecules of solid water (**ice, that is**) to be aligned with O–H bonds lined up end to end with the hydrogen head pressed up against the oxygen of another molecule in a specific geometry. We can depict this with a dotted line to represent a hydrogen bond:

$$\begin{array}{cccccc} \delta\text{-} & \delta\text{+} & \delta\text{-} & \delta\text{+} & \delta\text{-} & \delta\text{+} \\ \text{O–H} & \cdots & \text{O–H} & \cdots & \text{O–H} \\ \text{H} & & \text{H} & & \text{H} \end{array} \quad \text{and so forth}$$

This three-dimensional orientation takes up a bit more room per molecule than if there were no hydrogen bond with its spatial requirements. Therefore, when water freezes, it must <u>expand</u> to accommodate the specific spatial orientations of the hydrogen bonds, and the solid becomes less compact (less dense) than its liquid form. Conversely, when ice melts, the solid lattice collapses. Consequently, icebergs and ice cubes float.

Few other materials do this. Pure elemental silicon (Si), gallium (Ga), antimony (Sb), and bismuth (Bi) expand slightly upon freezing, which is useful in making solder with bismuth alloys. Every other chemical substance except water contracts and becomes denser when it freezes. That is the normal way for nearly everything other than water.

The expansion of water when it freezes is lifesaving. Think of what would happen if water contracted upon freezing like everything else. For one thing, ice would be denser than liquid water and blade skates could not skate on it. Far more importantly, the ice would sink when water freezes, and entire lakes would freeze solid. Every winter would imperil species living in water. How would that affect aquatic species struggling to survive? Every Ice Age would cause mass extinctions.

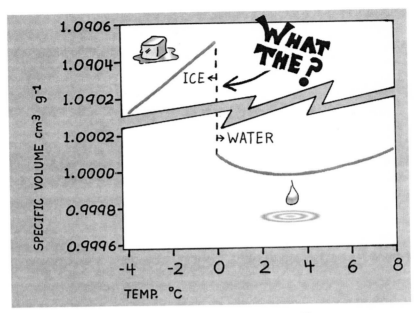

ANOMALOUS EXPANSION OF WATER UPON FREEZING

You may not have thought about it, but ice skating works only because of this curious feature of water. When you skate on ice, the thin blade of your skate presses down on this expanded lattice of solid ice. That pressure causes a thin surface of the ice to collapse into a liquid film directly beneath the skate blade. Since the liquid is far more fluid than the solid, it is more slippery, and you can glide along with much less frictional resistance. Once the skate blade has moved past this point, the super-cooled water immediately refreezes after the blade's pressure is removed. But if the temperature is too cold, the ice lattice will not collapse under the blade and you cannot skate on it.

Consider then what else would happen without hydrogen bonding between water molecules. Water's boiling point would be at a far lower temperature, and almost all of the water on Earth would be gaseous. There would not be enough condensation of rain to fill lakes and oceans. No known living species could survive that. You can see that it is a unique and vital feature of water that it has special intermolecular attractions due to hydrogen bonding. Otherwise, life would be far more tenuous. One can certainly wonder whether the hydrogen bond is just another super-lucky circumstance in an impersonal, purposeless world, or whether this is yet another example of an anthropic purpose to be added to all the other ways in which nature is consummately fine-tuned for life.

Hydrogen Bonding to Nitrogen

Can you stay with me for one more step about hydrogen bonds? I promise you will be glad you did. It is important that the electrical polarity of the O–H bond in water creates a special situation for dipoles to approach closer when the tiny H atom of one molecule lines up directly toward the O of another molecule. A weaker hydrogen bond works for certain molecules that have a <u>nitrogen</u> atom bonded to hydrogen.

The N–H covalent bond is not as polarized as the O–H covalent bond, because nitrogen is not as electronegative as oxygen and does not pull the shared pair of electrons toward itself as strongly as does oxygen. When I was in graduate school, hydrogen bonding was thought to be singularly exhibited by molecules (like water, alcohols, and sugars) with their O–H covalent bonds exposed out on their periphery. Now, it is well established that N–H covalent bonds, similarly exposed on a molecule's edge, can also have a hydrogen-bond effect, albeit weaker than for O–H. Compare the elevated boiling points of both NH_3 and H_2O on page 264.

The best and most important example is the internal structure that holds together the two strands of the double helix of deoxyribonucleic acid (DNA). Recall the fact that four nucleotide bases [cytosine (C), adenine (A), guanine (G), and thymine (T) in very specific pairs (only C:G or A:T)] form connective bridges between DNA's entwined coaxial helices (see page 164). In cell division the two strands are separated in order to generate two new identical double helices. For each of the original two strands, every cytosine (C) must match up with a guanine (G) nucleotide, and every (G) must match up with a new (C). Similarly, every adenine (A) from either of the two original strands must pair with a new thymine (T), and every T must match up with a new A. That's how chromosome replication works to produce two "daughter" DNA double helices, each identical with the original.

So what does this have to do with weak hydrogen bonds? It is indispensable and intrinsic. Each nucleotide in its place along either helical strand is attached to its own outer helical coil in such a way that one or two N–H covalent bonds are extended across the central axis of the DNA, and directly at a nitrogen or oxygen atom of the nucleotide with which it is paired. These relatively weak hydrogen bonds, N–H $\cdots$ N, or N–H $\cdots$ O, hold the two strands together at every cross-link. When the DNA replication process begins separating the two strands so that they can be reassembled into two new double helices, all that has to be broken are these weak hydrogen bonds of N–H $\cdots$ N and N–H $\cdots$ O across the DNA axis.

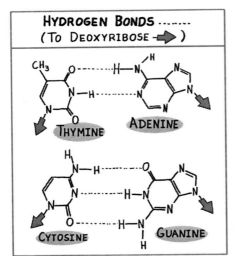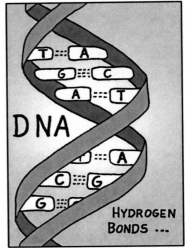

Hydrogen Bonding from Pyrimidine to Purine in DNA

Understanding this mechanism holding the DNA strands together raises a new anthropic coincidence. If the hydrogen bonds of N–H $\cdots$ N and N–H $\cdots$ O were nearly as strong as O–H $\cdots$ O, they would be far too strong for the rapid process by which DNA is unzipped prior to cell division. If they were too weak, the whole business could not hang together. It had to be not too weak and not too strong, but just right. Fine-tuning is everywhere.

Optical Activity and Louis Pasteur

This next illustration may be elusive, but see if you can absorb the essence of it. If the concept seems incomprehensible, just skip down to the last paragraph of this subtitle.

In 1815, Jean-Baptiste Biot studied the effect upon polarized light by solutions of various biological chemicals. In some cases, he found that the plane of the polarized light was rotated to the right (clockwise), and in others, to the left (counterclockwise). He had no explanation for this effect. In 1848, Louis Pasteur devised the correct theory based upon the three-dimensional molecular structure of carbon compounds.

To demonstrate this effect, take two pair of Polaroid® sunglasses. Hold them together so that the plane of either lens of one pair is parallel to and coaxial with a lens of the other pair. Through this alignment, with one eye you can see a lighted object through the two aligned lenses. Rotate only one of the lenses by turning it gradually vertical, keeping them coaxial in parallel planes and in line with the object. Notice that the image darkens to the point that nothing can be seen through the aligned lenses when one is rotated 90° from the other about their common perpendicular axis.

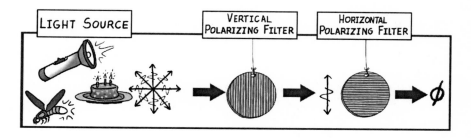

Light can be described as a wave with vibration in all directions lateral to the path of the beam of light. A Polaroid lens has the effect of blocking all vibrations except in one perpendicular plane. Polaroid sunglasses are aligned so that the horizontal components of light waves are blocked, and only the vertical vibrations pass through. Because vertical vibrations are absorbed better by the surface of water while the horizontal waves reflect cleanly, Polaroid sunglasses help by reducing glare from the water surface. If you rotate one pair of sunglasses (or you might rotate your head, tilting the plane of your eyes and sunglasses) 90° to either the right or the left, you will see an increase in the glare of sunlight reflecting from water.

In Biot's polarimeter (below), a polarizing prism was mounted on each end of a tube containing a solution to be examined with polarized light. With pure water in the tube, there is no effect upon the polarized light, and it passes through with no rotation. Experimentally, rather than judge degrees of brightness, it is easier to grade the degrees of darkness when the two prisms are rotated 90° from each other: the null condition.

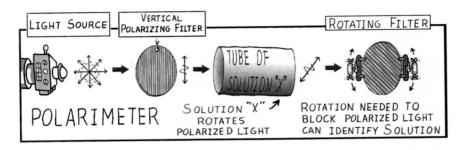

LIGHT SOURCE — **VERTICAL POLARIZING FILTER** — **ROTATING FILTER**

TUBE OF SOLUTION "X"

POLARIMETER

SOLUTION "X" ROTATES POLARIZED LIGHT

ROTATION NEEDED TO BLOCK POLARIZED LIGHT CAN IDENTIFY SOLUTION

With a solution of dextrose sugar in water, the prism nearest to the eye has to be rotated to a degree that is proportional to the concentration of the sugar in order to achieve the null point. Dextrose sugar rotates the polarized light to the right. The higher the concentration of the sugar, the greater the rotation. It was this apparatus that led Pasteur to discover that almost all biologically active organic compounds are also "optically active," meaning that in solution they cause rotation of polarized light about its directional axis. He was most excited to observe that tartaric acid crystals inside the neck of old wine bottles displayed recognizably asymmetric features.

Since this naturally occurring tartaric acid rotated polarized light to the right, its crystals were deemed "right-handed." Synthetic tartaric acid, however, was not optically active. Pasteur was able to grow crystals of this inactive tartaric acid and 12 of its salts, and in many cases these crystals had grown to be in two asymmetric forms that were mirror images. He sorted out those that he deemed "right-handed" and those that were "left-handed" into two separate piles. He found that a water solution of the right-handed pile rotated the plane of polarized light one way, and a solution of the other pile rotated polarized light the other way, and to the same degree.

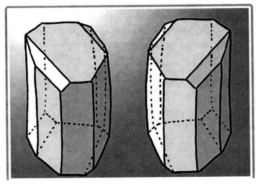

Outline of Mirror Image Crystals of D- and L-Tartaric Acid

Having two forms of the crystals implies that there are two forms of tartaric acid, differing only in their 3-dimensional molecular arrangement (**configuration**) in space. His attention focused on the two middle carbon atoms, each of which had four different groups (called **substituents**) attached. In the pictogram below, one –OH is up, the other down.

Molecular Tartaric Acid Mirror Images

Chirality: Molecular Asymmetry

Pasteur recognized a vital correlation: almost every known optically active compound had at least one carbon atom with <u>four different</u> substituents attached. It followed that the four attachments could not be at the corners of a square with the carbon at the center, for that has a plane of symmetry. Rather, the tetra-covalent carbon must be at the center of a triangular based pyramid known as the **tetrahedron**. This key structural arrangement (or "configuration") results in two nearly identical structures, differing <u>only</u> in that one is the mirror image of the other. Like your right and left hand, they are "non-superimposable mirror images." They are asymmetric, or "chiral." This new word, **chiral**, is derived from the Latin word for "hand," as in "right-handed."

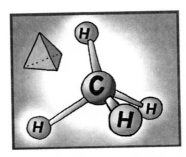

Tetrahedral Molecule of Methane, CH$_4$

A tetrahedron is a four-cornered geometric figure with four sides, each of which is an equilateral triangle. Examine the drawing (below) of a generic amino acid molecule having four different groups bonded to it at the corners of a tetrahedron. It has two stereo-isomeric forms. That is, it has two different three-dimensional configurations that are mirror-images of each other. You will experience one of those "Aha!" moments, when your mind develops a feel for this spatial arrangement, and you can visualize that the two forms are not completely identical in space. They are not super-imposable.

This is not as unimaginable as one might think. You are familiar with the obvious fact that your two hands are very similar but not quite the same. One apparent difference is that a left-handed glove will not fit very well on the right hand. The right hand is the mirror image of the left hand, and the left and right hands are "non-superimposable." This means that when you place one hand over the other, with both palms down (or both up), the thumbs do not overlap but point in opposite directions. Likewise, a pair of shoes are mirror images, so the left shoe will not fit the right foot. Once you begin to visualize this vital spatial relationship, you will see an astonishing new element in the cosmological debate among scientists. Amino acids have no hands; they are attached to R below for "handy" reference.

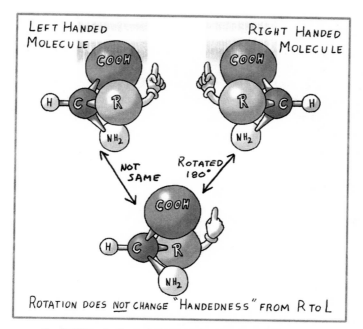

LEFT HANDED MOLECULE

RIGHT HANDED MOLECULE

NOT SAME

ROTATED 180°

ROTATION DOES *NOT* CHANGE "HANDEDNESS" FROM R TO L

**Left-Handed and Right-Handed Forms of a
Generic Amino Acid**

The essence of this section is the realization that in all of nature there is something so singularly unique about proteins and carbohydrates that the odds of this feature occurring by any random process has a probability of zero. One of nature's special secrets is that amino acids in proteins are all left-handed (following a standardized spatial convention). All naturally occurring carbohydrates are right handed. If we synthesize any amino acid from symmetrical reagents in the laboratory, we always get absolutely equal amounts of the left- and right-handed amino acid (Same for carbohydrates.). However, at some point very early in the origin of unicellular life, a chiral selection occurred, so that proteins contained only left-handed amino acids. This phenomenon and its profound implications have been analyzed thoughtfully by German theologian Hans Schwarz in his 2002 book *Creation*.

Nature has no left-handed carbohydrates. Consequently, because **2-deoxyribose** is a right-handed carbohydrate, the double helix of the DNA (of which it forms the backbone) spirals in a right-handed helical fashion, just like all common screws and bolts, never in the left-handed manner. The same is true for RNA, with a similar right-handed single helix due to having right-handed **ribose** in its backbone.

Now, let that settle in for a moment. Before we dig into this three-dimensional concept, what I am saying is that *at the very beginning of life on Earth, the most profound choice was made in pre-determining that life and its subsequent evolution of species would be based upon right-handed RNA, assembled from right-handed ribose, such that the ensuing proteins would be constructed only from left-handed amino acids.* It is a three-way chicken and egg riddle. In trying to understand that selection, the question frames itself: "What caused that? Who could have done that?"

Who, indeed! One thing is certain: it could not happen by chance.

Right Handed DNA, or Life with a Twist

Everyone is familiar with the universal asymmetric bias of screws and bolts, although you probably never thought about it in this way. When you drive a screw into wood, you must turn the handle of the screwdriver in a clockwise direction. Let me put that another way. If you are holding the screwdriver in your right hand, with your thumb generally pointing toward the screw, you must turn the screw driver in the direction of the fingers of your right hand. If you insist on using left-handed screws, they're hard to find!

The same is true of nuts and bolts at the hardware store, without exception. To tighten the bolt into the nut with a wrench, you must turn the wrench in the clockwise direction ("righty-tighty"). To loosen it, you turn the bolt the opposite way ("lefty-loosey"). It is also true of a wrench holding the nut on the other end: looking at it from the nut end of the bolt, you turn the nut in a clockwise direction to tighten. We say that all nuts and bolts (and screws) are threaded in the right-handed manner.

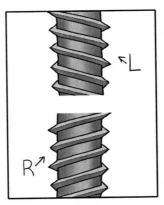 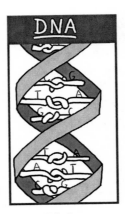

**Right- and Left-
Handed Screws**

**Right-
Handed DNA**

As you can easily test, the bolt can be started into either face of the nut as well as the other. You don't have to worry if the nut is upside-down. You never have to flip the nut over to make it fit. That is to say: the threads are right-handed in either direction!

I am oversimplifying this intentionally to make a point. Very probably, you have never seen a screw or bolt or nut with threads going in the other direction. In theory, a machinist could fashion nuts and bolts with left-handed threads; however, no one would want to buy them, except perhaps as a curiosity. Think of the mischief and confusion if you bought a random batch of nuts and bolts, half of which were right-handed and half left-handed. The right-handed bolts are mirror images of the left-handed bolts. Right-handed nuts cannot fit on left-handed bolts. You would have to sort them out to be sure that right-handed bolts were paired with right-handed nuts. Then you would probably throw away all of the left-handed sets to avoid further confusion. That is precisely why, very early in the Industrial Revolution, it became the accepted convention that right-handed nuts, bolts, and screws were specified exclusively. Right-handed threads became the inviolable, conventional standard. A purposeful choice was made.

[There are a few exceptions, each for a very good reason. When a band saw is assembled with a new blade, the threads of the locking nut are left-handed, so that the nut must be tightened in a counter-clockwise direction. That arrangement is essential, so that the clockwise spin of the shaft (viewed from the nut-side) will always tighten the locking nut and not loosen it. If the band saw blade had right-handed thread alignment, the clockwise turn of the axis could loosen the blade and spin out of it. Your familiar lawn mower blade is probably mounted the same way, with a shaft and nut having left-handed threads. You don't want these babies coming off at high speed. I have no idea why the hollow nut for attaching your gas grill's hose to its propane tank is left-handed, but it is.

There is another example from the motor sports field. In some racing models, the wheel is locked in place on the hub not by a set of five lug nuts, but with one single threaded spinner cap attached to the outer hub aligned with the center axis of the wheel. These are called "knock-off" wheels, because the spinner is loosened and removed by knocking with a soft hammer. This allows racing pit crews to replace tires faster in competition. The wheels on the left (driver's) side have to be threaded left-handed, so that the spinner cap will not spin off its threads upon braking. For the same reason, the wheel caps on the right side must be threaded right-handed. Some have said that this arrangement causes the forward spin of the wheel hub to tighten the spinner cap if the left side hub has left-handed threads, but that seems backward to me. More likely it is because a spinner cap with right-handed threads on the left side wheels could spin off upon braking.

According to "Steve Mags Speaks" in the www.moparmax. com website, knock-off wheels with left-handed spinners on the left side were standard with Jaguar E-Type models in the 1960s, as well as Corvettes from 1963 to 1966. If you have one, check it out. This site also reports that Chrysler products had five left-hand-threaded lug nuts on each wheel on the left side, although it attributes non-technical reasons for this confusing design "screw-up," which lasted from 1947 until the 1970 model year.]

This discussion may confuse someone who has difficulty imagining objects in three-dimensional space. It is worth the effort, as we will see with the three-dimensional structure ("stereochemistry") of amino acids, carbohydrates, and especially DNA and RNA. As with nuts and bolts and screws, the helical structure of DNA could, in theory, be "threaded" either in a right-handed or a left-handed manner. However, just as with nuts and bolts and screws, all DNA in every living organism has an absolutely exclusive preference for a right-handed helical alignment.

Why is that? How was that preference selected? Look at the illustration of a model of DNA, above. Notice the geometry of the DNA as it spirals upward. If you can imagine placing the fingers of your right hand around the grooves of the DNA model with your thumb pointed up, your fingertips would be aligned with the forward rising curvature of the helix. Your fingers will be slanted slightly upward in the direction that the helix ascends. Now, it might surprise you that if you were to turn your right hand over so that the thumb points downward, the fingers also would align tilted downward with the direction in which the helix descends. Aha! Like the bolt, the DNA helix is right-handed in either direction of its axis. Your left hand cannot fit its curvature the same way.

Why do you think all DNA would be right-handed, with no left-handed DNA in any living organism? It is as if some Great Machinist decided to prefer right-handed DNA when "Life's Industrious Revolution" began. This is a fundamental cosmological question, yet difficult for science to answer, although some have tried. Many will keep trying. One may choose to believe, of course, that this highly exclusive preference could have occurred without a purposeful choice. To do so requires an atheist to take a leap of faith at least as ballistic as any theistic believer <u>ever</u> has to make.

The backbone of the DNA helix is a sequence of alternating 2-deoxy-ribose and phosphate. The right-handed helix of DNA is a consequence of the fact that 2-deoxy-ribose (like all other natural carbohydrates) has the right-handed D-configuration, not the L-form. That conclusion was first reached by Watson and Crick when they correctly deduced the geometry of DNA, because they assembled it from D-2-deoxy-ribose scale models. Now this is going to be somewhat harder to visualize, but you will find it worth the effort to grasp this vital geometry of so many carbon compounds.

[As you might expect, some publications erroneously show DNA as a left-handed double helix, whether carelessly or innocently. This is not likely to confuse those who know the actual structure of DNA is like a normal right-handed bolt. In a way, since there is a 50:50 chance of an uninformed author getting it wrong or right, it may be that the incidence of this <u>error</u> represents only half of those who are clueless.

There is even a website on the Internet that is dedicated to "search-and-destroy" missions against publications showing left-handed DNA. This website is called "The Left-Handed DNA Hall of Fame," maintained by Tom Schneider at the National Cancer Institute. As of the last time I looked (June 2015), it had called out 808 or so errors and most had been corrected. Noble service! He even found a Doonesbury cartoon strip of a biology lecture in which the first frame shows a left-handed DNA model, and the second frame has it corrected. How cleverly ambidextrous!]

Rare Left-Handed DNA

As has been belabored repeatedly, the basic form of DNA is a right-handed double helix. That means that, like a normal right-handed screw or bolt, it spirals away from the observer in a clockwise fashion. It has a pitch (axial length) of 3.4 nanometers per complete turn, and a diameter of 2.1 nm. We refer to this as B-DNA, because that is what it is called by experts in genomics. It is the physiologically prominent form, and displays major and minor grooves around its surface. Our genetic language is B-DNA.

There is also another possible right-handed structure that can be constructed from scale molecular models, denoted as A-DNA. It is more compact, with a 2.46 nm pitch per turn, a diameter of 2.3 nm, and no minor grooves. It is found in dehydrated DNA.

Another curiosity is the rare Z-DNA. Brace yourself, for its structure is a transient left-handed double helix. Formed from the same D-deoxyribose, phosphate, and nucleotide pair components, Z-DNA winds those in a left-handed helical arrangement, twisting counter-clockwise away from the observer. It is longer, with a pitch of 4.56 nm/turn, and thinner at 1.8 nm in diameter. This form is thought to exist briefly as an intermediate during DNA transcription. One idea is that it may provide temporary relief from torsional strain. Think of it as the equivalent to "backlash" on a fishing reel!

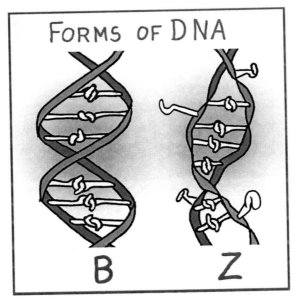

Right-Handed B-DNA is a Stable Form;
Left-Handed Z-DNA is an Unstable Transient

Let me emphasize that Z-DNA is not the mirror image of B-DNA. The mirror image of B-DNA can only be made from left-handed L-deoxyribose, the mirror image of D-deoxyribose. Compare the illustrations of the images of the B and Z-forms. In the latter (Z), not all purines (adenine or guanine) connect across to their pyrimidines (respectively thymine or cytosine).

This finding has created quite a stir in research circles. One group of collaborators from the University of Mississippi, Louisville University, and the University of Texas has found a potential drug that selectively binds to otherwise transient Z-DNA to stabilize it. Their goal is to block DNA transcription in cancer cells, and in this manner block cell division. They report that their drug converts B-DNA into pure Z-DNA. Careful, now!

There have been some ingenious attempts trying to explain what caused this exclusive preference for D-sugars, L-amino acids, and right-handed helical DNA and RNA; and how this got fixed so neatly for life on Earth. We will take a look at these hypotheses in chapters 15 and 16.

> *Organic chemistry just now is enough to drive one mad.*
> *It gives me the impression of a primeval forest,*
> *full of the most remarkable things,*
> *a monstrous and boundless thicket, with no way of escape,*
> *into which one may well dread to enter.*
>
> ——Friedrich Wöhler (1835)

Chapter 15

Revelation Through Biochemistry and Genomics

Research in biochemistry and medicine is action-packed these days, with so many jigsaw puzzles being solved as we speak. This book cannot cover all topics of interest, but will address some that relate to our main theme of revelation. As in earlier chapters, we will see that it is neither necessary nor valid for the believer to rely upon gaps in science as evidence of God. There are plenty of foundational elements well-established in science to support the belief that life is extraordinarily special. What we do know from biochemical science is enough to question whether life, in even its simplest expression, could ever emerge from a nonbiotic mixture of raw chemicals on any planet.

Back in the days when anatomical comparisons, including fossil specimens, revealed inductive evidence of evolution from common ancestry, it was enough to shake the faith of many who already had doubts about religion. It seemed to some that science might well supplant any need for belief in God. As biology and chemistry combined to reveal the molecular basis for evolution, two seemingly contradictory certainties soon emerged. First, the molecular interpretation of mutations arising from random errors in the DNA code added a compelling explanation for descent with modification beyond reasonable doubt.

But second, it also revealed numerical improbabilities so infinitesimal that the very existence of successful life points many of us toward our Creator. To reiterate Bonhoeffer, this is based on what we do know, not on what we don't know. The deeper we go in unraveling the many facts of biological structure and function at the molecular level, the more we encounter instances of what Paul Davies called "specified complexity" (page 227 above), far more profound than occasional Fibonacci ratios. Is science sending us a message of revelation?

Let's look first at some of the very basic concepts before we take on topics that are more difficult to decipher and describe. A good place to start would be a review of the descending levels of structure of DNA, from the microscopic to the molecular.

Two Dozen Thousand Genes in the Human Genome

There are 3.1 billion ($3,100,000,000 = 3.1 \times 10^9$) nucleotide base pairs, or DNA "rungs," in the **haploid** (half) human genome. This may be written as 3.1 Bbp. Someone clever has pointed out that if this were written down for brevity as a sequence of initials A, T, C, and G (for the four nucleotide bases on either side of the DNA double helices in 23 chromosomes), it would fill up 200 books the size of the Manhattan telephone directory with a thousand pages each. Of these nucleotide base pairs, 50 million (a mere 1.6%) are aligned in your approximately 23,000 protein-expressing genes.

A protein-expressing gene is a section of DNA whose code is transcribed in the production of a specific messenger-RNA (mRNA), which in turn translates the code to a specific protein. Of the ~23,000 human genes that express proteins, at least 4,000 (17%), when defective, control specific inherited diseases. Typically, the fault involves some error in one or more locations. DNA changes may occur via substitutions, deletions, insertions, or relocations from previous sequences. Generally speaking, humans have a considerably higher proportion of genes devoted to the central nervous system, particularly the brain. This could be a nice advantage, if we use it more effectively.

The rest have functions that are only partially deciphered, being mostly a mixture of non-coding-RNA genes, regulatory sequences, and **introns** (other non-coding DNA segments, formerly called "junk DNA"). Non-coding-RNA genes transcribe their code to RNA segments other than mRNA. Examples are **ribosomes** (the cells' protein factories) and transfer-RNA (tRNA). Each tRNA is like an usher, guiding a single, specific amino acid to mRNA as the latter feeds through the ribosome. Introns were once considered relics of neglected, once-operative genes, but now are thought to provide a way to increase diversity of proteins without adding more genes. Many introns function as regulators of protein-coding genes, enhancing or suppressing their effects.

The human genome groups these genes within 46 chromosomes, comprising 23 chromosome pairs. The average number of genes per chromosome is 652, with an average 103,360 rungs (base pairs) per gene, or 67.4 million rungs per chromosome. The chromosomes other than the sex-determining X and Y are numbered in order of size with the largest being:

- ➤ Chromosome 1   247 Mbp (million base pairs)
- ➤ Chromosome 2   243 Mbp
- ➤ Chromosome 3   199 Mbp
- ➤ Chromosome 4   191 Mbp

And so forth, with the smallest being:

- ➤ Chromosome 20   64 Mbp
- ➤ Chromosome 21   47 Mbp and
- ➤ Chromosome 22   49 Mbp (smaller than #21 due to shorter genes)

The X chromosome is medium-large with 153 Mbp, and the Y chromosome in males is among the smallest with 50 Mbp.

Chromosomes have been mapped to show what is known of the association of specific regions of each chromosome with particular diseases, disorders, and predispositions. Downs Syndrome, for example, is caused by an error that forms a triple copy of chromosome 21 instead of the normal pair. Search "chromosome regions" on the Internet to learn more about these chromosomal sites for specific diseases.

Genomic similarities across species (even across phyla) provide compelling evidence for evolution from common ancestry. The *hominin* subfamily (of which *Homo sapiens* is the only surviving species) is readily distinguishable from the subfamily of apes, although some close similarities are inescapable. Among the latter, the chimpanzee is closest in genomic similarity with humans. Even a cursory glance at the chimps' behavior, innate as well as learned, is convincing that these guys are like us in many respects, although not in other ways. It should not be surprising that the genomes of these two species are similar, but the similarity turns out to be astonishingly close. The chimpanzee genome has 94% of the sequences of the human genome. One highly significant difference is that the human large chromosome 2 is an apparent fusion of chimpanzee chromosomes 12 and 13 (see pages 240-241).

The genomes of the rat and mouse also have similarities to the human genome. A billion nucleotides, roughly 39% of each genome, are aligned similarly in all three species. Half of the rat genome is rat-specific, while another 28% is more generally rodent-specific. It has been estimated that these genetic lines for primates and rodents began to diverge genetically 59–75 million years ago (59–75 Mya), with most genes still mostly intact in all three species since the last common ancestor. Divergence of the rat and mouse lines began about 20 million years ago (20 Mya). Some rat genes that are not found in the mouse have special properties, such as pheromone production, detoxification and other immune functions, and proteolysis (digestion of protein).

[The laboratory method for estimating how long ago two classes, genera, or species diverged genetically is based on the number of substitutions, insertions, deletions, or relocations of sections of their respective genomes. In non-coding sections, these changes accumulate over time and are assumed to occur at a steady pace with exposure to cosmic radiation, thermal stress, and so forth. This process serves as a sort of "molecular clock," allowing genomicists to calculate the time back to divergence of species by counting the number of such changes.

Recent studies have found that the pace of these chromosomal changes for rats is three times faster than for humans. More work will need to be done to see if there are patterns for the speed of change among groups of classes or families in order to refine this molecular clock. Could it be a function of body surface or mass?

Meanwhile, this method can still give us rough but useful estimates of the relative timing of some major evolutionary transitions. For example, Waterstone *et al* ("Nature" 420, pp. 520–562, December 6, 2002) compared the gene sequences of mouse and human genomes and found 295 rearrangements of their chromosomes. Estimating that such rearrangements would occur at the rate of one every 200,000 years, they conclude that these two species diverged 295 x 200,000 = 59 Mya. Barbara Picone and Luca Sineo at the University of Palermo calculate 75 Mya as the earlier date of the divergence of (a) one group of primates (including humans), tree shrews and lemurs from (b) another group that evolved into rabbits, squirrels, mice, and rats.]

Synteny: Similar Order within Chromosomes

The domesticated horse has been the subject of considerable genomic interest, because of its extensive fossil lineage and its cultural connection with humans. One important characterization is the extent to which chromosome segments are in the same places in horses as in humans and other mammals. More than half of the horse chromosomes are arranged in the same order as the corresponding human chromosomes. This similarity is called **synteny**. There is a remarkable evolutionary connection between humans and horses, given the propensity for genes to be relocated and rearranged over vast time periods of evolution. This indicates a high degree of genetic kinship. For comparison, the degree of synteny between dogs and humans is less than a third.

For another example, "Genome News Network" reports that the female X chromosome in horses has nearly the identical order of genes as in humans. Horse chromosome-22 is a very close match for human chromosome-20 (both of which are only a partial match for the mouse chromosome-2). There is the same correspondence of horse chromosome-11 with human chromosome-17. The NIH website (www.ensembl.org), however, seems to accord only 55% <u>overall</u> correspondence between the horse and human chromosomes.

The distinction between (a) the sequential order of genes and (b) the synteny of chromosome arrangements causes some confusion. Here is one way of putting this in perspective: Gene sequencing is the analytical mapping of the order in which genes are located in a chromosome. Synteny is the comparison of how similar blocks of genes have migrated to different locations over evolutionary time. The more blocks of genes are in the same location, the higher the synteny. Similarities of gene blocks among genomes indicate the extent to which humans are syntenic with other mammals.

The common fruit fly (*Drosophila melanogaster*) has been studied frequently as a convenient genomic model. It has only four pairs of chromosomes, with 13.7 million base pairs, far less than the 3.1 billion in humans, forming 13,600 genes. It is worth pondering that some 60% of the same genes in fruit flies are conserved in humans, although not in the same order (low synteny). The implications of this are enormous and mind-boggling! Other genomic research models are shown in Table #15:

Table #15. Synteny among Animal Genomic Models

Species	Taxonomy	DNA Base Pairs	Genes	Human-like Synteny	Karyotype
Human	*Homo sapiens*	3.1 Gbp	23,000	99.8%	23
Chimpanzee	*Pan troglodytes*	3.0 Gbp	30,000	98%	24
Mouse	*Mus musculus*	2.6 Gbp	30,000	90%	20
Rat, Norway	*Rattus norvegicus*	2.8 Gbp	25,000	90%	21
Horse	*Equus caballus*	2.7 Gbp	~20,000	55%	32
Dog	*Canis familiaris*	2.4 Gbp	19,300	31%	39
Zebra Fish	*Danio rerio*	1.5 Gbp	30,000	85%	25
Fruit Fly	*D. melanogaster*	170 Mbp	13,600	--	4
Nematode	*C.s elegans*	97 Mbp	19,000	21%	6
Water Flea	*Daphnia pulex*	3.2 Mbp	31,000	--	6

(Gbp = billion base pairs)

[Ordinarily, fossils older than 40,000 years will have lost too much of their DNA from decomposition of this fragile molecular store of information. That means we are limited as to how far back science can reach in order to decipher DNA of fossils. For most purposes that limit has been about 40,000 years, but new methods are expanding that range. There are circumstances whereby the DNA of much older specimens might be preserved from the ravages of time, such as an insect imbedded in amber (as featured in the movie "Jurassic Park"). The oldest "fossil" from which DNA has been extracted is in fact a 100-million-year-old honey bee preserved in amber, found in Myanmar (Burma, if you prefer). Analysis shows that it had a total of about 10,000 genes, which is the same as today, although less than the modern mosquito or fruit fly. It is just not clear whether that means anything that we can understand.]

Molecular Structure of DNA

For many years following its discovery in pus-contaminated bandages, the function of DNA was unclear, and its structure even more obscure. At first, it was regarded as a curiosity, until it began to be recognized as the fundamental molecular basis for genetics. Its composition was shown to contain phosphate, 2-deoxyribose, two purines (adenine and guanine), and two pyrimidines (cytosine and thymine). Oswald Avery and his team at Rockefeller Institute for Medical Research found convincing evidence that DNA was the vital inheritance factor (1944). Hershey and Chase had previously demonstrated that protein could not be that heritable material.

Curiosity went ballistic when DNA's composition was determined by Austrian chemist Erwin Chargaff (1952) to contain identical amounts of the nucleotides **guanine** and **cytosine**, with about 30% of each, and identical amounts of **adenine** and **thymine**, with some 20% of each. These ratios varied from one species to another, but in every individual instance the guanine (G) and cytosine (C) were always equivalent, as were the adenine (A) and thymine (T). From this it was inferred that there was a dependency between paired G and C, and a different but similar correlation between A and T. In 1953, James Watson and Francis Crick, having learned this directly from Chargaff, correctly deduced that the G:C pair formed bridges linking the deoxyribose-phosphate polymers across a double helix, and the A:T pair did the same in other locations.

You may read their original article in all its glorious brevity as found in Origins (www.exploratorium.edu/origins/coldspring/ideas), the Internet website of San Francisco's Exploratorium science museum, with kind permission of the journal *Nature*, where it first was published: This version is laced with entertaining historical footnotes about the collaborative ingenuity and visionary insights that led to such phenomenal success for Watson and Crick.

A vital key was an x-ray diffraction spectrogram of DNA that Watson had seen. You only need to know that x-ray <u>diffraction</u> technology does not present a nice pictorial image of the material, but often reveals a useful pattern of x-ray scattering. For crystals of simple salts, by arduous and lengthy mathematical computations one might calculate backward to deduce the crystalline structure that would have caused the observed x-ray scattering. But 1952-53 was long before the advent of digital computers and the structural complexity of DNA could not be revealed by retro-calculating. All Watson had to go on was the recognition that the x-ray diffraction of DNA showed a pattern that had been associated with another, simpler, known **helical** structure. This "signature" was all he needed.

Watson and Crick (1953) with Their DNA Model
(Credit: A. Barrington Brown/Science Researchers)

Constructing molecular scale models from cardboard cutouts, Watson and Crick saw that the overall gap distance across the guanine-cytosine pair was exactly the same as for the adenine-thymine pair. They recognized this parity was profound, for it led deeper into the search for a complete model for DNA. When they applied these hydrogen-bonded nucleotide pairs as cross-links between two coaxial helical strands of deoxyribose-phosphate, they reached the correct solution to this complex puzzle. The ball-and-stick molecular model that resulted is the classic with which they posed.

In chapter 13, we saw that cell division is preceded by replication of the DNA code so that there will be two complete sets of chromosomes for each of the two daughter cells. Each cell contains a group of enzymes to facilitate this process. As part of the normal course of cell division, there is a preliminary process by which an enzyme called **helicase** separates each chromosome's double-helical structure step-wise from one end to the other. As each base pair uncouples in turn, a new DNA strand correlated with the old is assembled by another enzyme (**polymerase**), correctly pairing the sequence of each original strand. The polymerase enzyme double-checks its own work, even though its error rate is only 1 flaw in 10 million nucleotide pairs. If it finds an error, it usually makes the necessary correction. This generates a new DNA double helix from each of the original strands. Each is an exact duplicate of the original double helix.

The structure of RNA, incidentally, does not have the double helix of DNA. It is a single chain of alternating phosphate and ribonucleotides, with right-handed helical coils over some sections. In one related "great leap forward," Watson and Crick recognized that RNA's ribose component could not fit within the double-helical chain of DNA, because there is not enough room in the interior space for ribose's extra hydroxyl group ($-OH$) at the 2-position. How did ribose lose a hydroxyl group? It is generally presumed that RNA came first, and DNA later. How any evolutionary process of nature ever figured out how to substitute 2-deoxy-ribose in place of RNA's ribose (or *vice versa*) is beyond scientific revelation at this time. Otherwise, of course, we would not be here.

In chapter 14 we found important consequences of this unusual structure. When they published their findings in April 1953, Watson and Crick offered the following classic understatement: "This structure has novel features which are of considerable biological interest." Indeed! In a companion understatement, they declared:

"It has not escaped our notice that the specific pairing we have postulated immediately suggests a possible copying mechanism for the genetic material."

DNA Code: Unlimited Data Storage

Earlier, we noted that there are some 23,000 genes in the human genome, each of which codes for a particular protein. The mechanism is based on the finding that each amino acid incorporated into the protein is associated with a particular combination of three consecutive rungs of nucleotide pairs. The order in which amino acids are sequenced in a protein is determined by the sequence of nucleotide triplets (called "**codons**") in the gene.

In turn, messenger-RNA (mRNA) gets its code by transcription from a gene of DNA, and applies that code for a specific protein with nucleotides C, A, G, and U (uracil), the latter substituting for thymine. Each successive mRNA codon selects a specific amino acid, and delivers it for synthesis in the sequential order of the codons. A codon of three consecutive bases (C, A, G, or U, in any sequence) has $4^3 = 64$ possible combinations. This is a modest excess, as mRNA only needs to coordinate 20 amino acids for protein synthesis. So there is some redundancy, with more than one codon combination for selecting many particular amino acids. One specific codon (AUG) always keys the start of protein synthesis, while three others signal it to STOP. We will return to this concept of messenger-RNA in just a few pages.

These requirements raise a fundamental question: Are there a sufficient number of nucleotide pairs in DNA to code for the enormous number of inherited features within and among species? The short answer is: far more than enough. The DNA code is not the <u>number</u> of pairs in all of the chromosomes, but the order in which they are sequentially aligned. Each rung may be either the guanine-cytosine (G:C) pair or the adenine-thymine (A:T) pair, with each pair having two orientations (C:G or G:C, and A:T or T:A) as they span across the two coils of the double helix. For convenience and simplicity here, we can annotate the sequence of rungs of these base pairs by listing only the nucleotide bases of one of the two helical strands. In this way, the sequence (CCTAGT) tells us that the correlated sequence paired on the other strand is (GGATCA).

For each of four possibilities in the first rung, there are another four combinations for the second rung (i.e., 4 x 4 = 16). So for two rungs, there are $4^2 = 16$ possible combinations, and for three rungs, there are

$4^3 = 64$ possible combinations. Then for four rungs there are $4^4 = 256$ possible combinations, and for five, there are $4^5 = 1,024$ combinations, and so forth. Let that sink in for a moment, for we are about to follow this into incredibly large numbers of combinations.

Compare these exponential **quadrinomial** values (for C, G, A or T) with the exponential **binomial** (0 or 1) combinations upon which our digital computers are based. The combinations for coding in DNA are vastly superior to those of digital computers. For the latter, the exponential series is based on powers of two. For example:

$$2^{10} = 1,024 \qquad 2^{20} = 1,048,576 = 1.05 \times 10^6 \qquad \text{and } 2^{40} = 2 \times 10^{12}$$

For DNA, the exponential series is based on powers of four:

$$4^{10} = 1.05 \times 10^6 \qquad 4^{20} = 2 \times 10^{12}$$
$$4^{30} = 2 \times 10^{18} \qquad \text{and } 4^{40} = 2 \times 10^{24}$$

As you can see, the quadrinomial variety quickly rises to astronomically exponential heights:

$$4^{50} = 1.3 \times 10^{30} \qquad 4^{100} = 1.6 \times 10^{60}$$
$$4^{200} = 2.6 \times 10^{120} \qquad 4^{500} = 1.1 \times 10^{301}$$

Beyond this, my humble desk computer is inadequate, and requires special interpolations. It is possible, however, to recognize patterns in a table of such large exponential numbers, such that certain relationships recur periodically. For example, **as a close approximation**, $4^{10n} = 10^{6n}$

$$4^{10} = 10^6 \quad 4^{20} = 10^{12} \quad 4^{30} = 10^{18} \quad 4^{100} = 10^{60} \quad 4^{500} = 10^{300}$$
$$(n = 1) \qquad (n = 2) \qquad (n = 3) \qquad (n = 10) \qquad (n = 50)$$

We can see this approximation is off by a factor of 11 in the last example. I will spare you the mathematical gymnastics for more precise calculations, which follow.

From the foregoing math, we can derive an amazing illustration. If we took a short strand of hypothetical DNA with a mere 167 nucleic acid base pairs (n = 16.7), there would be more than one **googol** (10^{100}) of possible combinations! Consider this:

$$4^{167} = 3.5 \times 10^{100}$$

Now, this number 10^{100} is so large that mathematician Edward Kasner suggested it might serve as a practical surrogate for mathematical **infinity** in equations containing that term. The whimsical term "googol" was coined by his nine-year-old nephew Milton Sirotta. Of course, the googol convention has led some to a great waste of time defining even closer approximations to infinity.

To put this in perspective, the known universe is estimated to have no more than 10^{87} atomic particles or so; therefore, the googol should be sufficient for most practical purposes. To extend the comparison, a googol of hadrons might even accommodate 10 trillion (or 10^{13}) parallel universes (10^{87} x $10^{13} = 10^{100}$). That might be enough to satisfy even the fertile imagination of the eminent Stephen Hawking, who has suggested, without evidence, that there could be an infinite number of universes, one for every possible variation in all of the physical constants cited for the Anthropic Principle (see pages 89-97 above).

Ah, but you see, we are not concerned here with that many <u>particles</u>. We are talking about a few billion nucleotide base pairs in human DNA. That number is almost manageable at the limits of our imaginations as we have become accustomed to our federal government spending a few billion dollars a day. Nevertheless, we shall need to deploy much larger numbers than mere googols, because we have entered the realm of the vast number of <u>combinations</u> possible for a large but finite set of DNA base pairs.

For example, since there are on average 103,360 base pairs in a human gene, there would be $4^{103,360} = 1$ x $10^{62,229}$ possible combinations. Since the entire human genome consists of 3.1 billion base pairs, there must be on the order of 1 x $4^{3,100,000,000} = 4$ x $10^{1,866,385,973}$ possible combinations of the four nucleotides A, C, G, and T. Surely that is more than enough to organize life! But how did any correct, working combination ever get assembled?

Have your eyes begun to glaze? If you bail out at this point, for fear of boggling your mind, it is suggested that you skip over the next subsection of this chapter, and rejoin us for the subsequent scintillating mental excursion. If, however, you elect to stay with us here, just let your mind relax a bit for what follows. Go wash your eyes. Then take a deep breath. Are you ready?

By the Numbers

We can start with small numbers and work up slowly. We were looking at the number of combinations of base pairs, and had concluded that a short, little synthetic DNA double helix with only 10 rungs of base pairs could have slightly more than a million (10^6) different combinations. Twenty rungs would have a few trillion (10^{12}). If this imaginary DNA chain were to have 167 rungs, we saw that it would then have 3.5 googol (3.5×10^{100}) possible combinations.

If your mind is elastic enough to stretch a bit further, it can be shown that if 100 rungs have 10^{60} possible sequences, and 1,000 rungs has 10^{602} combinations, then you can accept the progression until 1,000,000 rungs would have $10^{602,060}$ combinations.

If you are speed reading through this section (just kidding!), you might assume mistakenly that $10^{600,000}$ is 6 thousand googol. However, it is incomprehensibly larger (like $10^{599,900}$ googol!). A thousand googol is "just" $1,000 \times 10^{100} = 10^{103}$ and a billion googol is 10^{109}. Although it may seem convenient to "round off" these large exponents, just be aware that it could throw them off by <u>billions of trillions</u> of googols!

Where does this lead us in the real world of DNA, which has many more than just a million base pairs? To reach these numbers, we cannot rely upon an extension of the foregoing approximation that for z base pairs there will be $4^y = 10^{0.6y}$ combinations.

[Footnote: It may be that some attentive mathematician will devise a better, more accurate formula for calculating the possible combinations of base pairs. That will deserve and have my appreciation, and contribute to an improved second edition.]

Since there are 67.4 million base pairs in an average chromosome, there would be $4^{67,400,000} = 1 \times 10^{40,578,844}$ possible combinations! Perhaps it is time to translate these numbers into the more convenient and modern scientific mathematical notations, whereby $4^{67,400,000} = $ 4^67,400,000 and likewise $10^{40,578,844} = $ 1E+40,578,844.

You can type those kinds of numbers (preceded without a space by the "equals" symbol =) into your spreadsheet software, and be pleased to discover that it works as long as you don't exceed 4^511 and 1E+308 or so. Okay? Let's try to put this in its mind-blowing perspective.

Suppose that you tried to write 1E+40,578,844 as its equivalent plain number: the integer 1 followed by 40,578,844 zeroes. Rapidly scribbling two zeroes per second, working 7.5 hour days (to allow down-time for your day job, sleep, food, and paying your taxes!), it would take you two full years to complete the task. That's just to write 40,578,844 zeroes, without the 13,526,281 commas! Check it out, as follows:

$$40,578,844 / (2 \times 60 \times 60 \times 7.5 \times 365) = 2.06 \text{ years (or 2 years, 3 weeks)}$$

You had better lay in a stock of a thousand or so ballpoint pens.

Similarly, the entire human genome, with its 3.1 billion base pairs, has the potential of $4^{3,100,000,000}$ different combinations, which we can approximate as 1E+1,866,385,973 if the above relationships hold for such large numbers. That would be 1 followed by almost 1.9 billion zeroes, which is a lot of zeroes. To write that out at the same pace as above (2 per second), you will have to give up your day job so you can devote 15 hours a day to this heroic task. It will take you over 47 years (and 333 <u>gross</u> of ball point pens) to do the job! That leaves no time to qualify for Social Security benefits. So let's just mimic comedian Steve Martin and declare: "Let's <u>don't</u>, and <u>say</u> we did!"

Keep in mind that whether we write 1E+1,866,385,973 or $10^{1,866,385,973}$ (or 1 followed by almost 1,866,386,000 zeroes), we are representing the number of times that we repeatedly multiply by 10, which in this case would be well over 1.866 billion times. That is an incredibly large number, but is it large enough for all the mutations that could possibly be needed to evolve us to where we are today? Apparently so, for here we are. Whether 3.5 billion years has provided enough time to work out the correct combinations for just a few million known species by random biochemical processes without outside help is another matter.

Telomeres Tell Your Age

The more detail that is revealed by DNA studies, the more ingenious it all appears. For one example, the very ends of chromosomes have special protective features. These end structures have been shown to protect temporarily against the aging of the organism.

Generally, for more complex organisms (*eukaryotes*), including all higher plants and animals, the DNA at the ends of each chromosome has non-coding patterns of base pair sequences. These end sequences are **telomeres** (TELL-*uh-mere* or TEE-*lo-mere*, from the Greek words for "end parts"). They typically have rather simple, repetitive sequences of the usual base pairs. These telomeric end sections are not associated with information coded into the DNA, but serve instead as disposable, "tear-away" padding.

The DNA replication process preceding cell division cannot perfectly copy the two terminal ends of a chromosome's DNA double helix. This error could prove lethal to the replication of DNA coding for the two cells being formed were it not for these end parts known as telomeres. Each successive replication damages part of the telomere at each end, causing it to be sacrificed in the process. This provides protection vital to the operative coding information in the rest of the DNA, but at an eventual cost. In effect, telomeres absorb the damage for many years until well past the person's reproductive lifespan (after which, evolution becomes inoperative, anyway!). It is hard to see how "descent with modification" would have any control of the telomeres' protective function past our reproductive years. So have we found yet another anthropic coincidence?

Over a series of cell divisions, the telomere structure is gradually used up, until it is consumed, and thereafter can no longer protect the coded sections of its chromosome. At that moment, we are in mortal trouble. Any further cell division without the unique protective shield of the telomeres will end up badly, with defective replication of the DNA code. This ultimate consequence is one of the causes of what we call "aging."

For a fascinating account of how this was discovered, you should read *The Immortal Life of Henrietta Lacks*, by Rebecca Skloot. It is the story of her fabulous *HeLa* cell line and the legacy of the woman whose cancer cells survive her today for the benefit of medical research. Cancer cells, like stem cells, tend not to consume their telomeres.

In pursuit of this riddle, it was discovered that cancer cells use the enzyme called **telomerase** to reverse this damage by rebuilding some of the sacrificial telomere. This led a group at Harvard to see if telomerase could repair the fraying telomere ends of healthy cells, in a kind of "telomere therapy." Sure enough, when aged lab mice were treated with telomerase, they got younger in certain respects. It will be interesting to see where this goes. Volunteers?

Another group under Aubrey de Grey has postulated seven different aspects or causes of aging, including "cell senescence," whereupon cells are no longer able to divide. He has established the Strategies for Engineered Negligible Senescence (SENS) Foundation, along with his earlier Methuselah Foundation, to support research in this field. Their objective is to combine gene therapy with regenerative medicine (see below) as a promising pathway for restoring body parts.

Mitochondrial DNA

While most DNA is found in the cell nucleus, a quite different form
is found in small, extra-nuclear bodies called mitochondria. These
are the agents (a few thousand within each cell) that convert food
energy into adenosine triphosphate (ATP), which powers the cellular
processes. Compared with human nuclear DNA, which has 3.1 billion
base-pair "rungs" connecting the coaxial double helices, mitochondrial
DNA (mtDNA) is diminutive, with only 16,600 base pairs (about one-
thousandth the size of the smallest of our 46 human chromosomes). Even
so, that allows for $10^{9,994}$ possible combinations, which is approaching
within range of googol to the hundredth power: $(10^{100})^{100} = 10^{10,000}$. Of
those combinations, only a few million exist in working order, which
implies something more selective than "survival of the fittest"!

Typically, in mammals this shorter mtDNA is a molecular ring, as
if two opposite ends had joined, with no need for telomeres. It expresses
a mere 37 factors needed for the cell's energy processes. Of these, 13
express protein enzymes and hormones, 22 are for transfer-RNA (tRNA),
and two guide assembly of the two halves of a ribosome (the "protein
factory").

It might astonish you to know that your mitochondrial DNA came
exclusively from your mother, regardless of your gender. Your mother
got her mtDNA from her mother, who got it from her mother, and
so on. This has excited speculation about where it started; i.e., the
mitochondrial Eve, ancestral mother of us all. The brilliant British
geneticist Brian Sykes has explored this riddle in *The Seven Daughters
of Eve*, based on the near-homogeneity of all human mtDNA. Relying
on an average of one mutation every 3,500 years, Sykes identified seven
basic clusters of genetic variants among Europeans alone. These resulted
from only a dozen or so mutations over the past 45,000 years, ending
approximately 10,000 years ago. Some contend this is contrary to the
notion of human descent from Neanderthal females, which had over two
dozen mtDNA variants from humans. It is a fascinating story that Sykes
tells very well.

Sykes later found another 29 mtDNA lines worldwide, of which
13 are in Africa. Significantly, only one of these 13 is an ancestral
line to those on other continents. From this evidence, Sykes inferred
a chronology, with the one African "mother clan" crossing up into the
Middle East 100,000 years ago, and on into Europe and Asia 50,000
years ago. This retraced the earlier migration of the Heidelberg and
Neanderthal species.

Your father, by the way, carried his mother's (and therefore, her mother's, *et sequitur*) mtDNA, but did not transfer it to you. Neither did his father transfer it to him. Nor did your mother's father, OK? The mitochondrial DNA line is exclusively maternal. That raises the question whether the sperm cell from the father had mitochondria. In fact, they do feature these little power plants, mostly in the tail appendage, working hard to propel the head of the sperm into the female's egg cell to complete the vital process of fertilization. Once the propulsive tail is broken off, the father's mtDNA can't get into the action. Any male mitochondria that do accidentally get into the egg carry a small protein tag called ubiquitin, which designates them for destruction within the egg. As you might expect, there is no recombination of mtDNA. Consequently, there is no scrambling or shuffling the deck from generation to generation. There's only the rare mutation.

If you wondered, there is a male line of ancestral DNA: it's the male Y-chromosome! This is one of the smallest human chromosomes, with a mere 72 protein-controlling genes. One of these is a unique and vital gene called SRY. This is the one that conveys certain masculine traits if it succeeds with XY pairing in the fertilized ovum. Similar ancestral analysis of the Y chromosome in European and Middle Eastern males corroborated Sykes's analysis. Peter Oefner and Peter Underhill and their Stanford group found a small number of "Sons of Adam," traceable back 89,000 years to the most recent common ancestor of all living men. That date was 23,000 years before the first human migration out of Africa.

Reading the DNA Code (to be read slowly and patiently!)

As discussed earlier, for each protein there is a specific section of DNA, called a gene, which transmits its code to RNA (*RIBO*-Nucleic Acid), which in turn directs the sequencing of amino acids into protein. In humans, there are about 23,000 protein-coding genes. The process for getting the protein sequence assembled correctly according to the gene code consists of two steps: (1) transcription and (2) translation.

Transcription is the method by which a special enzyme called RNA-polymerase reads the entire sequence of A, T, C, and G from a DNA gene in order to install the genetic code into RNA. RNA consists of a single-stranded chain of phosphate and <u>ribose</u>, instead of <u>deoxyribose</u>, to which are attached unpaired nucleotide bases. This vital distinction keeps the cell and its processes from confusing DNA and RNA.

Another distinction is that in the formation of the messenger-RNA (mRNA), with its nucleotide code transcribed precisely from one gene of the cell's DNA, another vital substitution is made: inserting a different pyrimidine base known as **uracil** to take the place of thymine in the sequence. While a partial nucleotide sequence of three triplets in one strand of uncoupled DNA might be CAT GTA GCG, when this code is transcribed onto the derived mRNA, it becomes <u>not</u> GTA CAT CGC, but GUA CAU CGC. This single-stranded mRNA has the unique capability to carry the message of its partial genetic code out of the cellular nucleus into the cytoplasm. Unlike DNA, it can never form a hydrogen-bonded double helix, because ribose is the wrong size.

SECOND BASE OF CODON

FIRST BASE OF CODON		U	C	A	G		THIRD BASE OF CODON
	U	PHE	SER	TYR	CYS	U	
		PHE	SER	TYR	CYS	C	
		LEU	SER	STOP	STOP	A	
		LEU	SER	STOP	TRP	G	
	C	LEU	PRO	HIS	ARG	U	
		LEU	PRO	HIS	ARG	C	
		LEU	PRO	GLN	ARG	A	
		LEU	PRO	GLN	ARG	G	
	A	ILE	THR	ASN	SER	U	
		ILE	THR	ASN	SER	C	
		ILE	THR	LYS	ARG	A	
	START → MET	THR	LYS	ARG	G		
	G	VAL	ALA	ASP	GLY	U	
		VAL	ALA	ASP	GLY	C	
		VAL	ALA	GLU	GLY	A	
		VAL	ALA	GLU	GLY	G	

Chart of Codon Selection of Amino Acids in Protein Biosynthesis

Each amino acid is selected in turn for its place in a protein by one or more triplet sets (called **codons**) of three RNA nucleotides. For example, histidine (abbreviated "his") is selected by either codon CAU or CAC. Similarly, alanine ("ala") may be selected by any of the following codons: GCA, GCU, GCC, or GCG. This coding redundancy works for 18 of the 20 proteinogenic amino acids. Two exceptions, methionine ("met") and tryptophan ("trp") are dependent upon one single codon, AUG and UGG respectively. There are $4^3 = 64$ possible codons (sets of three nucleotides), and 61 of them have been shown to code for one of the

20 amino acids. The remaining three codons signal protein synthesis to FULL STOP.

When mRNA enters the cell's **ribosome** enzyme, this protein "factory" reads the mRNA, always starting at AUG, and lays down methionine as the first amino acid in the protein sequence. It always starts with methionine. Thereafter, it continues to assemble the protein one amino acid at a time, translating the sequential order of mRNA codons into the protein's sequence of amino acids. This continues uninterrupted until the arrival of one of three terminal codons: UAA, UAG, or UGA. Any one of these codon triplets signals the ribosome to stop, having completed that protein.

Ribosome Protein Factory, with tRNA Delivering Amino Acids in Sequence to Match the Code of mRNA

A ribosome is a large device (organelle) inside cells that provides the chemical machinery for biosynthesis of proteins with the guidance of mRNA to translate its gene's transcribed code. Each ribosome consists of two sections, which combine *ad hoc* for the purpose of a protein synthesis, and then separate immediately upon its completion.

The smaller section of the ribosome reads the template pattern of the mRNA code, while the larger section assembles the amino acids in proper order and splices them together into protein by enzymes that form chemical bonds called peptide bonds. This is assisted by a **transfer RNA** (tRNA), each one of which collects only its specified amino acid for insertion into the ribosome processor when its turn comes.

Ribosomes were discovered by Albert Claude, Christian de Duve, and George Emil Palade at the Rockefeller Institute for Medical Research, for which they shared the Nobel Prize in Medicine in 1974. The chemical structure of each ribosome is a complex mixture of about 65% RNA (in its catalytic portion) and 35% various proteins (in the scaffolding part). The detailed atomic structure of a dozen or more ribosomes has been obtained via x-ray crystallography imaging. For this pioneering work, Venkatraman Ramakrishnan, Thomas Steitz, and Ada Yonath won the 2009 Nobel Prize in Chemistry.

Their images show large blocks of protein as scaffolding for an intestine-like tangle of ribosomal RNA (rRNA) in a precise architecture so that the mRNA and amino acids can pass through the processor. Of extreme interest, the coiling of all RNA is right-handed, just like the right-handed double helix of DNA. This has to be a consequence of the handedness (chirality) of the D-ribose in the RNA chain. One can speculate whether L-amino acids are selected exclusively in the biosynthesis of proteins because of the specific chiral twists of the mRNA (or the tRNA, or maybe the rRNA, or all three). Think about the immediate cause of each step in this sequence of chirality control.

(a) DNA is a right-handed helix <u>because</u> its coils are enzymatically constructed with right-handed deoxyribose as the attachment point for each nucleotide base.

(b) The code of DNA is transcribed to mRNA, which combines with tRNA, whose right-handed coils select only L-amino acids for biosynthesis of proteins in right-handed ribosomes.

(c) Enzymatic proteins (made of L-amino acids) control the chiral biosynthesis of exclusively right-handed carbohydrates, including D-ribose and D-deoxyribose.

(d) Go forward to (a) and repeat.

And so forth. Where did it start? The chicken-and-egg conundrum is simple by comparison. Which came first? We will return to this profound question in chapter 16.

Of course, it is more complex than that, but I wanted you to get some sense of what is involved in <u>transcribing</u> the DNA code into RNA language, and then <u>translating</u> that into the protein's amino acid sequence. The product protein is then folded in its proper functioning pattern by other enzymes.

Protein Folding

The sequence of L-amino acids in a protein is its <u>primary</u> structure. Each codon set of three consecutive nucleotides in the messenger-RNA feeding through the ribosome "protein factory" determines this primary sequence of amino acids. The way in which a section of the protein coils as a ribbon or folds as a sheet is called its <u>secondary</u> structure. This feature is held together somewhat loosely by hydrogen bonds (pages 262 ff.). These segments of ribbons and sheets are folded together in an inordinately complex manner: its <u>tertiary</u> structure. Finally, there are many examples in which two or more of these tertiary structures are bundled together in a <u>quaternary</u> protein structure, like hemoglobin.

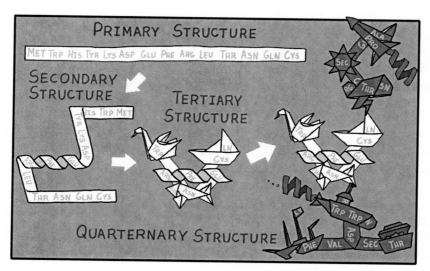

**PROTEIN-FOLDING, ILLUSTRATED ORIGAMI-STYLE
(In reality, it looks like a tangle of entrails!)**

The particular architecture of this elaborate protein-folding is vital to the biological function of each protein hormone or enzyme. If not folded in its critically precise way, the protein cannot carry out its specific mission(s), and may become toxic to its organism. This aspect of complex folding has surpassed research on primary sequence to the degree that most discussions of active proteins deal with cartoon drawings of the higher order structures, without bothering to show the individual amino acids.

The defining structure of each protein is set when it is synthesized through the ribosome factory in the cell. If not properly folded, it must be destroyed by protease enzymes assisted by ubiquitin and expelled as small harmless polypeptide fragments for future recycling. Elucidation of this process earned the 2004 Nobel Prize in Chemistry for two Israelis, Aaron Ciechanover and Avram Herschko, and an American, Irwin Rose. Illnesses such as neuromuscular diseases, Alzheimer's and Parkinson's syndromes, cancer and sickle-cell anemia have been associated with misfolded proteins.

If this does not strike you as incredibly and intricately sophisticated, then consider that a special enzyme, cleverly named *chaperonin*, has been found with the fantastic ability to refold certain protein enzymes into the correct conformation for their proper function. Whoa!

On pages 257-259, we examined the intricate porphyrin structures of chlorophyll and heme. As to the latter, heme is not the most complex part of hemoglobin. That distinction belongs to the globin proteins, in a precisely folded quaternary structure of four globin tertiary structures, each consisting of a coded sequence of about 150 amino acid units, with each globin attached to its heme, as represented below. (As you might suspect, chlorophyll is also associated around the perimeter of a large protein.)

The porphyrin portion (heme) is held in place rather loosely by a histidine ring (an amino acid unit in the globin structure), allowing just enough room for a single oxygen molecule on the other side, nestled between the iron cation of the heme and a second histidine. It takes no stretch to consider the manner in which O_2 is gently cuddled in hemoglobin to be yet another anthropic balancing act, perfectly tuned for mammalian blood. Slightly stronger or weaker—and we mammals would long ago have become extinct from asphyxiation.

This fragile attachment is vital for our respiratory and circulatory success. For example, carbon monoxide (CO) and cyanide ions (CN^-) are nearly the same size as O_2. They bond too strongly to the hemoglobin iron, lethally preventing it from transporting oxygen. As for oxygen, its attachment is pH dependent, such that the oxygen is held securely by heme in the slightly basic medium (pH > 7) of the lungs, and more weakly in the slightly acidic cellular environment (pH < 7) into which the oxygen is delivered and released. This is certainly fortuitous for our survival, and begs the question how many failed alternative protein structures were attempted during the Cambrian evolution before we got respiration just right.

Pictogram of Quaternary Structure of Hemoglobin

Other DNA Oddities

While the molecular geometry of DNA, with its incredibly large number of possible combinations, provides an elegant mechanistic explanation for the genetic variation aspect of Darwin's Evolution Theory, one might expect there to be a progression in the size and complexity of DNA with the corresponding size and complexity of the animal orders and species. This is not necessarily the case, for some worms have larger genomes than we humans do

It would be reasonable to expect that species that emerged early in the paleontological record would have simpler DNA than later (more advanced?) species. No DNA has yet survived from the earliest epochs, which leaves us with no evidence on this point. We can consider animals like worms, sharks, and crustaceans, which have survived from much earlier periods until modern times. They generally have DNA chains similar in length to more modern species. From this, one may conclude that DNA did not need to grow to accommodate a higher complexity of structure, neurology, or immunology. It has always been much longer than needed, with vast excess capacity in reserve for coordinating structure and function. The molecular structure of DNA and specific alterations here and there provide powerful evidence for the correctness of the Theory of Evolution. However, there is no clear explanation as to how evolution's random variation, coupled with natural selection, had any influence on the helical structure of DNA or its present size. Both must surely have predated the first genetic variation and selection.

Immune Aberrations

The **Immune Response** is highly developed in many animal species. The enormous complexity of this function is so bewildering that one can readily assume that evolution had something to do with it. The evolutionary history of these immune processes has been a rich lode for research. Even an introductory discussion of so complex a subject must be left to other texts. We will examine just a few anomalies.

Higher orders of animals have evolved with elaborate immune systems, featuring both molecular agents and cellular forms for defense against bacteria, viruses, and parasites. This protection is well-developed and complex in vertebrates, especially among humans. The great variety of weapons in our immune arsenal includes many with similar capabilities, making the immune system highly redundant and hard to overcome by invaders. For this reason, transplant surgeons have had to employ ways to suppress the immune system in order to inhibit its natural assault against transplanted foreign tissue.

It is exemplary for the purposes of this chapter, however, to point out three rather amazing exceptions in which the immune response appears to be naturally curtailed or even off-limits. It is a curious anomaly that, of all organs of the body, the eyes and male testes have special "immune privilege" whereby the entry of an antigen does not trigger an inflammatory response of the immune system. The same is typical of the uterine placenta and its fetus.

- In the unusual case of the eye, its structure involves its own impenetrable barrier, which prevents entry by immune agents as well as antigens. The cornea, for example, is not vascularized, and therefore is inaccessible to blood-borne immune responses. Whether this is an evolutionary consequence of selection to avoid inflammatory damage to its essential property of transparency, or just a result of its innate isolation, is a good question. Maybe both? The eye might not have evolved very far had it become opaque from scarring in the inflammatory battles between invaders and defenders. Some minimal protection is provided by the abrupt blink response of the eyelids and the cleansing function of tear glands.

- The fetus and its placental envelope are genetically different from the mother (since half of the chromosomes are from the father), and in some respects are like an allograft from another individual. Therefore, it is of great interest that the mother's immune system does not attack this "foreign" matter, which would be lethal to the reproductive scheme. Special molecules secreted from the placental envelope have been identified that restrain the immune responses of the mother, yet without interfering with the fetal protection and nutrition she provides.
- Perhaps most amazing of all are the Sertoli cells produced within the testes of all male mammals. Once thought to be "nurse maid" cells for the developing spermatocytes, we now know that they are uniquely vital in providing a safe, immune-privileged site. It is dimly understood how these Sertoli cells signal the immune system that their vicinity is off-limits. This unique capability has been studied as a potential procedure for transplanting allografts without employing immune-suppressive drugs.

Paul Gores at Carolinas Medical Center in Charlotte has worked with pancreas-impaired laboratory animals. These are deficient in islets of Langerhans, the cells that secrete insulin naturally to regulate the effects of excess glucose. In such induced diabetics, if a packet of islets of Langerhans from an entirely different genus is surgically implanted alongside of Sertoli cells from yet another mammalian genus, the repaired animal can function and survive for years without immuno-suppression or insulin injections. The implanted Sertoli cells are able to transfer their immune privilege to the immediate transplant site while the islets do their insulin thing. This may hold intriguing potential for transplant technology. Regardless, it bewilders our amazement.

Regenerative Medicine

One of the most remarkable developments in the science and technology associated with medical surgery is regenerative medicine. It is part of a broader field called "tissue engineering." Robert Langer at MIT pioneered the use of biodegradable polypeptide polymers (see page 255) to form suitable infrastructure for surgical repairs. He partnered with Harvard surgeon Joseph Vacanti to explore useful methods for regenerating body parts. Tissue taken from the patient can be enzymatically dissociated into individual cells. These harvested cells are grown in a culture dish to multiply the supply, which is then applied to polypeptide scaffolding formed in the shape of the intended body part. What follows is miraculous.

When this cell delivery device is implanted in the proper location of the body, the cells begin to assemble new tissue. Most remarkable is that the cells work as if they are directed what to do. They exchange **cytokine** chemicals with the surrounding tissue to send and receive signals directing the process. The surgeon cannot instruct the cells how or what to grow, but the patient's body tissues do that naturally by these cytokine signals.

[**Cytokines** are relatively small proteins (typically consisting of 100 or so amino acid units) that regulate the immune system, among other properties. They are released by most cells into the surrounding tissue in response to any injury or potential threat to the tissue. When you see a reference to interleukin, interferon, lymphokines, erythropoietin, growth factors, and tumor necrosis factors, these are cytokines in which there is a great deal of medical interest.

Once produced in response to a new stimulus, the cytokine delivers its "signal" to an adjoining cell by attaching or interacting with a receptor embedded in the cell wall. As you might expect, these receptors are themselves proteins, constructed by the cell for the sole function of being activated by the cytokine. It is essential that the cytokines and their corresponding receptor sites are folded in precisely the proper spatial configuration for their interactive parts to "mate." Otherwise, they will be useless, conveying no signal. If you wish to read more about these peculiar but vital proteins, there are some good articles in the Internet.]

As the implant cells grow and reconstruct the new body part, the biodegradable scaffolding temporarily holds everything in the proper three-dimensional space while it slowly dissolves. At the end of this process, the new tissue serves whatever was the function of the replaced or augmented tissue. One great advantage in this transplant method is that there is no need for any suppression of the patient's immune system, because the implanted cells are **autologous**—from the patient's own body. There is nothing alien for the immune response to reject except the temporary scaffolding.

The first successful human transplant of this kind was reconstruction of skin for burn victims. The infrastructure was a relatively simple film that was grafted onto the cleaned burn site. Another, more dramatic but with limited application, was Joseph Vacanti's implant of cartilage precursor cells (chondrocytes) in place of the sternum for a young man born without one. Not only did the new sternum take shape, but the boy's ribs grew forward to join up with the new tissue.

Typically, the new tissue takes the exact shape of the temporary biodegradable support structure. This has been demonstrated by Charles Vacanti, growing an odd appendage shaped like a human ear on the back of a mouse. There was no function for it at that location, of course, except "shock and awe." Many more challenges are encountered when the tissue to be replaced by regeneration is an organ with greater complexity.

Another leader in this field is Anthony Atala, once associated with Langer and Vacanti at Harvard, and now head of regenerative medicine at Wake Forest University Medical School. His early success was a method for reconstructing a partial bladder wall for bladder cancer patients and those with neurologic bladder dysfunction. He used autologous smooth muscle cells and/or multi-potent stem cells from the patient. He is expanding this procedure for reconstructing other tissues.

These and other investigators are now using modified inkjet printers programmed to "print out" the highly detailed micro-features of complex organs by laying down precise patterns of cells in the architecturally correct, biodegradable scaffolding. This is called **bioprinting**. An ultimate goal of this research is to be able to regenerate large, extremely complex organs such as livers, kidneys, and hearts. One can imagine that if "tissue engineered" organs can be successfully implanted and grown in patients using autologous cells, the Nobel Committee will not be able to ignore such creative inventors.

Adding to the excitement of this field, a Scottish team led by Will Shu at Heriot-Watt University in Edinburgh, Scotland, has a three-dimensional printer for layering human embryonic stem cells (once considered too fragile for bioprinting) into artificial tissue constructs. An immediate application has been proposed using these products as surrogates for toxicity testing of experimental drugs before clinical tests on humans.

These developments hold great promise. They also lead one to wonder further: by what random process was the animal anatomy preconditioned to accommodate and guide such a brilliant surgical method? The cytokine signals that can direct regeneration must have been the guiding agents for growing all of the natural, specialized organs, but when and how did they originate in the evolutionary processes? Every cell of an organism (such as you) has the same entire DNA code as every other cell of the same body. Yet something in those non-coding segments of chromosomes provides the "On/Off" switch controlling which processes are activated in which cells, and which are turned off. In this way, different organs and tissues are grown only in different, favored locations. Is that not amazing?

Recapitulation: To Life!

Here we see what a heavy burden confronts any explanation of life. We have encountered numbers so incredibly enormous that there is a vanishingly remote probability that random chemical reactions could ever have produced life with a DNA code just right for generating thousands of enzymes plus all the intron switches to activate and deactivate the proteins. If that weren't difficult enough, those proteins had to be folded in precisely intricate twists and turns, or else none of them would have any physiological effect. Add to that the necessity for the pre-existence of hundreds of large, complex, asymmetric types of organic molecules before any DNA, RNA, or proteins could be assembled. One might wonder whether 13.7 billion years is enough time to get just one simplest system organized for life.

For those who believe in multiverses, they might need something like a googol to the twenty millionth power in number of universes, which is written,

$$(10^{100})^{20,000,000} = 10^{2,000,000,000}$$

in order to have any chance of one of them hitting the DNA jackpot with its $10^{1,866,385,973}$ possible combinations. We might consider that possibility if and when one other alternative universe has been observed.

Make that at least two other observable universes (confirmed) before we accept such an imaginative hypothesis for how God did it.

Revelation
Through
Science

Part Four

Chapter 16

Abiogenesis and Molecular Evolution

Abiogenesis: Life from Nonliving Matter

Within the fields of biology, chemistry, and their hybrid biochemistry, we have found a degree of complexity that confounds any notion that life and its means of evolution could inevitably result by chance from random molecular collisions. In this chapter, we take up the ultimate question of **abiogenesis**: the improbable process by which carbon-based life might have arisen from nonliving natural chemicals. Impossibly improbable, but it did!

After its first one billion years, the earth had cooled down to a degree suitable for the stability of organic molecules. All matter was still naturally inanimate until single-cell microbes first began to register in the fossil record (from 3.5 Bya). This radical departure raises a fundamental question that cannot be ignored, although it is very difficult to answer. How could living organisms begin to organize from nonliving substances?

For centuries, the belief in **vitalism** held that all organic substances from living things contained some essence of life or "vital force," and, therefore, could never be synthesized in a laboratory from inorganic chemicals. In 1828, a German chemist named Friedrich Wöhler (who was the first to make elemental metallic aluminum from bauxite ores) was attempting to make ammonium cyanate ($NH_4^+ OCN^-$) from silver cyanate and ammonium chloride. What he got was an unexpected but familiar organic compound, urea (H_2NCONH_2), a constituent of urine. This chance discovery was a solid refutation of the chemical aspect of vitalism.

Spontaneous Generation

For two thousand years, it had also been generally believed that lower forms of life were generated naturally from decaying life with no parent involved. For example, rats and mice supposedly were formed from decaying dirt or slime by the heat of the sun, and fleas sprang from dust. This belief prevailed from its original conjecture by Empedocles and Aristotle until it was disproven by French chemist and microbiologist Louis Pasteur (in 1859, the same year Darwin published *On the Origin of Species*).

Bacteria had been discovered in 1683 by Anton van Leeuwenhoek, a Dutch merchant whose lack of education was surpassed by his curiosity and ingenuity grinding lenses for simple microscopes. Consistent with the Aristotelian view, many believed that these microbes could arise spontaneously from dead animal tissue, although the position of the Catholic Church was that every living being had parents.

What Pasteur did was simple yet ingenious. With his microscope, he had observed that bacteria were killed in boiling water. He placed broth with bits of meat in a round-bottomed flask (A), and heated the neck so that he could pull it into an S-curve, tilted 90 degrees. When he boiled the water to preserve the cooked meat, some of the water condensed in the dip of the S-curve, preventing the entry of air. This is the same principle as the trap at the base of a toilet or sink (a 1775 invention), which fills with water and blocks sewer gases from entering the bathroom.

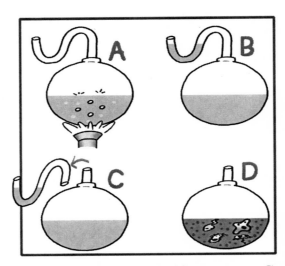

Pasteur's Experimental Disproof of Spontaneous Generation

Pasteur's cooked meat (A) did not rot and form new microorganisms as long as the water (B) blocked entry through the S-curve. But when he subsequently (C) broke off the S-curve or tilted the flask so that the sterile contents of the flask were exposed to external contamination, bacteria were observed growing in the broth (D), and the meat soon began to decay.

From such experiments, Pasteur concluded that life cannot arise from sterile conditions. He further developed his ideas about bacteria entering from the external air, not by spontaneous generation from the cooked meat. He figured that milk was spoiled by airborne bacteria, and perfected a method for heating the milk, then sealing it before it cooled, in order to protect it by sterilization, now called pasteurization.

After Pasteur, spontaneous generation was in disrepute, although his experiment had not contemplated waiting a billion years to see if something might come alive. We now explain the origins of all organisms by processes of cell division and reproduction from parents generally of the same **genus**. What, then, was the first origin of life?

The Urey-Miller Experiment

The question remains unsolved as to the mechanism(s) of abiogenesis by which life first arose from nonliving substances. Remember that Darwin's Theory of Evolution was an explanation of how a new species could emerge differing from its ancestral species. He reasoned that this process could evolve many species from some common ancestor, but he had no answer for how the first ancestral species came to be. Russian biochemist A.I. Oparin (1924) thought that the first examples of life on Earth could have been formed from simple, abiotic (nonliving) chemicals that were abundant in its primordial atmosphere and oceans. The next question was: "How?"

In slightly less than a hundred years after Pasteur, a prophetic question arose: could atmospheric lightning in that primordial sky have scrambled its atoms to generate a large number of more complex chemicals that are essential for living organisms? Our first reaction is that lightning does not raise life, but kills it, Mary Shelley's Gothic anti-hero *Frankenstein, or the Modern Prometheus* to the contrary notwithstanding. But wait.

Back in the day, my graduate school lecturer in organic synthesis was a distinguished and proper gentleman named Everett S. Wallis (1899–1965). He was the master of classical methods of laboratory synthesis of larger, more complex molecules from smaller, simpler molecules. Often this began with large reactor flasks filled with measured equivalent mixtures of predetermined ingredients, which we can symbolize as A,

B, and maybe C. Catalysts might or might not be useful, and this potion would be heated or cooled to the desired reaction temperature, usually stirred (rarely shaken!). With skill and luck (i.e., if the working theory of the synthesis were correct), one might recover the intended product, purify and test it, and confirm its structure. Throwing random reagents together from off the shelf was never an option (except for nature?).

Typically, the practical yield of intended product might be somewhere between 10% and 70% of the theoretical maximum yield. That is because such reactions usually synthesize other, unwanted side products. Special techniques must then be employed to isolate and purify the intended product. Often, the product purified from the initial reaction can then be mixed with other reactants under suitable conditions to modify it, converting it intentionally into a different compound.

There you have sequential organic synthesis. Even if you got pretty good results, say 40% yield at each step, a three-step synthesis might yield 40% x 40% x 40% = 6.4%. In another hypothetical three-step illustration, 70% x 20% x 25% = 3.5%. All you need next is a well-equipped laboratory and a good understanding of organic chemical structure and reactions, and off you go!

In one memorable lecture in 1958, Professor Wallis recounted a 1952 experiment at Cal Tech by Harold Urey and his enterprising graduate student Stanley Miller. While considering a list of possible research projects for his doctoral thesis, Miller was interested particularly in one for exposing a gaseous mixture of methane, ammonia, hydrogen, and water (CH_4, NH_3, H_2, and H_2O) to an electric spark and/or ultraviolet light on the off chance it might produce something exciting, as Oparin had predicted in 1924.

Dr. Urey (already the 1934 Nobel laureate for his studies of the deuterium isotope of hydrogen, ^2H, in "heavy water") was surprised that young Miller wanted to attempt a project with little likelihood of success. It definitely offered an extravagant appeal: to generate complex organic compounds from scratch. After all, that starting mixture was thought to resemble Earth's primordial, lightning-riven atmosphere about 3.5 billion years ago, after it had cooled down enough to retain these simple gaseous compounds. Undeterred by a high-risk, high-reward proposition, Miller was determined to try it.

Miller assembled his apparatus and filled it with his first mixture of ingredients to replicate his best estimate of the presumed primordial atmosphere, taking great care to exclude oxygen (O_2) to avoid an explosion. Within hours after he turned on his 50,000-volt spark generator, he noticed that the cloudy broth had turned a pinkish brown. This discoloration was his first sign of the formation of amino acids.

THE UREY-MILLER "LIGHTNING" EXPERIMENT

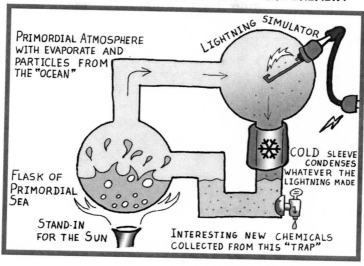

PRIMORDIAL ATMOSPHERE WITH EVAPORATE AND PARTICLES FROM THE "OCEAN"

LIGHTNING SIMULATOR

FLASK OF PRIMORDIAL SEA

STAND-IN FOR THE SUN

COLD SLEEVE CONDENSES WHATEVER THE LIGHTNING MADE

INTERESTING NEW CHEMICALS COLLECTED FROM THIS "TRAP"

Miller followed up with careful analysis, confirming that the resulting soup contained quite a few amino acids, the most abundant being glycine ($HOOC-CH_2-NH_2$), plus four others. There were even a few simple carbohydrates. This was an historic first: to simulate what may have been the lifeless atmosphere of early Earth, give it a crude electric shock, and thereby to "synthesize" some of the essential compounds required for physiologically active proteins. Published just a few weeks after the Watson-Crick paper on DNA structure, Miller's was one of the most exciting experiments in the annals of science, opening the supposition that life could erupt spontaneously after all in that energetic atmosphere.

Such an amazing discovery was also an irresistible target for skeptics and rivals. Typical of the competitive nature of science, each new breakthrough is a challenge not only to established concepts, but also to the reputations and theories of many rival laboratories. For one thing, there was criticism that Miller had found only a few of the 20 amino acids that constitute natural protein. To make matters worse, the prebiotic atmosphere was now believed to have been a different mixture containing water and methane, yes, but with carbon dioxide (CO_2) and elemental nitrogen (N_2) instead of hydrogen and ammonia. When electric sparks were passed through this more plausible candidate atmosphere, an even greater variety of amino acids was produced, especially in the presence of clay, a supposed naturally occurring catalyst.

Recently, a group of interested scientists wondered whether Miller had missed many compounds simply because of limitations in his available analytical methods. They were able to obtain sealed samples from Miller's research heirs, and applied new, more sophisticated analytical techniques that did not exist in the 1950s. Sure enough, they detected small but definite amounts of many more amino acids and sugars, as well as purines and pyrimidines; the latter two types being reminiscent of the structures of the nucleotide bases that form the rungs within the DNA double helix. With confirmation that many of life's building blocks were available, all that remains is to show how these components could be assembled into the extremely complex architecture of RNA, DNA, enzymes, cells, and tissues.

The Origin of Life Preceded Evolution

There has been a great deal of work and speculation about the earliest origin of life. One hypothesis for a starting point is that certain organic molecules could stick together to form nonliving, globular sludge (called **protobionts**, as if to confer a degree of pseudo-technical mystique). This might explain how cell-like shapes could form, but how it got from such humble precursors to the intricacies of a living cell is a huge question. It is reasonable that a nonreactive mixture of oily stuff could form a semipermeable protective crust. It is problematic, though, to expect it to evolve to where "it's alive!"

Theodore Gray has advanced an interesting hypothesis that the properties of soap could have contributed to the formation of pre-cellular protobionts. The long lipophilic hydrocarbon "tails" of fatty acid molecules can gather with other organic molecules in the center of a small ball, with the ionic-charged inorganic "heads" sticking outward for hydrophilic water solubility. Such a cluster of fatty acids and other organic molecules could form an external surface, which then might well serve as a kind of membrane around the rest.

Could it be that these micelle-like structures somehow led to living cells? This is a start, since all cells are encapsulated by a membrane. But there is a lot more complexity within a living cell than just a soapy membrane, not least of which is DNA. Among the ingredients collected within the soap micelle, was there some attribute that would arrange the nucleotides just so? Probably not.

Another partial hypothesis is that DNA was preceded by RNA, based on the reasonable assumption that the billion-year-old earth was still too hot for DNA. RNA might have first appeared as a function of viruses. Viruses inhabit and replicate within cells of organisms, and consist of a large segment of RNA with a protective coating of protein. Once these RNA strands proliferated, they might have inherently generated segments of the much longer DNA double helices, but only after a miraculous unassisted substitution of thymine for uracil and 2-deoxyribose in place of ribose. Where then did any viruses get their RNA, if not from nonexistent host cells? The purported RNA and any accompanying protein were not at all random in their sequences.

Were there preexisting polymerase enzymes available to synthesize the RNA? If so, what assembled each polymerase protein? Ordinarily, proteins are assembled by a "protein factory" ribosome, which itself is a highly complex protein, into which the amino acids are brought selectively by the messenger-RNA. Set aside for now how the mRNA could have the proper coding for the amino acid sequence for protein without prior transcription from the code of DNA. That still leaves an enormous question as to how the original viral (or any other) RNA could have been polymerized without some enzyme polymerase having previously been assembled. The implied preexistence of polymerase requires the prior availability of a properly coded m-RNA carrying the proteinogenic code. And so forth.

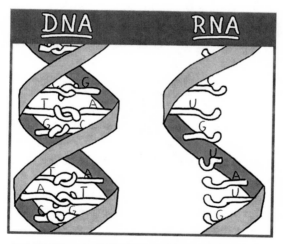

Right-Handed Helices of DNA and RNA
(Due to Right-Handed Sugar in the Backbone Coil)

The point is that biosynthesis can only succeed from an elaborate system of sophisticated ingredients, all of which must be present together at the beginning of life. Even if all the chemical components of RNA were mixed, is it likely that they would self-assemble in a coherent, coded arrangement resembling the complexity of the simplest coil of RNA? That would be an interesting chemical experiment if we had a few billion years to await its undirected consummation. My prediction is you don't need to wait that long. It won't happen.

Clearly, no one would mistake some nonliving micro-sludge for any kind of living cell structure. There had to be a lot more going on before any protobiont could reorganize as the first living organism capable of mobility, assimilation of nutrients, and reproduction by cell division. How did the first cell nucleus form? How could the first rudimentary RNA have been assembled and introduced? How would the first enzymatic proteins have been assembled? How remote are the odds for getting useful information coded into DNA by chance? What guided all this? Or is life so simple and inevitable that no directions are required for assembly?

Was this merely a matter of trillions of random chemical errors thrashing and churning about while attempting every suitable combination of factors, finally coming together all at once in a single convergence of life? How improbable would it be for such a scramble to hit the "jackpot of life"? This is far more complex than evolution of an eyeball from an organism that already has life. It dwarfs the improbable problem of monkeys typing the complete works of Shakespeare.

If we boldly assume the foregoing issues are not insurmountable, the remaining obstacles to simplest life are relatively minor. From that first protobiontic material, we can imagine that one thing led to another until prokaryote cells (lacking a nucleus) could have evolved. Any supposed, original cell-like material would have to function without oxygen, O_2, since the early atmosphere lacked molecular oxygen. By the time the earliest fossil evidence of bacteria was deposited 3.5 billion years ago, their predecessor, nucleus-lacking prokaryote cells, might have been around for a hundred million years or more. Cyanobacteria (blue-green algae) generated free oxygen, which then should have destroyed the hypothetical but oxygen-intolerant predecessor prokaryote cells.

A number of contemporary scientists are trying to answer these questions. Important questions about nature will draw the attention of the best scientists, eager to unravel yet another great mystery. Results so far are impressive, and even encouraging. There is little, though, that can lift the veil of mystery about the earliest origin of life. Still, one wonders:

    (a) If we really understood life, we could generate it in the laboratory;

    (b) We can't generate life from nonliving chemicals in the lab,

    (c) Therefore, we don't completely understand it <u>yet</u>.

Origin of Asymmetry

We have seen (pages 295 ff.) that when the cellular ribosome assembles amino acids into each particular protein it selects only L-amino acids. This is most likely due to the observed right-handed coiling of messenger-RNA and its partner transfer-RNA, which gather amino acids for the ribosome. This pathway through the ribosome ensures that only L-amino acid molecules could gain entry during **translation** to be sequentially polymerized into protein. Right-handed RNA and DNA got that exclusive preference, in turn, because the helical coiled spine is composed of right-handed D-ribose in RNA and D-deoxyribose in DNA. That all sugars and other carbohydrates have the D-configuration is believed to be due to having been biosynthesized in cells by enzymes exclusively composed of left-handed L-amino acids. This three-way "chicken and egg" algorithm explains each immediate cause in a cyclical, repeating sequence, but not their First Cause.

It is not clear from science how this preference for one chiral form of each came about. Professor Wallis amused us with one hypothesis that this asymmetric preference might have been induced by circularly polarized light acting obliquely on a pond's very slightly curved surface (representing its little fraction of the global curvature of the earth). This idea suffered for lack of supporting evidence, but it made us think. Even if such a proto-chiral effect did occur within ponds every morning across the Northern Hemisphere of the earth, the opposite effect would occur in the afternoon, with no chiral preference overall. The reverse sequence would characterize a similarly balanced outcome for ponds in the Southern Hemisphere.

More recently, Robert Hazen has shown that different mirror image surfaces of natural calcite crystals in contact with solutions of amino acids can accumulate either the L- or D-forms preferentially and facilitate their polymerization. On the left-handed faces of the calcite he found a 40% excess of L-amino acids, with the same for D-amino acids on the right-handed faces.

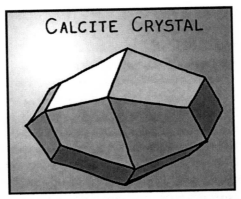

Idealized Facets of Asymmetric Calcite

That would cause no prebiotic preference overall, because for every right-handed face of calcite there would be a left-handed face (unless preferentially exposed—a clause that leads back to teleological constructs). There is also nothing about the structure of calcite that would direct any biologically active sequence of these amino acids. That is, this process might assemble random sequences of amino acids in random, non-coded polypeptides, but not the precise sequences or complex folding patterns of enzymatically active proteins.

Murchison Meteorite

There are reports that some meteorites contain encapsulated traces of amino acids that have survived the frigid temperatures and cosmic radiation of outer space, as well as the intense heat of atmospheric entry. Where this organic material might have originated is open to speculation.

Considerable attention has been given to the Murchison meteorite, a carbonaceous lump that fell in Australia in 1969. It was found to contain carbohydrates and amino acids, but no DNA. Indeed, it contains at least 70 amino acids, including 15 (but not all) of the 20 natural amino acids in Earth's living organisms. That raises a question: if the Murchison meteorite contains many more amino acids than exist naturally on Earth and yet does not contain all of Earth's protein-forming amino acids, what, if anything, could it possibly have to do with abiogenesis of life as we know it?

Even more startling was the discovery of a very slight chiral bias for one amino acid, L-isovaline, in the Murchison meteorite. This amino acid has a very long stereo-isomerization half-life of billions of years, which means that any slight preference of either stereoisomer would preserve its majority for a long time until, and after, it struck Earth. This small favoring of left-handed chirality has inevitably led to speculation that ancient meteorites might have implanted this L-amino acid bias several billion years ago, which then was "selected for" in the evolutionary process.

It is not clear what could possibly "select for" absolute exclusivity for all proteins from an initially modest excess of slightly more L-isovaline than the mirror-image D-configuration, especially if the very first enzyme would need all amino acids to be left- handed. More critical for this hypothesis is the fact that L-isovaline is (a) very rare in nature, and (b) not one of the 20 vital amino acids that make protein! Hmmm?

Earlier analytical studies of meteorites had been plagued with frequent contamination from terrestrial sources, such as careless scientists' hands. In the case of Murchison, the very presence of the 55 non-proteinogenic amino acids plus the chirality found only in the nonessential L-isovaline stand as convincing proof that no earthly contaminants were present. Nevertheless, there is nothing in this Murchison meteorite that could possibly explain the exclusive chirality of all proteinogenic L-amino acids. Of course, one could imagine that another meteorite might have arrived with a quite different mix of extraterrestrial amino acid dust, with L-chirality among some of its protein-forming amino acids. Even if so, from whence came its asymmetric preference?

Circularly polarized light (page 317 above) has enjoyed a revival as a possible explanation. The distinguished chemist Ronald Breslow (Columbia University, 2008) suggests that meteorites passing around a neutron star could be exposed to intense, circularly polarized radiation, emitted right-handed from one pole and left-handed from the other. On one side, this would preferentially destroy D-amino acids, leaving a slight enrichment of L-amino acids, and upon crashing into Earth could seed its surface with a small preponderance of L-configurations. If so, we have a new anthropic coincidence on our hands. For that to work, you see, would require that all amino-acid-laden meteorites be guided to Earth mostly passing by the D-smashing side of neutron stars, since the other side would destroy L-amino acids. If this were a random process, there should be equal destruction of both D and L!

Regardless of the source, what could amplify it to chiral exclusivity? Donna Blackmond at the University of Hull (UK) has shown (2008) that a mostly racemic (50:50) mixture of a DL-amino acid with a slight trace of excess L-form in solvent chloroform will crystallize out as

DL-pairs, leaving the dissolved L-amino acid enriched to 90% or more. This illustrates a possible pathway, assuming some biologically active, mostly racemic DL-compound could crystallize from water (since there was no ambient chloroform solvent in those days?). Timing would have been a problem, too, for if the remaining solvent evaporated before life commenced, it would leave the mixture right where it started, with no chiral enrichment. The idea is intriguing, although there is this fundamental problem: one or two (even ten) enriched L-amino acids would not come close to a biologically active protein assembled from up to 20 different types of exclusively L-amino acids.

There's another small question of what laced the meteorite with amino acids. How would they have been synthesized in outer space? Was there a reaction similar to the Urey-Miller experiment, energized by cosmic radiation or the hot entry into the ancient atmosphere . . . or what?

Robert Shapiro ("Scientific American" February 12, 2007) has pointed out that the process for replication of DNA cannot happen without guidance from **helicase** enzymes, whose function is to regulate the unzipping of the previous DNA double helix. Also, **polymerase** enzymes must be present to direct the synthesis of the new deoxyribo-phosphate polymer along each of the separated chains and insert the requisite purine or pyrimidine nucleotides to match the pre-existing ones. One would assume that the amino acid sequences in those protein enzymes were biosynthesized from the code of mRNA, which gets us back to the question of how that cycle of reciprocally dependent derivation ever got started.

We have seen (pages 209) that the first lifeforms (3.5 Bya) were prokaryotic cells and algae. These had no cellular nucleus, and consequently no replication of DNA to manage. As time arrived for these rudimentary prokaryotic phyla to transition to eukaryotic cells, how could they acquire nuclear DNA?

Shapiro raises an interesting proposition that the first DNA could have been preceded by spontaneous generation of ribonucleic acid (RNA). He believes that the necessary building blocks could have been caught between layers of some mineral membrane (protobiont?), which might protect fragile cytosine from degradation by water. I am sure I do not do justice to his hypothesis, and you might want to search the Internet for his article. He acknowledges that the odds of this are not favorable.

Asymmetric Amino Acids Revisited

Oddly enough, extremely small traces of a few D-amino acids have been found in some proteins. Khoury and colleagues at Princeton have tabulated the relative abundances of D-amino acids detected in the "Swiss-Prot" database of proteins, containing 187,941,074 amino acids. They count 837 D-configurations, or 4.5 in a million. This is the result of a biochemical modification, subsequent to polymerization from exclusively L-amino acids, that changed the size of the –R substituent, and therefore the chiral definition (based on the convention for the progressive sizes of groups attached to the asymmetric α-carbon). Here, the exceptions prove the rule.

It must be noted that the mirror-image D-amino acids do exist within living organisms, even if they are not utilized to form any protein. There are several reasons for this. Some unattached amino acids in either the D or L-configuration are not chirally stable. A pure sample of either one will slowly isomerize (transform) into its mirror image. As soon as a little D-amino acid is formed by isomerization from the L-form, some of it isomerizes back into the L-amino acid. This goes both ways until (given enough time) there is an equilibrium mixture with equal amounts of each mirror image.

This 50:50 mixture is said to be a **racemic** mixture, honoring the work of Louis Pasteur with racemic acid from grapes (*racemus* is Latin for grape.). So while there is a small amount of D-amino acid present in any organism, it is ignored by the right-hand coiled RNA as it produces protein only from the L-configuration. Once incorporated into the polymeric chain of the protein, the L-amino acid units are no longer able to isomerize to D-forms.

During the digestion of food, any protein consumed is smoothly and efficiently broken down (hydrolyzed) into its constituent amino acids. This is due to the action of gastric enzymes called **proteases**. There are also intestinal bacteria that digest any D-amino acid that might have been present. Some beans have significant quantities of unattached D-amino acids. One theory is that this could be a remnant from early evolution, but it may be due simply to the isomerization cited above. This bacterial digestion breaks the amino acid down into carbon dioxide (CO_2) gas. In case of ingesting some D-enriched beans, it may be sufficient to cause mild flatulence. Beg pardon?

One highly beneficial curiosity in nature is the fact that one particular D-amino acid (D-alanine) occurs in the cell wall of bacteria, but not in humans and other mammals. Penicillin is an antibiotic by virtue of its ability to bind to and destroy this D-alanine, which dooms the bacterial cell. How this D-alanine ever got in the bacterial cell wall is unknown, but is thought to be an evolutionary defense mechanism for the bacteria. If so, it ironically allowed a selective countermeasure for humans and domesticated mammals.

This miraculous antibiotic was discovered somewhat by accident in 1928 by Alexander Fleming. Examining a culture of *Staphylococcus* that had been contaminated by a green *Penicillium* mold, he saw that the bacterium was being killed near specks of the mold. Suspecting that the mold was releasing some chemical with antibacterial potency, he isolated the active ingredient, which he named penicillin. Nine years later, Howard Florey and Ernst Chain worked out the structure and antibiotic mechanism of penicillin, and developed a method for manufacturing large quantities of this mold extract, as well as synthetic versions. This work earned for these three the Nobel Prize for Medicine in 1945.

Time Magazine later dubbed Fleming one of the "100 Most Important People of the Twentieth Century." As a Scottish medical corpsman during World War I, he had observed that the antiseptic remedies then available (which worked well for surface infections) were lethal for soldiers with deep wounds, killing more than were killed by the infection. He found that in deep wounds, the anaerobic bacteria were not affected, but the antiseptic dose was enough to impair the patients' immune systems, with deadly results. His new medication is estimated to have saved 200 million lives.

As for Howard Florey, upon his death, he was honored with a memorial service in Westminster Abbey, with a marker recognizing his contributions placed there beside the tombs of two great eminences, Charles Darwin and Sir Isaac Newton.

Panspermia

Remember that the term "Big Bang" was coined by Fred Hoyle as a disparaging reference to the main rival to his own theory. Hoyle apparently leaned toward atheism at the time, and was troubled by the logical inference that a sudden instant of creation implied the prior existence of a Creator. His personal view of the universe ("according to Hoyle," a phrase associated with Edmond Hoyle, the British authority on card games) favored the concept of a "steady state," in which matter and energy were continuously being interconverted so that the universe was eternal and had no beginning.

It was only later that Hoyle was driven to a thoughtful reconsideration of his philosophy while reflecting upon the statistical improbability of the high-energy state needed for the nucleosynthesis of carbon in stars. He wrote:

Would you not say to yourself, "Some supercalculating intellect must have designed the properties of the carbon atom, otherwise the chance of my finding such an atom through the blind forces of nature would be utterly minuscule?" Of course you would.

A common sense interpretation of the facts suggests that a superintellect has monkeyed with physics, as well as with chemistry and biology, and that there are no blind forces worth speaking about in nature. The numbers one calculates from the facts seem to me so overwhelming as to put this conclusion almost beyond question.

This idea that there was some guiding force out there so troubled Hoyle, who also had his doubts about evolution, that he became attracted to the notion of **Panspermia**. This was the belief that life as we know it could have been "seeded" by dormant microbes brought to Earth on the rubble from a catastrophic collision of another planet already having lifeforms, a few of which might survive the long, frozen journey here. Alternative versions suggested that advanced civilizations on other planets could have brought it here, or perhaps it was their garbage that got life planted on Earth. That, of course, leaves unanswered and experimentally moot the question of how carbon-based life might have originated on that remote exoplanet before its destruction. In any event, it was enough to turn many leading thinkers against Hoyle, who gamely, needless to say, fought back.

Hoyle's protégé, Professor Chandra Wickramasinghe at the University of Cardiff, Wales, has continued to develop their theory of Panspermia. Hoyle's original idea was that we might have experienced "Evolution from Space." The Cardiff group has pursued a more modest variation on this theme. They contend that the ingredients of life could have come here from asteroids or comets to inoculate Earth with the life-bearing raw materials that could be assembled into living, replicating organisms here. Earth was visited after all; not by alien UFOs, but by comets and stardust!

To support their case, they calculated that the odds for one <u>single</u> enzymatic protein being formed by random processes, even in a rich ocean full of amino acids, is 1 in 10^{20}, which is one infinitesimal improbability. Consequently, random assembly of some 2,000 physiologically active proteins necessary for the simplest organism would have dismissively ultra-low odds of 1 in $10^{40,000}$ to be overcome without guidance.

The Panspermia answer is that the process got a jump-start by being seeded from outer space. It may be that if we can afford to keep looking on remote asteroids and comets, someday we will discover DNA and/or proteins out there. Won't that still leave the more inaccessible question of how and when it got there fully coded?

Wickramasinghe has published an interesting reverse variant on this, in which a comet or asteroid strikes the earth and splashes microorganisms among the debris cast far out into space. Most large organisms cannot survive the harsh cold and radiation, but certain bacteria can do so. Thus, in his retro-seeding theory, Earth could be the source of fledgling colonies of organisms on other planets or moons where temperature and water availability are conducive to life. This will be hard to verify and prove, but if true, would support the expectation that interplanetary transfer of life is inevitable, either from Earth or from another origin. Spattered Earth would not account for the Murchison meteorite.

You may draw your own conclusion. This Hoyle/Cardiff Panspermia Theory might appeal to some as one highly imaginative possibility. Still, it leaves unanswered the fundamental question of ultimate origin. Indeed, this is the barrier facing any theory about biogenesis from nonliving chemicals.

One appeal of Panspermia is that it tries to bypass the overarching question: is Earth old enough for any and all of these improbable steps to occur? It is certain that Earth is 4.55 billion years old. The same age is rather firmly determined for the rest of our solar system of the sun and all its planets. The same applies to the bands of asteroids encircling our sun. Asteroids are no older than Earth. *So why presuppose life based on DNA and proteins as arising from incoming asteroids? It's hard enough to figure out a prebiotic process on Earth . . . where life has been discovered!*

In 2005, NASA launched the *Deep Impact* artificial satellite to probe nearby space, and directed it to the passing comet "Tempel I." It detected clay and water, which should not be noteworthy, except for the theory that clay might have served as a catalyst for high-energy synthesis of amino acids. Far greater interest attached immediately to the fact that it also found hydrocarbons. In 2004, the "Stardust Mission" to the comet known as "Wild Two" had found a wider range of complex hydrocarbons. These findings raise again the question of how did that get there. What does it mean?

What Does It All Mean?

Here is the fundamental question for us to ponder: let's suppose that we could mix all of the chemicals whose molecules and ions constitute the composition of a living organism. That would include every constituent carbohydrate, amino acid, purine, and pyrimidine nucleotide base, phosphoric acid, pyrrole, surfactant fatty acid, mineral, *et cetera, et cetera* (you name it, it's in there). Add as much clay, calcite, and any other possible inorganic catalyst as you like. How long would it take for the first life to appear? Four billion years might not be long enough.

Cell division could not succeed without the elegant process of DNA replication, which could not happen without the enzymes that guide the replication. How would the first molecules of DNA (or RNA) be assembled before there were any polymerase enzymes to connect deoxy-ribose (or ribose) with phosphate and connect the correct sequences of nucleotides? Where would the first polymerase enzymes come from if there were no ribosome protein factories or anything programmed to assemble the ribosomes?

Our best efforts to rationalize the origin of left-handed amino acids by means of meteorites, asymmetric crystals, curved surfaces, and even neutron stars, all fail to take into account that none of that matters. Every cell has abundant access to both left- and right-handed amino acids, but only the left-handed ones are ever selected for protein biosynthesis. That is because right-handed ribose configures only right-handed mRNA and tRNA, which can bring only left-handed amino acids into the ribosome.

How would any predecessor protein obtain the functionally correct sequence of amino acids before RNA or DNA were infused with just the right sequence of codon triplet nucleotides? Where would the DNA or RNA get the correct code sequence for even one protein, much less 23,000 of them? DNA or RNA could not be assembled without their respective right-handed sugars. Sugars are not synthesized in cells without special enzymes, assembled from exclusively left-handed amino acids. And how would a correctly sequenced protein become folded into the only proper spatial arrangement in which it could function as an enzyme? In a few nutshells:

- There would be no DNA without a preexisting sugar, deoxyribose.

- There would be no RNA without a specific, preexisting sugar, ribose.
- There would be no sugar without preexisting enzymatic proteins.
- There would be no proteins without preexisting RNA.
- There would be no proteins without preexisting ribosome proteins.
- There would be no DNA replication without preexisting proteins.
- So, what came before all of that?

Perhaps we can now answer the question posed earlier (page 299) regarding the three-way "chicken/egg" riddle. To be functional, every living cell must have:

(a) thousands of right-handed messenger-RNA molecules, each with its code transcribed from a specific gene in pre-existing DNA,

(b) thousands of proteins, each composed of hundreds (or thousands) of left-handed amino acids in a precise sequence controlled by the code of mRNA, and

(c) right-handed ribose and deoxyribose, which confer right-handed chirality on RNA and DNA respectively, and get their own right-handedness solely through biosynthesis by special left-handed protein enzymes.

Which, then, came first in the original living cell: (a) RNA and DNA, (b) proteins, or (c) ribose and deoxyribose sugars? The only workable answer is (d) all of the above---fully formed, correctly sequenced, and mutually interdependent---in the very first organism. What's the chance of that?

Thanks to Louis Pasteur, it is no longer permissible to imagine that in raw nature some nonliving, prebiotic chemicals have an innate tendency to assemble RNA in the wild, yet decline to do so in the laboratory. How could all these mutually dependent processes start up at the same time without guidance? Among the more reasonable answers is this: "They couldn't!"

A puzzling, enigmatic quandary? You bet!

Chapter 17

Are we alone?

Two possibilities exist: either we are alone in the universe, or we are not. Both are equally terrifying.

——Arthur C. Clarke

Of all the subjects that make up the general question of life on Earth, none quickens the public attention more than extraterrestrial intelligence. Especially in the United States, we have a fixation on any news report that some ordinary citizen has had a "close encounter" of any kind. Official denials from government agencies are discounted as just another cover-up.

Contrary to the intriguing idea that we inhabit a rather ordinary planet orbiting an unexceptional star in a remote corner of a typical galaxy, the direct experience of western civilizations would tend to predispose many of us to assume that we are so special in the eyes of our Maker that we just have to be *sui generis,* one of a kind. As apparent confirmation, there is no indication that any other sentient creature than our genus has ever evolved on this earth. This only adds excitement to any report or rumor that intelligent beings from another planet have been sighted.

Which planet? Our solar system has nine. In order of distance from the sun they are Mercury, Venus, Earth, Mars, Jupiter, Saturn, Uranus, and Neptune—plus the former planet, little Pluto, recently downgraded to dwarf planet, much to its chagrin. Now there's evidence (January 2016) of a new Planet Nine, a Neptune-sized giant so far beyond Pluto that it can only be inferred by the effect of its gravity having pulled six planetesimals (Pluto-sized) into grossly anomalous solar orbits. It will be named when visually confirmed. Several big telescopes have been dedicated to the search.

A frenzy of curiosity has been jacked up by scientific speculation that one plausible origin of life on Earth could have been the organic waste left behind by earlier visitors. Perhaps we had been colonized! One version of this is the modern legend that our low-brow *hominin* ancestors acquired self-awareness, language, fire, and tool-making from contact with some early messengers from outer space—perhaps genetically from their seed.

An entirely different hypothesis for the origin of life on Earth followed the discovery of a number of fundamental chemical components of DNA in several meteorites. This is treated more completely in chapter 16, but is not nearly as provocative as the speculation about alien creatures visiting from distant planets. Besides, DNA is not just a random collection of its components that just fortuitously happened to have thousands of correctly coded protein-expressing genes.

For whatever reason, many believe that we definitely have been visited from outer space by beings with superior intelligence and technology. They must have been far more advanced than we, simply because we have no means for visiting their home planet. That little syllogism works nicely if you stipulate the claim that they have been here. As of today, however, we still don't know if, who, or where they are. That's downright unacceptable!

Who's on Mars?

Ever since H.G. Wells wrote his hot classic *The War of the Worlds* (1898), science fiction has conditioned us to anticipate, and even accept, the existence of other lifeforms on distant planets. Actually, his horror story was not the first about interplanetary visitation. In 1752, Voltaire wrote *Micromegas*, a tale of two curious visitors from Saturn and Sirius. These fictional aliens were merely inquisitive about the follies of human society, likely reflecting Voltaire's own opinions. At least one signer of the U.S. Constitution in 1787, Hugh Williamson of North Carolina, believed that most stars had planets with intelligent inhabitants.

Johannes Kepler had composed earlier an imaginative fiction about the way hypothetical moon dwellers might contemplate Earth from their lunar-centric perspective. It was Wells's Martian creatures, however, with their frightful mechanized walking tripods in *The War of the Worlds* that set the menacing standard for hostile invasion and displacement of mere humans.

Science had just begun to search for evidence that some kind of life was really out there. This heightened the excitement. In 1877, 21 years before publication of *The War of the Worlds*, Italian astronomer Giovanni Schiaparelli (uncle of the celebrated fashion designer Elsa Schiaparelli) had been observing Mars through his telescope in Milan. He reported seeing a pattern of lines, which he described as *canali*, meaning "channels." This was mistranslated to be <u>canals</u>, by which it was presumed the intelligent Martians could have brought water down from the Red Planet's poles.

This notion was soon championed by the distinguished American astronomer Percival Lowell, who published drawings of an extensive array of lines he had seen (1895). Other astronomers protested their own inability to see them, suggesting the "canals" were but an optical illusion, or perhaps just a reflection of the blood vessels in the back of Schiaparelli's and Lowell's eyes. It seems unlikely that such experienced astronomers would make such a rookie mistake. Such unkind disparagements only fueled the counterclaim that their rival detractors were more envious than dubious.

Barely one year after Wells brought forth his Martian invasion, the eminent inventor Nikola Tesla, an American immigrant from Croatia, reported (1899) that he had detected simple numerical patterns of radio signals from the general direction of Mars. Not to be outdone, Guglielmo Marconi, the rival Italian inventor (1895) of the radio, soon announced that he, too, had received such "messages" with his own apparatus. This was electrifying, but doubts soon arose as to the authenticity of both claims.

["Who is John Galt?" But who was Nikola Tesla? In 1943, the U.S. Supreme Court ruled that Tesla's radio patents (filed in 1897) had prior claim over those of Marconi. Tesla's inventions had become the prized intellectual property of his employer, Westinghouse Corporation, the competitor of Thomas A. Edison's General Electric Company. In an extended "War of Currents," Tesla had championed wiring America with alternating current (AC) for Westinghouse in vigorous competition with Edison's advocacy for direct current (DC) on behalf of GE. We are fortunate that Tesla and Westinghouse prevailed. His iconic legend was enhanced by rumors that he had a secret invention that could harness energy from the atmosphere without fuel consumption. He also claimed to have invented a "death ray" particle gun. Could his reputation, built on these claims, have contributed inspiration for Ayn Rand's monumental fictional hero John Galt in *Atlas Shrugged* (1957)?]

329

H.G. Wells had studied biology under T.H. Huxley, the noted English zoologist, anatomist, and agnostic. Consequently, he was well grounded in Darwin's Theory, which Huxley had vigorously defended against opponents from both the scientific and religious establishments of the Victorian era. Wells had a full grasp of the implications of "survival of the fittest" versus highly intelligent beings, implacable as sharks with superior technology. He understood also the vulnerability of any species previously unexposed to humble earthly microbes, against which they had no immunity. Wells was thus a gifted pioneer for a host of science-fiction writers with a ready audience for their amazing fantasies of visitations from remote civilizations.

As the twentieth century awoke to speculation about such horrors, there was no scientific refutation to prove the negative and calm the jitters. H.G. Wells had a narrow window of opportunity through which to pounce. Look at his contemporary timeframe:

1877.	Schiaparelli sees *canali* on Mars
1895.	Lowell adopts the notion of Martian life
1895.	Marconi proves the concept of radio communication
1897.	Tesla files patent claims for radio
1898.	H.G. Wells publishes *War of the Worlds*
1899.	Tesla reports Martian radio signals, echoed by Marconi
1938.	Orson Welles narrates *War of the Worlds* on CBS radio
1938–39.	Nazi Germany occupies Czechoslovakia and invades Poland
	(That last entry was a reminder that fear of invasion was timely.)

The motion-picture industry perfected its fabulous technology for creating anatomically horrifying monsters for the viewing public, and we were hooked. Life as we had known it was threatened in films like *The Day the Earth Stood Still* and episodes of *Star Trek* and *Star Wars* and their many spinoffs. *Close Encounters of the Third Kind* and *E.T. the Extra-Terrestrial* restored the idea that planetary visitors might well be rather friendly and curious, as with Voltaire's characters. These amiable attributes certainly did not suffer at the box office.

Our space technology has placed probes on the surface of Mars, but <u>no</u> life of any kind has been detected there, let alone sentient, communicative, canal-building, death-tripod-driving cultures. The latest scientific rover, named *Curiosity*, was sent in search of traces of methane as a possible decomposition product from ancient organisms. Astronomers on Earth had observed a gusher of methane in 2003 and a smaller gush in 2006. If a puff of methane at the 2003 level were released from ice melting with every year's warming season, ultraviolet radiation would decay part of it, establishing a steady-state equilibrium calculated at 20–35 parts per billion (ppb). So far, *Curiosity* has sniffed no methane.

Gullible Travesties

In a popular modern invention, dozens of unauthenticated tales of UFO sightings and even escapes from the clutches of space aliens have promoted the notion that we are not alone. Americans' fascination with conspiracy theories has led 40% of respondents in one survey to agree that "the federal government is withholding proof of the existence of intelligent life from other planets." In a 2012 survey for its "Chasing UFOs" TV series, National Geographic Channel found 11% who claim to have seen an actual UFO.

After all, UFO is an acronym for "Unidentified Flying Object." That covers any phenomenon observed in the sky that cannot readily be correlated. There is nothing wrong with a healthy skepticism about our government, but a fraction of that distrust should be reserved for claims of visitations from another planet. No government agency or any other expert authority has confirmed evidence that we've been visited by alien spacecraft. Nor has any secret documentation been leaked. After all, that is a rather daunting distance to travel, even at "warp speed."

An embarrassing personal confession is in order here. When I first ran for Congress in 1972, the producer of my campaign's television ads was a talented and creative fellow named Don Ringe. Don was then producing the popular NBC-TV documentary *In Search of Ancient Astronauts* (1973), narrated by Rod Serling. The material was based on Erich von Däniken's explosive book *Chariots of the Gods* (1968). Both the book and the TV documentary interpreted numbers of ancient paintings and figurines, the petroglyphs of Stonehenge and Easter Island, and the strange geoglyphs on the high plains of Nazca, Peru, as artifacts of interplanetary visitations.

I was thus predisposed when our 13-year-old son and his buddy, in what I mistook for youthful awe and wonder, showed me an indistinct photograph they had taken of what appeared to be a "flying saucer." By that time, I was in my first term in Congress and a new member of the House Committee on Science and Astronautics. Surely it was my patriotic duty to deliver a copy of this astonishing photograph to the Air Force office in charge of examining these claims. My excitement gave way to chagrin when I read the gently drafted official response informing me that my son's "discovery" was not a saucer at all, for the enhanced image showed the lid of a Maxwell House coffee can suspended by monofilament fishing line, tilted slightly for effect! Let's hope Don Ringe never finds out.

Searching for Extra-Terrestrial Intelligence

Science, meanwhile, has not left the issue to the imaginative or gullible classes. The new field of astrophysics has found for itself an irresistible opportunity for studies of "signals" from extraterrestrial sources. It may be hard to believe today, but in 1924 there was an effort to coordinate a search for radio messages from the good people of Mars. For one 36-hour time span, when Mars was in its nearest proximity to Earth, Americans were asked to silence every radio at hourly intervals so as not to interfere with any incoming messages. Conspiracy theorists probably thought we were being distracted so we would not tune in and hear these amazing interplanetary exchanges. What if some suspicious citizens turned on their parlor radios anyway? If so, they got an earful of silence and static.

There remained some anxiety that, with millions of habitable planets out there, with a likelihood that some would have produced sophisticated societies with colonizing intent, our relatively modest technology might leave us rather vulnerable. If one such superior civilization anywhere in our galaxy had rocketry capable of achieving even one percent of the speed of light, would they not have conquered a substantial galactic empire?

That is known as the *Fermi Paradox*. In a 1950 lunchtime conversation with Edward Teller and others about such speculation, Enrico Fermi (1938 Nobel laureate in physics for studies of radioactivity) challenged the concept that so many nearby stars had planets populated with intelligent life. If so, he calculated it should only take a few dozen million years for such an advanced civilization to gain forcible dominion over a vast, colonized empire. If so, he wondered, "Where is everybody?" Many scholarly papers were offered in response to this Fermi Paradox. Could the superior aliens be averse to the impulse for conquest? Or what?

Our radio technology by 1960 had become far more sophisticated. We were determined to find out who was out there. In that year, from one of our greatest bastions of science at the University of California at Berkeley, there came the bright idea to launch an all-out coordinated search for any incoming space messages. There, the Space Sciences Laboratory hatched their Search for Extra-Terrestrial Intelligence, known by the acronym, SETI. They employed the Arecibo radio telescope in Puerto Rico as soon as it became operational in 1963. If any intelligent species from other planets were trying to reach out to us, it was our duty to decode their message and see if they were friendly or hostile. If no trigger-happy citizen on either side started shooting, surely we could learn a lot from each other.

Regrettably, after a decade of fine-tuning, no incoming message was detected. Maybe nobody was at home. Maybe their transmitters had the wrong frequency range. Maybe they had the technology, but just had not thought there might be any other inhabited planet but their own. Maybe they had other things to do. Well, then, it was up to us to contact them, to let them know that we are here, and wish them no harm (having long since repressed our own colonizing tendencies?). Undeterred, we would initiate the first ever interplanetary communication. Many questions about this search and what happens if we do make contact have been addressed in an entertaining and provocative series on TV's Science Channel. It is called "Through the Wormhole with Morgan Freeman," produced and narrated by that distinguished actor and featuring many leading thinkers on this topic.

There are two divergent points of view about this. Many believe it is inevitable that life has emerged on almost every suitable planet, and that sentient, intelligent life was bound to follow. This is the obvious position for those who believe there is nothing special about Earth and its inhabitants—that we are about average and our place in the universe is one of mediocrity. We have seen this referred to as the Mediocrity Principle. Some find this Mediocrity Principle also ingrained in Darwin's Theory of Evolution: that *Homo sapiens* is just another species of animal, or so they say.

Furthermore, they point out that our Milky Way Galaxy has some 200 billion stars (2×10^{11}), and there are at least 100 billion (1×10^{11}) Galaxies. If our Milky Way is only average, it would mean there are 2×10^{22} stars out there. Surely, billions of those stars must have sophisticated civilizations nearby. That's not counting any overlapping multiverses. What if there were life out there and we didn't check it out?

Others believe that the extreme difficulty of assembling monocellular life is compounded when it comes to higher forms, and that it would be a rarity of the highest order for any other planet to get this far. Some on both sides have elevated this issue to a test of Divine Creation, which it isn't. Whether life is detected elsewhere or not does not prove unequivocally either theological premise. Nevertheless, this is a really big question.

Thus it came to pass that, after careful preparation, SETI broadcast from Arecibo in 1974 a strongly enhanced and directional radio signal aimed straight at the spectacular globular cluster of stars known as M13. The best minds had convened for the purpose of figuring out just what sort of symbols might be decipherable to our neighbors out there. Surely, among images of mathematics, the Periodic Table of Elements, art, anatomy, and civilization, something would ring a bell with anyone tuning in from M13.

Perhaps Earth was overly eager to hear from our distant extended family, but we were not to be disappointed. In 1977 (just 33 months later), scientists at another observatory reported that they had received an interplanetary response. Though trembling with excitement, that claim did not hold up . . . and for good reason.

Hello?

There were, you see, two rather fundamental problems with this search for the family of young E.T. over in M13. First, that star cluster is some 25,000 light-years away from Earth! Our radio transmissions could not exceed the speed of light, which means that they could not reach the possibly life-bearing planets of M13 for 25,000 years. By the time the imagined sentient creatures among the M13 planets figure out what this is all about, and consider whether it was a ruse, perhaps a misdirecting prelude for our invasion of their peaceful kingdom, it would then take another 25,000 years for their reply to get back to us. Would there still be anybody here 50,000 years after 1974 to take down their message? Then what?

The second problem is even more intractable. M13 has moved laterally from where its light (visible today) originated 25,000 years ago. By the time our focused radio signal broadcast in 1974 reaches its target 25,000 years after its transmission, M13 will have moved even further, well out of the line of trajectory of our signal. Unless they had left behind some sort of trolling antenna, their radio receivers would miss our call.

This is a real problem. Or were we just pretending to "reach out and touch" M13? Was it enough just to show we had the capability of sending such a message? Or was this pseudo-science? Or budget manipulation? Next time, we must be sure to "lead" our target enough to allow for the galactic rotation of our Milky Way.

Fortunately, the cost of these follies has not yet been too extravagant, as Big Science so often can be. The time devoted to this intragalactic sporting gesture was but a small fraction of the operating time at Arecibo. Many of its other contemporaneous projects have been much more fruitful. For example, this giant radio telescope has detected numerous pulsars and binary pulsars. Astronomers there have been able to determine the precise period for axial rotation of Mercury as 59 days, a slow-poke compared with our circadian 24-hour day! It is likely, one would expect, that Arecibo must have yielded useful military information as well.

As a sequel to this valiant effort to ring up our neighbors, a more advanced radio antenna system was built in northern California: the Allen Telescope Array (ATA), originally designed to link together 350 directional antennas. Regrettably, the project suffered the fate of many governmental enterprises due to the weak economy and tight Federal budgets after 2008, and was "moth-balled" until happier days are here again.

A private rescue led by Microsoft co-founder Paul Allen and inspired by actress Jodie Foster (after dramatic success in *Contact*, a motion picture about SETI), has raised significant private funds for growing and operating ATA, currently under auspices of the Stanford Research Institute. ATA's survival from the 2014 California wildfire could be another good omen.

Suitable Planets

We will not be dissuaded from this noble quest. Canadian astronomers reported in 1989 the discovery (independently confirmed in 2002) of the first observed planets outside our sun's planetary system. The first planet associated with a so-called main-sequence star (one like our sun, small-to-medium in relative size and therefore relatively long-lived so that its hydrogen fusion reaction would not overheat and consume its fuel too soon) was detected by a Swiss group in 1995. This has since become a very productive field of endeavor, employing a half-dozen ingenious techniques. Improved astrophysical technologies have enabled discovery of more and more planets. In 2009, after preliminary exploration with the Spitzer space telescope, NASA launched the **Kepler Project**, deploying the Kepler space telescope synchronized with a number of large, ground-based telescopes to hunt for exoplanets in the region of constellations Cygnus and Lyra.

335

Most of the confirmed exoplanets have been "observed" as a result of their passage across the face of their star, briefly dimming the brightness of the star by less than 0.1 %. This is the method of the Kepler space telescope as it daily scans a fixed field of 150,000 stars, looking for that abbreviated dip in luminosity to indicate a planetary transit. This method can only detect a planet whose orbital axis is perpendicular to us, for otherwise it would never pass between us and its star.

Before the Kepler telescope shut down (2013) it had examined 42,000 stars. Its data allowed Geoff Marcy *et al* at the University of California at Berkeley to project that some 8–11 billion Earth-sized exoplanets may exist in our Milky Way Galaxy alone. That's a pretty large number, but doesn't differentiate whether any of these are habitable. Marcy is searching for signs of an irregular transit of a star, indicating possibly a giant space ship. He drolly suggests that our radio message should say, "We taste bad!"

A few exoplanets have been observed directly by special photographic imaging. Some have been detected indirectly as an oscillation of the star's emission spectrum. The gravitational pull between the star and planet causes a slight cyclical "wobbling" of the star's position. As the planet pulls its star away from us and then toward us, the resulting Doppler Effect produces a measurable variation, or quaver, in its wavelength. The technique was perfected by the Berkeley group (above) led by Geoff Marcy.

Because several more are being confirmed per week, it is necessary to qualify any numerical count with the date of the report. Accordingly, it can only be said that as of September 1, 2016, there had been confirmed a grand total of 3,518 distant planets, not counting the eight or nine circling about our sun. As of that date, the new Kepler satellite telescope had already identified another 2,740 <u>candidate</u> exoplanets, yet to be confirmed. One such blithe prospect was observed directly in 2008 by the Earth-orbiting Hubble telescope. A photographic image was captured of a reflecting exoplanet orbiting Fomalhaut, a bright star only 25 light-years away. The Hubble telescope was set up with a screen called a "coronagraph" to block precisely the star's light, so that the planet's reflected light could be detected by its motion within the dust cloud around Fomalhaut.

At about the same time, one of the newest technologies to become available was the Gemini Planet Imager, consisting of a programmed pair of 8-meter telescopes, one in Hawaii and the other partner in Chile. This setup enabled operators from UC Berkeley to obtain extremely high-contrast images of both the star and its planet (as the star is a million times brighter than the reflected light from its planet). Such images are difficult to resolve, but when achieved can provide data about the surface and atmosphere of the subject planet. With this equipment, three more planets have been observed near the young star HR-8799, showing the size, temperature, and some of the atmosphere believed to be necessary for life. The sophisticated technical term for this is the "Goldilocks Zone," meaning it's "not too large and not too small, not too hot and not too cold . . . but just right!"

*NOTE: PLANETS IN ACTUAL UNIVERSE MAY NOT LOOK LIKE BEARS...

The Hubble telescope had earlier (2007) found spectral evidence of methane (CH_4) in the atmosphere of a planet nicknamed "Little Fox." It is in the constellation Vulpecula, some 63 light-years away. Methane is one of the chemical materials believed to be part of the primordial atmospheric synthesis of amino acids before life could commence (see chapter 16). Little Fox is about as large as Jupiter, and is probably too hot for carbon-based life. The importance of this discovery was that it first established the validity of the coronagraph method employed using the Hubble telescope.

Another possibility is Gliese-581, a "red dwarf" star 20.5 light-years from Earth in the constellation Libra. It has a nice rack of seven or so planets, one of which, discovered in 2010 by the Lick-Carnegie Exoplanet Survey, given the notation Gliese-581g, is thought to have just the right temperature for carbon-based life somewhat like that found on Earth.

This planet has a swift 37-day orbit because of its proximity to its sun. Since its sun is a red dwarf, it was assumed to have survivable surface areas. It is very close to its star, so this particular planet revolves in a synchronized manner, like the tides, with its period of axial rotation being identical to its orbital period.; Consequently, the same side is always facing the red dwarf (and is too hot), while the opposite side is always in shadow (and too cold). In between perpetual light and dark there has to be a somewhat cylindrical collar that is always in a sort of twilight (which may turn out to be "just right," for immobile life). The other six planets of Gliese-581, however, are not so fortuitous for life. Gliese-581g, by the way, weighs in at three to four times the mass of Earth, which may or may not be an advantage. This discovery has not been independently confirmed by other observatories, so until that is resolved it is still in the "candidate" category.

In 2008, a high-powered radio signal carrying a new "Message from Earth" (TRUMPETS, OFF) was beamed at the star Gliese-581. Since it is a mere 20.5 light-years away, we may expect an answer in 2049—if there is someone alert with a radio on one of the Gliese-581 planets (and if there is someone still alert on Earth in 2049!). I can't wait . . . literally!

December 2011 brought some really exciting discoveries. The Kepler Project team announced the first exoplanet confirmed to be within the Habitable Zone of its star. About 600 light-years away, it was denoted as Kepler-22b. It was detected by the method of measuring the slight dip in intensity of its star, Kepler-22, as it made a transit two years earlier, shortly after the Spitzer telescope was launched. It was confirmed only when three consecutive transits had been observed, showing that it had a 290-day period of orbital rotation, almost as long as Earth's 365-day orbit. Since the star (Kepler-22) is about the same size and intensity as our sun, this means that its planet, Kepler-22b, is almost the same distance from its star and receives about the same radiant energy as we.

The Kepler Project estimates that the mean surface temperature on Kepler-22b is 72° Fahrenheit. Not bad for a start, but others were sure to follow. Historically, this was the first planet to have been proven to have all the right conditions to hold an atmosphere with water, essential for initiating and sustaining life. Because of its great mass, it may be entirely underwater, which could limit technology matching if there is some form of intelligent life and they try to reply. Although it has not yet been observed that life actually exists on Kepler-22b, it is exciting to know it's possible. We can anticipate that some group will apply the Hubble telescope and its coronagraph screen to tell us more about the atmospherics out there on Kepler-22b. Meanwhile, radio telescopes are already trained on this neighbor, waiting for a sign.

The First Discovered, Habitable Exoplanet
Kepler-22b (Kepler Mission 2011)

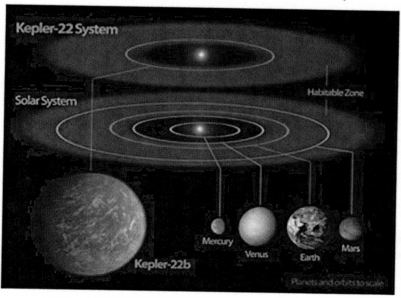

Image Credit: NASA/Ames/JPL-Caltech

Within weeks, the Kepler Project reported that two more exoplanets of interest, Kepler-20e and Kepler-20f, had been confirmed. These were the first planets right in the size range of Earth and Venus, but both are too remote from their star, Kepler-20, and consequently too cold for much biological development. Of the 2,740 or so <u>candidate</u> exoplanets, 400 or so are expected to be Earth-size, so there is a lot of excitement awaiting a few more orbital transits for some of these to be confirmed. In 2013, two planets orbiting Kepler-62 (slightly dimmer than our sun) were calculated to have just the right size and distance. Kepler-62f is 40% larger than Earth and orbits in 267 Earth-days, while sister Kepler-62e is 60% larger with a 122-day year. Each should have the right balance of retained atmospheric water. The biggest drawback is that these two are 1,200 light-years away, which handicaps prospects for communication. But are they inhabited?

As of September 2016, a total of 38 possibly habitable exoplanets have been identified, 10 of which are not much larger than Earth. Of these, seven have been independently confirmed. In the constellation Scorpius, there is a faint star Gliese-667C (also designated GJ-667C), 23.7 light-years from us. It has a complement of 7 planets, 3 of which (c, e, and f) are Earth-size or slightly larger, and all within the Zone. Among this promising "nearby" array, GJ-667Cc appears to be most Earthlike in atmosphere and surface qualities. Overall, the most likely prospect so far is Kepler-452b, a rocky planet discovered July 2015 in the habitable zone of a sun-like star. Although 1,400 light-years away, Kepler-452b already has the attention of the Allen Telescope Array. As yet, no radio signal has been detected.

Does this raise theological questions? Well yes, almost everything does. But is it problematic? The best short answer is: "not necessarily." If any kind of life is found on another planet, it might strain the belief system of some but not others. It is more likely to shake the faith of someone who has come to rely upon the singular uniqueness of life exclusively on Earth as if that were proof of a Creator-God. For others who accept whatever science offers as revelation of the handiwork of God, it will be startling, to be sure, but need not shake their faith.

Surely, if God chose to create conditions suitable for the emergence of life on another planet, He would not be bound by our imaginations or wishes (or computerized calculations) in the matter. What, then, if He chose to evolve life elsewhere? And what if He chose NOT to create life elsewhere?

It is worth consideration that while our *Homo ergaster* ancestors developed a complex language, our *Homo neanderthalensis* cousins did not. Would that undermine a conclusion that language was inevitable, or even somewhat probable for any other suitable planet?

Probability of Life Elsewhere

Any probability can be stated as a number between zero and one. We know that life is abundant here on Earth, so the probability here is 1, the maximum probability. We also know the probability of life on the moon is zero. What is the probability that life has emerged anywhere else in the universe? Is it somewhere between 0 and 1? Good guess!

Stephen Hawking and others have argued that the fact that life <u>has</u> evolved on Earth requires that there be comparable life on some other planets somewhere out there. Their reasoning is that the universe is so vast in its dimensions, with trillions of stars, many of which will have planets with conditions suitable for life, that the same spark of life must have been ignited somewhere else. Alan Boss at the Carnegie Institute extrapolates that there could be 100 billion planets in the Milky Way Galaxy alone. Surely some of these will have life? Boss supposes there could be thousands of civilizations out there. Nevertheless, until such life is actually detected, that conclusion, lacking evidence, remains premature, if not equivocal.

One may accept the conjectures of Hawking and Boss, or reject them, or just wait and see if anyone returns our call. If you want to keep track of the amazing progress in this exciting field of study, you might want to monitor the excellent summary articles on the Internet, such as "extrasolar planets" or several of the many links under "exoplanets."

Another contrary argument to Hawking *et al* might go like this. One tenet of modern Darwinism, based upon similarities among genomes of different organisms, holds that all species evolved from one single common ancestor. If we believe that, then it follows that it must have happened only once on Earth; otherwise, such descent would have to be from an array of multiple common ancestors. The only established instance of **abiogenesis** (emergence of life from nonlife) occurred very early as soon as Earth's surface and atmosphere had settled into favorable thermal conditions.

This raises a difficult question: if spontaneous generation were thought to be inevitable and commonplace, why did it not start thousands of times in different locales on Earth, creating many alternative ancestral lines? If abiogenesis of primordial life is so easy for natural processes, why was the start-up not repeated numerous times? There is in fact no confirmation that it originated more than once. Craig Venter has disclosed one instance of a microbe with an abnormal process for protein synthesis (chapter 10). This singular exception deserves more scrutiny. In any case, it seems not all that inevitable and easy after all, but extremely difficult and rare. In chapters 13–16, we discussed various factors that make the natural probability of this process so remotely small . . . even though we <u>are</u> here thinking about it!

Furthermore, only one <u>intelligent</u> genus (*Homo*) of any phylum has appeared on Earth in 4 billion years. That singular achievement of evolution occurred only in Africa, and nowhere else. Clearly, intelligent life is not that easy to evolve, else it would have emerged on Earth more than once, and on other continents.

Ernst Mayr has noted that the evolution of eyesight occurred more than 40 separate times (although from the same set of light-sensitive genes from a common ancestor), while the evolution of sentient intelligence occurred but once. Many biologists and paleontologists are coming to the view that the pathway from life to intelligent life is neither obvious nor inevitable. Nor is it likely to be replicated often out there. SETI has turned up no clue. Mars may have amino acids, maybe microbes, maybe even bugs, but maybe not. There likely will be no evidence of sentient Martians.

Despite the extreme complexity of life, here we are. If an Intelligent Creator could arrange a system to bring forth life on Earth, that same omniscient, omnipotent Deity could choose to repeat this again elsewhere—or <u>not</u>. That decision is not ours to make. We can only search. To believe, however, that such an improbable event could have occurred elsewhere by random chemical interactions is quite a stretch. And if you agree with that statement, then you have to wonder whether such an improbable event could ever have occurred <u>here</u> by random, unguided chemical interactions. Aha!

Even if sentient life were to be discovered someday on some remote planet, what would that tell us about God? Would that prove that it merely happened by chance, or would it prove that God had plans for more than just us? Such a finding could readily be argued as evidence of an intelligent, supernatural Creator-God, who chose to repeat a very difficult feat. Scientists who profess a belief in God could readily accept such a discovery as part of the growing revelation of God's power and purpose.

On the other hand, what if all we find are microbes? Will that satisfy our search for companionship? Will that settle our deepest longings? What if we find nothing but a few intriguing chemicals? Which would be the more miraculous: to find that life emerges on every habitable planet, or only rarely on a few, or exclusively on this rare earth?

Until Then, for All Practical Purposes . . . We're on Our Own

It is mathematically unreliable trying to extrapolate from one single data point—in this case, life on Earth. This problem has been addressed with sobering logic by Harvard astrophysicist (and former Chair of Astronomy at The Smithsonian Institution) Howard A. Smith in *American Scientist*, Vol. 99, pp.320–327 (July, 2011). He shows that for all practical purposes we are very probably "on our own."

Smith first proposes that we confine our anxious attention to the likelihood that there's any extraterrestrial intelligence (ETI) close enough to Earth to matter. That means we disregard all planets more than 1,250 light-years away. That parameter would allow 2,500 years for us to wait for a roundtrip of interplanetary communication exchanged with some neighbor. This timeframe is based on the idea that any wait beyond 100 human generations (with an average reproductive span of 25 years per generation) is impractical. Perhaps tongue-in-cheek, Smith pegs that as the down-to-earth limit of human impatience. Already we are a little outside that range with top prospect Kepler-452b.

Our Planet
Hunting
Neighborhood

Sun →

Most of the planets found to date lie within about 300 light-years from our Sun.

Image Credit: NASA/JPL

Setting aside the question whether any extraterrestrial neighbors in this vicinity are friendly and willing to become our "pen pals," it could be countered that Smith is being generous by at least a factor of 10. Surely, ten generations (250 years) is long enough to expect us to wait. I end the phone call after five unanswered rings! His first condition should then have started out with a roundtrip radius of 125 light-years. But as we shall soon see, it would not affect much the outcome of his calculation. So, let's stretch our horizon out to a sphere with a radius of no more than 1,250 light-years (LY), as Smith has proposed. That is a minuscule fraction of our Milky Way Galaxy, but it contains something on the order of 30,000,000 stars (including Kepler-62 and GJ-662C above). As a technically practical matter, most discoveries have been within 300 LY.

To introduce further rationality to this puzzle, Frank Drake (1961) proposed a matrix of eight factors for estimating the number of civilizations "out there." For simplicity and convenience, we can condense these into five factors. Now, some of this may seem highly esoteric, even vague, but one has to start somewhere. So here goes.

Drake's Formula

The five elements postulated by Drake (as modified by Smith and me) are:
1. The number of suitable stars
2. The number of suitable planets around each suitable star
3. The probability of life emerging on any suitable planet
4. The probability that any life can evolve to become intelligent
5. The typical lifetime of an intelligent civilization compared to the lifetime of its star

If each of these factors is assumed to be finite (somewhere between zero and one), it is assured that the calculated answer will be finite. When Drake proposed this to stir up the debate, he assumed that every planet that was suitably situated for life would evolve life. This assumption would make the third factor have the maximum probability of 1, which is far too high. It is obvious that the mathematical product of factors 1 and 2 is extremely large. We might imagine that the product of multiplying together the last three factors will be very small. What, then, is the product of all five factors? You have come this far, so I encourage you to "hang on," as this is quite an exhilarating ride!

Factor 1: Taking Smith's lead, the first element of the modified Drake Equation is that we have approximately 30,000,000 stars in our hundred-generation envelope. There are estimated to be another 10^{22} stars in the entire visible universe outside our "bubble of impatience," but we can disregard those, because they are well beyond our intragalactic neighborhood. That doesn't mean there is no ETI out beyond 1,250 light-years. It simply means that we really don't care since we're not likely to find out within the next 100 generations of our descendants.

Of these 30 million stars, most are too small, and a planet would need to be very close in order to receive the right amount of radiant light and heat. If that were the case, the planet could be locked into a tidal orientation, with the same face always toward its star, as is our moon relative to Earth. Only its peripheral circle, always angled horizontally at dusk, would have the right temperature for life to survive. Examples are Gliese-581g and our nearest known exoplanet *Alpha*-Centauri-Bb, alias Proxima-b. Proxima-b orbits very close to a red dwarf, and only its shadowed peripheral circle could sustain life. It holds interest for a proximal target colony from Earth.

Most of the remaining stars are too large, and will burn out too soon. This leaves only 10%, or roughly 3 million **main-sequence** stars, that are in the "suitable" range between 0.7 and 1.7 times the mass of our sun. Many of these are too young for the 4.5 billion years it took for us and our radio technology to evolve on Earth. Others are too old, and their internal nuclear fusion reaction will have faded. Even so, let's go with 3 million suitable stars, which is a pretty big number.

Factor 2: The next issue is to estimate how many suitable planets, if any, are connected with these 3 million suitable stars. That's a little harder. What we can do is to look at a reasonably large sample and try to extrapolate from that. As discussed above, most of the stars studied so far have no detectable planets, but 3,518 exoplanets have now been confirmed and another 2,740 unconfirmed candidates have been identified as of this printing, mostly in the field of view of the Kepler Project. And the counting has just begun.

It is sobering to note that of those detected exoplanets, most are too massive, such that gravity would be excessive for anatomical structures and strengths of body types with which we are familiar. Roughly a tenth of them (called "mesoplanets") have about the same mass as Earth. Nine out of ten would have surface gravity far too great for bones, muscle, and sinew to grow larger than small shrews.

One must keep in mind that the principal techniques and instruments upon which these early discoveries rely is not capable of detecting planets too small to occlude or block a discernible fraction of light from its star during transit or cause a Doppler wobble for its star. Most will probably be too small to be suitable anyway, for Smith figures only 13% of planets in close orbits are within the right size range of 0.7 to 1.7 times the mass of Earth. That would be the global mass necessary to attract an atmosphere, but not so large that vital plate tectonics (the movements and collisions of planetary crust, like the fracture of Earth's continents) would be suppressed or entirely underwater.

Furthermore, no planet could ever be detected by this method if its orbital axis were not perpendicular to our line of sight, an absolute prerequisite for transit between its star and our telescopes. So the next few thousand or so may be harder to confirm.

This cuts the known planets and candidates down to a hypothetical few hundred or so within all parameters of the Habitable ("Goldilocks") Zone. Again, only nine have been confirmed thus far. However, it is still early in our search. At least 38 known "Warm Terran" exoplanets may be in the Zone. This number could be raised a bit, since large planets like Jupiter may have <u>moons</u> in the prescribed mass range.

Table #17. Potentially Habitable, "Warm Terrans" (09/03/2016)

Planet	Star Class	Relative Mass	Suitable Atmosphere	Rel. Orbit Radius	Stellar Flux	Distance from Earth
Earth	**G**	**1.00**	**Perfect 1.00**	**1.00**	**1.00**	N/A
Kepler-452b	G	~ 5	Very Likely	1.6	1.20	1,400 LY
Kepler-438b	K	1.3	Likely	1.1	1.38	473 LY
Kepler-296e	M	3.3	Likely	1.5	1.22	1,692 LY
Gliese-667Cc	M	3.8	Likely	1.5	0.88	22 LY
Kepler-442b	K	2.3	Likely	1.3	0.70	1,115 LY
TAU Ceti-e *	G	4.3	Likely	1.6	1.51	12 LY
Gliese-667Cf	M	2.7	Likely	1.4	0.56	22 LY
Kapteyn-b	M	4.8	Likely	1.6	0.43	13 LY
Kepler-62f	K	2.8	Likely	1.4	0.39	1,200 LY
Kepler-186f	M	1.5	Likely	1.5	0.34	561 LY
Proxima-b	N	1.3	Limited	0.05	0.10	4 LY

(* TAU Ceti-e is included due to its proximity to Earth, as yet unconfirmed.)
(Approx. temperatures of Star Class G = 6,000°, K = 5,200°, M = 3,700°)

To be habitable, a planet's orbit has to be nearly circular, like that of our Earth, so that it doesn't spend much time very close (hot) or very far (cold) from its star. In 90% of the known cases, the elliptical orbit is too eccentric, which trims our list to only a few dozen. Even that is still hypothetical, by the way, because few exoplanets have been confirmed so far with enough Earthlike characteristics. The search goes on.

It has been suggested that a lucky planet would benefit also by having a giant neighbor, like our Jupiter and Saturn, available to help sweep up the interplanetary debris of large asteroids. This would help shield the Goldilocks planet and its fragile early life from frequent cataclysmic collisions. The last thing (literally!) that incipient life needs would be frequent, continual mass extinctions to interrupt progress.

Factor 3: Trying to figure the probability of life being generated on any of these planets is highly conjectural. One factor believed to be essential is the presence of water vapor in the atmosphere and in liquid form on the surface. If the conditions of mass and orbital eccentricity in the preceding section are met, there is then the question of the orientation of the planet's axis of rotation relative to its orbital axis of revolution around its star. This property should be fairly random, since it is the consequence of an accumulation of major collisions during the formative period of the planet.

Earth's spin axis is tilted 23.5 degrees from its orbital axis, which is nearly ideal for Goldilocks. This allows the surface of each pole to be exposed to sunlight in due season, so that every region is habitable within the temperature range for plant and animal life. Within our solar system, Earth and Mars fit this condition. We might assume, as a generous and useful working approximation, that a third or so of planets tilt about 20–30 degrees from their orbital axes.

It would be essential, according to Smith, for the planet to have an abundance of carbon compounds (any organic chemist would list that first!), silicon, iron, calcium, phosphorus, and many others across the Periodic Table. The heavier elements are not formed in early stages of thermonuclear reactions of a young star, but are created in significant quantities just before a supernova explosion. Its wreckage then aggregates by gravity to form the new star and its planets, asteroids, and dust. For each exoplanet, this composition can be inferred from the emission spectrum from its own star. The abundance of these heavier elements has been shown to be uneven within the Milky Way, decreasing with greater distance from the center. Stars and planets farther out in its arms will have insufficient elements for life. On the other hand, planetary systems too close to the galactic center will not be habitable because of intense radiation from the black hole at the center. Our sun and solar system are just the right distance for supernova incidence, as would be all candidate exoplanets in our 1,250 light-year bubble of interest. Maybe our location is not so mediocre after all?

Getting from these favorable conditions to the actual generation of life from raw, nonliving chemicals is a special challenge. If only life could occur by random natural interactions, one would think we could duplicate that in the laboratory. So far, we have not come close. Just consider the ultimate improbability of spontaneous generation. In a series of experiments begun in 1953 (see pages 313 ff.), Harold Urey and his graduate student Stanley Miller were able to synthesize a few amino acids, nucleotide bases, and sugars by exposing an atmosphere of nitrogen, methane, carbon dioxide, and water to electric sparks and ultraviolet light. However, only a few of the necessary components were formed in useful quantities.

Furthermore, these experiments invariably yield exactly equal amounts of (right-handed) D- and (left-handed) L-amino acids. There is no plausible mechanism for generating only L-amino acids that are the exclusive asymmetry found in living, natural protein. That's why a great deal of excitement properly attended the discovery that some meteorites contain small traces of amino acids. They are generally present as the 50:50 DL-mixture however, and besides, do not transport any bacteria or bugs. For a more complete review of this asymmetry issue, return to chapters 14 and 15.

An equally difficult problem for unguided random abiogenesis is the incredible size and highly **specified complexity** of DNA in all species. There is a considerable range of genomic size in nature, but the DNA of the round worm, one of the simplest of macroscopic species, is every bit as large and complex as that of humans. All plants and animals have the same kind of sacrificially protective telomere end pieces on their DNA. Some of the oldest living multi-cellular species have just as large and complex DNA as the more sophisticated primates. This evidence strongly suggests to some that the extreme complexity of DNA emerged intact at the beginning of life, and not as any gradual progression of sequential assembly of longer DNA from shorter segments. Others would dispute this, but this problem is not inconsequential (no pun intended!).

A contrary argument could be made based on the smaller size of many bacterial genomes. James Van Etten has pointed out (*American Scientist*, Volume 99, p. 304) that the smallest free-living bacterium, *Mycoplasma genitalium,* has just under 600,000 base pairs, and codes for just 482 proteins. Far smaller is the cicada's bacterial parasite, *Hodgkinia cicadicola*, whose DNA has just 140,000 base pairs, coding for only 169 proteins. This is much smaller than our human genome, with its 3.1 billion base pairs, and its 23,000 protein-coding genes. This midget microbe *H. cicadicola* lives entirely within the friendly but noisy confines of cicada cells, extracting presynthesized nutrient from its host, allowing it to thrive without having its own protein-expressing tools. It must have good earplugs!

Some have imagined that carbon chemistry might not be the only basis for organizing sustainable life. In the next row of the Periodic Chart, silicon (Si) falls directly beneath carbon. Silicon is also tetravalent (forming four covalent bonds to other atoms), and some see it as the molecular basis for alternative lifeforms. Rubbish! Silicon does not form the variety of covalent bonds that carbon does. Its covalent bonds do not have the reactive polarity of many of carbon's bonds. Silicon is superior to carbon for making silicate rocks and semiconductors. It does not come close to carbon in providing structures for the complexity of organizing life. Trust me on this.

Factor 4: Drake's fourth criterion is the probability that incipient life on a planet would evolve into sentient, intelligent beings capable of developing radio or any other communications technology. Once the most rudimentary form of single-cell life emerges (Factor 3), what probability is there that evolution will raise that spark of life to the level of at least one intelligent species? If life were the inevitable product of mixing enough chemicals at the right temperature and gravity for a billion years or so, and if another two billion years is all it would take to upgrade the prototype to an intelligent species, then Drake figures there could be "1 in 10 million stars with a detectable civilization." That works out to 3 in our 30 million sample.

Stephen Jay Gould was even more direct, saying that our abiogenesis was so extremely random that it could probably never repeat. One could well ask: "If life is so remotely improbable, how could it arise even this once?" Well, it did! The apparent fact that sentient life did arise on Earth need not surprise us. However, if such advanced life had not succeeded here, nothing could surprise us. Or is that thought too subtle?

It has been suggested that evolution was accelerated by whatever triggered the appearance of so many new phyla during the "Cambrian Explosion." This speculation refers to the fossil evidence that most animal body plans very suddenly appeared 545–525 million years ago, but not one new phylum since that door opened and closed. This would seem to imply some manner of "threshold conditions" during that brief geologic time span, without which evolution might never have generated the first vertebrate (of the *Chordate* phylum) and then climbed beyond that to our *hominin* level. Was 20% atmospheric oxygen the trigger?

For these and many other reasons, it is hard to justify a probability fraction much bigger than one in ten thousand (0.0001) for this factor, which is arguably very generous, since less than one in a million species on Earth made it (chapter 12).

Factor 5: Not much is left to say about Drake's fifth factor: the likely duration of a civilization compared to the lifetime of its star. We know that our *hominin* subfamily began to descend from tree-climbing antecedents some 4.5 million years ago. Earth fortunately did not have an intervening mass extinction before we could get this far. We know that our civilization has had its radio communication technology barely a hundred years. How commonplace that might be among exoplanets is hard to imagine. Once again, we are limited in being able to generalize from the one example of Earth, the only planet which is known to have been occupied by what we like to characterize as intelligent life.

Drake's guess is that a technologically communicative species might survive 10,000 years. We have run a very small fraction of that. Carl Sagan fears our span would be abbreviated substantially by nuclear war or some environmental catastrophe. He has a point. What if an intelligent civilization evolved on a nearby planet a million years before we did? Would it also be extinct by now? Harvard's Howard Smith sums it up quite succinctly:

There will be no civilization if a star is too large or too small,
    -if a planet's orbit or obliquity (i.e., axial tilt) is wrong,
    -if its size or chemical composition is ill-suited,
    -if its surface is ill-equipped,
    -if its geologic and meteoric history is inauspicious,
    -if the powerful chemistry needed to generate the first life forms is
      too intricate...or too slow,
    -if evolution from proteins to intelligence is too often aborted
    -or directed into sterile tangents,
    -or if civilizations die off too easily.

Smith then adds:
If we are to have company in our volume of the galaxy, the likelihood on average for each of these conditions has to be pretty high . . . better than 20 percent. If the probability of some, such as the chances for life to form, evolve or survive, is much smaller, then even if the others are 100 percent certain, it is unlikely there are any stars near us hosting intelligent beings.

Whimsically, he calls this his **Misanthropic Principle**. The odds are stacked against any ETI, at least within our reach of 100 generations. It could be argued that we are supposing too many handicaps in the way of life. Yet, until we actually find more complex structures than just a few naturally occurring ingredients (a few amino acids in a few meteorites), it is appropriate to maintain a measure of skepticism against wishful thinking.

In short, we may be down to just one ideal planet for intelligent life within our little 1,250 light-year bubble, and that planet (herald trumpets off) is our very own Earth. Here abundant life has been detected, even what we consider to be intelligent life. At most, only a couple more are likely to be within range. Drake himself speculated that there could be as many as ten in our entire galaxy. That estimate would be consistent with no more than just one or two (Earth and one other) in the 100 generation bubble of space recommended by Smith. So let's keep a watchful eye on Kepler-452b!

Let us not forget that there are several uncertainties in the assumptions we plugged into the modified Drake formula. There was speculation in the range of numbers at each step. This leaves us room to allow that there could be 2 ± 2 equals 0 to 4 more life bearing planets out there. In any case, we are not going to stop searching any time soon. Besides, what if someone on M13 star cluster decided 25,000 years ago to send a signal our way? We had better keep our scanners on. So far, all we have heard is static.

In *God's Universe*, Owen Gingerich characterizes the Search for Extraterrestrial Intelligence (SETI) as a grand experiment to select between two divergent theories:

- Abundant life and creative intelligence are inevitable; versus
- Life is highly improbable and intelligence borders on the impossible.

If SETI succeeds in discovering intelligent life on some other planet(s), does that really invalidate one theory or the other? One still could believe it's inevitable, or that it is unlikely. Moreover, what does that tell us about God? From the viewpoint of the theistic scientist, it only means that we will have achieved further Revelation about the purposes and handiwork of God. So far, we are left with the Fermi Paradox (page 332): Where is everybody?

PLUS ULTRA

Before Columbus (1492), Spanish coins carried the bold motto: NE PLUS ULTRA, signifying "no more beyond." This expressed not only the military power of Spain, but also the prevailing view about the known world. It was the nautical warning posted at Gibraltar on the Pillars of Hercules ("as far as you should go"). After Columbus returned from the New World, subsequent coinage dropped the negative, proclaiming PLUS ULTRA: "more beyond."

> *Psalms 8:4–6* raises a question for those who think there is no more beyond the physical realm: *What is man that Thou art mindful of him?*
> Does it lower our self-esteem? Does it express our relative mediocrity according to the Copernican Principle? I think not. The Psalmist answers: *Thou hast made him a little lower than the angels And crowned him with glory and honor.*

We are an impossibility in an impossible universe.
——Ray Bradbury

Chapter 18

Science and Politics

The First Amendment

If you ask whether the U.S. Constitution provides "a wall of separation between church and state," many Americans will answer: "Yes, of course!" There is a fundamental organizing principle of this great nation that reveres the freedom of religion from control by the government. And also *vice versa*. Many of our original colonies were founded upon a determination to be free from persecution for one's religious beliefs and affiliation.

But is that what the Constitution says, . . . *a wall of separation*? The First Amendment, enacted in 1789 as part of the "Bill of Rights," reads in relevant part:

Congress shall make no law
respecting an establishment of religion
or prohibiting the free exercise thereof; . . .

The rest is about free press, speech, assembly, and the right to petition for redress. There's no mention of any "wall of separation," a pet phrase of Thomas Jefferson, which the framers of the Bill of Rights would not accept. While widely revered, Jefferson was not a Member of Congress during the adoption of the first ten amendments, known as the Bill of Rights, although he was a strong advocate.

That's all it says on this subject, but that says a lot. It really provides two protections: the first being the "anti-establishment" clause; the second being the "free exercise" clause. As you can imagine, these two clauses at times can be in conflict, requiring careful balancing. Try to imagine one without the other. One person's right to be free from the dictates of an established religion or having to support it with taxes can often impact another's free exercise. The first part has been upheld by

353

the U.S. Supreme Court by knocking down establishmentarian practices such as the use of public property for Christmas manger scenes or crosses, or more recently overturning state bans on same-sex marriages. In other cases, the Supreme Court has favored protection of free exercise by allowing "released time" for public school students to attend religious instruction in parochial schools. A review of thirty or so conflicted cases (analyzed in James Reichley: *Faith in Politics*, 2002) shows that each clause was given preference about half the time.

Recently (2014), the U.S. Supreme Court has acknowledged that opening governmental board meetings with prayer is permissible as long as the governing body invites clergy on an ecumenical basis, which had become the congressional standard. When my father was invited to lead the opening prayer for a session of the U.S. House of Representatives, he was "coached" by Speaker Tip O'Neill to be ecumenical. Pop closed his prayer with this gem: "We make our prayer each in his own way . . . and many of us in the name of Jesus! Amen!" Respect for others' religious views did not require him to demean or disrespect his own. The Speaker got a hearty laugh out of that pearl.

The phrase ". . . no law respecting an establishment of religion" clearly meant that Congress may not establish a favored religion or any religious test or obligation. There was to be no federal law for or against such a relationship. In the context of that time, it is clear that this provision of the First Amendment was never intended to apply to the states. It clearly expressed restrictions only upon the Congress and, by extension, the federal government. Had the original purpose been to apply this stricture to the states, there were enough states with religious establishments to reject the amendment. Indeed, half of the fledgling states in 1789 still had their own established churches, and would not have ratified any federal interference upon states' rights. In that light, "no law respecting an establishment of religion" expressed a non-Jeffersonian meaning.

That interpretation no longer stands today. It was reconstructed in light of the Fourteenth Amendment (adopted 1866), which was intended solely to protect the rights of newly freed slaves from discriminatory persecution by the states. Not until four decades later, the Supreme Court found that the Fourteenth Amendment had grown to cover a broader range of restrictions against states as well as local governments than originally conceived. In *Lochner v. New York* (1905), that state's law limiting the number of hours that bakery employees could work was struck down in part on the basis of the "Due Process" clause of the Fourteenth Amendment.

This new interpretation of the Fourteenth Amendment was more clearly settled in *Meyer v. Nebraska* (1922), which overturned that state's law prohibiting the teaching of any foreign language before the ninth grade and requiring that all classes be taught in English. No argument arose that the Nebraska law had imperiled any former slave. New semantics had revealed that the language of the Fourteenth Amendment somehow cloaked an unintended broader meaning, hidden within its Equal Protection clause for 56 years.

What does this have to do with science and religion? Plenty! The famous Scopes trial in Dayton, Tennessee (see chapter 9), raised the crucial test whether a state could penalize someone for teaching evolution or any theory contrary to the Biblical story of Creation in public schools. That celebrated case (1925) never made it to the federal courts because of a technicality, but laws in Arkansas and Louisiana provide clearer test cases.

Forty-three years after "Scopes," a teacher named Susan Epperson brought a lawsuit against Arkansas on First Amendment grounds, invoking the Fourteenth Amendment to restrain her state and overturn its similar law enacted in 1928. Although no one had yet been prosecuted, such laws on record in many states had the proverbial "chilling effect" on teachers and textbook publishers. Upon the Epperson challenge, the Arkansas law was held to be unconstitutional by the U.S. Supreme Court in 1968 as an invalid establishment of religion. Often referred to as "Scopes II," its reach was quickly applied to other states. That did not quite settle the matter, however.

Creationists had begun a careful counter-attack. If states could not ban the teaching of evolution, then they would require something called "creation science" to be taught along with evolution with an allowance for equal time or a balanced treatment. In 1977, both Louisiana and Arkansas enacted "equal time" laws. The Arkansas law was challenged by a group of churches and parents in federal court, which held in 1981 that creation science did not meet any standard of science. Judge William Overton developed a legal precept of science, and ruled the law unconstitutional for promoting a particular religious viewpoint. While this was an important precedent and was the first opportunity to get scientific testimony on record before a court, *McLean v. Arkansas* did not reach constitutional finality. Arkansas Governor Bill Clinton, an opponent of the creation science law, could not in good conscience make a case to reinstate it, and therefore could not appeal.

The next year, a similar suit was brought in federal court against the Louisiana law by biology teacher Don Aguillard. Upon Judge Overton's precedent in Arkansas, this law also was held to be unconstitutional. Since Louisiana Governor Edwin Edwards did support the law, he appealed the ruling to the U.S. Supreme Court, where the lower court was affirmed, 7–2. While the majority opinion in *Edwards v. Aguillard* allowed that it was permissible to teach alternative scientific theories, it accepted the opinions of 72 Nobel laureates that creation science was not one of them. Thus it came to pass that American law was finally settled that no state may require non-science to be taught as science in the name of religion or otherwise.

In *Rocks of Ages*, Stephen Jay Gould recounts a number of amusing anecdotes about these trials, in one of which he was a scientific witness. In the Arkansas trial, a young male second-grade teacher described his use of a considerable length of string to illustrate geologic time, with tape at points to mark the origin of life, the rise of dinosaurs and their extinction long before humans appeared, etc. The Arkansas Attorney General, hoping to undermine this image, asked: "and how would you teach this if the earth was only 10,000 years old?" The reply was brief: "Shorter string!" The A.G. had neglected the lawyerly dictum that you should not ask a question unless you know the answer.

Another witness for the state was Fred Hoyle's protégé (page 323 above) Chandra Wickramasinghe, who opposed evolution on alternative scientific grounds. When asked what he thought of Darwin's theory, he replied: "Nonsense!" Alas, the eager barrister went one rhetorical bridge too far, inquiring what the witness thought of the belief that the earth was younger than a million years old. The terse response: "Worse nonsense!"

Bipartisan Nonsense

One keen observer of today's culture, American Chemical Society President Bassam Shakhashiri describes a "science-rich sector" (universities, national science labs, military, healthcare, telecommunications, transportation, and technology industries) and a "science-poor sector" (everyone else), and says the gap between the two is widening. To some, this dichotomy presents a partisan political advantage, ready to be seized.

Here's an easy question for which anyone probably has a ready answer. Which political party is anti-science? A quick response to this question might reveal your own political orientation. Before we move on, then, let me ask you to think again about this. Alex Berezow, editor of *RealClearScience*, has posed a different answer, in which he concludes that partisans of both stripes are equally abusive of science and technology, albeit on different topics and issues. Before we see if he makes good sense, ask yourself if you readily picked as "most anti-science" the party other than the one with which you usually align and vote. If you picked your own party, you are probably in a small minority of Republican voters who worry about those few GOP candidates who have been called out for being dismissive of the best science. Democrats don't attribute anti-scientific views to their candidates. Nor do the mass media. They err.

Berezow cites the videotaped and apparently set-up encounter in which a youngster in Iowa asked 2012 Republican presidential candidate Governor Rick Perry of Texas about the age of the earth. How's that for your atypical youthful political inquiry? Actually, this is a handy surrogate question about evolution, because one's belief about the age of the earth is a crucial test for young-earth creationism. Anything less than a million years is clearly insufficient for Darwin's Theory of Evolution. If you believe that the earth and the entire universe were created only six thousand or so years ago (see chapters 4 and 11 for a deeper exposition of this subject), you have to reject the best scientific evidence that the earth was created 4.5 billion years ago, and the universe 13.7 billion years ago.

A great deal of what we know about evolution could have woven the texture of life as we know it in the intervening 3.5 billion years since the earth's surface cooled enough to be barely habitable. If I may be permitted an understatement: evolution could not have gotten very far in six thousand years. For that and other reasons, many of our neighbors who reject evolution hold fast to a young earth.

The news videotape shows a cautious candidate Perry trying to mutter that in Texas both creationism and evolution are taught. That might come as a surprise to the American Civil Liberties Union, although the Supreme Court, in prohibiting government from <u>requiring</u> equal time for creationism alongside of evolution, has not yet restricted a teacher's academic freedom to present both. The young boy's mother seemed to be the instigator, as the video recorded her prompting her son to pin him down with the killer question, "Ask him why he doesn't believe in science."

Berezow closes his preamble with the rhetorical question and answer: "Is the Republican Party anti-science?" He answers his own question: "Yes. But so are the Democrats." In a later interview, he contends that politicians should debate the ethical and policy implications raised by science, but "**let science be science**."

Error on the Right

Let's consider Berezow's bipartisan criticism, starting with my Republicans, many of whom often take science-averse positions like:

- Earth is a young 6,000–10,000 years old
- Evolution is just a theory
- Global warming is a myth, and
- Embryonic stem cells should not be used for research or therapy

The first two bullet issues are treated extensively in chapters 11 and 10, respectively, and as follows:

Earth is 4.54 billion years old. The universe is 13.7 billion years old.

Evolution is a highly credible, unifying theory of all biology.

If you reject these positions, it does test your understanding and acceptance of science.

Moving to Berezow's third point, most atmospheric scientists believe the evidence is overwhelming that industrial, residential, and transportation uses of fossil fuels (coal, oil, and gas) have added a substantial increment of carbon dioxide (CO_2) to the atmosphere. This is confirmed by analytical chemistry. Global trends in temperature are consistent with their theory that these molecules absorb and trap radiant heat from the sun, contributing part of the rise in ambient temperatures worldwide, and all that goes with that. Think of shrinking glaciers, melting polar ice caps, rising ocean levels. Most Republicans dispute that outright, which puts them in a difficult position, facing taunts about a "flat earth." Meanwhile, some catastrophist alarmists on the other side tend to "predict" the higher end of a range of temperature forecasts, albeit without evidence, which keeps the deniers lathered.

There are other contributing factors, of course. Decimation of tropical forests surely reduces a major "sink" for carbon dioxide removal. This deserves our commitment to better practices. Volcanic activity comes and goes, as do the El Niño and La Niña cycles, deep currents that affect the Pacific Ocean climate. Not much we can do about it.

A more fatalistic hypothesis has come from astrophysicists Adam Frank (University of Rochester) and Woodruff Sullivan (University of Washington): that life on Earth is constrained by fundamental laws of planetary life. Just as the early success of archaea and algae caused a dramatic rise in atmospheric oxygen two and a half billion years ago, the successful rise of our industrialized, energy-harvesting species has inevitably created its own problems of sustainability, regardless of which political parties hold power in any nation. By studying other planets (Venus, Mars, etc.), they hope to find a path to more sustainable longevity for life, both ours and other species', on this planet.

Then there is the little known Milanković Theory (1941), the highly predictable cycle of eccentricities in the earth's orbit around the sun. In addition to the tilt of the axis of rotation (a phenomenon that warms some latitudes but cools others seasonally), and its precession there is said to be a slower distortion of its nearly circular orbit. Gradually every 100,000 years, Earth glides temporarily into a more elliptical trajectory due to combined gravitational effects from Jupiter and Saturn (cf. "Planet Nine" on page 327). This periodic excursion is thought to have caused past Ice Ages in that cycle, when the warming and cooling effects did not balance out. Instead, the larger ice cap in winter would persist longer and efficiently reflect solar radiation and minimize its warming effect in the spring.

Of immediate concern, the 21,000-year cycle of a displacement of the earth's rotational axis relative to radiation from the sun is in a prolonged pattern that for the last two thousand years had produced a steady cooling trend. According to the National Center for Atmospheric Research, that reversed sharply in the early twentieth century, resulting in a pronounced warming effect. Instead of the prehistoric trend that had cooled Arctic climate (revealed in ice cores) by 0.5° Centigrade, Arctic temperatures have warmed a full degree above what had prevailed two millennia ago. That's a total shift of 1.5° C (or 2.7° F), so other factors must be at work. It doesn't mean that carbon dioxide is not a problem. It just means there are also other contributors we can't control.

Instead of futile denial that excessive carbon dioxide from combustion of coal and oil contributes to global warming, Republicans should "let science be science" and focus on better approaches to policy. It would be more defensible scientifically and politically to weigh the oppressive cost of any major correction, plus the loss of measurable benefits following a collapse of the economic miracle of capitalism. Denial is indefensible.

Forward thinking electric utilities have rolled out windmill farms, photovoltaic converters, exemplary energy-efficient office buildings, and all manner of expensive scrubbers to clean up their coal-fired generators' exhausts. Despite the political pressure and subsidies to achieve a substantial fraction of electricity from windmills, photovoltaics and the like, little has come of it. Reformed former Greenpeace activist Bjorn Lomborg (author of *The Skeptical Environmentalist*) produced a pessimistic estimate that wind and solar technologies by now would generate a little over 3.2% of electricity. According to the 2013 statistical analysis by *EurObserv'ER*, a mostly European consortium promoting "renewable" energy, wind and solar produced about 2.9% worldwide in 2012.

Hydroelectric generation added a solid 16%, but there are few real opportunities left for damming rivers and tides. All other "renewable" sources for electricity generated another 1.9% of capacity. This means we can't do much to reduce greenhouse gases unless and until we build more nuclear power plants, currently generating 11%. Global demand still depends on fossil fuels for 68%. Nuclear electric power could, by 2050, economically achieve about half of the carbon dioxide reduction target endorsed by the United Nations climate summit in Paris (late 2015*). If we cannot accept nuclear power as an irreplaceable part of the solution, how serious are we about the problem?*

"Green" does have nice clean natural symbolism, of course. It reallocates cost, but so far has shown more aptitude for restraining economic growth than for stimulating it. Conservative political thinkers need to focus on the more realistic alternatives. Same for liberals. Let science be science, but let economics be economics.

It is noteworthy that some senior biologists don't seem to worry too much about it. Daniel Botkin points to the mitigating fact that an abundance of species has adapted quite well to far greater swings in ambient temperature than anything observed or predicted so far. Plants and animals can adapt by moving with the shift to favorable *terroir*, and so can we. Others counter that those earlier temperature shifts were gradual over long time spans, and that this may be too abrupt. It may be especially tough for polar bears on receding ice floes. That scenario is troubling, but its proof is not yet clear.

Similar reasoning can be applied to stem cell research. The kernel of this dispute is not about all stem cells, just embryonic stem cells. Modern medicine can enhance reproductive success for childless couples by harvesting a reserve supply of embryonic material shortly after *in vitro* fertilization. Once the best prospect is selected, there remain all the surplus samples in a form technically suitable for research. While some opponents may object sternly to any use of the leftover embryo, it is hard to argue that using it for beneficial research is worse than destroying it as a biohazard. The real fear for most of those who would ban embryonic stem cells is that they might be used in actual therapies. Viable embryos could thus present a marketable commodity, leading to a real and substantial potential for unethical commercialization and exploitation of human embryos.

For one thing, while not generally understood, human embryonic stem cells are not likely to be approved for use in medical therapies until medical researchers can find a way to down-regulate the tendency of lab-animal embryonic stem cells to form cancers in their hosts. It is for that reason that leading laboratories in the field are devoting more time to using placental and/or adult stem cells for therapeutic applications. Adult stem cells are ordinarily nowhere near as versatile or potent as embryonic stem cells. Fortunately, there are methods for up-regulating them so that they are almost as effective as the controversial embryonic type but less risky.

Adult stem cells have the additional major advantage that they can be harvested as needed from the individual patient, who later might receive an implanted device made from his/her own cells (see pages 303 ff.), thus obviating any need for suppressing the patient's immune system. For that reason, it might be prudent to preserve placental cells from each newborn for later availability. The point here is that by failing to make the distinction between embryonic stem cells and enhanced adult stem cells, conservatives miss an opportunity, and leave themselves at a disadvantage.

What, then, about our Democrat friends?

Error on the Left

Berezow points to other science issues for which many Democrats are the ones rejecting the best science. To be fair and even-handed, we might offer unsought advice to these anti-scientific Democrats, just as we did for their Republican counterparts. While the following statements do not characterize all progressive Democrats, it is from their ranks that we find those most likely to seek to:

- "Protect" us from vaccination
- Oppose food additives on the grounds that synthetic chemicals are bad for us (implying falsely that natural chemicals are always better for us)
- Ban genetically modified foods, contrary to the best scientific evidence
- Block the construction of nuclear power plants (see the related discussion about Republicans above) and the proper disposal of radioactive wastes, and
- Prohibit the use of lab animals for medical research

As for vaccination, at least two Republican presidential candidates (in 2015) have stumbled on the antithetical side of that, and members of both parties have been spooked by periodic news reports trumpeting erroneous alarms that the measles vaccine causes autism. It doesn't, but scientific denials never get the same coverage. Even so, it is a test of faith mainly for progressive Democrats. At the other extreme, one Australian writer, Ian Sinclair, thinks "germs are our friends." Well, some are (see page 210).

Statistical studies have shown that 100% participation is not required. Not everyone needs to be vaccinated in order to interrupt successfully an outbreak and spread of a viral or bacterial disease. Depending upon the nature of the disease, vaccination of 80–90% of the at-risk population is often enough, but that doesn't leave much leeway for many exemptions. It depends upon factors like the duration of susceptibility of carriers and the velocity of spreading, and whether the agent is stable in air or water (think of sneeze particles), or requires intimate contact with an infected person or carrier. Once enough individuals are vaccinated, the kinetics of the epidemic is disrupted sufficiently, its run-out will diminish, and there would be less need to vaccinate the hold-outs.

In some states, specified exemptions are allowed for categories for whom there are serious concerns about vaccination, such as those with impaired immune systems (organ transplant, cancer chemotherapy, and HIV patients, as well as infants), plus those with religious objections. They would be at greater risk than those who comply, but will be personally safer, ironically, if almost everyone else participates.

It is argued that no vaccination is 100% effective and risk-free, but that is also true of most medical therapies, without which life expectancy would be much shorter. History does affirm many magnificent successes for vaccination:

- **Polio, diphtheria** and **whooping cough** have been almost eradicated.
- **Smallpox** has been substantially suppressed. Previously its death toll was 2 million a year globally. Introduced to Mexico in 1520 during the invasion led by conquistador Hernan Cortés, it decimated the Aztec population. In the eighteenth century, smallpox killed 60 million Europeans. Only the virulent bubonic plagues in AD 542 and 1350 ("Black Death") have been more devastating to humankind.

- **Influenza** has been largely countered, but remains an ever-present threat because of its ability to evolve and spread new viral hybrids that require new vaccines. Every year, public health authorities have to choose the three most likely flu strains, because only three vaccines can be widely supplied. Despite best efforts, flu varieties still kill some 400,000 per year worldwide. In 1918, the Spanish Flu **pandemic** (i.e., a global epidemic) killed nearly 50 million. It is now largely controlled by vaccines.

We must never lose sight of the fact that these diseases are still out there in a latent state, quietly awaiting any weakening of public health measures. We saw that in the 2015 outbreak of measles, when groups of infants less than one-year-old (thus exempt from vaccination and unprotected) became infected by one willfully unvaccinated adult carrier who had been exposed at an amusement park.

Instead of opposing any use of vaccines, a better stance for liberals would be to join polar-opposite libertarians to protect a few parents' and adults' right to opt out. After all, many conservatives don't want government telling us what to do . . . except maybe in the bedroom. This latitude for waivers does lead to a sizeable fraction of "free riders" who, with some risk, benefit from the "herd immunity" induced by vaccination of the majority. They risk fewer infectious contacts.

If, however, excessive social mimicry and "anti-vaxxer" activism results in more than 20% of the community choosing to avoid vaccination, that could tip the kinetics of contagion back toward rampant epidemic. As Ari Brown, author of *Baby 411*, has cautioned: "You can't hide in the herd when the herd isn't protected."

My personal physician Charles Rich offers this appeal to reluctant patients: "If not for yourself, then for those closest to you, get vaccinated. If not for them, then as a moral obligation to society and especially the immune impaired, please do it."

One last bit of advice for those of either party or no party who still conscientiously refuse vaccination: if you manage to get legally excused, it is in your best interest to just be quiet about it, lest you stir others similarly inclined to abdicate the herd immunity.

On another front, it is interesting that in advanced countries the food supply is safer than ever, yet public distrust is' higher. This has heightened the appeal of "organically grown" meat and vegetables. All food is organic (in the organic chemical sense), but the point of difference is the avoidance or minimization of additives and pesticides. Organic farming has its advantages, but adequate supply to feed burgeoning populations is not one of them. Global needs can only be met with commercial fertilizers, pesticides, and the development of hardier hybrids. The political debate has moderated, thanks to governmental quality control, and we seem content to let others eat "organic" or not, according to each one's personal preferences.

More aggressive attitudes arise regarding genetically modified (GM) food. This is mitigated somewhat by the fact that civilizations have long been crossbreeding all kinds of food sources, plant and animal, for improved stocks. For example, more than 80% of corn, beets, soybeans, and cotton grown in the United States come from genetically hybridized strains. Today's focus of concern is targeted at food made from genetically modified organisms (GMOs). GMO sources have had their DNA altered by addition of genes from other plants or animals to confer resistance to specific pests, pathogens, applied herbicides, or other factors that affect yields. Most consider these practices beneficial as long as no risk is found. One Swiss success was the insertion of a carrot gene into rice to make carotene-enriched "Golden Rice." It could save millions of deaths a year from Vitamin-A deficiency, but fear-mongering from Greenpeace and others has so far blocked it from worldwide availability.

One complaint is that any altered DNA or RNA in our food might survive the consumer's stomach acid and affect our genes and their functions (while ignoring the equally alien DNA of unadulterated "organic" foods). The DNA in food we digest cannot be incorporated into our genome. If it did, vegans might soon become plants. Given today's population burden, GMO innovations may be the only way to avoid widespread famine. For those unalterably opposed to food modifications, a Swiftian "Modest Proposal" might be the abandoned, formerly progressive fetish of eugenics (pages 131-133: "Francis Galton") and euthanasia, or even simpler, passive reliance on mass starvation. For now, the best position to take on genetically modified foods is to be sure the Food and Drug Administration is adequately funded to evaluate the safety and nutrition of new food products.

Expansion of nuclear power capacity is another magnet for the fury of progressive Democrats. It is an easy target for "Not in my Back Yard" (NIMBY) campaigns and fundraisers for radical environmental groups. It is encouraging from my point of view that a few of the more moderate environmental groups have seen an opportunity to build a broader common front with industries by trading certain major goals. If (a) industry will support energy efficiency and expansion of renewable energy sources, (b) some of the environmental side will accept expansion of new nuclear power facilities. The payoff is synergistic in that both approaches will help reduce carbon dioxide generation without having to bash each other in arguments over the relative risks and benefits of doing so.

A similar tack might be more productive for folks on the left like People for the Ethical Treatment of Animals (PETA). Lab animals are thought by most people to be irreplaceable surrogate subjects for studying diseases and injuries. Instead of blocking their use in medical research, PETA might well focus its considerable energies on advocating best ethical lab practices and on opposing animal research that has nothing to do with healthcare. They would then be in step with 93% of scientists. More importantly, they would not risk alienating those who have lost loved ones to diseases that someday might become curable through research. PETA's response has been to advocate "thought experiments," designing computer models to forecast results instead of actual outcomes with laboratory animals. The problem with their approach is that real life is extremely complex. Reliance on imaginative guesswork is not likely to conjure up all the right parameters for the computer, or enter all the correct data without knowing how biologically similar surrogate animals actually respond.

So, Berezow concludes: "for every anti-science Republican, there is at least one anti-science Democrat. Neither party has a monopoly on scientific illiteracy." Whether you agree with that may depend upon your own political ideology, and you are entitled to your opinion. It does help every now and then to consider respectfully the opinion of the other side and the basis of their position. You just might begin to realize that they are not the only obstinate ignoramuses—at least not all the time!

Red Genes *versus* Blue Genes

Writing in *Scientific American* with similar examples, Minnesota filmmaker Shawn Otto concluded that Republicans take the anti-intellectual prize, especially after one Tea Party candidate (2012) opined that rape cannot cause pregnancy, and another said that if it does it must be accepted as God's will. Neither opinion represents most Republicans, who dismissed them as aberrations. While these absurdities were denounced by most Republicans, they were broadly attributed to the Republican Party, much to its chagrin. Otto does not ignore Democrats' denial of science, especially those who fear cell phones and synthetic chemicals. He correctly worries where we are headed if both parties devalue the objectivity of science.

365

To this elevated debate has now been added a new fantasy: that Republicans are genetically inferior. Try using that label on any other minority group! Chris Mooney has written *The Republican Brain: The Science of Why They Deny Science—and Reality*, wherein he promotes the self-aggrandizing notion that liberals are more intelligent than conservatives. Mooney seems to be a science writer with a constructivist fixation on "The Republican Brain," a frequent topic that has earned him a nice niche among forums of the left. As expected, there are some right-wing kooks (thankfully less visible) who harbor similar suspicions about genetic inferiorities of Democrats. Then there's the Green candidate for president who would ban Wi-Fi in case all radiation is dangerous.

A more balanced interpretation comes from the Cultural Cognition Project at Yale Law School (www.culturalcognition.net) led by Dan Kagan. Their thesis is that both sides of every hot political debate have equivalent intelligence and access to the same science, but each side gives greater credence to facts that best fit its respective ideology, as that reduces the personal discomfort of **cognitive dissonance**.

Free Health Care

From time to time, some will advocate federal, single-payer health insurance as a way to provide better quality care for more people at lower cost. The same wishful thinking characterized the enactment of the so-called Affordable Care Act of 2010. This reminded me of the classical Gas Laws of chemistry and physics, wherein the pressure of a contained gas at constant volume is proportional to its absolute temperature. An increase in temperature will increase the gas pressure (P), expressed as:

$$P = R \times T, \qquad \text{or simply, } P = R\,T$$

where T is the Kelvin (absolute) temperature, multiplied by R, the gas proportionality constant. Similarly, Boyle's Law states that at constant temperature, the gas pressure (P) is inversely proportional to its volume (V), so that an increase in pressure will compress the volume. The formula for this states that the product of P *times* V is a constant:

$$P \times V = R, \qquad \text{or simply: } P\,V = R$$

A more generalized Ideal Gas Law for a given amount (n) of a gas follows:

$$P\,V = n\,R\,T$$

What does this have to do with health care cost? A reasonable thought-experiment would suggest that the cost (C) of health care is proportional to access (A), such that doubling the number of covered patients will double the overall cost. Thus, we have:

$$A = K\,C \qquad \text{with K being the proportionality constant.}$$

After the same fashion, it can be argued that cost is roughly proportional to quality (Qu) of the care provided. In other words, you get what you pay for:

$$Qu = K\,C$$

If you are thinking ahead, you might anticipate that there would be an Ideal Health Care Law, combining the two preceding formulas into:

$$\textbf{Qu A} = \textbf{C K}$$

If so, those who say they can provide (a) better quality health care to (b) more people at (c) lower cost may be indulging a bit of free-lunch economic **"Quackery."** It's like an **Iron Law** of healthcare economics.

"Golden Fleece"

There was one issue that cropped up during my time in the U.S. Congress that was irresistible to a bipartisan pair of respected colleagues. Both were opposed to federal taxpayer funding of basic scientific research. Senator William Proxmire (D-WI) wrote a comical diatribe against any research that had a funny name or a purpose that was easily ridiculed. Proxmire was famous for alerting citizens that they had been "fleeced" again. According to *Wikipedia*, his "Golden Fleece" awards blasted research on:

- How airline stewardesses arranged their knees while seated
- Whether combat soldiers should carry umbrellas
- Why prisoners want to get out of prison
- Best ways to teach college students how to watch television, and
- Mating habits of tree frogs.

This probably enhanced his reelection campaigns, although he was very popular and didn't need it. Once, he even objected to the radio signals beamed in the Search for Extraterrestrial Intelligence (chapter 17) until Carl Sagan talked him out of it.

Meanwhile, over on the Republican side, Representative John Ashbrook (R-OH), a founder of the American Conservative Union, launched an amendment to eliminate appropriations for basic research. His argument was that federal funds should only be spent to support "practical" applied research that had some likelihood of an immediate benefit. There was a certain innocent but false appeal to the Ashbrook restriction. This was in the mid-1970s, and my colleague Mike McCormack (D-WA) and I took to the House floor as a bipartisan "tag-team" against what we felt was a misguided policy proposal.

McCormack and I were the only two Members of Congress at the time with advanced degrees in science. He had worked at the Hanford Atomic Energy facility, and I had taught organic chemistry at Davidson College. Our arguments emphasized that there was less need for Congress to fund applied research (except for military purposes and NASA), because private investment protected by patent rights was a better way to find and develop practical benefits. On the other hand, private investment was not as likely to support basic research, for which the outcome was less certain. On this occasion, our colleagues listened to our bipartisan rebuttal and the Ashbrook amendment was defeated.

Still, one could wish that research scientists would try to be more circumspect with less bandying of clever titles for publications and grant proposals.

The Saccharin Saga

News item: Ralph Nader and Sidney Wolfe, MD support the FDA!

The U.S. Food and Drug Administration (FDA) is charged with responsibility to protect us from harmful ingredients in our food and medicine. This is authorized under the Food, Drugs and Cosmetics Act (1906, as amended), so they also have responsibility for our cosmetics. As for food, their emphasis is on food additives, while the Department of Agriculture has principal jurisdiction over farming practices.

Since FDA's inception, there has always been controversy about the regulation of new medications, with some partisan bias most of the time. Usually, Republicans tend to argue for faster approval of a new drug if early evidence supports its safety under phase I clinical trials, or if European regulators had approved it for some ailment for which there's no alternative therapy. Democrats are more likely to come down on the side of waiting to see if phase II and phase III clinical trials show a definitive medical benefit before approval is given. It's a healthy demarcation line for policy debate, but not all Republicans or Democrats always follow the party line.

It is a good policy that some leeway has been built into laws for so-called **orphan drugs**. This term applies to medications that show potential efficacy for a disease or condition that affects relatively few patients, and consequently may not serve a large enough market to justify the huge expense of a full-scale research program. This category has been favored as well with certain advantages under the patent law.

In 1958, Congress enacted a provision that came to be known as the Delaney Clause, named for its distinguished author and principal advocate Representative James Delaney (D-NY). Its noble purpose was to protect us from the addition of any known **carcinogens** to our food supply. It was worded in very simple and straight-forward language to which no one (except chemists) could possibly object:

The Secretary of the Food and Drug Administration shall not approve for use in food any chemical additive found to induce cancer in man, or, after tests, found to induce cancer in animals.

Who could not support such a well-intended law? What principled politician could risk being labeled as "in favor of a little bit of cancer"? Yet, this law with such benevolent intent soon became immersed in heated controversy.

Within a year of enactment, the Delaney Clause was applied to cranberries, found to contain traces of 3-aminotriazole, also called 3-AT, a potent herbicide used in Oregon and Washington. This chemical scare decimated the cranberry market just weeks before Thanksgiving. More recently, in 1989, the detection of traces of another pesticide, Alar, in apples torpedoed that year's apple market. Rival fruit-producing industries were suspected of scare tactics, but were probably innocent, fearing the same standard might destroy them as well. In each case, the affected industries were defended by their state's political leaders and even by a few scientists who contended that such small traces would have little or no effect. They, of course, became subjected to vile *ad hominem* attacks.

The Delaney Clause, however, allowed no exception for small traces. It was interpreted to have an "absolute zero risk tolerance," allowing no detectable amount of any suspected carcinogen to be added to any food product. At first, that standard was safe from rebuttal. Few political aspirants dared challenge a law that protected us from even the smallest added cancer risk, and besides, the Honorable Jim Delaney was Chairman of the House of Representatives Rules Committee. Say no more.

As a graduate student in chemistry (1957–60), I was aware of the Delaney Clause and its intent. I was also aware that advances in analytical chemistry were reaching previously impossible levels of detection. When chemical analysis was limited to no better than a few parts per thousand, zero tolerance seemed reassuring. As the limits of detection became more and more sensitive, reaching a few parts per million, zero tolerance seemed even more reassuring to some. To others, it raised a specter of over-intrusive regulation that eventually would impact most of the food supply.

One might not worry about carcinogens that could not be detected. Let's imagine that a popular food product contains one part per billion (1 in 10^9) of a chemical additive suspected to be a carcinogen. In the days when analytical techniques could detect no better than 1 part per million (that is 0.0001%, or 1 in 10^6), there would be little concern as long as the contaminant was below the threshold of detection. Now suppose advances in analytical instrumentation could improve that threshold down to a few parts per trillion (2 in 10^{12}), and the previously unseen carcinogen was now detected. Did the risk change? Common sense might indicate that without evidence of actual injury, there was no reason to ban that food product. The Delaney Clause, however, had no such nuance.

Whatever risk there was for such a low trace amount when it was too small to be measured, it set off legalistic regulatory zeal once improved analytical techniques were able to detect it. The societal perception shifted once that same contaminant could be detected at a few parts per billion or a few parts per trillion. The advance of analytical chemistry into these rarified levels began to raise alarms among knowledgeable scientists about regulatory excess, while also raising new opportunities for legal parsing among regulators. As a policy issue, it was coming down to how determined you were to impose stringent safety judgments on the free choices of others, even if benefits exceeded risks. Then along came saccharin.

Just prior to my first term in Congress (1972), the FDA had removed the artificial sweetener saccharin and its effective ingredient benzoic sulfimide from FDA's list of food additives "generally regarded as safe" (GRAS). This step was preliminary to invoking the Delaney Clause once again. Animal tests had confirmed that laboratory rats would develop excess bladder tumors when they were fed large doses of the otherwise inert and harmless substance. There was some doubt expressed as to how these surrogate animal experiments could be translated to the small amount of saccharin consumed by humans, but the law allowed no discretion. And so it was that humble saccharin was about to be **banned** *"at the drop of a rat."*

Having some scientific understanding of the problems inherent in an absolute-zero risk standard, the more I considered this issue, the more concerned I became that we had moved onto a foolish, dangerous precipice. The suicidal proclivities of lemmings provided an excellent metaphor for where we were headed. If any and every health risk comparable to or greater than that of saccharin were to be banned on similar evidence,

(a) there would not be much food of any kind left to eat,
(b) we could not go outdoors (cosmic radiation) or indoors (radon gas),
(c) we would not be allowed to travel or gather in auditoriums or stadiums,
(d) we could not touch each other in any meaningful way.

Statistically, these risk comparisons were valid. Their risks were acceptable, but the FDA insisted that saccharin was covered by the law and these other risks were not. It seemed to me that, if it would be wrong and foolhardy to prohibit by law all these comparable risks, then it was wrong to apply such a pointless standard to saccharin. I was about to get embroiled in a political risk far greater than the cancer risk of saccharin.

In a timely stroke of good fortune, the political balance abruptly tilted my way. The Juvenile Diabetes Association (JDA) weighed in against the ban. Millions of moms of kids with Type I Diabetes were furious that our own government was going to prohibit diet drinks and any chance of peacefully limiting sugar intake. Without the only artificial sweetener then available, their children would resort to clandestine consumption of sugar-sweetened drinks, with inevitably tragic results.

In March 1977 the final ban was published by FDA, to take effect three months later. It only applied to diet sodas and packaged foods. Oddly, the little pink packets of Sweet'N Low® would stay on the market, because this dry form of saccharin had not yet been added to food by any manufacturer. Each consumer could decide whether to stir it into a drink or not. A frightening warning label would be required on each small packet:

The Food and Drug Administration has found that saccharin causes cancer in laboratory animals.

As the only outspoken opponent of the now evident consequences of the Delaney Clause, I received numerous invitations to speak at JDA rallies against the ban. When the national news media picked up on the issue, I had a bigger platform. They wanted to publish the views of opposing sides, and that was how I got to know and appreciate a distinguished adversary, Sidney Wolfe, MD. He was head of the Health Research Group of Ralph Nader's organization, Public Citizen. His position was (a) that the Delaney Clause should be left as it was and enforced rigorously against any known carcinogenic food additives, and (b) that saccharin had no nutritive value and deserved no exception.

As the series of debates warmed up, I was fortunate to have the backing of some of the ablest and most respected scientists, who provided me with useful ammunition that proved effective in arguments against the ban. Irish physician John Higginson was the distinguished head of cancer research at the World Health Organization (WHO). He supplied me with many examples of how we needed to apply our defenses against more significant hazards, and not fritter our resources on inconsequential risks like this inert artificial sweetener that quickly passes through our alimentary system without danger of metabolizing. Higginson argued that it was counter-productive and detrimental for regulators to "cry wolf!" about extremely low risks when there were some real wolves out there. If Sidney Wolfe caught the ironic pun, he never let on.

Harvard nutritionist Elizabeth Whelan encouraged me with evidence from current research in her field. Especially useful was information about many natural foods that were far more carcinogenic than any claim about saccharin. Many others provided me with examples of relative risks that were readily and knowingly accepted by most people. The work of British-born Harvard physicist Richard Wilson was especially helpful.

Among the most compelling research findings at that time were:

- several large epidemiological studies that found no evidence of excess cancer of any kind among people who had consumed diet drinks over a long period,

- convincing evidence that any repetitious irritation of any kind at one spot of tissue (even an implanted coin) often induced cancer at that spot; and coupled with that,
- the finding that large doses of saccharin fed to these low-water laboratory rats formed abrasive crystals in the rat's bladder, an unlikely outcome at human dose levels.

On the rhetorical side of the debate, it was helpful to point out that for a human to ingest the same amount of saccharin relative to body weight would require drinking 850 cans of diet soda per day. No one came near that. Besides, you could never drink that many, because the first 50 drinks on Day One would drown you . . . with 800 cans to go!

It was also credible and effective to point out that many natural food ingredients were carcinogens. Dr. Wolfe responded that the FDA had no authority to control natural carcinogens in food, which was technically correct, but his legalism proved my point. He also alleged that the human body could adapt safely to potential hazards in natural foods, but could not adapt to synthetic chemicals. That was conspicuously false, as evidenced by the fact that a few of these natural food artifacts (nitrosamines and aflatoxin) were among the most potent known carcinogens. After 200,000 years, where was the adaptation?

As a further irony, many pharmaceutical pills were coated with saccharin to offset the bitter taste of the medicine. For that practice to be prohibited would likely result in widespread noncompliance with necessary medicinal prescriptions.

It was useful in debate to imagine where this would lead, as laboratories found more ways to overdose sensitive little rodents with every known chemical. The only substances that would escape a zero-tolerance carcinogen ban might be lethal poisons like potassium cyanide. No one would be able to overdose lab animals with cyanide or strychnine long enough to produce a cancer.

Legislators' support began to come forward steadily with more co-sponsors, thanks to prodding from the JDA moms in every congressional district. It was still difficult to get the Commerce Committee to take up any remedial legislation, as Mr. Delaney was still Chairman of the gate-keeper House Rules Committee. Nevertheless, after four years of pressure from the grassroots, in 1977 we were able to pass the "Saccharin Study and Labeling Act." It was introduced in the Senate by Senator Edward Kennedy (D-MA) one week after the ban finally went into effect, which helped get key Democrats as co-sponsors. It provided a two-year moratorium, during which the warning label had to be on every container. The moratorium was extended every two years until 1991, when FDA withdrew the ban. While the prescribed label was frightful enough, it was too small to read on some packets and posed a greater risk of discrediting the value of warning labels. The label requirement was revoked by Congress in 2000.

Meanwhile, other competitive artificial sweeteners were coming on the market. At first, there was some suspicion that rival manufacturers would join the attack against saccharin and support the FDA ban. As it turned out, however, they realized that the same method of forcibly overdosing sensitive laboratory animals could also be directed at their products, with similarly misleading but disastrous results. Consequently, the entire food industry was united in favor of the more sensible application of <u>relative</u>-risk standards instead of Delaney's absolute zero-risk tolerance.

That is how it came to pass that today there are numerous brands of artificial sweeteners on the market. Often, they are sold as mixtures with lesser amounts of each ingredient to reduce the implied but unproven risks that each is alleged to have. Take a look at their labels. Not one, not even humble saccharin, has any scary warning about cancer. That is because it is now understood that normal use does not cause cancer. The legend on the pink Sweet'N Low packet these days carries no hint of the past scare tactics, just this in fine print:

*"**Information: 1 packet contains the sweetness of 2 teaspoons of sugar**."*

As a rule, we disbelieve all the facts and theories for which we have no use.

———William James

Chapter 19

Personal Journey

This personal reflection is presented last for a good reason. Should you find my personal witness bland, even boring, having to sort through it at the beginning might have cooled your interest. If you can muster little patience for a brief autobiography, you are excused, with thanks for reading this far. For a fuller, independent account, see *Catalyst: Jim Martin and the Rise of North Carolina Republicans* by John Hood (John F. Blair, Publisher, Winston-Salem 2015). The essence of my faith and philosophy may have been evident herein, but it is not certain that I will have an opportunity to write another book. So before we close, here is what I believe.

What I believe

I believe that the Holy Bible is the received word of God, the Creator and Sustainer of the universe and of any life that it holds, on Earth or elsewhere. I believe the Bible is our best guide to faith and practice. It is not a scientific textbook. As indicated throughout the foregoing chapters, I believe there is, and can be, no irreconcilable conflict between science and religion, for they are revealed from the same God. Even more than that, as a Christian, I believe that God is most clearly revealed in the life and teaching of Jesus Christ. Furthermore, I firmly believe that a loving God intended us to have the capacity to observe and interpret nature, so that we would grow in understanding the majesty and mystery of His creation and all that followed.

In the fullness of time (that is, in the last few centuries), God has given us the capacity to examine and understand many aspects of His creation through science, its methods and technologies. This has raised our comprehension to a level that explains many former mysteries, although many remain to be explained. Evidence accumulated in this fashion has even given us new revelations of God's way.

At the same time, God has shown us other mysteries that are unexplained and perhaps unexplainable by science. Let me suggest two kinds of examples:

- Religious Revelation: Christ's virgin birth, resurrection, and miracles of healing; and the pervasive moral order recognized in every human society in recorded time.
- Scientific Revelation: The Big Bang of creation, exclusively right-handed asymmetry of DNA, and fine-tuning of numerous physical constants and other anthropic coincidences.

If God could cause the second kind of unfathomable phenomena and more, could He not also cause the first kind—and more?

My view is that science is a modern and valid means of revelation of God's great power. Science observes and explains the nature of God's work in His universe and in us. The Old and New Testaments and other religious documents reveal to us the relationship between God and His people. That is what I believe as a Christian. You may have a different belief. I respect your belief, and expect the same courtesy.

I grew up in the Presbyterian manse in Winnsboro, South Carolina, the second son of the Reverend Arthur Morrison Martin and Mary Martin, *née* Mary Julia Grubbs, both of Savannah, Georgia, where I was born. With their loving guidance, I benefited from the mutual support and competition typical among four brothers, from each of whom much was expected. This nurtured our responsibilities and rivalries. All four of us graduated from Davidson College, as did Pop, and earned advanced degrees in different fields:

- Arthur Morrison Martin Jr., Davidson 1956, with his MD from Duke University, is a pathologist in Butler, Alabama. If you call, don't ask for "Dr. Martin," ask for "Dr. Bubba." As an all-state football star, and our family's only Phi Beta Kappa in college, he set high standards for his brothers in both academic and athletic achievement.
- Joseph Bacon Martin, Davidson 1962, with a PhD in English from Duke University, was a key executive of North Carolina National Bank guiding its novel, pioneering interstate expansion to become Bank of America. Almost totally paralyzed for twelve years with amyotrophic lateral sclerosis (ALS, or "Lou Gehrig's

Disease") until his death in 2006, Joe wrote two books with the help of EyeGaze® technology.

- Neal Anderson Martin, Davidson 1967, earned his MS in library science at Emory University, and recently retired as librarian in the Mooresville North Carolina Public Library, after serving Francis Marion College and Coker College. We are fortunate to have kept close family ties over the years, now living as neighbors across a cove on North Carolina's Lake Norman.

Shortly after my Davidson graduation, Dorothy McAulay Martin of Columbia, South Carolina, and I were married. We had met and become acquainted at Presbyterian Church youth meetings, and at summer church camp on the shores of Buzzards Roost Lake near Greenwood, South Carolina. Neither of us considered that to be romantic at the time. Love blossomed while she was a student at Queens University of Charlotte.

When Dottie and I moved to Princeton in 1957 for my graduate studies, I realized for the first time that most scientists in those days were not religious at all. With a few exceptions among my fellow chemistry colleagues, most were aloof and did not care particularly one way or the other. It was not a subject for ordinary conversation, and one didn't talk much about it. You either went quietly to church, or you quietly did not. Coming from Davidson College and Presbyterian tradition, it was a new experience.

The Davidson student body certainly had its share of doubters and religious rebels. A majority objected to required chapel three days a week and having to return for Sunday Vespers (now discontinued). Those programs gave us valuable exposure to some of the leading thinkers of the day, but rebellion has its own agenda. We were also required to take two introductory Bible courses, Old Testament in the first semester and New Testament in the second. There was not much objection to that requirement, as we knew Davidson was a special place when we enrolled. The same applied to its Honor Code: *A Davidson student will not lie, cheat, or steal, or tolerate those who do.*

Certainly, you could find dorm discussions among the upper intelligentsia on many philosophical questions. As a young chemistry major, involved in a good many extra-curricular activities, I was not particularly disturbed or interested.

I was also aware of religious conversions among my fellow students, some more celebrated than others. One popular star athlete generated quite a stir by proclaiming vividly to a dormitory hall packed with students eager for inspiration how he had sinned, and was now a new person. A few months later, word circulated that he had gotten converted yet again, and this time the crowds were overflowing to hear him repent his intervening sins and escapades . . . in awe-inspiring detail!

My graduate school career was in a milieu of many different religions and non-religions. In the Southern United States, there were closet atheists who were quiet about it. In the North they were less reticent, yet not particularly aggressive about it. These seemed to be distinctively different cultures. At least, they were in the 1950s. Fortunately for me and my faith journey, my graduate studies were supported by a fellowship from the Danforth Foundation of St. Louis, Missouri, from the good people who brought us Purina animal "chow" and Ralston cereal products.

There were three special requirements for Danforth Fellows. One was that each of us would be committed to a teaching career upon receiving the doctorate. The second requirement was that each had to profess a genuine religious commitment. The third was that we would get to know other Danforth Fellows socially and intellectually and attend a summer week at Camp Miniwanka on the shores of Lake Michigan. The first two standards reflected how the late William H. Danforth dared us to carry our faith as a moral and spiritual armament into the classroom. The third requirement introduced me to a lasting friendship with the distinguished poet, novelist, and Davidson English professor Tony Abbott, my editor. It also enlisted us into a special support group long before such mutual associations were found to be very valuable for medical patients with shared illnesses. The fellowship within the Danforth society encouraged and strengthened me in my faith as well as in my intention to become a good chemistry teacher, although the latter got side-tracked by politics a decade later.

It was at Princeton that my fascination with the three-dimensional asymmetry of natural product chemicals, especially steroids, proteins and sugars, and the abiotic origins of life took flight. My doctoral thesis was guided by Richard K. Hill, the leading expert on the molecular structures of aphrodisiacs, a gifted teacher, and a wise and perfect gentleman. We sorted out the stereochemistry of the Diels-Alder reaction, in case you wondered. I remember clearly the adroit manner in which Professor Everett Wallis used his lectures on organic synthesis to introduce the Urey-Miller experiment (pp. 313 ff.) in which assorted amino acids were generated by passing a spark through a gaseous mixture of simplest chemicals. Wallis later raised questions of how the exclusive asymmetric bias for natural sugars and proteinogenic amino acids ever could have originated without direction.

I must confess that I am not among those fortunate enough to have gained a deeper faith by confronting and overcoming early intellectual doubts. I truly admire those who have been victorious in that quest, and wonder whether I could have found my way home. Perhaps that leaves me with a void as to any full understanding of the journey through the valley of skepticism or the "slough of despond," deprived of a healthy process that has surely helped reconstruct sturdier philosophical foundations for others. There is no need, however, to let that bother me, as I can only work from personal experiences of my own. I was not converted to Christianity, having never believed otherwise or entertained any fundamental disbelief.

Did I miss something by not having worked through serious doubts that many students have been fortunate to resolve? Perhaps, but I just never felt the appeal of doubt. Besides, for Mary Martin's sons, that was not an option! I did worry that for many colleagues an overconfidence in the eventual omniscience of science might lead them to have little use for religion, the God of Abraham and Moses, or Jesus as Savior. That is why I welcome the contemporary movement among theistic scientists, both Christians and Jews, who believe in a God-ordained and guided creation and evolution of life. My perspective on religion from the vantage point of my training as a scientist has always been grounded in the belief that there really is no fundamental or irreconcilable conflict between science and religion. None.

Not all scientists are comfortable with acknowledging their faith. In speaking on this subject in forums of academic scientists and religion scholars, I have observed the curious tendency of so many to disavow any religious commitment when discussing religious implications, as if to avoid the appearance of bias. It is as if one must foreswear any taint of belief in order to be accepted as certifiably open-minded on matters of pure professional scholarship. There seems to be a prevalent obsession that peer approval requires a renunciation of any belief in order to be worthy of collegial respect.

I can only marvel that so many have devoted themselves to fields of study in which they feel it would be disqualifying to reach or express any uplifting (or reverent, especially) conclusion. Or is it just personal? Perhaps they merely enjoy testing the resilience of my reasoning.

What Do You Believe?

Religious faith partly reflects an acceptance of the examples and teachings of others who have found a belief in God as revealed in the wonders of the world around us and in the special wonder of human life and thought. It is partly a matter of letting trust and worship draw us into a very personal relationship with God. We may have it or we may not. Each of us has to accept it or work it out to our own satisfaction . . . or not.

There are indeed other venues of truth, most certainly including literature and the arts. They guide us to a deeper understanding of human nature and the mysteries of life. The full meaning of life is revealed to us in various ways, which we can sense but not readily articulate.

Literature helps us by verbalizing keen emotions and intuitions that may have been lurking, unresolved and unspoken, in the recesses of our own preoccupied minds. Literature applies its special gift of language art to every aspect of human existence, yet nowhere more profoundly than matters of love, wisdom, religion, and spirituality. This mode of revelation can be especially effective in its more interactive genres of drama and poetry. Both, it seems to me, require penetrating insight and an exquisite combination of talent and courage to say what we so deeply need to hear.

Music, in its almost infinite variety, has the widest possible range for expressing our inner feelings. It can inspire us to greater determination, or calm us with distraction. In classical music, we have many examples of works that evoke deep emotion. One cannot listen to Elgar's "Nimrod Variation" or Barber's "Adagio for Strings," Mozart's "*Lacrimosa*," Verdi's "*Agnus Dei*," or Lloyd-Webber's "*Pie Jesu*" without being passionately moved. You might search for and enjoy these on the Internet.

In science, we have a particularly effective method for applying both theory and practice to improve our knowledge and understanding of the universe and everything in it. It enables us to unravel nature's secrets for our advantage. Science can only seek natural explanations. While characterizing materials and processes and behaviors, science gathers evidence and interprets it with mathematical, mechanistic, and structural explanations. The familiar concept of the atom, with its electrons orbiting about the nucleus, is not our most sophisticated version, but is a useful metaphor as we begin to comprehend the once-hidden nature of atoms.

Science can develop our best answers as to how things happen and discern the immediate and direct, proximal causes of events. Science cannot answer (or even ask) questions about whether there is any purpose involved, or <u>why</u> something has a certain structure or pattern of behavior. *Science cannot reach back to the primal causes, being unable to conceive such concepts and hypotheses or methods for testing them. This limitation is a quintessential strength of science, but it can lead some to the mistaken conclusion that purpose is absent and, therefore, irrelevant.*

For reasons inherent in these attributes, some conflict between science and religion may have been inevitable. Earnest advocates on both sides rarely miss any opportunity to aggravate the frangible relationship. And yet, from this classic stress between thesis and antithesis, might there not emerge a new synthesis? Could we not rise above the fray to build bridges of understanding between science and religion?

Because we process thoughts and ideas in so many different ways, each with our own little nuances and idiosyncrasies, there is a full spectrum of philosophical positions concerning all the theological issues here. Ted Peters and Martinez Hewlett (in *Can You Believe in God and Evolution?*) have reduced this from a bewildering array of possible philosophies to a simpler list of major points of view, for which you can substitute your own terms or simply add as many sub-headings as you like. I have <u>adapted</u> their original "Spectrum of Faith" as a valuable framework with slight divergence for my own reflections upon each category. You would benefit from the perceptive clarity of their original version.

RAINBOW SPECTRUM OF RELIGIOUS FAITH
(adapted after Peters and Hewlett):
- **Creationists**
- **Intelligent Design Advocates**
- **Tolerant Separatists**
- **Theistic Scientists**
- **Deists**
- **Pantheists**
- **Atheists**

Creationists contend that the Holy Bible is literally inerrant as to the young age of Earth, and that all species, both extant and extinct, were fixed during six days of Creation. Their objective is to counter the arguments and influence of activist atheists by opposing the science

381

of the evolution and "Big Bang" theories. Their view is that to believe in God, one must reject evolution and its scientific basis. That is unfortunate.

They have pressed to have laws enacted to prohibit the teaching of evolution or any scientific theory in conflict with the creation story of *Genesis* in the public schools. The U.S. Supreme Court has held such laws to violate the First Amendment (see pages 355 ff.). A case could be made that this played into the hands of the atheists, and that the creationist strategy lost more converts to atheism than it won to Christianity. Whose victory would that be?

Advocates for **Intelligent Design** arose to find a way around the constitutional restraint. In order to advance a supernatural explanation contrary to the findings and methods of science, they campaigned to have their intelligent-design principle taught as an alternative to evolution. Their legislative tactic has been to require intelligent-design concepts to be taught alongside evolution, and if necessary without mentioning God. Their "equal time" or "balanced" approach has also been found to be unconstitutional.

Some, but not all, who promote intelligent design do accept the scientific evidence that the earth is extremely old. Some in this movement have begun to show indications that they can present respectful arguments that can be tested in keeping with the Scientific Method. This approach can be much more constructive, in my opinion.

Tolerant Separatists accept science and religion as an independent duality of truth, or in Stephen Jay Gould's phrase: Non-Overlapping Magisteria (NOMA). This stance is one of benign neutrality. Science does not overrule religion, and religion does not overrule science. In Francis Collins's phrase, neither can trump the other.

The two may coexist in harmony. This is essentially the position taken by the "Clergy Letter Project" that was initiated in Wisconsin (2004) by Michael Zimmerman. Its intent was "to demonstrate that religion and science can be compatible and to elevate the quality of the debate of this issue." From a localized initiative with 200 signatories, it has grown to become a nationwide petition with over 14,000 signatures in 2016.

Theistic Scientists comprise a new movement of scientists who heretofore have been quiet about their religious convictions, who realize they have left the debate mostly to those at the opposite poles of this spectrum. Many have begun to come forward in the last two decades with scientific concepts and principles that help to reconcile modern science with religion based solely on the science, without dependence upon Scripture. This view often conflicts with the ideals of atheists and creationists. These revelations do not differentiate among most religions, for which one must rely on other foundations.

As a general precaution or disclaimer, theistic scientists acknowledge that we have no hard scientific proof of the existence of God, and don't expect or need to find any. We contend that science, beyond merely being compatible with faith, does reveal abundant evidence pointing us to God; evidence whose meaning can be disputed, but should not be ignored or discounted.

Some adversaries tried to ridicule this movement by calling it "theistic evolution," which Francis Collins sought to counter by calling it BioLogos. His term suffers only from being a synthetic, composite word, without a familiar meaning in common parlance. It is, however, a quite felicitous name for his BioLogos Foundation, which encourages expressions of reason into the relationship between science and religion. Whatever the phraseology, it is sufficient that here is a system of belief that works well for me, and it seems to be drawing the acceptance of many other scientists, some of whom otherwise might be lost to faith. My preference is to say that we are theistic scientists, or scientists who firmly believe in God. Why back down from the taunts of bullies?

Deists hedge many imponderable issues by the clever premise that after God created the heavens and Earth He then wandered off to tend to other responsibilities and left us fend for ourselves. This stance avoids having to defend many important theological principles. As for what happened long after the first instant of creation, deists must rely on the extreme improbabilities of chance. They would be quite comfortable with deistic interpretations of most anthropic coincidences that were fine-tuned in the beginning. They might not accept those associated with abiogenesis, genomics, or chirality. Deism is said to describe the faith system of Thomas Jefferson and certain other Founders of the American Republic.

Pantheists see Divinity in all of nature and as the essence of the driving force of nature, but as an impersonal God who can be served mainly by defending Mother Earth. This brings intensity to those whose paramount commitment is to the environmental sanctity of this planet. This theme has been featured in several major motion pictures, most recently *Avatar*.

In a remarkable fourteen-part television series *Cosmos*, Carl Sagan took a different stance on spirituality that many find very appealing. He said: "For we are the local embodiment of a Cosmos grown to self-awareness. We have begun to contemplate our origins." Then he put it metaphorically: "We are a way for the Cosmos to know itself." Was he saying that <u>we</u> are the ultimate manifestation of the Cosmos? Was he also implying that the Cosmos is all there is? If so, this would seem to have definite overtones of religion of a pale, pantheistic kind at best. Elsewhere, after the rhetorical question, "Who speaks for Earth?" Sagan answered: *Our loyalties are to the species and the planet. We speak for earth. Our obligation to survive is owed not just to ourselves but also to that Cosmos, ancient and vast, from which we sprung.*

This is a clear and inspiring statement. While it would quicken the heartbeat of any absolute environmentalist, it goes deeper than that. The use of the word "species" may be ambiguous by intention, for the same word may be either singular or plural. He could have meant loyalty to the species *Homo sapiens* or, more likely, he could have referenced all taxonomic species. Either way, "our obligation to survive" expresses a debt owed to cosmic evolution by all humanity on behalf of all organisms. Many theists of every faith feel that commitment as well.

Atheists are those who have concluded and do believe that there is no God. They believe instead that everything has a natural explanation and that life has no purpose. They believe that Darwin's Theory of Evolution explains adequately how we got here, and some wield this as an intellectual hammer and wedge against religion. Most atheists seem content to keep their own counsel, and want to be left alone without any intrusion from religion, and especially from government on behalf of religion.

Very few feel burdened with an aggressive responsibility to discredit religion and to disabuse believers of the tenets of their faith. Such atypical activists seem especially eager to proselytize Christians in order to convert as many as possible to atheism. A better term for these more combative individuals is that coined by Scottish theologian Robert Flint: **antitheists**. This was the attribute taken by the late Christopher Hitchens in his *Letters to a Young Contrarian* (2001) in a statement that allows for little ambiguity about his meaning or purpose:

> *I am not even an atheist so much as I am an antitheist; I not only maintain that all religions are versions of the same untruth, but I hold that the influence of churches, and the effect of religious belief, is positively harmful.*

The foregoing is not and cannot be a complete summary of viewpoints on the subject, but hopefully helps put it in perspective. Each of the seven categories has much more depth than can be distilled into any brief description. There may be objection to some detail or other, but this should be sufficient to sketch the general picture. It does not include those who have not settled into a personal faith, such as **skeptics**, who may be searching but are troubled by inconsistencies all around. Nor does it include **agnostics**, who admit they do not have a satisfactory answer as to whether there is a God. Those who "don't know and don't care" might well be termed "**apatheists**." If they espouse any belief, it is that arguments for or against God are both inconclusive and inconsequential.

Creationism Revisited

Peters and Hewlett acknowledge a beneficial contribution from creationists' opposition to Darwinism in that it raised a counterforce to the lure of atheism, as it often is promoted as synonymous with science. It is not. Rather, atheism is a contrarian faith. As you have seen in the earlier chapters, atheism today is not without its own considerable "leap of faith" to accept, explain, or deal with many of the concepts we have examined.

I have no quarrel with the religious beliefs of others, and claim no superiority with regard to personal conviction. If the faith of anyone is sustained by a belief that earth was created in six days of 24 hours each some 6,020 years ago, I have no partisan or mischievous agenda to disturb that. Either belief system referred to as "Creationism" or "Intelligent Design" is clearly helpful to those who believe in a young earth. My one *caveat* is that it not be confused with science.

It does seem ironic that had leading theistic scientists first formulated the meaning of "Intelligent Design," that phrase might have become a label with which many good scientists could find comfort. That semantic term had been co-opted by good people, many of whom happen to believe that Earth is rather youthful and that evolution is a fraud. Under the First Amendment, and with good will, they are entitled to their view. The objection I would have about the system of principles they have attached to those terms is simply that it cannot be regarded as scientific and should not pretend to be.

Science requires that each hypothesis or theory must be falsifiable: capable of being tested by experiment with the potential for being disproved. Anything else may be arguable, with its own inherent merit, but is not science. I recognize that this distinction is a convenience, but it is a powerful one, without which technical progress is not possible. It need not displace other belief systems. It simply defines and qualifies what the Scientific Method is and how it must operate. In his new book, *The Great Partnership*, chief rabbi of the United Kingdom Jonathan Sacks makes this further distinction:

Science takes things apart to see how they work.
Religion puts things together to see what they mean.

I find no antithetical conflict in that. I do find encouragement in the success of a growing number of scientists in presenting what Francis Collins in his subtitle has called scientific "evidence for belief."

Another difficulty has been addressed by Peters and Hewlett: once a religious movement takes the position that one cannot believe in evolution and God, its adherents must either choose to abandon the best principles of science or risk an erosion of their faith. What is to be won by that approach? Is it a victory for advocates of religion if their aggressive dictates cause some young scientists to abandon their faith and drift toward agnosticism or atheism? The goal and purpose of the religious side of this debate should be to counter the arguments of atheists in order to save doubters, not to drive those who respect science into the ranks of disbelievers.

Final thoughts

In closing, I do hope that you have found much to ponder in this review of the early conflict between science and religion, and how it is manifested even today. We have taken a tour of various scientific disciplines and some of the amazing discoveries within each, gathering a lot to think about. We have seen how dozens of highly fortuitous scientific "coincidences" have led to a concept of an "Anthropic Principle" that has energized a movement of theistic scientists to speak out more confidently in affirmation of their own faith. And we have seen many examples of how science can bring us a modern revelation of God's creative power.

- We have considered whether Creation, and especially its origin and evolution of life, reveals purpose.
- We have reviewed the early moments and fine-tuning of the Big Bang.
- We have examined the momentous evolutionary anomaly of the Cambrian Explosion.

- We then analyzed the miraculous complexity of the DNA structure and code, and how it gets replicated, transcribed to RNA, and translated into many thousands of vital proteins.
- We encountered the ineffable uniformity of exclusively right-handed sugars and left-handed proteins, working hand-in-glove, and how that correlates with the architecture and function of DNA and RNA.
- We have weighed the incandescent uniqueness of these and many other known singularities that abound in nature, and point us to our Maker.

In doing so, we have engaged our minds around the many compounded improbabilities for life to have originated here or elsewhere without some guiding light or purpose.

If this has been a useful voyage of discovery for you, it will have fulfilled the purposes of this book. If you have been able to work through (or around) some of the nearly "impenetrable thickets" of the deepest labyrinths of science and come away with awe and wonder, it should delight us both. If you have come to understand better and accept that science need not be an impediment to the faith of any believer, it would be highly satisfying. If you grew to a new perception of how science reveals the majesty of God's creation, it would be truly rewarding enough for the six years devoted to its writing.

The wisest among us have reached varying philosophical conclusions about cosmology, its meaning, and whether a higher power was its First Cause. In the view of many, the beauty and structure and intricate function of the universe, the earth, and all its lifeforms is fully consistent with an omnipotent and omniscient and purposeful Creator, whom we call God, whose benign intervention has never ceased. So when we consider the fundamental improbability of how this world, as we know it, could have happened by chance of random collisions, or in any other undirected, purposeless way, perhaps the **Answer** has always been right in front of us.

When, in the revelations of science, we find realities of nature that point us to God, we might thank God for science.
——Jim Martin, 2016

Implied Anthropic Coincidences and Conditions

<u>Fine-Tuned Physical Constants</u>

1. Big Bang of Instantaneous Creation
2. Gravitation Force
3. Strong Nuclear force
4. Weak Nuclear Force
5. Electromagnetic Force
6. Critical Density
7. Cosmological Constant
8. Planck Constant
9. Quantum Mechanical Constants
10. Speed of Light

<u>Fine-Tuned States</u>

11. Anti-Matter initial abundance
12. Low Initial Entropy
13. Hoyle State
14. Heisenberg Uncertainty Principle

<u>"Goldilocks Zone" in Astronomy</u>

15. Mass and Age of Earth
16. Mass and Age of Sun
17. Distance from Earth to Sun
18. Proximity of larger, blocking Planets
19. Age and Size of Universe

<u>Fortuitous Chemical Coincidences</u>

20. Abundance of Chemical Elements

21. Specified Complexity of Tetravalent Carbon
22. O-H···O Hydrogen Bonding in Water
23. N-H···N Hydrogen Bonding of Paired Nucleotides in DNA
24. Atmospheric Oxygen Equilibrium
25. Concentration of Dissolved Oxygen in Water
26. Porphyrins: Hemoglobin and Chlorophyll

Geological Coincidences

27. Cambrian Explosion (530 Mya)
28. Mass Extinctions
29. Chicxulub Asteroid and Cretaceous Extinction
30. Tectonic Plate Shifts and erosion of granites releasing Cu, Mb and Zn
31. Half-life of U-238

Biochemical Coincidences

32. Chiral exclusivity of DNA, carbohydrates, proteins
33. Irreducible and Specified Complexity of DNA Code
34. Substitution of 2-deoxyribose in DNA (ribose too bulky)
35. MYH-16 Gene Defect Allowed Brain Expansion
36. Chromosomal Evolution
37. Telomere protection of each chromosome's DNA code
38. Ribosome function and allied enzymes
39. Irreducible Complexity of Protein Folding
40. Ubiquitin removal of misfolded protein
41. Chaperonin repair of misfolded protein
42. Complete set of complementary Enzymes for each living organism
43. Mitotic Enzymes

Anatomical and Physiological Coincidences

44. Irreducible Complexity of the Eye
45. Irreducible Complexity of *Coliform* Flagellum
46. Irreducible Complexity of the Heart
47. Multiple Redundancy of Immune Function
48. Acid-Base Dichotomy in the Gastrointestinal Tract
49. Immune Privilege of Eyes, fetal Placenta and Testes
50. Specified Complexity of Fibonacci Patterns

Roster of 31 Nobel Prizes Referenced Herein

1902. Emil Fischer (Chemistry): biochemical "lock and key" model.

1906. J.J Thomson (Physics): discovered electrons.

1907. Albert Michelson (Physics): measured the speed of light.

1908. Ernest Rutherford (Chemistry): nature of radioactivity.

1909. Guglielmo Marconi and Karl Braun (Physics): invention of the radio.

1911. Marie Curie (Chemistry), also 1903 (Physics): discovered radioactivity.

1918. Max Planck (Physics): quantum theory.

1921. Albert Einstein (Physics): theoretical physics and the photoelectric effect.

1922. Neils Bohr (Physics): theory of atomic structure.

1923. Robert Millikan (Physics): oil-drop experiment measured the charge of an electron.

1929. Louis de Broglie: (Physics): dual nature of electrons as waves and particles.

1930. Erwin Schrödinger (Physics): wave equations for electrons of atoms.

1932. Werner Heisenberg (Physics): uncertainty principle and quantum mechanics

1933. Hunt Morgan (Physiology and Medicine): chromosome studies of fruit flies.

1934. Harold Urey (Chemistry): heavy hydrogen and other isotopes.

1935 Irene and Frederic Joliot-Curie (Chemistry): synthesis of heavy elements.

1945. Alexander Fleming, Howard Florey and Ernest Chain (Physiology and Medicine): penicillin.

1949. Hideki Yukawa (Physics): predicted mesons.

1950. Otto Diels and Kurt Alder (Chemistry): Diels-Alder cyclo-addition synthesis.

1962. Max Perutz and John Kendrew (Physics): x-ray crystallography of heme structure.

1962. James Watson, Francis Crick and Maurice Wilkins (Physiology and Medicine): structure of deoxyribonucleic acid (DNA).

1964. Dorothy Hodgkin (Chemistry): x-ray crystallography for structure of insulin, penicillin and vitamin B_{12}.

1965. Robert B. Woodward (Chemistry): Syntheses of Organic Natural Products, e.g., chlorophyll.

1974. Albert Claude, George Palade and Christian de Duve (Physiology and Medicine): electron microscopy of cellular structure, and discovery of ribosomes.

1978. Arno Penzias and Robert Wilson (Physics): Big Bang echo.

1979. Sheldon Glashow, Abdus Salam and Steven Weinberg (Physics): theory of the Weak Force.

1983. Fred Hoyle's collaborators (Physics): Hoyle state of carbon.

2004. Aaron Ciechanover, Avram Herschko and Irwin Rose: mechanism of biodegradation of improperly folded proteins by protease enzymes (proteasomes) assisted by ubiquitin.

2009. Venkatraman Ramakrishnan, Thomas Seitz and Ada Yonath (Chemistry): ribosome structure and function via x-ray crystallization.

2013. Peter Higgs and François Englert (Physics): theory of mass and the Higgs Boson.

2015. Tomas Lindahl, Paul Modrich and Aziz Sancar (Chemistry): DNA repair mechanisms.

Glossary of Less Familiar Terms
(as used in this book)

Abiogenesis: Formation of living organisms and/or their component biochemicals from non-biological precursors.

Acrocentric: adjective for a chromosome having its constricted centromere away from its center.

Agnostic: one who does not know whether or not there is a God.

Anthropic: adjective relating to human beings and our existence; or anything that advances, or is compatible with the interests of, mankind.

Antitheist: one who actively opposes any religion or belief in God.

Apatheist: one who doesn't know and doesn't care whether there is a God.

Apoptosis: cell death.

Armillary: an open spherical device for displaying the positions and trajectories of heavenly objects (stars and planets).

Asteroid: large mineral object orbiting the Sun, much smaller than the smallest planet.

Asymmetric: an aspect of three-dimensional structure denoting the lack of any point, axis or plane of symmetry (see chirality).

ATA: the Allen Telescope Array in California.

Atheism: the system of belief that there is no God and no first cause.

Atheist: one who believes there is no God or supernatural creator.

Atomic Mass: a number assigned to an element to define its relative mass on a scale adjusted so that the mass of an atom of carbon-12 is precisely 12; or, atomic mass of $^{12}C = 12$. It is very approximately the number of protons and neutrons in the atom's nucleus.

Atomic Mass Unit (amu): the mass of an atomic isotope of an element

Atomic Number: the number of protons in each atom or an element.

Atomic Weight: a term in older literature for atomic mass. In chemistry, it denotes the weighted average mass of the natural abundance of isotopes of the element.

Autologous: adjective denoting cells or tissue being implanted in the individual from which they were obtained, typically after being expanded by culturing.

Autosome: any chromosome other than a sex-determinant X or Y.

Baryon: any subatomic particle composed of three quarks: thus, protons and neutrons. Baryons and mesons are two types of hadrons.

Baryonic matter: all atomic material composed mostly of baryons, includes all larger atomic nuclei and whole atoms.

Big Bang: The astronomy theory that this entire universe was created all in one instant from one relatively small but otherwise undefined space.

Billion: a thousand-million = $1,000,000,000 = 10^9$.

Bio-printing: use of advanced three-dimensional ink-jet (or other) printers to construct viable biodegradable scaffolding laced with autologous cells in regenerative medicine.

Black Hole: in astronomy, a super-massive object with enough gravitational attraction to hold its surrounding galaxy together, and to trap light from being emitted (hence the name).

Boson: one of four forces that operate upon the six quarks and six leptons.

Cambrian Explosion: the sudden flourishing, unprecedented and unrepeated, of new body forms (phyla) approximately 535 million years ago, revealed by fossil evidence.

Catalyst: a chemical substance that accelerates reactions of other chemicals without itself being changed.

Canonical: pertaining to books of *The Bible* that have been accepted and approved by scholarly councils ordained by religious authorities.

Catastrophism: a concept of early geology and cosmology that Earth's composition and its living beings were fixed in sudden bursts of creativity within a few thousand years.

Centigrade: the temperature scale, defined in scope such that $0°$ is the freezing point of water, and $100°$ is the boiling point of water under average atmospheric pressure at sea level. The lowest theoretical (absolute zero) temperature is $-273°$ C.

Centromere: the narrow section of a chromosome that holds two copies of the replicated chromosome (sister chromatids) together during cell division. It ensures that no daughter cell will receive more than one copy of the chromosome.

Chirality: a distinction of an asymmetric molecular structure, such that one spatial arrangement is not superimposable with its mirror image, often referred to as having right-handedness or left-handedness.

Chromatin: the apparently dispersed order of chromosomal matter within a cell during an interval between stages of cell division (mitosis).

Class: a taxonomic rank for similar <u>Families</u> such as sharks, skates and rays; or all mammals, or all birds; between <u>Phylum</u> and <u>Order</u>.

Codon: a set of three consecutive nucleotide bases in messenger-RNA, transcribed from the corresponding triplet in DNA, which is translated in a ribosome to select the sequence of amino acids in protein synthesis.

Copernican Concept: heliocentric theory of a planetary system around the fixed Sun.

Cosmos is an orderly system, generally applied to the universe.

Cosmology: the study of the universe, its origin and first cause, and its orderly description.

Covalent Bond: a shared pair of electrons between two atoms in a molecule, which holds them at a characteristic distance from each other and at specific angles from other atoms in the molecule.

Chromatin is a mixture of nucleic acids and proteins in the cell nucleus, which condenses to form <u>chromosomes</u> just prior to cell division.

Chromosome: a grouping of DNA that comes together within the nucleus of a cell just before, and to facilitate, cell division and reproduction.

Configuration: in organic chemistry, the three-dimensional molecular arrangement of atoms (or groups of atoms) attached to a particular carbon atom.

Creationism: the doctrinal belief that the universe was created six thousand years ago, when all living species were fixed in their present form.

Cytogenetics is the study of cell structures, primarily chromosomes.

Cytokines: relatively small proteins involved in identification and trigger signaling among cells.

Cytokinesis: the singular step of cell division by which the cell irreversibly splits in two.

Dark Energy: a term for the force believed to be causing expansion in the remote universe.

Deistic: adjective pertaining to belief in an omnipotent, impersonal God who is no longer involved in our world and lives.

Deuterium: a less abundant isotope of hydrogen, having a nucleus with one proton and one neutron; also called "heavy hydrogen."

Density: the mass of an object divided by its volume.

Diploid Cells: have two sets of all chromosomes, in pairs.

Disanthropic: Adjective for anything that opposes, or is contrary to, the interests of mankind.

Disorder: the degree of randomness in a system.

DNA: deoxyribonucleic acid, the molecular carrier of all genetic code in plants and animals; a double helix structure, consisting of two entwined polymers of deoxyribose and phosphate radicals, to which are attached complimentary bridges of coded purines and pyrimidines.

Domain: the highest taxonomic level of living organisms, above kingdoms: differentiated among *prokaryota, eukaryota, bacteria* and *archaea.*

Doppler Effect: shift in wavelength (e.g., of light or sound) as its source moves toward or away from the observer.

Electronegativity: the relative affinity of an atom for shared or acquired electrons

Element: one of 118 substances that cannot be broken down or converted into any other substance by chemical reaction. All atoms of an element have the same number of protons.

Endemic (adj.): pertaining to a species unique to one isolated geographic locale. Cf. indigenous.

Entropy: in the Second Law of Thermodynamics, the universal tendency of any isolated system to become less orderly. It thereby gives direction to mathematical concepts of time.

Enzyme: Any one of a number of natural proteins generated by RNA controlled processes that are active as biochemical catalysts.

Epicycles: in Ptolemaic astronomy, the imaginary device conjured up to account for retrograde motion of Mars, Jupiter and Saturn.

Epigenetics: the study external effects that modulate the gene-expression of DNA, without altering its code.

Epistemology: the study of knowledge. What do we know, and how do we know it?

Eugenics: the study and practice of methods to improve human heredity by adverse selection.

Eukaryote: any organism whose cells have a membrane-enclosed nucleus containing genetic material organized as chromosomes.

Exoplanet: a planet outside our solar system, orbiting a remote star.

Family: any taxonomic rank of major groups between Order and Genus of plants and animals, such as *hominids*, which includes genera of apes, chimpanzees and hominins (humans).

First Cause: the cosmological concept of the original contributor or source of a given subject or its derivative successors.

Flagellum: a whip-like appendage of certain single-celled organisms, the spinning of which drives locomotion.

Galaxy: a system of billions of stars, revolving around a central <u>black hole</u>.

Gamete: a <u>spermatocyte</u> or an <u>oocyte</u>. Human gametes have 23 <u>chromosomes</u>, one from each pair.

Gene: a section of DNA that carries the vast code of successive codons (nucleotide triplets) for synthesis of a specific protein (enzyme or hormone). A gene is said to "control for" a protein.

Genus (genera, pl.): a taxonomic rank within a <u>Family</u> that includes a group of related species, such as the Homo genus, which includes modern humans, and Neanderthals and Peking Man.

Geocentric: Ptolemy's theory of the planetary system with the sun, moon and all other planets revolving around the fixed earth.

Globin: a massive protein associated with heme in hemoglobin.

Gluons: one of four boson elementary particles, being the one that carries the strong nuclear force.

Gold Foil Experiment: Rutherford's experiment for "measuring" the volume of an atomic nucleus.

Golden Ratio: the ultimate ratio of consecutive higher Fibonacci numbers, often associated with partial anatomical structures of certain organisms, and with pleasing features of art and architecture.

Goldilocks Zone: in astronomy, the habitable zone for a planet orbiting a star: "not too hot, not too cold; not too large, not too small; just right!"

Googol: an arbitrary large number (10^{100}) proposed as a practical surrogate number for infinity.

Hadrons: baryons (protons and neutrons) and mesons.

Haploid Cells: (e.g. gametes) have half the number of chromosomes of the parent cells.

Helicase: an enzyme with the vital function of separating the double helix of DNA into single strands, just ahead of other (polymerase) enzymes constructing duplicated DNA "daughters."

Heliocentric: the planetary system of Copernicus, with all planets, including Earth revolving around the Sun (*Helios*).

Hematology: the study of the composition, function and diseases of blood.

Higgs Boson: the elusive, fundamental "particle" that provides mass to all other particles.

Hominid: all modern and extinct humans and great apes, including chimpanzees, bonobos and gorillas; but not orangutans or gibbons, which are a different family.

Hominin: all human-like species, including modern and extinct ancient species, from the *genera: Homo, Australopithecus* and *Ardipithecus.*

Hormone: any internally produced compound, or a synthetic derivative thereof, that affects the action of organs and tissues in another part of the body. Examples are proteins like insulin and hemopoietin, and complex cyclic hydrocarbons like steroids and adrenaline.

Hydride: a chemical compound of hydrogen with another element.

Hydrogen Bond: a special attraction between molecules of water (H_2O) that confers its higher melting point and boiling point than would be inferred from similar hydrides of the same periodic family as oxygen. It is also a special feature of the pairing of nucleotide bases in DNA.

Hypothesis: a scientific explanation for a process or structure or other feature of some object or occurrence, as yet unconfirmed by experiment.

Imidazole: a heterocyclic (a ring containing nitrogen and carbon) aromatic structure with two nitrogen and three carbon atoms in a ring. This structure is part of all purines and the amino acid histidine.

Indigenous (adj.): native to one or more regions, without having been introduced. Cf. <u>endemic</u>.

Infinity: a mathematical concept for an unlimited quantity, larger than any real number: $1/0$

Inquisition: Congregation of the Holy Office, part of the Vatican Curia empowered to suppress heresy, active from the 13th Century to the 17th.

Intron: non-coding section of DNA, once considered "junk DNA," now thought to be possible activators for coded, proteinogenic DNA sections called genes. Introns may provide separation between consecutive genes, either to allow chemical exposure or to protect the gene.

Irreducible Complexity: a controversial assertion that major anatomical structures are so complex that evolutionary assembly from simpler components might be impossible.

Isomerize: to transform a particular molecular substance into a slightly different molecule with a different configuration or arrangement of the same atoms.

Isotope: a variety of a given element, differing from other isotopes of the same element only by the number of neutrons in the nuclei of its atoms.

Karyotype: the total number of chromosomes of an organism.

Kelvin Temperature: absolute temperature scale, with the freezing point of water at 273° K, and its boiling point at 373° K. Hence, the minimum temperature (absolute zero) is 0° K.

Leptons: particles with low mass, such as electrons, neutrinos and muons.

Macroevolution: a theory of changes at taxonomic levels higher than species and genera, leading to new phyla, classes, orders and/or families. (See microevolution.)

Meiosis: Reproductive cell division.

Mesons: in particle physics, fundamental hadronic particles composed of one quark and one anti-quark, thus 2/3rds the size of protons; observed from high energy collisions.

Metacentric: adjective for a chromosome having its constricted centromere near its middle.

Metaphysics is the philosophic consideration of the world and the nature of existence and being, without reliance on experimental observation (*meta* = "beyond"). It would include "First Causes" beyond Science.

Meteorite: rocky residue of a meteor that strikes the surface of Earth.

Microevolution: a theory of heritable changes in structure and/or function within a species, leading to a new species or genus. (cf. macroevolution.)

Milky Way: the vast <u>galaxy</u> of which our Sun is one of several billion stars; also the hazy streak of light across the night sky, containing the nearest stars, including the constellations of the Zodiac.

Mimicry: heritable, defensive, anatomical traits of a given species that closely resemble a distinctive feature of another dangerous or bad-tasting species with advantages of survival.

Misanthropic: in cosmology, an adjective relating to anything that deters the origins, or is contrary to the interests, of mankind.

Mitochondria: components of eukaryotic cells involved in the metabolic processes converting carbohydrates and oxygen into energy. The genome of a mitochondrion has DNA that is (a) unrelated to that in the chromosomes of the cell nucleus, (b) derives solely from the maternal ancestral line, and (c) does not recombine in reproduction.

Mitosis: a stage of chromosomal realignment preceding ordinary cell division.

Monoploid Cells: have one set of unpaired chromosomes, such as in gametes from diploid cells.

Multiverse: the hypothesis, supposition or conjecture that there may be many overlapping or parallel universes, perhaps an infinite number, as yet unobserved.

Ontology: the study of Reality, and Existence.

Oocyte (oh-oh-site): an egg cell.

Oogenesis: reproductive meiosis in the female parent, preparing an egg cell (oocyte).

Orbital: the wave equation for the energy level of an electron or pair of electrons in an atom or molecule.

Organic Chemistry: the study of structure, function, and reactions of carbon compounds.

Order: a taxonomic rank, such as primates and owls, between <u>Class</u> and <u>Family</u>.

Paleontology: the study of fossils and their accompanying relics.

Pandemic: a global epidemic.

Pangene: a 19th century notion regarding an undetected, microscopic essence that carried information about cell structure and function.

Panspermia: the belief that life on Earth was "seeded" by unknown life from outer space.

Pantheism: the naturalistic belief that God is the synonymous expression of nature.

Paradox: something that appears internally contradictory or incredible; that seems to have conflicting meanings.

Parthenogenesis: the production of viable offspring of a multicellular organism without any paternal contribution of fertilization.

Peptide: a union of two amino acids, joined at the amino (-N-) end of one and the carboxylic unction (-CO-) of the other, as –N-CO.

Periodic Table: an orderly arrangement of chemical elements according to sequential atomic number, so as to reflect similar chemical properties.

Photon: the particle nature of light.

Phylum (**phyla**, pl.): the level of taxonomic description that codifies distinctive body forms, such as chordates, invertebrates, etc.

Ploidy: the number of sets of chromosomes in a cell or organism (e.g., diploid cells have two sets of all chromosomes).

Polarized Light: luminosity (typically in the visible spectrum) with vibrations restricted to one single plane perpendicular to the direction of its motion. It is obtained by passing a beam of light through filters that block wave oscillations in all other planes.

Polymath: a person having the Renaissance ideal of being expert in many fields and abilities.

Polymer: large organic compound with a long chain of monomer units joined end-to-end.

Polymerase: an enzyme that assembles new DNA molecules from the "unzipped" portion of their identical predecessor DNA. (See helicase and DNA.)

Polypeptide: a polymer composed of a chain of amino acids.

Polyploidy: having multiple sets of chromosomes, greater than two: e.g., triploidy, (3 sets) tetraploidy (4 sets).

Porphyrin: one of an assortment of large organic molecules (e.g., chlorophyll and heme) formed from four bridged pyrrole rings, each consisting of a ring of five atoms, one of which is nitrogen oriented toward the center and typically bonded to a central metallic ion.

Primeval Atom: the hypothesis of physics conceptualizing the compressed supermass from which the Universe emerged in the Big Bang.

Prokaryote: a unicellular organism that has no cell nucleus.

Protease: any enzyme that can hydrolyze (break up) protein into its constituent amino acids.

Proteasome: a complex enzyme that, degrades improperly folded proteins by hydrolysis (severing) of the peptide bonds.

Protein: a polypeptide in which the sequence of amino acids is precisely defined by the DNA code of a gene, and which exhibits a precise folding arrangement.

Protobionts: crude, inanimate emulsions of non-functional organic mixtures, thought by some to be precursor pathways to form living cells.

Pseudo-Genes: DNA sequences that may have had but lost the ability to code for proteins.

Ptolemaic: the geocentric planetary system with Sun, Moon and all other planets revolving around Earth.

Purine: a heterocyclic (i.e., a ring containing at least one nitrogen among the carbon atoms) organic compound formed from a pyrimidine ring sharing two carbons with a five-membered imidazole ring. Examples are adenine and guanine.

Pyrimidine: a heterocyclic aromatic organic compound of four carbon and two nitrogen atoms in a six-membered ring (e.g., cytosine, thymine and uracil).

Pyrrole: a heterocyclic aromatic organic compound with one nitrogen among the four carbons forming an unsaturated five-membered ring. Examples are found in heme and chlorophyll.

Quadrillion: a "million billion" or $1,000,000,000,000,000 = 10^{15}$.

Quantum: the small energy differential between atomic orbitals for an electron. It is the energy of a photon emitted when a thermally excited electron returns to its atomic orbital.

Quantum Mechanics: the complex mathematical treatment of the wave properties of (a) atomic nuclei and subatomic particles, and (b) the electrons composing the external part of an atom, outside of, but influenced by, the atomic nucleus.

Quark: one of 17 elementary particles, being associated with gluons to form protons and neutrons.

Quasars: early, extremely massive stars with luminosity comparable to some entire galaxies.

Racemate: a 50:50 mixture of mirror image (chiral) forms of the same organic compound.

Red Shift: the displacement of refracted light from distant galaxies toward longer wavelengths.

Retrograde Motion: the apparent reversal in the motion of planets more distant than Earth from the Sun, as Earth, in its faster orbit, passes between them and the Sun.

Ribosome: a large cellular enzyme that assembles protein from amino acids; a "protein factory."

RNA: ribonucleic acid, a polymer of phosphate and ribose, to which are attached purines and pyrimidines in a coded order derived from DNA.

Saltation: a term for sudden spurts of evolutionary activity at higher taxonomic levels. (See Cambrian Explosion and macroevolution.)

Serendipity: the good fortune of seeking one objective and instead finding another, based on a Persian folk tale of the "Three Princes of Serendip." Serendip is an old name for Sri Lanka.

SETI: search for extra-terrestrial intelligence using technology

Singularity: an unequalled and unduplicated phenomenon or condition.

Specified Complexity: a concept or feature that seems to have a particular irregular pattern not readily explained by natural causes. It is used in Intelligent Design arguments.

Spermatocyte: a sperm cell.

Spermatogenesis: reproductive meiosis in the male parent, preparing multiple sperm cells (spermatocytes).

Spontaneous Generation: nineteenth century belief that insects, vermin and microscopic organisms could arise from dead animal matter without the prior necessity of ancestral parentage (disproved by Pasteur).

Standard Model: in particle physics, an established mathematical treatment of the nature of the composition and interactions of subatomic particles.

String Theory: a set of mathematical models for one-dimensional vibrations to account for the attributes of fundamental particles of matter, and thus the foundation of everything.

Substituent: as used in organic chemistry, an atom or group of atoms attached to a carbon or nitrogen atom of an organic molecule.

Supernova: the bursting of a large star that had diminished hydrogen fuel; and which contracted to a density in which elements higher than lithium were produced, scattering those heavy elements across the surrounding space.

Synteny: the extent to which different genera, families or other taxonomic groups have chromosome segments in the same relative locations.

Tautology: a circular argument that neither explains nor predicts.

Taxonomy: the characterization and naming of categories of grouped plant and animal types, from Domain to Kingdom, to Phylum, to Class, to Order, to Family, to Genus, to Species, with many sub-categories.

Teleology: Purpose.

Telomere: the terminal end of a chromosome that is gradually sacrificed by ongoing cell division, and which thereby serves to protect the survival of the operative DNA code.

Telomerase: an enzyme in cancer cells that repairs its sacrificial telomeres.

Terran: in astronomy, a term for any rocky planet about the size and rockiness of Earth.

Tetrahedral: a molecular structure in which a central atom (typically carbon) is bonded to four atoms attached at the corners of a tetrahedron

Tetrahedron: a geometrical solid with four corners, four triangular sides and six edges.

Theistic: adjective pertaining to a faith-based belief in an omnipotent and personal God

Thermodynamics: the study of heat, work and energy of chemical processes and systems.

First Law of Thermodynamics: Energy can neither be created nor destroyed.

Second Law of Thermodynamics: Heat flows from a higher temperature to a lower temperature system.

Third Law of Thermodynamics: matter cannot be cooled to absolute zero temperature, unless it is a perfect crystal with zero entropy.

Transcription: the transfer of part of the genetic code of DNA to a derived RNA molecule.

Translation: the cellular process by which ribosomes "read" the codon sequence of RNA and guide the assembly of proteins from a specific sequence of available amino acids.

Trillion: a "million-million" = 1,000,000,000,000 = 10^{12}.

Tychonic: the planetary system with the Sun and Moon revolving around the fixed Earth, with all other planets revolving around the Sun, devised by Tycho Brahe.

Ubiquitin: a protease enzyme that assists in removal of improperly folded protein by "tagging" the unwanted protein for degradation by proteasome enzymes.

Uniformitarianism: the concept of early geology and cosmology that past changes in the composition of Earth and its inhabitant species occurred by the same (mostly slow) processes that are observed today.

Valence: In molecular compounds, the number of shared electron pairs, or the number of covalent bonds.

Vitalism: 19th century belief that all organic chemicals found in living organisms were imbued with some kind of "vital force" not found in inorganic chemicals (disproved by Wöhler).

Zygote: a diploid cell formed by fertilization of a monoploid egg by a monoploid sperm cell.

Bibliography of References

SCRIPTURE

The Holy Bible: *King James Version, Scofield Reference Bible* (Oxford University Press, New York 1909-1945)
The Holy Bible: *The New King James Version* (Thomas Nelson, Nashville 1984)
The Living Bible, Paraphrased (Tyndale House, Wheaton 1973)
Quran, *A Reformist Translation* (by Edip Yuksel *et al*, Brainbow, USA 2007)

BOOKS CITED

John Barrow and Frank Tipler: *The Anthropic Cosmological Principle* (Oxford Univ. Press, New York 1994)
Karl Barth: *Dogmatics in Outline* (Harper & Row, New York 1959)
Marcia Bartusiak: *The Day We Found the Universe* (Random House, New York 2010)
Daniel Botkin: *Discordant Harmonies* (Oxford Univ. Press, New York 1990)
Sean B. Carroll: *Into the Jungle* (Pearson Benjamin Cummings, San Francisco 2009)
Sean B. Carroll: *The Making of the Fittest* (Norton, New York 2006)
Marcus Chown: *Magic Furnace* (Random House, New York, 1999)
Francis S. Collins: *The Language of God: A Scientist Presents Evidence for Belief* (Free Press, New York 2006)
C.A. Coulson: *Science and Christian Belief* (Fontana, New York 1958)
Harvey Cox: *The Future of Faith* (HarperCollins, New York 2009)
Michael Cremo and Richard Thompson: *Forbidden Archaeology* (Torchlight Kindle 2011)
Erich von Däniken: *Chariots of the Gods* (Penguin Putnam, New York 1968)
Richard Dawkins: *The God Delusion* (Mariner, Boston 2006)
Charles Darwin: *On the Origin of Species by means of Natural Selection* (original 1859, reprinted by Penguin Classics 1985)
Charles Darwin: *The Descent of Man, and Selection in Relation to Sex* (Dover, London 2010)

Paul Davies: *The Fifth Miracle* (Touchstone New York 1999)

David Deutsch: *The Fabric of Reality: Towards a Theory of Everything* (Allen Lane, London 1997)

Timothy Ferris: *Coming of Age in the Milky Way* (Doubleday, New York 1988)

Thomas Fowler and Daniel Kuebler: *The Evolution Controversy* (Baker, Grand Rapids 2007)

Galileo Galilei: *Dialogue Concerning the Two Chief World Systems* (translated by Stillman Blake, Univ. of California, Berkley 1962)

Karl Giberson: *The Wonder of the Universe: Hints of God in Our Fine-Tuned World* (InterVarsity, Downers Grove 2012)

Owen Gingerich: *God's Universe* (Belknap, Cambridge USA 2006)

Stephen Jay Gould: *Ever Since Darwin* (Norton, New York 1992)

Stephen Jay Gould: *Rocks of Ages* (Ballantyne, New York 1999)

Stephen Jay Gould: *I Have Landed* (Three Rivers Press, New York 2003)

Stephen Jay Gould: *The Living Stones of Marrakech* (Harmony Books, New York 2000)

John Gribbin: *The Scientists* (Random House, New York 2004)

Joshua Gilder and Anne-Lee Gilder: *Heavenly Intrigue* (Doubleday, New York 2005)

Paul Halsall: *The Crime of Galileo: Indictment and Abjuration* (Internet Modern History Sourcebook, Internet 1998)

Brian Hare and Vanessa Woods: *The Genius of Dogs* (Penguin, New York 2013)

Stephen Hawking: *A Brief History of Time* (Bantam, New York 1988)

John Hood: *Catalyst: Jim Martin and the Rise of North Carolina Republicans* (John F. Blair, Winston-Salem 2015)

Robert Jastrow: *God and the Astronomers* (Norton, New York 1992)

Timothy Johnson: *Finding God in the Questions* (InterVarsity, Downers Grove 2004)

Jerome Lawrence and Robert Edwin Lee: *Inherit the Wind* (Random House, New York 1977)

Bjørn Lomborg: *The Skeptical Environmentalist* (Cambridge Univ. Press, Cambridge 2001)

Earl Mac Cormac: *Metaphor and Myth in Science and Religion* (Duke Univ. Press, Durham 1976)

Adrienne Mayor: *The First Fossil Hunters* (Princeton Univ. Press, Princeton 2000)

Eric Metaxas: *Bonhoeffer: Pastor, Martyr, Prophet, Spy* (Thomas Nelson, Nashville 2010)

Ted Peters and Martinez Hewlett: *Can You Believe in God and Evolution?* (Abingdon, Nashville 2006)

Ted Peters and Gaymon Bennett: *Bridging Science and Religion* (Fortress, Minneapolis 2003)

John Polkinghorne: *The Faith of a Physicist* (Fortress, Minneapolis 1996)
A. James Reichley: *Faith in Politics* (Brookings Inst., Washington 2002)
John B. Rogers, Jr.: *The Birth of God* (Abingdon, Nashville 1987)
Jonathan Sacks: *The Great Partnership* (Hodder & Stoughton, London 2011)
Giorgio de Santillana: *The Crime of Galileo*, translated (Univ. of Chicago Press 1955)
Hans Schwarz: *Creation* (Eerdmans, Grand Rapids 2002)
Neil Shubin: *Your Inner Fish* (Random House, New York 2008)
Rebecca Skloot: *The Immortal Life of Henrietta Lacks* (Random House, New York 2010
Dava Sobel: *Galileo's Daughter* (Walker, New York 2011)
Lee Strobel: *The Case for a Creator* (Zondervan, Grand Rapids 1952)
Bryan Sykes: *The Seven Daughters of Eve* (Norton, New York 2001)
Colin Tudge: *The Link* (Little, Brown, New York 2009)

JOURNALS WITH RELEVANT ARTICLES

American Scientist
National Geographic
Nature
Science
Scientific American

ANY MODERN TEXT BOOK

Astronomy
Biology
Chemistry
Geology and paleontology
Physics
Religion

INTERNET SOURCES

Wikipedia (for a balanced introduction to most topics)
CERN website (high energy physics)
NASA website (research satellites and exoplanet news)
Ensemble (NIH website)
RealClearScience
Answers in Genesis (among website for creationism)
Talk Reason and *Uncommon Descent* (among websites against creationism)
Golden Number (website for Fibonacci curiosities)

Index of Names

U

Udall, Morris "Mo," 5
Underhill, Peter, 295
Urban VIII (pope), 39–40, 42, 44
Urey, Harold, 312, 348, 391
Ussher, James, 190–91

V

Vacanti, Charles, 305
Vacanti, Joseph, 304–5
van der Marel, Roeland, 67
van Etten, James, 348
van Leeuwenhoek, Anton, 310
Venter, Craig, 179, 230, 341
Viviani, Vincenzo, 26, 44
Voltaire, 328
von Däniken, Erich, 331
von Humboldt, Alexander, 116

W

Wacey, David, 209
Wallace, Alfred Russel, 124–25, 127,
    133, 137, 148
Wallis, Everett S., 311–12, 317, 378
Watson, James, 163–64, 277, 285–87,
    313, 392
Wedgwood, Josiah, II, 115
Weinberg, Steven, 93, 95, 392

Wells, H. G., 328–30
Whelan, Elizabeth, 372
White, Tim, 141
Wickramasinghe, Chandra, 323–
    24, 356
Wigner, Eugene, 88
Wilberforce, Samuel, 134–35
Wilkins, Maurice, 164, 392
Wilson, President Woodrow, 158
Wilson, Richard, 61, 66, 372
Wilson, Robert, 60, 392
Wöhler, Friedrich, 279, 309
Wolfe, Sidney, 368, 372
Wood, Rachel, 204
Woodward, Robert Burns, 260

Y

Yonath, Ada, 298, 392
Yukawa, Hideki, 80, 391

Subject Index

CPSIA information can be obtained
at www.ICGtesting.com
Printed in the USA
FFOW02n1401020617
36329FF